MW01196688

International Political Economy Series

Series Editor

Timothy M. Shaw, Visiting Professor, University of Massachusetts Boston, USA and Emeritus Professor, University of London, UK

The global political economy is in flux as a series of cumulative crises impacts its organization and governance. The IPE series has tracked its development in both analysis and structure over the last three decades. It has always had a concentration on the global South. Now the South increasingly challenges the North as the centre of development, also reflected in a growing number of submissions and publications on indebted Eurozone economies in Southern Europe.

An indispensable resource for scholars and researchers, the series examines a variety of capitalisms and connections by focusing on emerging economies, companies and sectors, debates and policies. It informs diverse policy communities as the established trans-Atlantic North declines and 'the rest', especially the BRICS, rise.

Titles include:

Eleonora Poli
ANTITRUST INSTITUTIONS AND POLICIES IN THE GLOBALISING ECONOMY

Andrea C. Simonelli
GOVERNING CLIMATE INDUCED MIGRATION AND DISPLACEMENT
IGO Expansions and Global Policy Implications

Victoria Higgins
ALLIANCE CAPITALISM, INNOVATION AND THE CHINESE STATE
The Global Wireless Sector

Andrei V. Belyi
TRANSNATIONAL GAS MARKETS AND EURO-RUSSIAN ENERGY RELATIONS

Silvia Pepino
SOVEREIGN RISK AND FINANCIAL CRISIS
The International Political Economy of the Eurozone

Ryan David Kiggins (*editor*)
THE POLITICAL ECONOMY OF RARE EARTH ELEMENTS. RISING POWERS AND TECHNOLOGICAL CHANGE

Seán Ó Riain, Felix Behling, Rossella Ciccia and Eoin Flaherty (*editors*)
THE CHANGING WORLDS AND WORKPLACES OF CAPITALISM

Alexander Korolev and Jing Huang
INTERNATIONAL COOPERATION IN THE DEVELOPMENT OF RUSSIA'S FAR EAST AND SIBERIA

Roman Goldbach
GLOBAL GOVERNANCE AND REGULATORY FAILURE
The Political Economy of Banking

Kate Ervine and Gavin Fridell (*editors*)
BEYOND FREE TRADE
Alternative Approaches to Trade, Politics and Power

Ray Kiely
THE BRICS, US 'DECLINE' AND GLOBAL TRANSFORMATIONS

Philip Fountain, Robin Bush and R. Michael Feener (*editors*)
RELIGION AND THE POLITICS OF DEVELOPMENT
Critical Perspectives on Asia

Markus Fraundorfer
BRAZIL'S EMERGING ROLE IN GLOBAL SECTORAL GOVERNANCE
Health, Food Security and Bioenergy

Katherine Hirschfeld
GANGSTER STATES
Organized Crime, Kleptocracy and Political Collapse

Matthew Webb and Albert Wijeweera (*editors*)
THE POLITICAL ECONOMY OF CONFLICT IN SOUTH ASIA

International Political Economy Series
Series Standing Order ISBN 978–0–333–71708–0 hardcover
Series Standing Order ISBN 978–0–333–71110–1 paperback

You can receive future titles in this series as they are published by placing a standing order. Please contact your bookseller or, in case of difficulty, write to us at the address below with your name and address, the title of the series and one of the ISBNs quoted above.

Customer Services Department, Macmillan Distribution Ltd, Houndmills, Basingstoke, Hampshire RG21 6XS, England

---

The Gulf States in International Political Economy

Kristian Coates Ulrichsen
Baker Institute Fellow for the Middle East, Rice University, USA

© Kristian Coates Ulrichsen 2016

First published 2016 by
PALGRAVE MACMILLAN

Palgrave Macmillan in the UK is an imprint of Macmillan Publishers Limited, registered in England, company number 785998, of Houndmills, Basingstoke, Hampshire RG21 6XS.

Palgrave Macmillan in the US is a division of St Martin's Press LLC, 175 Fifth Avenue, New York, NY 10010.

Palgrave Macmillan is the global academic imprint of the above companies and has companies and representatives throughout the world.

Palgrave® and Macmillan® are registered trademarks in the United States, the United Kingdom, Europe and other countries.

ISBN: 978–1–137–38560–4

Library of Congress Cataloging-in-Publication Data

Ulrichsen, Kristian Coates, author.
   The Gulf States in international political economy / Kristian Coates Ulrichsen, Baker Institute Fellow for the Middle East, Rice University, USA.
      pages   cm. —(International political economy series)
   ISBN 978–1–137–38560–4
   1. Persian Gulf States—Economic conditions.   2. Persian Gulf Region—Foreign relations.   3. Persian Gulf States—Politics and government.
   4. Globalization—Persian Gulf States.   5. Gulf Cooperation Council.   I. Title.
   HC415.3.U47 2015
   337.536—dc23   2015021434

Contents

List of Tables

Acknowledgements

I would like to thank Professor Timothy Shaw for commissioning this book and for his support throughout the writing process. Christina Brian and Judith Allan were also extremely helpful points of contact at Palgrave Macmillan and I thank them for their assistance. I thank also my colleagues at Rice University's Baker Institute for Public Policy, namely Ambassador Edward P. Djerejian, Marwa Shalaby, Ben Stevenson, Ariana Marnicio, and Jim Krane, as well as at Chatham House in London, whose 'Future Trends in the GCC' project was particularly useful in generating new ideas about the direction of travel in the Gulf States. My friends and family in the United Kingdom, Greece, and Norway provided much-needed encouragement, as did my wife, without whose support this book could not have been written. Every academic career has to begin somewhere, and mine began with my doctoral work at the University of Cambridge under the supervision of Professor Sir Christopher Bayly. Chris passed away suddenly three days before I completed this manuscript and it is to his memory that I dedicate this book, for he taught me to think across academic disciplines and national and regional boundaries.

List of Abbreviations

AAOIFI	Accounting and Auditing Organization for Islamic Financial Institutions
ACD	Asia Cooperation Dialogue
ADGM	Abu Dhabi Global Market
ADIA	Abu Dhabi Investment Authority
ADIC	Abu Dhabi Investment Council
ADNOC	Abu Dhabi National Oil Company
AFESD	Arab Fund for Economic and Social Development
AHAB	Ahmad Hamad Algosaibi and Brothers
ALBA	Aluminium Bahrain
AQAP	Al-Qaeda in the Arabian Peninsula
Aramco	Arabian American Oil Company
ASEAN	Association of Southeast Asian Nations
ASPA	South American-Arab Countries Summit
BAPCO	Bahrain Petroleum Company
BCCI	Bank of Credit and Commerce International
BOT	Build, Operate, Transfer
BRIC	Brazil, Russia, India, China
CEDAW	Convention on the Elimination of All Forms of Discrimination against Women
CENTO	Central Treaty Organization
CIC	China Investment Corporation
CNOOC	China National Offshore Oil Company
COP	Conference of the Parties
CSB	Central Statistical Bureau (Kuwait)
DFSA	Dubai Financial Services Authority
DIFC	Dubai International Financial Centre
DIFX	Dubai International Financial Exchange
Dubal	Dubai Aluminium
ECFR	European Council on Foreign Relations
EEC	European Economic Community
EDB	Economic Development Board (Bahrain)
EITI	Extractive Industries Transparency Initiative
EIU	Economist Intelligence Unit
EM	Emerging Market
ENEC	Emirates Nuclear Energy Corporation

EU	European Union
FDI	Foreign Direct Investment
FGF	Future Generations Fund (Kuwait)
FIA	Fédération Internationale de l'Automobile
FSA	Financial Services Authority (United Kingdom)
FTA	Free Trade Agreement
GCC	Gulf Cooperation Council
GDP	Gross Domestic Product
GECF	Gas Exporting Countries Forum
GLMM	Gulf Labour Markets and Migration
GOSI	General Organization for Social Insurance (Saudi Arabia)
GRF	General Reserve Fund (Kuwait)
GRI	Global Redesign Initiative
GTL	Gas-to-Liquids
ICT	Information and Communications Technologies
IFDI	Islamic Finance Development Indicator
IIRO	International Islamic Relief Organization
IMF	International Monetary Fund
IOM	International Organization of Migration
IONS	Indian Ocean Naval Symposium
IPIC	International Petroleum Investment Corporation
IPO	Initial Public Offering
IRA	Independent Regulatory Agency
IRENA	International Renewable Energy Agency
ISIS	Islamic State of Iraq and Syria
ITUC	International Trade Union Confederation
KAC	Kuwait Airways Corporation
KA-CARE	King Abdullah City for Atomic and Renewable Energy
KAEC	King Abdullah Economic City
KAFD	King Abdullah Financial District
KAUST	King Abdullah University of Science and Technology
KCIC	Kuwait-China Investment Company
KEPCO	Korea Electric Power Corporation
KFH	Kuwait Finance House
KFUPM	King Fahd University of Petroleum and Minerals
KIA	Kuwait Investment Authority
KIO	Kuwait Investment Office
KNOC	Korea National Oil Corporation
KOC	Kuwait Oil Company
KPC	Kuwait Petroleum Corporation
KPI	Kuwait Petroleum International

LNG	Liquefied Natural Gas
MICE	Meetings, Incentives, Conferences, Events
MSCI	Morgan Stanley Capital International
OBU	Offshore Banking Unit
ODA	Overseas Development Assistance
OECD	Organisation for Economic Cooperation and Development
OIC	Organization of the Islamic Conference
OPEC	Organization of Petroleum Exporting Countries
PACI	Public Authority for Civil Information (Kuwait)
PDRY	People's Democratic Republic of Yemen
PETRONAS	Petroliam Nasional Berhad (Malaysian National Petroleum Company)
PFLOAG	People's Front for the Liberation of Oman and the Arabian Gulf
PIF	Public Investment Fund (Saudi Arabia)
PLAN	People's Liberation Army Navy
PPP	Public Private Partnership
PSG	Paris Saint-Germain
QAPCO	Qatar Petrochemical Company
QFC	Qatar Financial Centre
QFCRA	Qatar Financial Centre Regulatory Authority
QIA	Qatar Investment Authority
QNFSP	Qatar National Food Security Programme
QSI	Qatar Sports Investment
QIPCO	Qatar Investment & Projects Development Holding Company
RAF	Royal Air Force (United Kingdom)
RUSI	Royal United Services Institute
SABIC	Saudi Basic Industries Company
SALIC	Saudi Agricultural and Livestock Investment Company
SAEV	Saudi Aramco Energy Ventures
SAMA	Saudi Arabian Monetary Agency
SCAF	Supreme Council of the Armed Forces (Egypt)
SIDF	Saudi Industrial Development Fund
SoCal	Standard Oil Company of California
SOE	State-owned Enterprise
SQU	Sultan Qaboos University
SRI	Stanford Research International
SWF	Sovereign Wealth Fund
TIP	Trafficking in Persons
TRIPS	Trade-Related Aspects of Intellectual Property Rights

UAE	United Arab Emirates
UN	United Nations
UNFCCC	United Nations Framework Convention on Climate Change
USSR	Union of Soviet Socialist Republics
WECG	World Economic Centre of Gravity
WEF	World Economic Forum
WIPO	World Intellectual Property Organization
WTO	World Trade Organization
WWF	World Wildlife Fund

Introduction

This book examines the changing position of the Gulf Cooperation Council (GCC) states within a global order which itself is in a state of flux. Against the backdrop of deep shifts in the structure and balance of geopolitical and geo-economic gravity, the Gulf States have become increasingly assertive centres of regional power and influence. Beginning in the 1990s, the GCC states became increasingly integrated with the world economy, gradually opened up to foreign direct investment, and eventually acceded to the World Trade Organization. Since the turn of the century, and backed by the world's fastest-growing airlines and by governing methods that resemble a corporate structure grafted onto the principles of hereditary rule, Dubai, Abu Dhabi, and Doha have imprinted themselves on the global consciousness, their exposure magnified by the acquisition or sponsorship of landmark assets and prestige events across the world. Moving far beyond the longstanding role of Saudi Arabia in stabilising international oil markets, the Gulf States emerged in the 2000s as more muscular participants in attempts to rebalance and reshape the world around them. This process accelerated after the sudden outbreak of the Arab Spring upheaval in 2011, as the Gulf monarchies took unprecedented measures to contain and control the processes of change in the Middle East and North Africa, and peaked with the Saudi-led coalition that formed to conduct Operation Decisive Storm in Yemen in March–April 2015.

For many observers of international affairs, the awarding of the hosting rights to the 2022 FIFA World Cup to Qatar in December 2010 symbolised the rapid, even startling, rise of the Gulf States as regional powers with global reach. This breakthrough event took place in the wake of the global financial crisis and a series of high-profile investments by Gulf-based sovereign wealth funds and private investment vehicles. Within a

1

bewilderingly quick time, it appeared to many commentators that 'Gulf money' was everywhere, snapping up iconic global brands and investing in world-renowned institutions such as Harrods, Porsche, Ferrari, the Chrysler Building in Manhattan, the London Stock Exchange, Barclays Bank, Citigroup, and the 'Shard' skyscraper that towered over the skyline of London. Sports fans learned to navigate a new lexicon as they shuttled between Arsenal's Emirates Stadium and the Etihad Stadium of Abu Dhabi-owned Manchester City, while the most famous team in the world, FC Barcelona, took the field bearing the logos of the Qatar Foundation and Qatar Airways. Indeed, the quarter-final of the 2015 UEFA Champions League saw Qatar-sponsored FC Barcelona take on (and defeat) Qatar-owned Paris Saint-Germain, whose shirt sponsor is Emirates airline, also the shirt sponsor of the defending European champions, Real Madrid.

Even more remarkable than the material manifestation of Gulf capital is the pace and scale of economic – if not political – development that has propelled the Gulf States to prominence within just two generations. This means that some of the most remarkable and all-encompassing socio-economic transformations in recorded history have been distilled into the space of a single human lifetime. In *Rags to Riches: A Story of Abu Dhabi*, the prominent Emirati businessman Mohammed al-Fahim described the circumstances of his 1950s childhood as a place where

> the permanent and seasonal residents of Abu Dhabi island still lived in barasti huts built of palm fronds harvested from the date trees. The exceptions were a few wealthier residents and the ruling family who lived in earth or clay houses . . . The houses were clustered together for security, companionship, and warmth during the cooler months.[1]

In a similar vein, Khabeer Khan, a Pakistani advisor recruited by Sheikh Zayed bin Sultan Al Nahyan to work on agricultural development, described his first arrival in Abu Dhabi in 1962 as 'like stepping back into the Stone Age.'[2] Writing in 1995, al-Fahim added that 'the changes that have taken place throughout the Emirates over the past three decades have been incredible, difficult to believe even for those who have seen them with their own eyes.'[3]

As recently as the 1950s and 1960s, there was very little infrastructure in the small cities on the Arabian Peninsula as institutional mechanisms evolved slowly to absorb growing oil revenues. Saudi historian 'Abd Al-Aziz ibn 'Abd Allah al-Khwaiter offers the following description of rule in Saudi Arabia at the time of the creation of the kingdom in 1932:

The king was the source of power. He had the final word, which was bound solely by the power of the Sharia. He relied on no systematic administrative bodies other than the employees in his council, whose job was to submit to him the various matters that were raised in council, then to carry out his orders in addressing those matters. The king decided on administrative, political, military, economic, and social matters, and referred what concerned the Sharia to the relevant authorities.[4]

Indeed, as late as 1952, the only 'government' ministries in Saudi Arabia were those dealing with finance (founded in 1932), foreign affairs (1933), and the interior (1944).[5] In 1959, mail from Kuwait to the newly emerging oil centre of Al-Khobar in eastern Saudi Arabia still took around 30 days and virtually no international telephone lines existed in the kingdom.[6] Bureaucratic arrangements in many cases were limited to the presence of 'gatekeepers,' usually of foreign origin, who controlled access to the ruling sheikh and wielded enormous influence over the conduct of policy; examples of such personalised networks were those of Abdullah Suleiman, Fuad Hamza, and Yusuf Yassin in Saudi Arabia, Mulla Saleh in Kuwait, Charles Belgrave in Bahrain, and Abdullah Darwish in Qatar.[7] Even as late as 1990, a remarkable photograph of the main thoroughfare running through central Dubai, Sheikh Zayed Road, showed only a few scattered buildings surrounded by desert, in remarkable contrast to the road's centrepiece in an intensely built up 'global hub' just two decades later.[8]

Economic activity expanded rapidly with the growth of the oil industry following the discovery of oil in the 1930s, and the beginning of commercial extraction and export in the 1940s, following a hiatus during World War Two. Oil revenues transformed the political economy of the Gulf States, shaped the nature of state-society relations, and determined their subsequent development, while also enabling the sheikhdoms to evolve from little more than city-states dominated by local coalitions between ruling families and merchant elites into modernising and increasingly centralised states. However, certain rulers, such as Sheikh Shakhbut bin Sultan Al Nahyan in Abu Dhabi and Sultan Said bin Taimur in Oman, resisted the trappings of modernisation well into the 1960s, accounting in no small measure for their eventual toppling by more ambitious members of their immediate family. In 1965, for example, what is today the Abu Dhabi International Airport consisted of 'little more than a sand landing strip and a single small building that was cooled by a wind tower' with only a soft-sand track to connect it with the town.[9] Meanwhile Oman experienced what Marc Valeri describes as the 'decade of remoteness' as the Sultan withdrew from public life in the 1960s and sought to block all modernising influences, limiting running water and electricity, for example, to his royal palaces and the homes of a select group of trusted associates.[10] In addition, just three schools existed in the entire country in 1970, with a total enrolment of 900 boys and an illiteracy rate of 66 per cent among Omani adults.[11]

The central aim of this volume is to describe the processes by which the Gulf States have become embedded in the global system of power, politics, and policymaking over the past four decades. A key question is the extent to which the far more active – and assertive – involvement of individual Gulf States in international institutions and global governance is merely adding another dimension to otherwise little-changed structures or leading to something qualitatively new as coalitions of emerging economies challenge the hitherto Western-centric global order. This is closely related to a further dimension of the Gulf States' uneven engagement with the processes of globalisation, namely the degree to which the patterns of conspicuous consumption that have become characteristic of modern Gulf cities such as Dubai and Doha are gradually being augmented by productive integration into global economic structures and flows. A recent article in *Race and Class* summarised the ambivalence surrounding the political economy of the contemporary Gulf States by suggesting provocatively that the United Arab Emirates (UAE) and Qatar have in fact been 'consciously constructed as specialised geographic zones for the global elite and transnational capitalism.'[12]

Although the export of oil has connected the Gulf to the world economy for more than 60 years, far predating the great acceleration of economic globalisation from the 1970s on, the processes by which the Gulf States have 'gone global' nevertheless have proliferated beyond recognition since the 1990s. A rigorously interdisciplinary approach drawing upon historical development, international economics, international trade and international relations, comparative politics, and globalisation studies will situate the Gulf States firmly within their twenty-first-century context. Proceeding from the starting point that contemporary issues in global politics transcend traditional disciplinary boundaries, the book examines the complex interdependencies that mark the region as such an integral component of international affairs.

In addition, the book documents the thickening webs of inter-regional linkages between the Gulf States and major developing nations that are creating new 'coalitions of convenience' among rising powers with a shared interest in reshaping the post-1945 international architecture. Patterns of global engagement and the pursuit of internationalisation are reconfiguring the position of individual states within the global order and injecting new dynamics into inter-regional and international relations. This is by no means a phenomenon unique to the Gulf States, as made clear by the deep divisions within the European Union over the handling of issues such as the Greek debt crisis or the response to a more assertive Russia, both of which highlight the resilience of bilateral approaches to foreign policymaking. Nevertheless, the great diversification of the GCC states' geopolitical and geo-economic interests does represent a significant juncture in the process of internationalising the Gulf and repositioning it within the changing global order.

In common with many other 'non-Western' discourses, officials in the GCC states have embraced partial aspects of economic globalisation and focused on the practical measures of global engagement, over any attachment to theoretical or normative concepts of 'global governance.' Rather than posing a systemic threat to contemporary structures of international governance, the GCC states operate in a pragmatic manner designed to maximise influence and leverage in the existing architecture of world politics in which contemporary power and influence is dispersed among a greater number of active participants spread across a wider political and economic spectrum than before. This is also part of a broader trend whereby normative foundations of the international system – from governance and political reform to transparency and accountability – are increasingly seen through a prism that diverges from what may be termed the 'Western-centric' lens that characterised the post-1945 institutions of global governance and the political element of globalisation itself.

Yet such scepticism towards the more political (or cultural) dimensions of globalisation has not distanced the GCC states from acting as international players or from participating in the broader rebalancing of the global order. On the contrary, the Gulf States have become increasingly visible and proactive in setting international policy agendas on a wide range of issues, ranging from financial and energy governance to global aviation and food security. As set out in the following chapters, this holds important implications for the continuing evolution of international institutions in a polycentric environment with multiple centres of influence and competing policy objectives. It is also significant in terms of the regional reordering triggered by the political upheaval across much of the Arab world and the active policy responses of individual Gulf States to the disorder in North Africa and the Levant.

Although this book covers the GCC (Bahrain, Kuwait, Oman, Qatar, Saudi Arabia, and the UAE) as a whole, it is important at the outset to highlight the significant differences that exist among the six member states. What is often termed 'the Gulf' is neither a monolithic bloc of major oil-producing Arab states nor a case of 'Saudi Arabia plus five' smaller states. On the contrary, three broad categories readily become apparent in terms of resource endowments and policy projection. These are the aggressively internationalising approaches of Qatar and the UAE (and specifically Abu Dhabi and Dubai within the seven-emirate federation); the niche-level significance of Saudi Arabia and Kuwait in the global energy and investment landscape; and the lesser importance of Bahrain and Oman, both comparatively resource-poor states that are grappling with the immediate challenges of transitioning towards a post-oil economy. While these categories are neither static nor unchanging, they are evolving as the Gulf emerges as the pivot around which broader shifts in global economic activity are occurring. Thus, any examination of the international political economy of the Gulf States inevitably focuses more on Saudi Arabia, Qatar, the UAE, and Kuwait than on Bahrain and Oman. Yet the latter two states are far from insignificant actors on the regional stage, as the book makes clear.

The Gulf States in international political economy

Recent years have seen an explosion in the academic literature on the Gulf States, much of it rooted in political science, comparative politics, international relations, and security studies. While the majority of publications focus on a specific discipline, several edited volumes since the mid-2000s have examined the global emergence of the Gulf States through the prism of globalisation studies. A pioneer in this regard is *Globalization and the Gulf*, published in 2006, which offered innovative perspectives on the interaction within the global system of the processes of globalisation with the deeply held traditions of Gulf society and culture. As the three authors write in their introductory essay, 'no part of the world has come into the global market more rapidly and with more change in material abundance than the Arab Gulf oil states.'[13] Five years later, *The Transformation of the Gulf: Politics, Economics and the Global Order*, published on the very cusp of the Arab Spring, explored the mechanisms by which the GCC states were both shaping, and being reshaped by, globalisation. The volume outlined a roadmap of their repositioning in a global order itself in a state of flux following the 2008–2009 world financial crisis. It also provided material for a new theoretical approach to global studies by analysing the region as a barometer of globalisation, and a cockpit of transformative shifts in standards and patterns of living within a highly compressed time period.[14]

Three research articles by the present author have further investigated the global profile of the Gulf States. In *Rebalancing Global Governance: Gulf States' Perspectives on the Governance of Globalization*, I detailed how officials in the Gulf States evolved in their perspectives on the 'governance of globalisation' that differ significantly from Western-centric norms of 'global governance.' A second article, *The GCC States and the Shifting Balance of Global Power* surveyed the motivations and objectives behind the Gulf States' rise to international prominence in the first decade of the twenty-first century, and examined the implications for the future of global and regional politics in light of the growth of new interregional blocs and linkages. In a third article, *Repositioning the GCC States in the Changing Global Order*, I provided important historical context not only to the rebalancing of global power around multiple centres of political and economic influence, but also to the newfound set of pressures generated by the Arab Spring. In a separate article for the *Brazilian Journal of Strategy and International Relations*, I explored the multifaceted and lengthy integration of the Gulf States within frameworks of South-South relations, going back to the 1950s and 1960s when Saudi Arabia and Kuwait made important religious and humanitarian contributions to Arab and Islamic causes across the world.[15]

Similarly, the field of international political economy has matured and broadened significantly in the last decade. A comprehensive review of the literature is beyond the scope of this study, but it is sufficient to note some of the more important recent works. Research by Thomas Oatley has analysed the interplay between domestic and international politics, and surveyed the complex array of interests and institutions that together constitute the 'rules of the game' within which state and non-state actors pursue wealth and power. His work emphasises the importance of integrating the political and economic dimensions of the global economy, which itself is a competition that produces both winners and losers. As he notes in his overview textbook on the subject, 'politics in the global economy revolve around enduring competition between the winners and the losers generated by global economic exchange.'[16] In *Debates in International Political Economy*, Oatley also provides an accessible overview of the major theoretical and empirical debates on the nature of the contemporary international system, trade and migration patterns, the role of multinational corporations and sovereign wealth funds, international finance and monetary issues, and the global politics of climate change.[17]

In *Analysing the Global Political Economy*, authors Andrew Walter and Gautam Sen conduct a wide-ranging survey of critical areas of international political economy, with an emphasis on the importance of economic theory. Walter and Sen engage rigorously with the political economy of finance and financial integration, the international monetary system and foreign direct investment, and the evolution of a multilateral trading system. By bring economics 'back in' to the core of the study of international political economy, the book complemented and added value to much of the existing literature that prioritised political science and international relations-based approaches.[18] Other significant contributions to recent literature are a spate of works addressing the global political economy, with an eponymous volume edited by John Ravenhill one of numerous examples. This examined issues such as regionalism and the impact of globalisation in the Global South in another wide-ranging survey of contemporary issues of international political economy.[19]

Robert Gilpin's *Global Political Economy: Understanding the International Economic Order* (2001) built upon the author's path-breaking 1987 work, *The Political Economy of International Relations*, which did much to provide the conceptual underpinnings for the breakthrough and subsequent maturation of international political economy as an academic discipline. His books explored the intensifying interdependence of national economies, the rise of regional and inter-regional economic cooperation, and the ways that political, economic, and technological forces have transformed the world. In addition, they integrate political and economic analysis with historical and theoretical insights to produce a nuanced examination of the complex interaction between nation-states and the world economy. In a third study, *The Challenge of Global Capitalism: The World Economy in the 21st Century*, Gilpin argued that secure political foundations, wise leadership, and a set of fair rules were urgently required to ensure the stability of the international capital system.[20]

A different yet innovative approach to contemporary global issues has been provided by Richard Beardsworth in *Cosmopolitanism and International Relations Theory*. Beardsworth links the concerns of cosmopolitanism to international relations and world politics on the grounds that 'specific problems facing actors in the field of world politics are of an increasingly global nature, and since the solutions to them call for both global cooperation and global vision.'[21] This builds upon earlier research into what David Held labels 'the paradox of our times' – namely that 'the collective issues we must grapple with are of growing extensity and intensity, yet the means for addressing these are weak and incomplete.'²² In *Global Covenant*, Held identifies two major challenges for policymakers: identifying the economic, political, and security realms in the global arena, and moulding public institutions to regulate and manage these connections. Held argues that solutions to these dilemmas are required in order to support the rapid growth not only in mutual interconnectedness but also vulnerability in a world where 'the fate and fortunes of each of us are thoroughly intertwined' in virtually every facet of modern-day life.²³

Greater attention also has been paid to the transnational role of civil society and non-governmental organisations, in recognition of the fact that these constitute critical stakeholders that operate beyond the territorial constraints of nation-states. As Fred Halliday noted in 2003, on many issues ranging from political prisoners, the environment, and landmines, 'it is non-governmental organisations which have (within countries and internationally) developed the policies of global institutions.'²⁴ This forms part of what Jan Aart Scholte has labelled a 'more polycentric [system of] governance' whereby sub-state actors and suprastate agencies coexist alongside nation-states, albeit with some autonomy from them.²⁵ Meanwhile, work by Mary Kaldor and others in the series of *Global Civil Society* yearbooks has added depth to the concept and understanding of global civil society. This they define as the development of 'new forms of civic participation and involvement in a globalising world' through connecting people, organisations, values, and ideas located 'in some trans-national arena, and not bound or limited by nation-states or local societies.'²⁶

Building on this brief overview of recent approaches in critical concepts of international political economy, the need for a focused study on the role of the Gulf States in the broader global rebalancing becomes clear. Combining elements of international relations, international economics, comparative politics, and historical approaches, this book maps out and analyses the myriad patterns of Gulf States' engagement with the regional, inter-regional, and international system. Within the overarching shifts in geopolitical and geo-economic power, the Gulf States often stand out by virtue of eye-catching and headline-grabbing policy pronouncements, but deeper issues also lie behind their greater engagement. These factors are explored in the sections and chapters that follow, and collectively amount to a desire among policymakers in the Gulf States to proactively participate – on their own terms as far as possible although also through the creation of informal coalitions with other groups of emerging economies – in the shifting distribution of regional and international power (which itself is being redefined as a concept).

Structure of the book

There are two parts to this book which each address a different aspect of the Gulf States' interaction with the global arena. Part I, entitled 'Globalisation and the Gulf,' consists of four chapters that provide an introduction to the major theoretical and empirical units of analysis. The opening chapter offers a historical overview of the Gulf States' interaction with the global economy. It describes how the Gulf region has for centuries been a commercial and strategic pivot located astride the major trade routes linking India, Africa, and Europe, and connected to each through a dense network of transoceanic influences. Powerful processes of migration and acculturation shaped a cosmopolitan identity and externally focused trading mentality long before the discovery, extraction, and export of oil integrated the region firmly into the international economic system.

This leads into Chapter Two, which explores the evolving role of small states in world politics and international relations as the acceleration of global processes has opened up new possibilities for the exercise of power and influence. Kuwait and Saudi Arabia have, for decades, been embedded in networks of South-South relations through the generous provision of overseas development assistance and leadership in the pan-Islamic arena, but since the end of the Cold War the complexity of the Gulf States' connection with the international system has grown exponentially and far exceeded the Global South. Closer examination of Qatar and the UAE illustrates how, in both states, neither their territorial limitations nor their small population has constrained the projection of power and influence at levels that far outmatch many much larger and more conventionally 'powerful' states. This calls into question some of the dominant assumptions regarding international structures and power in the global age, as both are being radically reconfigured.

Chapter Three analyses the mechanisms of the Gulf States' projection of power and influence at a regional and global level through the prism of 'state capitalism' and the creation of national development plans and strategic niches. Emphasis is placed on specific niche developments in the Gulf, with particular emphasis on renewable and alternative energy in the UAE and Saudi Arabia, refined products and petrochemicals in Saudi Arabia, and higher education and research in Qatar and, to a lesser extent, Oman. The final chapter in this opening section explores the motivations and objectives that have underpinned Gulf officials' strategies of global engagement, not least in how policymakers have sought to derive maximum advantage from economic globalisation while minimising the spillover of its political and cultural dimensions.

In Part II, 'Changing Patterns of Global Engagement,' five chapters address the Gulf States' changing patterns of engagement with the global system. Chapters Five and Six focus on international finance and the enmeshment of GCC states in global trade. The development of GCC states into regional financial hubs for both conventional and Islamic finance is detailed in Chapter Five, which contextualises their growth against the deeper shift in global economic power from west to east and from the market to the state. A key feature of the chapter is the internationalisation of Gulf-based Islamic financial institutions and new acquisitions patterns of sovereign wealth funds, which are creating durable new connections between the Gulf and Southeast Asia, in particular. Such ties are examined more fully in Chapter Six, which delves into the significant diversification of Gulf States' trade relationships not only with existing states such as those in Pacific Asia, but also with new partners in South and Southeast Asia during the 2000s. The chapter ends with an extended case study of the emerging 'nexus' of food and energy security that is creating durable new connections between the Gulf States and a range of partners across Africa and Asia.

Chapter Seven consists of a case study of global aviation as the arena in which the Gulf States have been the most visible and dynamic generators of global change. It compares and contrasts the startling rise of Emirates, Qatar Airways, and Etihad and describes how these three airlines have redefined traditional aviation markets. Operating without the political or workplace constraints of 'legacy carriers' and benefiting from their hosts' 'state capitalist' models of development, the Gulf States' airlines have reshaped global aviation around the hubs of Dubai, Doha, and Abu Dhabi, turning them into 'super-connectors' capable of linking any two points on the globe with a single stopover in the Gulf. Moreover, the announcement of a series of record airplane orders provides further leverage to Gulf airlines as their business assumes ever-greater importance to manufacturers such as Boeing and Airbus at a time of contraction and consolidation elsewhere in the industry. Nevertheless, the chapter ends on a note of caution as it assesses whether three aggressively expanding competitors can be sustainable in such a concentrated market.

Chapter Eight explores how mass inward migration has resulted in a highly stratified workforce underpinning a distinctive form of 'Gulf capitalism' built upon rigid hierarchies of power that are subject to endemic and often systematic abuse. Flows of remittances create overlapping webs of human and socio-economic ties linking labour-sending countries in South and Southeast Asia with the Gulf, but in fundamentally unequal ways. These have contributed to a tense relationship with international non-governmental organisations and global civil society groups over calls for greater scrutiny of working conditions and transparency in protecting migrants from human rights violations.

Chapter Nine ends by examining how the themes outlined in this book, such as the internationalisation of the Gulf and the projection of different forms of power and influence across the regional and global economy, nevertheless coexist uneasily alongside potent existing and potential new sources of insecurity. This is part of a changing approach to the concept of security, in which non-traditional and longer-term challenges to stability are reshaping regional security agendas with the rapid rise of the Islamic State of Iraq and Syria (ISIS) only one of numerous policy challenges facing Gulf policymakers. Others include threats from state failure in neighbouring states, resource insecurity arising from the over-consumption and depletion of oil reserves, the difficulty of overhauling patterns of unsustainable economic development to cushion the eventual transition to a 'post-oil' era, and the new challenges presented by the post-2011 Arab Spring upheaval across the Middle East.

The conclusion will draw attention to the 'Gulf paradox' – that the global emergence of the Gulf States and the new challenges posed by the Arab Spring constitute two profoundly diverging trends for the contemporary Gulf. The interaction of these two diverging trends will shape the dynamics of the Gulf States' political economy and international relations in the years and decades ahead. New domestic priorities may temper some (but not all) of the Gulf States' global positioning that appeared to reach its apotheosis in December 2010. Nevertheless, the shifts in geo-economic power do present the Gulf States with opportunities to increase their leveraging influence in a global order in flux and to create or thicken mutual interdependencies with a multiplicity of partners. This is already leading to new inter-regional realignments and portends a future in which the Gulf States' traditional political and security alignment with the US and Western powers will coexist alongside economic (and possibly ideational) reorientation towards a variety of new partners in Asia, Africa, and even Latin America.

Part I
Globalisation and the Gulf

1
The Gulf and the Global Economy

The opening chapter in this book assesses the multifaceted reasons behind the Gulf States' uneven record of integration into the global economy. It begins by documenting how the ties binding the Gulf States into the global economy are both deep-rooted and long predate the discovery and extraction of oil in the twentieth century. Rather, the opening section highlights the historical interconnectivity of the transnational flows that tied the region into a broader economic hinterland spanning the Indian Oceanic world. Nevertheless, these processes were patchy and subject to partial reversal during the early oil years. Thus, the second section in this chapter examines the entrenched dynamics that also served to limit the Gulf States' relationships with the international system, both politically and economically. Such dynamics included the conservative leanings of many of the 'post-traditional' governing systems in the (Arabian) Gulf, and the Gulf States' enmeshment in Western political and military spheres of influence, during the period of prolonged British protection and following the passage to independence.

In the second half of the chapter, the focus shifts to the role of energy in framing the role of the Gulf in global economic structures and international trade and investment flows. Beginning in the 1940s, oil exports integrated the Gulf States firmly into the international economic system as Gulf oil became a motor of Western economic growth in the post-World War Two era. Securing stable access to regional supplies and the Western guarantees of security that underpinned this became the pillars that structured the international relations of the Gulf after 1945. Oil from the Gulf, particularly Kuwait, supplied 51 per cent of British requirements in 1971, while Saudi Arabia and the US enjoyed a similarly symbiotic relationship. The chapter ends by describing how the Gulf States were only partially impacted by the broader acceleration of economic globalisation in the 1970s and 1980s and by the rapid spread of global interconnections in the 1990s.[1]

An inter-regional crossroads

By virtue of its geographical location, both the Arabian and Persian shores of the Gulf and its hinterlands have been inter-regional crossroads for centuries. Powerful processes of settlement and exchange tied the area into a cosmopolitan network of inter-regional trade and migration. Such social and commercial links extend back into antiquity and the pre-Islamic era. Archaeological discoveries of imported Persian ceramics and seals at many sites in modern-day Kuwait and Bahrain indicate the presence of thriving traffic between the two coasts of the Gulf as far back as the third millennium BC. In about 2000 BC, the island of Failaka, lying just off the Kuwaiti coastline, was inhabited by colonists from the Dilmun civilisation, centred on modern Bahrain, who developed it into a commercial and trading outpost for the entire region.[2] Later, the Gulf's geographic location astride the meeting-point of the Middle East, Africa, and Asia was instrumental in shaping economic development in the region. The lucrative frankincense trade routes that linked Oman and Yemen with the Levant, North Africa, and the Mediterranean were one early example of inter-regional networks in operation; another example was provided by the *dhows* and *booms* that from the seventeenth and eighteenth centuries sailed among the Gulf sheikhdoms, the coast of western India, and the port cities of East Africa. *Dhows* and *booms* departed each season from Basra and the coastal settlements on both sides of the Gulf for the east coast of Africa and the west coast of India, laden with goods and binding the region into a much broader 'transoceanic' maritime community.[3]

In the latter half of the nineteenth century, important new export markets for Gulf dates and pearls emerged in Europe and as far away as North America. Global demand for both commodities boomed in the later years of the century, as international seafaring trade networks proliferated. The value of the date export trade in Muscat (today the capital of Oman) doubled between 1899 and 1906 and increased two-and-a-half times in Bahrain in the same period. Meanwhile, lifestyle changes and the expansion of the middle and upper classes in industrialised countries generated a substantial boom in demand for pearls, and the total value of pearls exported from the Gulf as a whole trebled between 1893 and 1904.[4] The Kuwaiti historian Fahad Ahmad Bishara has documented how:

By the early twentieth century, as the boom reached its zenith, the merchants and mariners of the Gulf had established sizeable communities in a number of western Indian ports, including Karachi, Bombay, Goa, and Calicut, with some venturing further into the interior and taking up residence in such trading centres as Hyderabad and Poona. Western India quickly became a cornerstone of the Indian Ocean world of Gulf merchants, providing them with access to foodstuffs such as rice, sugar, tea, and spices as well as textiles, building materials such as Indian teak and other types of timber, which were vital to the burgeoning dhow-building industry in the Gulf.[5]

The powerful merchant families of the Hejaz (including the Ali-Rida, Zainal, Shobokshi, and Jamjum) constituted the mainstay of economic power in the Arabian Peninsula, together with immigrant merchants, many of whom came from Hadramawt in Yemen (the Bin Mahfouz, Bin Ladin, Bin Sakr, and Ka'aki families being prominent examples). These early economic elites operated within a broad transnational sphere stretching from East Africa to India and were cosmopolitan in their outlook and connections to international economic interests. In his seminal study of the major Gulf merchant families, Michael Field described how one of the scions of the Alireza family (in modern-day Saudi Arabia), Mohammed Ali, visited Paris for the first time in 1920.

> Drawing on the help of business friends, he opened an office at 62 rue La Fayette, on the edge of the main shopping area of Paris . . . From the early 1920s, Mohamed Ali made it his habit to spend several months at a stretch in Paris each year – he bought a house on the Champs Elysees . . . During the height of his career in pearls, he lived almost permanently in Bombay and Paris.[6]

Writing about Bahrain's most prominent merchant family of the nineteenth century, the Safar, James Onley provides an evocative description of a relentlessly trans-regional family hailing from Hillah in modern-day Iraq but putting down deep roots across Bahrain, Iran, and India.

> Hajji Mirza Muhammad Ali Safar (1778–1845) was born in Bushehr; lived in Hillah, Mochah, Bahrain, Bushehr and Bombay; was a Persian, Ottoman and possibly British Indian subject; wrote his letters in Farsi and Arabic . . . His brother, Hajji Muhammad Jafar, was born in Bombay to a Persian mother from Shiraz, lived in Bombay and Bushehr, was a British Indian subject, dressed in the style of an

Indian merchant in Bombay, and probably spoke Farsi, Arabic and Hindi.[7]

Such movement (and opportunity) was restricted to elites and was not generally available to the majority of the inhabitants of the Arabian Peninsula but, in addition to the intermixing of merchant elites and economic migrants, tribal movements were also fluid, as allegiances and relationships shifted over time, and in response to localised factors.[8] A case in point was the movement of large numbers of people as a result of the collapse of the pearling economy in the Gulf in the aftermath of the Great Depression in 1929 and the Japanese introduction of cultured pearls. Socio-economic hardship and conditions of near-famine caused more than one-third of the population of Qatar at the time to migrate to neighbouring states in search of work and sustenance.[9]

Countervailing forces of conservatism

The intermixing of peoples and cultures described above had a strong influence on the emergent states and societies in the Gulf. This rich geographical history belies any notion of the region as peripheral to world history in the pre-oil era or any attempt to define the Gulf solely by its possession of some of the largest energy reserves in the world. Nevertheless, the integration of the coastal Arabian Peninsula sheikhdoms into the network of British protected states between 1835 and 1916 profoundly influenced the region's subsequent political development. Beginning with the signing of a General Treaty of Peace in 1820 and a 'perpetual' Maritime Truce in 1835 and motivated by imperial considerations of safeguarding the coastal flanks of the maritime route to India, British officials representing the (British-controlled) Government of India concluded individual treaties with the Trucial States (now the UAE) in 1835, Bahrain in 1861, Kuwait in 1899 and again in 1914, and Qatar in 1916. Together, the agreements enmeshed the emerging proto-state entities into an inward-oriented, sub-regional unit in which British 'protection' was extended in return for exclusive political and economic relations.[10]

British protection elevated and formalised the roles of the ruling families in each sheikhdom, as Lisa Anderson documented in her important article on the 'resilience of monarchy' in the Middle East in 1991. This external protection additionally gave ruling elites in the Arabian Peninsula – whether members of the ruling families or the British political officers – a considerable stake in maintaining the conservative status quo. A prime example of this conservatism in practice occurred in Kuwait in 1938, where the powers of the ruler, Sheikh Ahmad al-Jabir Al Sabah, were threatened by a vigorous reform movement that culminated in the election of a Legislative Council in June of that year. Under the leadership of a senior member of the ruling family, Sheikh Abdullah al-Salim Al Sabah (himself a future ruler of Kuwait between 1950 and 1965), the new body immediately involved itself in the administrative and financial governance of Kuwait and made unprecedented demands on the ruler's power. Most notably, they forced Sheikh Ahmad al-Jabir Al Sabah to consent to Article One of the law that established the Council, which stipulated that the people were the source of power as represented by elected members of the Legislative Council. Article Five further stated that the head of the Council would exercise executive authority in Kuwait.[11] These were meaningful powers to give away, and the Legislative Council rapidly sought to take responsibility for both Kuwait's external affairs and collective state revenues. However, when these developments inspired similar reform movements in Dubai and Bahrain, they began to alarm British officials as much as the ruler himself. With power seemingly slipping away from the carefully constructed group of British-protected Sheikhs up and down the Gulf, Britain supported Sheikh Ahmad al-Jabir Al Sabah when he dissolved the Council in December 1938 and violently suppressed its elected replacement in March 1939.[12]

A slightly different set of circumstances prevailed in Oman and Saudi Arabia although the end result was broadly similar. In Oman, British influence was informal yet pervasive, as opposed to the formal establishment of protected state relations with Kuwait, Qatar, Bahrain, and Oman, yet it maintained a determined grip over the regime of Sultan bin Taimur (ruled 1932–1970).[13] British officials in the early decades of the twentieth century also sought to build relationships among the competing claimants of power in the Hejaz and Nejd. However, Britain's backing of the Sharif of Mecca during and after the Arab Revolt during World War One failed eventually to prevent the Hashemite leader from being defeated decisively by Ibn Saud (Abdulaziz bin Abdulrahman Al Saud) in 1925. The expansion of Ibn Saud's rule across the Arabian Peninsula culminated in the creation of the modern Kingdom of Saudi Arabia in 1932 and the subsequent development of close relations with the US. In February 1943, President Franklin Delano Roosevelt declared that the defence of Saudi Arabia was vital to American security, following a series of long-distance Italian bombing raids against oil installations in Saudi Arabia and Bahrain, and his administration designated Saudi Arabia eligible for Lend Lease assistance. Two years later, on Valentine's Day 1945 and shortly before his death, Roosevelt journeyed from the Yalta conference to the Great Bitter Lake in Egypt for the fabled meeting with Ibn Saud that formed the cornerstone of the 'oil-for-security' bargain between the US and Saudi Arabia ever since.[14]

During this period, before and after World War Two, British officials scrambled to protect their political allies in the smaller coastal sheikhdoms who were otherwise vulnerable to Saudi expansionism to the peripheries of the Arabian Peninsula. After 1945, the growing web of political and military ties between Saudi Arabia and the US constituted a new strategic challenge to Britain's regional primacy. Initially, British officials tried to resist the growth of American influence in the Gulf only to come closer together in the early 1950s as the shared sense of Cold War threat increasingly preoccupied American and British attention, although differences in approach remained a factor in regional policymaking, particularly towards Yemen.[15] While the gradual transition from British to American influence was far from seamless and unfolded over a period of four decades from the 1940s to the 1980s, the Western political and security umbrella did provide shelter for Saudi Arabia and the smaller Gulf States, and buffered their rulers from the political cross-currents of Arab nationalism and socialism.[16]

Although not monolithic in political structure, and capable of including progressive political leaders such as the 'Free Princes' and Abdullah al-Tariki (the 'Red Sheikh' and the co-founder of the Organization of Petroleum Exporting Countries [OPEC]) in Saudi Arabia, the Gulf regimes nevertheless developed a reputation for political caution as they transitioned into fully fledged independent states. This contrasted sharply with popular and radical movements of national liberation among post-colonial entities elsewhere in the world between the 1940s and 1960s, and it required the Gulf rulers to adopt a delicate and – at times, awkward – balancing act between their reliance on British protection and the need to appease politicised local groups within society.[17] Nevertheless, the pragmatic pursuance of strategies of survival enabled the ruling families to manage quite effectively the transformational socio-economic impact of incoming oil revenues on their polities. The capture of such processes of change enabled Gulf rulers to defy the arguments of social scientists such as Karl Deutsch and Samuel Huntingdon, who predicted their imminent demise in the 1950s and 1960s. Huntingdon's 'Sheikh's Dilemma' put forward the case that most remaining 'traditional' monarchies would collapse under pressures for political reform and that modernising forces that would overwhelm the supposedly 'weak' polities.[18]

Internal and external considerations therefore reinforced a conservative political stance that distinguished the Gulf States from the majority of other developing countries during the post-colonial period following the end of World War Two. The divergence in world views became clear during the Marxist-supported rebellion in the Omani province of Dhofar from 1965 to 1975. Officials from the People's Democratic Republic of Yemen (PDRY) – the only Marxist state ever to exist in the Arab world – supported the Popular Front for the Liberation of Oman and the Arabian Gulf (PFLOAG) in its struggle against the Omani Sultanate. Oman eventually defeated the rebellion, but only after high levels of British political and military assistance, including deployment of SAS battalions that extended well beyond Britain's formal military withdrawal from the Gulf on 30 November 1971. Such high levels of external assistance – which also came in the form of Iranian military support provided by the Shah – enabled PDRY officials to portray the Dhofar campaign as a 'war of liberation against foreign occupation' from the 'puppets of colonialism in Oman' and its 'client Government,' propped up by British (and Iranian) assistance.[19]

The Dhofar war and its regional repercussions visibly illustrated the extent of the Gulf States' divergence from political trajectories then dominant in much of the developing world. Moreover, the struggle to prevent the spread of revolutionary Marxism into the neighbouring Gulf States was an illustration of how broader Cold War tensions played themselves out on a local scale. By pitting British- and Iranian-backed government forces against rebels armed with Chinese and Soviet weaponry, the campaign demonstrated the interplay among competing local, regional, and international interests in framing the nature of the conflict in the southern flank of the Arabian Peninsula.[20] The strategy of rolling back any ideological threat to regional stability was made more significant by the failure of Western-led attempts to create a durable security pact that would act as a bulwark against the spread of Communism in the Middle East. Both the short-lived Baghdad Pact (created in 1955 by Britain, Iraq, Iran, Pakistan, and Turkey) and its successor, the Central Treaty Organization (CENTO) foundered after the revolutions that swept away conservative monarchical rule in Iraq and Iran in 1958 and 1979 respectively.[21]

This intersection of Gulf States' and Western security interests from the 1950s through the 1970s complicated and delayed the growth of tangible links with the Soviet Union and major emerging economies such as China, which actively supported the anti-imperialist, revolutionary movement in Dhofar and the PDRY. Kuwait was the earliest of the Gulf States to establish diplomatic relations with the Union of Soviet Socialist Republics (USSR) and China in 1963 and 1971 respectively.[22] Until the 1980s, Kuwait was the only regional state to maintain a working political, financial, and military relationship with the USSR, with Saudi Arabia only establishing diplomatic relations with Moscow after the Iraqi invasion of Kuwait in 1990. With China also, the normalisation of ties did not occur until after Deng Xiaoping announced a moderation of Chinese policies away from the ideological rigidity of the Mao era in 1978, after which Oman established diplomatic relations with China in 1978, followed by the UAE in 1984, Qatar in 1988, Bahrain in 1989, and Saudi Arabia, again, in 1990.[23]

The bifurcation between the Gulf States and much of the developing world, including other Arab and Islamic states, was reinforced by a Saudi-led policy of actively resisting the political currents sweeping the region in the post-war years. The Al Saud family led the way in the 1960s and 1970s in encouraging the formation of Islamic organisations to counter left-wing or secular oppositional alternatives. Under King Saud (ruled 1953–1964) and King Faisal (ruled 1964–1975), Saudi Arabia engaged also in an 'Arab Cold War,' broadly pitting the region's conservative monarchies against its revolutionary republics led by Egypt's charismatic President Gamal Abdul Nasser, as Saudi and Egyptian military forces backed competing proxy factions in Yemen.[24] Moreover, the inflow of oil revenues into Saudi Arabia facilitated the creation of an array of international Islamic institutions and networks that extended transnationally the kingdom's 'soft power.' Notable examples were the creation of the Muslim World League in 1962, the Organization of the Islamic Conference (OIC) and the World Assembly of Muslim Youth in 1972, and the International Islamic Relief Organization (IIRO) in 1975.[25]

The oil 'revolution'

The pre-oil economy of the communities distributed along the shoreline of the Gulf was dominated by the pearl industry. Pearling structured social relationships and hierarchies within a segmented labour force broken up into merchant-moneylenders, ship captains (*nakhodas*), and the divers and haulers who undertook the dangerous tasks of collecting the pearls from the seabed. It also spawned a derivative service economy that supported and sustained it. Not for nothing has the pearl become the heritage symbol of the modern Gulf States, found on banknotes and monuments throughout the region and fondly recalled in heavily sanitised folk histories that usually downplay pearling's harshness, inequalities, and dangers to life and limb. Prior to the discovery of oil in the 1930s and the commencement of exports in the 1940s, pearling constituted the major economic activity for decades, and its sudden demise created conditions of real hardship. This occurred in the space of just a few years after the onset of the Great Depression in 1929, as the international demand for pearls collapsed, while the introduction of Japanese cultured pearls left Gulf producers unable to compete on cost. One chronicler of Qatar described it as 'a disaster which almost overnight removed the one export on which the people of the Gulf could rely to bring in foreign earnings.'[26]

The smaller Gulf States' reliance on a single economic sector for the majority of incoming revenues curiously foreshadowed their later dependence upon oil receipts. Although the pearling and oil industries are completely different in scale, organisation, and economic and techno-political complexity, they both represented volatile streams that fluctuated according to external factors and international demand, both of which were beyond the control of local officials. This was at its most pronounced in Qatar, where the impact of the collapse of the pearling industry was magnified manifold by the near-absence of any other form of economic activity, as it lacked the entrepôt trade of Kuwait, Bahrain, or Dubai. Their greater dependence on pearling had dramatic results, as Crystal estimates that between one-third and a half of the population chose to emigrate during the decade that elapsed between the end of the pearl era and the subsequent onset of the oil era. They included many members of the business class: only two major merchant families – the Darwish and the al-Mani – remained behind.[27]

Oil was first discovered in the Middle East in southwest Persia (modern-day Iran) in 1908 and later was found in commercial quantities in northern Iraq near Kirkuk in 1927. Exploration quickly began in the neighbouring Gulf sheikhdoms, where geological conditions were similar to those where oil had been struck in Iran. On 31 May 1932, the newly created Bahrain Petroleum Company (BAPCO), a British-controlled subsidiary of the Standard Oil Company of California (SoCal), struck oil in Bahrain. Production began the following year, and in 1933 SoCal (today's Chevron) was awarded the concession to search for oil in the new Kingdom of Saudi Arabia.[28] Five years later, oil was discovered in the Dammam Dome in the Eastern Province, near the western shoreline of the Gulf, and following a decade-long interruption due to World War Two, large-scale Saudi oil exports commenced in 1948. Government revenues immediately surged from the US$13 million to US$16 million range annually between 1938 and 1946 to US$53.6 million in 1948 and US$100 million in 1950.[29] This required the urgent creation of a system of functional governing ministries, coordinated by the establishment of a Council of Ministers in October 1953, and capable of absorbing and spending the incoming monies. This took place in the final weeks of Ibn Saud's life, and followed closely on the creation of the Saudi Arabian Monetary Agency (SAMA) as a means of institutionalising mechanisms of monetary and fiscal control.[30]

Elsewhere in the Gulf, events followed a similar pattern with the exception of the Trucial States and Oman, where oil only became a significant factor several decades later, as Table 1.1 shows. In Kuwait, a concession to explore for oil was granted to the newly formed Kuwait Oil Company (a joint venture founded in 1934 by the Anglo-Persian Oil Company and America's Gulf Oil). Large quantities of oil were located at Burgan in 1938, nine days before the discovery of oil in Saudi Arabia, but, as in Saudi Arabia, full exploration and development was delayed until after 1945. Commercial exports from Kuwait started in June 1946 and production nearly tripled in the first year alone, from 5.9 million barrels in 1946 to more than 16 million barrels in 1947.[31] Similar conditions pertained in Qatar, where Petroleum Development Qatar Limited – a forerunner of the present state-owned oil company, Qatar Petroleum – was formed in June 1935 by a consortium that included Royal Dutch Shell and the Compagnie Française des Pétroles (today's Total). As in Kuwait and Saudi Arabia, the first oil was found in Qatar in late 1939 but further exploration and production came to a halt until the end of the war, whereupon exports began, admittedly at a tiny rate initially, in 1947.[32]

Table 1.1   Oil discoveries in the Gulf States

Country	Date
Bahrain	1932
Kuwait	1938
Saudi Arabia	1938
Qatar	1939
UAE (Abu Dhabi)	1958
Oman	1962 (commercial grade)
Dubai	1966

Source: Information collated by Kristian Coates Ulrichsen

The exploration and extraction of oil in the Trucial States/UAE and Oman occurred later than elsewhere in the Gulf. After several false starts in the 1950s, oil was finally discovered in the emirate of Dubai in the early 1960s and exports commenced later in the decade. Further onshore and offshore discoveries pushed oil production in Dubai to a peak in 1991, after which production levels began an inexorable and steady decline.[33] Dubai's reserves paled in comparison to those in neighbouring Abu Dhabi, which today accounts for more than 90 per cent of total UAE oil reserves. The first oil in Abu Dhabi was located at Umm Shaif in 1958 and the first exports from Das Island occurred in 1962, but production only took off after Sheikh Zayed bin Sultan Al Nahyan replaced his brother as ruler of Abu Dhabi in 1966 and set in motion the full development of the emirate's resources.[34] Similar to Abu Dhabi, the discovery of oil in Oman between 1962 and 1964 had to await political change at the apex of the state, as production remained tiny prior to the replacement of Sultan Taimur bin Said by his son, the present ruler, Sultan Qaboos, in July 1970.[35]

Once production got underway the, level of exports increased rapidly. A case in point is Saudi Arabia, where oil dominated the economy after exports commenced in 1948. By 1959, the sector accounted for 85 per cent of government revenues and 90 per cent of foreign export earnings, in addition to financing almost all commercial and infrastructural development.[36] During the subsequent decade, production approximately doubled and revenues tripled from 1962 to 1970, at a time when the posted price of oil remained fixed at US$1.80.[37] Similar dynamics were at play in Kuwait also, as the country initially became the largest oil producer in the Gulf in the early 1950s. This occurred in part as Kuwait replaced Iran as a major supplier of oil to Western markets after the Iranian government's nationalisation of the oil industry in 1951 and a resulting boycott of Iranian oil. In the space of just seven years, Kuwait's oil revenues soared from US$760,000 in 1946 to US$169 million in 1953.[38] By the time of the first oil price boom in 1973, oil revenues had reached US$9.8 billion and accounted for 70 per cent of Kuwait's total Gross Domestic Product (GDP).[39] Imports also surged, particularly after the 1973 oil price shock created a new class of affluent consumers virtually overnight; the number of registered vehicles in Saudi Arabia, for instance, rose 65-fold between 1970 and 1984 from 60,000 to 3.9 million.[40]

Revenues from the export of oil transformed the socio-economic structures and development patterns in the Gulf States. At first, the rudimentary traditional patterns of administration that held sway across large parts of the Arabian Peninsula until the 1930s and 1940s were incapable of managing the integration of the young new states into the global oil market. Thus, the challenges involved in absorbing and utilising enormous sums of money led to the rapid creation of institutional frameworks that often coexisted uneasily alongside the traditional measurements of power and authority, particularly in the early years.[41] Oil began to be exported in commercial quantities in the late 1940s and production rose rapidly in the 1950s and 1960s. This coincided with the formative passage to independence of Kuwait (1961) and the UAE, Bahrain, and Qatar (1971), and the early processes of modern state formation in Oman and Saudi Arabia.

Particularly after the first oil price shock of 1973, the resulting surge in government revenues provided the growing state structures with the financial wherewithal to reformulate traditional tribal structures into modern forms of governance. Pete Moore has noted that, as a region, the Middle East and North Africa outperformed all other regions in the developing world with regard to income growth and redistribution in the period between 1960 and 1985.[42] In the specific context of the Gulf States, the redistributive mechanisms of socio-political control that emerged did so within a highly stratified economic framework encompassing nests of rentiers flowing downward from the state at its apex.[43] Thus, the impact of oil rents became intertwined from the start with emerging state structures and decisions on how to absorb and utilise the revenues, thereby giving rise to pronounced regional socio-economic peculiarities (Table 1.3).[44]

Over the course of the second half of the twentieth century, the flow of oil from the Arabian Peninsula also became a critical component in the growth of the world economy. Table 1.2 illustrates the magnitude of GCC states' proven crude oil reserves in regional and global comparison, and indicates also how small Bahrain's indigenous reserves are by comparison to those of its GCC neighbours (Bahrain's production of 40,000 barrels per day [in 2011 figures] is boosted significantly by the allocation of an additional 150,000 barrels per day from Saudi Arabia's offshore Abu Safa field operated by Saudi Aramco [Arabian American Oil Company]).[45]

Led by the US and the post-war economies of Western Europe and Japan, industrialised countries embarked upon two decades of economic growth after 1945. With this period constituting also 'the golden age of Middle Eastern exploration,' the amount of oil sourced from the Gulf region, encompassing also Iran and Iraq, grew rapidly in both absolute and relative terms.[46] Indeed, by 1960, the Gulf States were producing

Table 1.2 Proven crude oil reserves, 2014

Rank	Country	Proven reserves (barrels)
1	Venezuela	297,700,000,000
2	Saudi Arabia	268,400,000,000
3	Canada	173,200,000,000
4	Iran	157,300,000,000
5	Iraq	140,300,000,000
6	Kuwait	104,000,000,000
7	UAE	97,800,000,000
8	Russia	80,000,000,000
9	Libya	48,470,000,000
10	Nigeria	37,140,000,000
11	US	30,530,000,000
13	Qatar	25,240,000,000
24	Oman	5,500,000,000
69	Bahrain	124,600,000

Source: CIA World Factbook

Table 1.3 Natural resource rents as percentage of GDP

Country	2010	2011	2012	2013
Bahrain	10.5	10.9	10.0	11.0
Kuwait	52.8	60.2	59.2	59.1
Oman	39.3	44.1	39.5	38.0
Qatar	41.5	43.4	36.7	34.6
Saudi Arabia	46.9	51.6	48.7	46.2
UAE	23.2	27.5	26.2	23.7

Source: The World Bank, http://data.worldbank.org/indicator/NY.GDP. TOTL.RT.ZS

15 per cent of the world's oil and a decade later this figure had approximately doubled to 30 per cent. Most remarkably, in the case of the United Kingdom, Britain's dependence on oil from the Middle East (including Algeria) peaked at 81 per cent in 1950 (as against 1.5 per cent in 2012).[47] These figures catapulted the commercial and strategic importance of the Gulf region – hitherto expressed largely in terms of the security of the British Empire and the protection of the land and sea routes to British-ruled India – up the agendas of international policymakers.[48]

Gulf oil revenues held an additional importance to the British economy as it struggled to adapt to the post-1945 decline of the

United Kingdom. Oil prices for the British-protected states in the Gulf were fixed in sterling and, initially, in the 1950s, the majority of imports also came from the United Kingdom as well. The intersection of political and financial ties between Britain and the Gulf States acted as a vital prop to successive British government attempts to maintain the value of sterling. Indeed, by 1959, it was estimated that the value of Gulf assets in the United Kingdom amounted to more than one-quarter of Britain's total gold and foreign exchange holdings. Kuwait, especially, emerged as a vital linchpin in British government efforts to prevent a precipitous decline in sterling. Although the small Gulf States continued to back sterling by holding their surplus oil income in London well into the 1960s, the situation ended abruptly in 1967 following the 16 per cent devaluation of sterling. This hit Gulf foreign assets hard and led to the diversification of the latter's foreign holdings and an end to the use of sterling as a major reserve currency.[49]

As oil prices soared following the 1973 Arab–Israeli war and the subsequent Arab oil embargo, the revenues pouring into Gulf treasuries multiplied. Across the region, oil rents were used to create an all-encompassing welfare state, as the government became a distributor to, rather than an extractor of wealth from, citizenry. The average price of crude oil surged from US$2.04 a barrel in 1971 to a high of US$32.50 in 1981, as the 1973 rise in prices was followed by a second spike in 1979–1980 in the wake of the Iranian revolution and the outbreak of the Iran–Iraq War. Simultaneously, the six Gulf States' combined crude oil production rose by 77 per cent between 1970 and 1980, resulting in a massive inflow of oil revenues, which increased from US$5.2 billion to US$158 billion during the period.[50] They entered into a society, however, still characterised by poverty and under-development, with low absorptive and human capacity to manage the sudden wealth, and ruling elites prone to commissioning extravagant and wasteful 'white elephant' prestige projects. Indeed, during the 'freewheeling' decade of the 1970s, almost all of the additional income generated by the oil price increases was spent immediately, rather than being saved for future generations, heightening Gulf States' subsequent vulnerability to the slump in prices to a low of just US$10 a barrel in 1986.[51]

With the massive influx of incoming revenues into Gulf economies in the 1970s, the flows of oil rents provided the emerging state structures with the financial wherewithal to create redistributive or 'rentier' states. Here, the 'no taxation without representation' paradigm was seemingly reversed as regimes sought to co-opt socio-political support through the spread of wealth, and exhibited varying degrees of autonomy from societal demands or pressures. Classical rentier state theory developed in the 1970s and 1980s to examine the impact of external rents such as oil on the nature of states such as Saudi Arabia and their interaction with society. Hazem Beblawi argued that a rentier economy developed when the creation of wealth was centred on a small fraction of society, while in a rentier state the government is the principal recipient of the external rent, and plays the central role in redistributing this wealth to its citizenry.[52] Giacomo Luciani extended this analysis of rentierism by distinguishing between allocative and productive states, in which the external origin of income derived from the export of oil frees allocation states from their productive economic base.[53] State autonomy from domestic taxation and societal extraction was expected to change the political 'rules of the game,' as the absence of the taxation/representation linkage would, it was postulated, lessen the incentive for mobilisation around programmes designed to change political institutions or policy.[54] With its petroleum sector accounting for 89.29 per cent of budget revenue and 41.5 per cent of GDP at the end of the first oil price boom in 1981 yet a mere 1.5 per cent of civilian employment (in 1980), Saudi Arabia came to represent an example of an oil state par excellence.[55]

Yet since the 1990s, a number of critiques of rentier theory moved beyond the structurally deterministic 'no taxation without representation' axis to emphasise the importance of local agency and decision-making in the creation of contemporary Gulf polities. These critiques put forward a more nuanced and multi-causal approach to the study of the formative period of state-building in the Gulf during the 1950s and 1960s. Examining such processes in Saudi Arabia, Steffen Hertog documented the dynamic interplay among elite politics, factionalism, and patronage networks alongside the growth of administrative structures. He described a period of considerable institutional fluidity within the Kingdom, in which competing centres of power led to the formation of a segmented bureaucracy featuring numerous and often-overlapping 'states within a state.' Over time, bureaucratic stasis ossified these initially fluid arrangements into rigid institutional structures although well-managed technocratic enclaves – such as SAMA and the Saudi Basic Industries Company (SABIC) – also emerged in parallel.[56]

Patterns of competitive institutionalisation and proliferating bureaucracies reflected the multiple circles of influence within Gulf ruling families. These intensified after the death of the patriarchal 'founding father' figures such as King Abdulaziz in Saudi Arabia in 1953 and, more recently, Sheikh Zayed of the UAE in 2004, as each had multiple sons among whom power and responsibility was divided. Moreover, factional intra-family struggles were long a characteristic of Qatar's ruling Al Thani dynasty, which saw contested successions in 1913, 1949, 1960, and 1972, and have been prominent in Bahrain since the death of the longstanding Emir of 38 years, Isa bin Salman Al Khalifa, in 1999. Gwenn Okruhlik has emphasised the significance of political choice and the interaction between structural rentier state theory and personal rule in explaining the political economy of oil states. She argued that rentier theory alone could not explain the rise of oppositional dissent in Saudi Arabia, Bahrain, and Kuwait from the 1950s on, and consequently the state's financial autonomy did not translate into immunity from civil pressures or societal contestation.[57]

In all the Gulf States, workers' demands for political and economic rights proliferated as oil revenues flooded in. In Qatar, these took the form of a petition in 1963 that contained 35 demands for reform. One of the most prominent and vocal advocates of change, Dr Ali Khalifa al-Kuwari, who worked in Qatar's oil and gas sector as vice chairman of the Qatar Liquefied Gas Company and as vice chairman of the National Company for Petroleum Products before joining Qatar University as a professor of economics, described what happened next:

> Strikes, imprisonments and expulsions that preceded it and the subsequent pledge by the then ruler to enact reform and ratify the majority of the petition's demands. Demands for reform did not stop there, however, but continued at a lower intensity . . . before finally emerging into the light in 1992 in the form of two petitions. The most important of these petitions' demands was the election of a consultative council, appointed and tasked to draw up a permanent constitution. As a result of this, the signatories were punished with prison sentences, travel bans, the denial of their rights and the threat to rescind their Qatari citizenship.[58]

Similar pressures arose in Saudi Arabia and Bahrain. The reign of King Saud (1953–1964), in particular, witnessed prolonged periods of labour unrest emanating from oil workers protesting over conditions at Aramco camps in Saudi Arabia's Eastern Province. Major demonstrations began in October 1953 with a three-week strike by 13,000 workers in the oilfields around Dammam. The strike was suppressed violently, although pay and general conditions subsequently improved slightly. Three years later, a workers' protest during a visit by King Saud to Dhahran in June 1956 also was met with state violence, while a decade later, a wave of unrest broke out in Riyadh and other cities between November 1966 and

February 1967.[59] Neighbouring Bahrain experienced a lengthy period of unrest between 1954 and 1956, which became fused with Arab nationalist and anti-British sentiments in the turbulent aftermath of the Suez Crisis in November that year. Oil workers were later involved heavily in a strike of BAPCO workers that paralysed Bahrain in March 1965. This escalated rapidly into a general strike and the formulation of a platform calling for the right to hold political meetings, the release of all political prisoners, an end to the state of emergency in place since the 1956 troubles, and the recognition of the right to form labour unions.[60]

The impact of oil on Bahrain and Kuwait had an additional, spatial, dimension, through the construction of 'company towns' in Awali and Ahmadi respectively. These new 'colonial' towns reshaped notions of urban space and patterns of lifestyle and consumption. Awali was constructed by BAPCO in 1937 and, over time, emerged as 'an integral part of an inclusive urban public culture that was the unique creation of oil and embraced both indigenous and foreign workers' in Bahrain.[61] Moreover, as Nelida Fuccaro has demonstrated, the oil boom in the 1950s had the effect of empowering a young and largely radical new generation of commercial workers and white-collar professionals who increasingly called into question the traditional governing practices of the ruling family and formed the vanguard of the ideological ferment centring around nationalism, communism, and Ba'athism that came to characterise urban life in Manama.[62] Ahmadi was built by the Kuwait Oil Company (KOC) in 1947 as part of a four-year Kuwait Building Plan intended to organise and rationalise the infrastructure needed to expand oil operations in the country. KOC commissioned James Wilson, a British architect who had worked as an assistant to Sir Edward Lutyens in the planning stages of New Delhi between 1913 and 1916. Wilson remained heavily influenced by his mentor and by the principles of 'Garden City' design and the result was a landscaped slice of greenery (and 'regular garden competitions') set somewhat incongruously in the desert outside Kuwait City.[63]

Limited initial impact of globalisation

With oil having become central to the post-war world economy in the 1950s and 1960s, the oil revenues that cascaded into Gulf treasuries following the 1970s price shocks were magnified by the nationalisation of the national oil companies during the decade. In Kuwait, the state took control of the KOC in 1975 and five years later created the Kuwait Petroleum Corporation (KPC) as an umbrella organisation integrating the various upstream and downstream operations under government control. The newly independent government in Qatar established Qatar Petroleum in 1974 and nationalised all oil companies in 1977, while Qatargas was created in 1984 to produce liquefied natural gas for export to Japan. In Saudi Arabia, the nationalisation of Aramco took place in stages between 1973, when the government first acquired a 25 per cent share of the company, and 1980, when it took full control (and formally changed its name to Saudi Aramco in 1988 when it also took over all remaining operational functions in the kingdom's oil and gas fields). The staggered process was notable for taking place in relative harmony with the four American concessionaires that made up Aramco, three of which (the now merged Exxon/Mobil and Chevron) continue to operate in Saudi Arabia today, albeit in a different capacity, as providers of technical services.[64] A similar harmony was apparent in Abu Dhabi, where Sheikh Zayed resisted full nationalisation of the oil sector and maintained good relations with international oil companies as part of the broader modernisation of the fledgling infrastructure of the UAE.[65]

Against this backdrop, a distinctive form of 'Gulf capitalism' emerged as incoming oil revenues intersected with the rapid expansion of infrastructure and urban development. This grew out of the traditional 'merchant family' business elites that predated the discovery of oil. Cut out by the ruling family/government from direct participation in the development of oil and gas resources, 'Gulf capitalists' (which are examined in greater detail in Chapter Five) pursued business opportunities in other industries that were either derivative to the oil sector or initiated with state assistance from accrued oil revenues. The most important of these opportunities initially were service and construction contracts granted to local companies by governments and foreign multinationals, either in the oil sector directly or for the infrastructural and industrial projects that formed the backbone of economic diversification programmes. Many of these groups today are characterised by their continued involvement in these types of service and basic contracting activities, which remain the core of their businesses even as they have diversified and developed extensive interests in other sectors, such as retail and finance.[66]

The most prominent merchant families developed cross-border ties that spanned and far surpassed the Gulf States. Examples included business groups such as the Kanoo, al-Fardan, al-Zamil, and al-Qusaybi that drew together the Eastern Province of Saudi Arabia, Bahrain, and Qatar. International exposure initially was concentrated in the 'agency' or franchising process, whereby brands needed a local partner in order to be able to set up shop within the Gulf, as well as in the formation of joint ventures, particularly in the construction industry.[67] Remittances from migrant labourers working in the Gulf also tied the economic fortunes of resource-poor states across the region to the oil-producing states. Countries in this 'secondary-rentier' category included Egypt, Syria, Palestine, Jordan, and Yemen, where the impact on the local economies of North and South Yemen from the remittance flows from the 1.2 million Yemenis working in Saudi Arabia alone was most pronounced, as Chapter Eight documents.[68]

And yet, despite these linkages and the flow of oil that made the Gulf indispensable to industrialised economies during the post-1945 period, the Gulf States, as with much of the broader Middle East region, was to a high degree untouched by the deeper processes of globalisation as they accelerated in the 1970s and 1980s. This was due, in large part, to the fact that the oil sector operated largely in isolation from the wider economy and so shielded domestic markets from the full force of the international system; moreover, oil revenues acted as a cushion against international economic pressures, particularly after the 1970s oil price shocks.[69] A paradox developed whereby both individuals and societies in the Gulf rapidly absorbed what John Fox et al. labelled 'the material benefits of globalisation' albeit in carefully controlled ways that limited and restricted the broader political or social penetration of global market forces.[70]

An often-uneasy symbiosis thus developed between local and global patterns of change as they interacted and fed off each other. An example of the political ramifications was the evolution of Islamist narratives of resistance to globalisation in the years immediately prior to the 9/11 terror attacks in the US. Other, less cathartic but still disruptive, manifestations of the tensions that occasionally surfaced came in the tangled webs of state-business relations when they intersected with international financial and corporate networks. Overlapping ties between the state and the new business elites produced frequently opaque governing arrangements. Members of ruling families often served as silent partners in business enterprises or became major business figures in their own right. The line between state funds and private capital was blurred further by the representation – usually in a 'private capacity' – of ruling family members on company boards.[71] Other characteristics of state-business ties in Gulf States included the allocation by the state of multinational franchising to local groups linked to major merchant families as well as the importance of 'brokers' and 'gatekeepers' who controlled and provided direct access to prominent decision-makers in the state apparatus.

It has been taken for granted by many observers of Gulf business patterns that senior figures in ruling families participate actively in business decisions, with key individuals frequently being singled out for their allegedly rapacious involvement in commercial affairs.[72]

Several murky episodes in the 1980s and 1990s fostered a negative reputation among international stakeholders and potential investors over the difficulties of distinguishing between public and private money and chaotic ownership structures. These included the Grupo Torras affair between 1986 and 1992, which concerned a series of investments made by the Kuwait Investment Office (KIO – located in and operating out of London) in Spain. The KIO established a holding company, Grupo Torras, to manage its increasingly aggressive investments in Spain. Torras grew quickly into one of the largest conglomerates in Spain, controlling several of the largest companies in the country, from chemicals to paper manufacturers, property developers, insurance companies, and textiles. A detailed investigative report compiled by *The Independent* newspaper documented the subsequent investment patterns:

> To avoid being identified as an investor, the KIO would buy shares in Spanish companies indirectly through offshore accounts. Once the price of the shares had risen, it would sell them on to Torras and book the profit. Torras would become the eventual owner of the shares at a relatively high price, which it borrowed money to pay. The strategy was designed to keep Torras functioning at a low profit level, therefore paying low taxes, while the KIO benefited from the share deals.[73]

In 1992, the system collapsed as investor confidence in Grupo Torras plummeted and political opinion in Kuwait turned on the KIO in anger. A new leadership of the KIO accused its predecessors of making irregular profits from the buying and selling of the shares through shell companies based in Gibraltar and the Netherlands. In July 1992, the then Crown Prince and Prime Minister of Kuwait, Sheikh Saad al-Abdullah Al Sabah called in KPMG to audit the KIO's funds and examine its Spanish investments. The subsequent investigation uncovered losses of more than US$4 billion in mismanagement and fraud and resulted in the censuring of former KIO head Sheikh Fahad Mohammad Al Sabah, as well as harsh criticism of another senior family member, Ali Khalifa Al Sabah, who as oil minister in the 1980s and finance minister during and after the Iraqi occupation in 1990, had become 'the main proponent of the KIO operating with autonomy, so that it could dedicate itself to making money without being hampered by the bureaucracy from which most Kuwaiti investment institutions suffer.'[74]

This chapter has documented the linkages between the Gulf States and the global economy as they evolved during the twentieth century. Between the 1930s and the 1950s, the extraction and export of oil transformed the political economy of the small coastal sheikhdoms and of Saudi Arabia and dramatically reconfigured state-society relations within the newly independent polities. While the network of political and security ties with the West distinguished the Gulf States from other post-colonial settings and largely shielded them from revolutionary upheaval, the phases of engagement between the Gulf and its regional and international partners were not static. Rather, they ebbed and flowed as the century progressed before reaching a watershed moment in 1990–1991 with the Iraqi invasion of Kuwait on 2 August 1990 and the subsequent liberation of Kuwait by an international led coalition in January–February 1991. This was a moment of profound change in the international system and coincided with the end of the Cold War and the acceleration of global political and economic change. Over the two decades that followed, the links with the international system would broaden and deepen as the Gulf States became more active participants in the global economy in ways that moved far beyond the hydrocarbons sector.

2
Small States in World Politics

Building on the analysis of the Gulf States' changing role in the world economy, this chapter examines the new possibilities for the exercise of power and influence by small states in the global era. Earlier assumptions of vulnerability and lack of resilience have been eroded as opportunities for small states to make their voice heard have proliferated in an intensely globalised environment in which leverage is projected through multiple channels and is less reliant than ever before on territorial size. This general trend has been magnified still further in the case of resource-rich small states possessing both the *intent* and the *capability* to shape globalising forces to their own advantage. Both Qatar and the UAE, led by the entrepreneurial leaderships of Doha, Dubai, and Abu Dhabi, have proven adept at delinking territory and power, and consequently have emerged as regional powers with international reach. This turns on its head much conventional thinking about the role of small states in world politics and international relations.

The chapter opens by documenting how the impact of globalisation has reconfigured concepts of power and called into question previously dominant assumptions regarding the structure and balance of the international system. Although regional disparities in resource endowment and wealth mean that the Gulf States cannot be treated as a monolithic bloc, there is a certain degree of similarity about the mechanisms deployed to enhance their international standing. Thus, the second half of this chapter documents the enabling factors that have underpinned such new approaches to the conduct of international affairs in the GCC states. These include the advent of a younger generation of leaders to power in the late 1990s and early 2000s and the projection of 'soft power' and cultural influence, particularly in global sport. With systemic changes to the world order shifting the centre of geo-economic gravity towards the 'Global South,' not only Qatar and the UAE but also the GCC as a whole emerged as a visibly proactive pivot around which the broader rebalancing of global power was taking place. The chapter concludes with a case study of branding at work in Gulf States' interaction with global sporting events and personalities.

International system in flux

The great acceleration of global forces from the 1980s onwards presented policymakers the world over with a new set of challenges as well as opportunities. Chief among them was the rise of a multipolar international system in which power was both more diffuse and spread across overlapping layers of national, regional, and global governance. The evolution of a web of multilateral institutions, transnational agreements, and formal and informal networks constituted a dynamic response to the complexity of global interdependence.[1] As a new form of 'global politics' developed, it highlighted, in the words of David Held and Anthony McGrew, 'the richness and complexity of the interconnections which transcend states and societies in the global order.'[2] A proliferation of new participants – state, non-state, interstate, and transnational has provided innumerable new points of entry for the leverage of power and influence on specific issues and policy challenges.[3] In virtually every economic and political sphere, the rapid emergence of the Global South has reformulated existing relationships among states and weakened greatly lingering divisions between 'core' and 'periphery' actors.[4]

The developments listed above have profoundly changed the landscape across which international affairs had been conducted for the majority of the twentieth century, encompassing the Gulf States' formative years of independence. During the Cold War, the study of great power politics in a bipolar international system dominated much of the historiography of international relations. Within these broad structural parameters, the international politics of the Middle East largely focused on the interaction between outside powers and local states.[5] 'Strategic cross-currents,' such as the US' political and strategic interests in Israel and simultaneous reliance on oil from the Gulf, complicated the reciprocal relationship between the international system and the regional sub-system in the Middle East.[6] Small states leveraged their influence predominantly by exercising their collective voice through the one-member one-vote system at the United Nations, and through such organisations as the Non-Aligned Movement and the Group of 77 (G77).[7]

An early example of the attempt by 'Third World' countries to align was the New Economic International Order that was put forth in a set of proposals by developing countries in the 1970s. These sought to revise the post-1945 Bretton Woods system created by leading industrialised economies by collectively promoting Third World interests on issues such as improving the terms of trade and reducing developed-country tariffs.[8] In May 1974, the UN General Assembly adopted their demands in the *Declaration for the Establishment of a New Economic Order* following concerted pressure from developing countries for changes to the management of the world economic system. However, in spite of this declaration of intent to raise the prices of raw resource exports and accelerate technological transfer to developing countries in addition to preferential trade access to rich country markets and greater aid to least developed countries, the New International Economic Order foundered in large part owing to a lack of cooperation among signatory states.[9] By 1979, the complete stalemate of the 'North-South' dialogue on the new international economic order sounded the death-knell to the initiative a mere five years after its launch.[10]

A decade later, the Iraqi occupation of Kuwait in 1990 underscored the vulnerability of small states to the rapacious designs of their larger and more powerful neighbours. Saddam Hussein's invasion fell into a pattern of large state/small state tension in the Gulf that persistently undermined attempts to band together in the name of developing country solidarity. During much of the twentieth century, a recurring feature of security policy in the four small Gulf States (Bahrain, Kuwait, Qatar, and the UAE) was how to balance ties with the three regional powers of Iraq, Iran, and Saudi Arabia. Although specific threats waxed and waned, the smaller Gulf States had to balance cooperation and engagement with the maintenance of national autonomy and protection from attempted interference in domestic affairs.[11] Although the attack on Kuwait was the most serious instance of the breakdown in this fragile equilibrium, both the UAE and Qatar had unresolved and acrimonious territorial disputes of their own with Saudi Arabia. These led to confrontation between Abu Dhabi and Saudi Arabia in 1954 (at Buraimi) and deadly border skirmishes between Qatar and Saudi Arabia as late as 1992 and 1993.[12]

The US-led international coalition which mobilised so rapidly to condemn the Iraqi invasion and liberate Kuwait in 1991 also carried a significant lesson for small states in general and for the GCC states in particular. This was that states with tangible interdependencies with powerful international partners could count on their support during times of crisis. Never was this more powerfully demonstrated than during the chaotic first few days after Iraqi troops overran Kuwait, when sceptics inside the George H. W. Bush administration who suggested that the US accept the Iraqi invasion as a *fait accompli* were convincingly – and quickly – overruled.[13] In its aftermath, all the GCC states moved to upgrade their bilateral security relationships with the US. Kuwait, for instance, signed ten-year defence agreements with the US on 19 September 1991 and with the United Kingdom on 11 March 1992. The value of these agreements quickly became clear as the US hurriedly deployed Patriot missiles and additional troops to Kuwait in August 1992 and October 1994 after Saddam Hussein again massed Iraqi troops on the border.[14]

Hence, the Gulf War of 1991 marked a watershed moment in the GCC states' international posture. Kuwait's liberation by a multinational coalition of 34 countries coincided with the end of the Cold War and with the acceleration of global political and economic change, just at the moment that the utility of robust interconnections with international partners became powerfully clear. These developments imparted greater depth to international political economy in general, and increased the range of pathways to inter-regional and global enmeshment open to emerging powers and states. A case in point was the proliferation of ties with rising powers India and China following several decades of deep-freeze. As mentioned in Chapter 1, diplomatic relations between China and all six GCC states were only established in 1990, with the normalisation of ties with Saudi Arabia. Ties with India also had been characterised by sustained frigidity during the 1970s and 1980s, as India turned inward under the leadership of Indira Gandhi and her immediate successors. These changed markedly after 1990, as rising energy consumption turned both China and India into major oil and gas importers increasingly dependent on the Gulf as a critical source of supply.[15] Crucially, economic relations also diversified far beyond the energy sphere to the extent that by 2014, 70 per cent of all manufactured goods leaving China by sea were shipped first to Dubai before being either allocated to regional markets in the Middle East or sent on to European and African markets.[16]

Two statements by senior Indian and Chinese policymakers in the mid-2000s captured the extent to which the Gulf was becoming pivotal to both countries' international relations. Although in both cases the sentiments revolved around energy security, they were buttressed by thickening bilateral linkages, investments, and joint ventures in myriad other sectors as well. Indian Prime Minister Manmohan Singh laid out the many connections binding India and the Gulf in a globalising world in a lecture in January 2005 marking the inauguration of the Centre for West Asian Studies at Jamia Millia Islamia University in New Delhi:

Ongoing processes in West Asia will have a critical impact on the global strategic environment. Strategic thinkers the world over will weigh the possible impact of the large and growing extra-regional presence in West Asia, or the possibility of radical religious groups seeking to create and fill a political vacuum in this region. Needless to say, the impact of any negative development on India will transcend the obvious political and security repercussions, as it will also greatly affect our economy, with our energy security strategy being the first to come under threat.[17]

Three years later, Singh used a visit to the Gulf in November 2008 to announce that India viewed the region as an interim part of its broader neighbourhood as he signed a range of defence and security agreements with Oman and Qatar. Energy security lay behind this statement, as India currently imports about 75 per cent of its total oil requirements, of which some 80 per cent originate in the Gulf States. In 2008, the sharp increase in oil prices alarmed Indian officials and contributed to a decision to move beyond reliance on imported oil and to seek 'equity access to foreign oil and gas reserves and achieve strategic energy security.' This decision also enhanced the importance of maritime security to India in ensuring stable and uninterrupted access to oil and gas supplies from the Gulf.[18]

Chinese approaches to the concept of energy security also evolved as dependence on Gulf imports grew in the 2000s. The debate among domestic policymakers was brought on by emerging anxieties at the country's high reliance on imported supplies of energy. An integral part of this conversation revolved around the naval capabilities and force projection that would be necessary to ensure China's secure maritime access to overseas energy sources. High-ranking members of the People's Liberation Army Navy (PLAN) emerged as advocates for an enhanced 'Far Sea Defence' (*yuanhai fangwei*) policy. Thus, the PLAN deputy political commissioner, Yao Wenhuai, argued in December 2007 that China's reliance on seaborne energy imports required a powerful navy to defend its strategic interests:

Particularly for oil and other key strategic supplies, our dependence on sea transport is very great, and ensuring the security of strategic seaways is extremely important. We must fully recognise the actual requirements of protecting our country's developmental interests at sea, fully recognise the security threats our country faces at sea, and fully recognise the special status and utility of our navy in preparing for military conflict.[19]

Although it is a much longer-term partner than China and India, the evolving nature of South Korea's relationship with the Gulf States, and particularly with the UAE, provides a further illustration of the changing inter-regional relations at work. Ties between South Korea and the UAE proliferated after the mid-2000s, beginning with a US$20 billion agreement signed in December 2009 between the Emirates Nuclear Energy Corporation (ENEC) and a consortium led by the Korea Electric Power Corporation (KEPCO) to construct four nuclear power reactors in the Western Region of Abu Dhabi.[20] This landmark deal was soon followed by a number of other strategic and commercial partnerships between the two countries. They included an oil storage agreement placing up to six million barrels of Abu Dhabi crude oil in Korea's Strategic Petroleum Reserve;[21] the provision of Korean military training to UAE soldiers in counter-insurgency and counter-terrorism operations;[22] and a lucrative oil exploration deal assigning two onshore and one offshore block (cumulatively covering 10 per cent of Abu Dhabi's territorial mass) to the Korea National Oil Corporation (KNOC).[23] The chief operating officer of KNOC, Seong Hoon Kim, declared: 'We don't have any natural resources but very modern high technology. If we combine together, it will be a very good combination for both countries.'[24]

Generational leadership shift

Table 2.1 illustrates how between 1995 and 2006 the leadership of every GCC state bar Oman changed hands as longstanding rulers died in Bahrain (1999), the UAE (2004), Saudi Arabia (2005), and Kuwait (2006). In Qatar, the equally long-serving ruler was overthrown by his son in a bloodless palace coup in 1995. With the sole exception of Sultan Qaboos in Oman (who had himself been a generational outlier when assuming power at the age of 29 in 1970), the generation of leaders that had been in power since the 1970s and early 1980s, and in the case of Bahrain, Qatar, and the UAE had overseen the transition from protected state to full independence, was succeeded by a group of 'millennial' rulers in a broader region-wide process that also included the young new leaders of Morocco (1999), Jordan (1999), and Syria (2000). To be sure, widely differing dynamics underpinned the particular transition in each individual state, and the notion of a generational shift was inapplicable to Saudi

Table 2.1 Succession in the Gulf States, 1995–2015

Country	Year of succession	New ruler	Age at succession
Qatar	1995	Emir Hamad	43
Bahrain	1999	Emir/King Hamad	49
UAE (Abu Dhabi)	2004	President Khalifa	56
Saudi Arabia	2005	King Abdullah	81
UAE (Dubai)	2006	Sheikh Mohammed	56
Kuwait	2006	Emir Sabah	76
Qatar	2013	Emir Tamim	33
Saudi Arabia	2015	King Salman	79

Source: Public records compiled by Kristian Coates Ulrichsen

Arabia and Kuwait, where slightly younger half-brothers succeeded their octogenarian siblings in power. Nevertheless, the trend was sufficiently pronounced as to give rise to hopes that previously ossified political and governing structures would, at the very least, be modernised in a carefully controlled process of top-down reform, just as the rebalancing of global power described in the previous section was taking place.[25]

The region's new leaders settled into power at a momentous time as the George W. Bush administration adopted a new foreign policy doctrine in the turbulent aftermath of the September 11 terrorist attacks on the US. Of the 19 hijackers on 9/11, 17 were GCC nationals (15 Saudis and 2 Emiratis) as was, by birth, the founder of al-Qaeda, Osama bin Laden. The links with the 9/11 perpetrators delivered a cathartic shock to GCC policymakers, as they not only warned of the existence of radical discontent with the status quo but also highlighted the need to open up to political and economic reform. This was particularly important in engaging with the US administration (and public opinion) as both the 'Bush Doctrine' and much neoconservative opinion emphasised the need to support 'freedom' and 'democracy' on a global basis to better secure American interests. Thus, the Middle East Partnership Initiative (MEPI) was announced by US Secretary of State Colin Powell in 2002 during the ideologically charged opening phase of the 'War on Terror.' This was followed in November 2003 by a highly publicised speech by President Bush at the National Endowment for Democracy that stressed the need to spread democracy to address the freedom deficit in the Middle East.[26]

During the early 2000s, each GCC state launched cautious programmes of reform aimed at updating traditional channels of state-society relations and introducing a minimal standard of political pluralism. The measures included the establishment of municipal elections in Qatar in 1999 and a new constitution in 2003; provision for direct election to the Consultative Council in Oman in 2000 and universal suffrage in 2003; a new constitution and bicameral legislature in Bahrain in 2002; expansion of the Consultative Council and the holding of municipal elections in Saudi Arabia in 2005; the enfranchisement of women in Kuwait in 2005 and the liberalisation of the media landscape in 2006; and very limited elections to the Federal National Council in the UAE in 2006.[27]

To be sure, the reforms neither changed the balance nor the structure of political power in the Gulf, and none met Marina Ottaway's definition of a 'political paradigm shift' governing relations between, on the one hand, state and society, and, on the other, the location of the source, distribution, and exercise of political power.[28] As Gerd Nonneman has observed, 'reform and liberalisation do not equate to democratisation – nor do they necessarily lead to it.'[29] In this respect, the measures amounted to an exercise in political 'decompression' that was a common feature of the 'liberalising autocracies' documented by Daniel Brumberg.[30] This did not, however, prevent or hold back the formulation of sweeping new visions of the Gulf States' place in a globalising world, particularly among the energetic new leaderships in Dubai and Qatar. A case in point was an observation by the Emir of Qatar, Sheikh Hamad bin Khalifa Al Thani, in a November 2000 interview with the *New Yorker* magazine. Speaking before 9/11, the Emir displayed a prescient understanding of the complexity of the information age, and the way it tied internal and external challenges together as never before:

> We have simply got to reform ourselves. We're living in a modern age. People log on to the Internet. They watch cable TV. You cannot isolate yourself in today's world. And our reforms are progressing well. In a tribal country like Qatar, however, it could take time for everyone to accept what we've done. But change, more change, is coming.[31]

In the case of Dubai, Martin Hvidt has documented the combination of factors that propelled the freewheeling model of the 'developmental state' that emerged in the 2000s. This occurred under the guidance of Sheikh Mohammed bin Rashid Al Maktoum, who formally became the ruler upon the sudden death of his older brother in January 2006 but had in fact been the driving force behind Dubai's development since the 1980s. Dubai's growth into an *entrepôt* economy rested on an aggressively streamlined 'government-led' model centred on the ruler as 'CEO of Dubai, Inc.' and able to make rapid decisions and fast-track development projects.[32] In his account of Dubai's startling rise, journalist Jim Krane quotes the ruler's uncle, Sheikh Ahmed bin Saeed Al Maktoum (the head of Emirates Airline), describing him thus:

> He is pushy. He is aggressive . . . He is the main driver behind pushing everybody. He wants things to happen yesterday if you decide today. But at the same time he gives you all the support you need. He will push you to do things but he will always be there to support you.[33]

Mohammad Alabbar, the outspoken chairman of Emaar, one of the largest property and real estate companies in the entire region, described a similar relationship with the Ruler of Dubai in a wide-ranging April 2015 interview with ArabianBusiness.com:

> I do not do anything without me talking to HH, he is the man who gave me unimaginable opportunities, and he gave me a chance to be who I am. And to trust me. And to create my career and my personality. And when I make mistakes he comes and pulls me up again. So I don't do anything without talking to him.[34]

The 'can-do' approach was supported by a powerful branding and marketing operation as Sheikh Mohammed oversaw the creation and internationalisation of a service economy that took full advantage of Dubai's geographical location astride the major East-West trade routes linking Europe, Asia, and Africa. Moreover, the launch of innovative 'free zones,' such as the Dubai International Financial Centre, represented attempts to gain the confidence of the international investor community by bypassing cumbersome local bureaucracies.[35]

In a similar vein in Qatar, the Heir Apparent, Sheikh Hamad bin Khalifa Al Thani, gathered around him a dynamic cohort of younger ministers, among them the future Prime Minister, Hamad bin Jassim Al Thani, from 1989 onward. Sheikh Hamad's modern education and professional training (as a graduate from Sandhurst military college in the United Kingdom) differentiated him from the earlier generation of Gulf rulers who guided their countries to independence but struggled with the challenges of constructing and consolidating bureaucratic and institutional frameworks.[36] The relationship between the Heir Apparent and his father, Emir Khalifa bin Hamad Al Thani, deteriorated after Sheikh Hamad undertook a further Cabinet reshuffle in 1992, and began to press for the accelerated development of Qatar's enormous yet untapped natural gas reserves. Although by this time Sheikh Hamad was the de facto leader, exercising political authority and control over government business, the uneasy stasis lasted until 27 June 1995. Then, taking advantage of his father's absence on a visit to Switzerland, Sheikh Hamad formally asserted control in a bloodless palace coup. Once in power, the new emir quickly moved ahead with measures that introduced a degree of political reform and economic liberalisation. These began with the abolition of censorship over the media in 1995 and the establishment of the Al Jazeera satellite television network the following year, and continued with the dismantling of the Ministry of Information in March 1998, the introduction of quadrennial elections to a 29 member Central Municipal Council in March 1999, and the adoption of a new constitution by popular referendum in April 2003.[37]

Significantly, Qatar's new leadership also initiated steps to liberalise the Qatari economy, particularly in the energy sector, to attract greater levels of foreign direct investment (FDI) and involve foreign technological expertise in developing Liquefied Natural Gas (LNG) and associated projects, such as gas-to-liquids (GTL).[38] These built upon the rapid development of the North Field gas field, which began in earnest soon after Sheikh Hamad took power, although as Heir Apparent he had been pushing to exploit Qatari gas reserves since the 1980s, and came to rely heavily on partnerships with international partners.[39] During the multi-year investment programme which followed, Qatar spent more than US$120 billion on its LNG infrastructure, the majority of which it borrowed from banks and industry partners such as ExxonMobil.[40] The first export of LNG cargo took place in 1995 and the pace of development was such that in 2006 Qatar overtook Indonesia to become the largest exporter of LNG in the world. In December 2010, production reached its developmental target of 77 million tons per year, by which time Qatar accounted for between 25 and 30 per cent of global LNG exports.[41]

It is, nevertheless, important not to over-generalise, as similar generational change in Bahrain had a very different trajectory. Emir Isa bin Salman Al Khalifa died suddenly in March 1999 after a 38-year rule and was succeeded by his (also Sandhurst-educated) son, Hamad bin Isa Al Khalifa. During the 1990s, Bahrain had experienced a prolonged period of domestic unrest that rumbled on intermittently between 1994 and 1999. Within two years of taking power, Emir Hamad surprised many in Bahrain by announcing sweeping political and constitutional reforms intended to draw a line under the 1990s troubles. In particular, detailed negotiations between the ruler and opposition leaders were initiated in December 2000, following the release of 300 political activists the preceding May. This resulted in a document, the National Action Charter, which laid out a roadmap for reinstating parliamentary rule (which had been suspended in 1975 after only two years) and restoring Bahrain to a constitutional monarchy. In February 2001, the Charter was overwhelmingly approved by 98.4 per cent of voters in a public referendum. Simultaneously, the repressive State Security Law, in place since 1975, was lifted, and parliamentary elections were scheduled for October 2002.[42]

However, early promise was soon overtaken by growing disillusionment as the Emir unveiled a new constitution in 2002. In addition to turning Bahrain into a Kingdom and shifting Hamad's title to that of King, the constitution significantly watered down the political concessions made in the National Action Charter. Most importantly, the National Assembly was to consist of two houses rather than one, with an appointed upper Consultative Council counterbalancing an elected Chamber of Deputies. This move enraged opposition figures, who pointed also to the concentration of authority in the executive branch as the King was granted the power to appoint and dismiss ministers, amend the constitution, and propose new legislation. In protest, four political opposition societies representing Shiite and liberal interests boycotted the parliamentary election in 2002, resulting in a largely pro-government assembly.[43]

The Bahraini experience, as well as the pattern of succession in Saudi Arabia and Kuwait, highlights therefore the enduring importance of ruling family dynamics in determining how and when generational change takes place. In the Bahraini case, the advent of a new ruler in 1999 was more than offset by the fact that much political power remained in the hands of his uncle, Prime Minister Sheikh Khalifa bin Salman Al Khalifa. The brother of the late emir, Sheikh Khalifa assumed the post of Prime Minister after Bahrain's independence in 1971, making him the longest-serving such official in the world. During the rule of his brother, Emir Isa, a *modus vivendi* developed whereby the Emir reigned but Sheikh Khalifa directed the affairs of state. This arrangement embedded the Prime Minister within a vast network of political and economic patronage that proved impossible to dislodge in the 2000s when the young and reform-minded Crown Prince, Salman bin Hamad Al Khalifa, attempted to do so in 2006 with the creation of the Bahrain Economic Development Board.[44]

In both Saudi Arabia and Kuwait, generational change proved to be a misnomer as the succession passed among half-brothers upon the deaths of King Fahd bin Abdulaziz Al Saud and Emir Jabir al-Ahmad Al Sabah in August 2005 and January 2006 respectively. In each country, the selection of the heir typically is governed by the principle of seniority rather than primogeniture, and has led to a gradual ageing of the ruling incumbent. Saudi Arabia is still ruled by the sons of its founder, more than 60 years after King Abdulaziz's death in 1953, even as the age of incoming Kings rose inexorably from 51 in 1953, to 62 in 1975, and 81 in 2005, before dropping slightly to 79 when King Salman ascended the throne in January 2015. In Kuwait, the last generational shift in the ruling Al Sabah family occurred in 1950, since when succession has passed among different groups of half-brothers and cousins.[45]

Soft power, cultural influence, and state-branding

The shifting contours of the global order and the emergence of a new cadre of Gulf leaders also intersected with changes to the very concepts of *power* and *influence*. Together, these opened up new possibilities and directions for the projection of influence, both unilaterally and by coalitions of emerging economies coalescing around select issues in global governance. The acceleration of globalising processes during the 1990s and 2000s led to what David Held and Anthony McGrew have labelled 'a significant shift in the spatial reach of social relations and organisation' as constraints of notions of 'distance' and 'geographical space' weakened and shrank.[46] Also significant was the reconfiguration of the concept of what *power* is and how it is utilised, in addition to an appreciation that power comes in many different forms and is itself distinct from *influence* and *ambition*. As Thomas Juneau has written in relation to the US, power is multidimensional and relative, and is derived from the assets that a state can leverage to shape developments in international politics in pursuit of national interests, whereas influence 'is defined by what a state achieves with those assets' and ambition 'consists of the intensity of a state's interests.'[47]

Most notably, Joseph Nye pioneered the study of 'soft power,' which he described as the ability to appeal to and persuade others using the attractiveness of a country's culture, political ideals, and policies. Although Nye first introduced the concept as early as 1990,[48] he explored in detail the phenomenon of co-optation rather than coercion as a means of persuasion in international politics in his 2004 book *Soft Power: The Means to Success in World Politics*. Nye described how states or other actors in world politics (such as non-governmental organisations) seeking to accrue soft power should set the agenda and attract others in world politics, and not only to force them to change by threatening military force or economic sanctions. This is soft power – getting others to want the outcomes that you want co-opts people rather than coerces them.[49]

Nye added that soft power resources consist of the assets that induce co-optation, and that it is a complex tool that governments must build up over time as they develop a reputation for credibility in a particular field.[50] The concept of 'soft power' thus was refined at the height of the George W. Bush presidency's attempt to resolve international challenges through military interventions in the Middle East and Central Asia. The Bush administration's failure to reorder Afghanistan and Iraq through the use of force highlighted the flaws inherent in the prioritisation of coercion over consent in contemporary world politics. The upsurge in terrorist and insurgent attacks during the ill-conceived 'war on terror' visibly demonstrated the limitations of traditional 'hard power' and also underlined the importance of actions being seen by the international community to be legitimate in and consistent with the norms of international law.[51]

Other iterations of the concept of 'power' include Nye's subsequent development of the label 'smart power' to describe 'the combination of the hard power of coercion and payment with the soft power of persuasion and attraction.' Examples of states that have proven adept at 'smart power' are Norway and Switzerland, with Norway, for example, deploying unprecedented military force in addition to diplomatic and humanitarian instruments in the NATO-led intervention in Libya in 2011 that ousted Colonel Gaddafi.[52] Moving to the specific context of the Middle East, a typology of soft power was published by the Dubai School of Government in 2010. Lawrence Rubin noted that use of the term *al-quwwa al-naima* (soft power) increasingly had entered local and regional discourse over the past decade.[53] Writing about Qatar and drawing on insight gleaned from his leadership position at the Georgetown School of Foreign Service branch campus in Doha, Mehran Kamrava introduced the notion of 'subtle power' – 'the ability to exert influence from behind the scenes.' Subtle power, Kamrava suggested, was a multipronged approach that involved 'a combination of bringing resources to bear, enjoying international prestige derived from and commensurate with norm-entrepreneurship, and being positioned in such a way as to manipulate circumstances and the weaknesses of others to one's advantage.'[54]

New forms of power projection therefore shifted the ways that regional structures of power were organised. These occurred against the backdrop of two significant developments in global politics and international relations. First, the emergence of the multiple poles of geo-economic gravity and centres of influence in the international system has opened up new possibilities for new coalitions of states and intra- and inter-regional realignments. In such a context, the future of 'global governance' is likely to be characterised by moves towards the creation of a new and more responsive institutional architecture that balances the rapidly changing global framework with the competing objectives of a larger array of major stakeholders.[55] Second, geographical territory has become less important to the projection of power, as the latter became more variegated in the 2000s, while the evolution of information and communications technologies (ICTs) created opportunities for new actors to stake an international role disproportionate to their geographical or population size. This was a significant new development that eroded many of the constraints hitherto imposed on 'small states' in the international system and made it possible to evade the 'international cliency' that hitherto formed the dominant framework structuring the relationships between strong states and weak states.[56]

A wide array of new opportunities hence opened up for small states seeking to leverage their limited political, economic, and strategic assets and overcome some of their spatial or geographical constraints. Moreover, in the Arab world, the decline of 'traditional' regional powers such as Egypt, Syria, and Iraq in the 1990s created a vacuum in which smaller states could exercise unprecedented leadership. This took very different forms in each of the Gulf States. Saudi Arabia and Kuwait built up networks of soft power throughout the Arab and Islamic world through the funding of international Islamic institutions and through generous aid and development programmes respectively. Yet, as the section above on generational change made clear, by the 1990s, ageing leaderships in both states were resulting in ossified power structures and a deepening resistance to change or innovation. The smaller resource-rich states of Qatar and the UAE provided a stark contrast as the dynamic new generation of rulers moved rapidly to take advantage of the systemic fluidity that opened up. Significantly, neither their small territorial extent nor size of population held back the projection of influence at levels that far outmatched many much larger and conventionally more 'powerful' states. Officials in Doha, Abu Dhabi, and Dubai forged instead what J. E. Peterson has labelled 'strategies of survival' for small states based on enlisting a powerful external protector (the US) as a security guarantor while developing strategic niches that facilitated and underpinned the rise to global prominence.[57]

The projection of cultural influence also developed as an object of study as emerging economies and non-state processes became more pro-active and visible participants in globalising flows in the 2000s. In a foreword to a British Council report on culture and soft power in the twenty-first century published in 2013, the then UK Foreign Secretary William Hague described how 'Foreign policy today is no longer the preserve of governments.' Instead,

> there is now a mass of connections between individuals, civil soci-ety, businesses, pressure groups, and charitable organisations which are also part of the relations between nations. It is more important than ever before to tap into these new human networks around the world.[58]

In a separate report on 'the global race for influence and attraction,' the British Council observed that the role of the state 'does not have primacy in the development of a country's soft power' as such influence 'stems largely from factors outside the direct control of governments.'[59]

While organisations such as the British Council, the Alliance Française (AF), Germany's Goethe-Institut, and Spain's Instituto Cervantes all orig-inated as state-backed entities committed to promoting national culture and language, over time their focus gradually become less state-centric and more internationalist. By contrast, in the Gulf States, the projec-tion of cultural influence is still resolutely top-down – either directly from state institutions or filtered through the state-owned enterprises that populate the political and economic landscape. In the case of Saudi Arabia, there is an additional religious dimension to the leverage of new forms of power and influence as the kingdom is home to the two holiest sites of Islam in Mecca and Medina. The decision in 1986 by King Fahd bin Abdulaziz Al Saud to title himself (and his successors as monarch) as 'Custodian of the Two Holy Mosques' attests to the symbolic impor-tance that the Saudi ruling family attach to their religious position as a source of domestic and international legitimacy. As such, there is a significant difference in the conception and deployment of soft power and cultural influence as understood in the specific Gulf context, where both remain resolutely top-down and subject to close control by senior circles of ruling elites.[60]

An important element of the enabling environment for soft power and cultural influence has been the concept of 'state-branding.' Peter van Ham has examined the growth of branding as a political phenomenon in world politics that operates at the intersection of media, marketing, and brand management with the international political arena. Van Ham describes branding as part of 'an effort to use strategies developed in the commercial sector to manage, if not necessarily wield, the soft power of a geographical location.'[61] Moreover, branding forms one of the components of 'a wider spectrum of postmodern power' alongside 'soft power' and also public diplomacy.[62] Van Ham concludes with the observation – highly relevant to the study of the global emergence of the Gulf States – that

> for both place branding and public diplomacy, a key element is to build personal and institutional relationships and dialogue with foreign audiences by focusing on values, setting them apart from classical diplomacy, which primarily deals with issues.[63]

Two points are relevant here as they influence the use of state-branding in Gulf States. The first is the weakness of public diplomacy in all GCC states and the second is the absence of common value systems, at least politically, with target Western audiences. In a context in which most major policy decisions are taken by an elite circle of ruling family members and senior officials and imposed, top-down, on ministries for implementation, there is almost no custom of explaining or justifying the particular choices made. Moreover, in an authoritarian political context, there are few avenues for holding the executive to account, with the notable exception of Kuwait's vocal parliament. In addition, the intervention of frequently competing ruling family factions in policy-making adds another layer of volatility to the decision-making process, as outcomes often reflect an internal struggle for influence over particular issues. The result is an intricate 'guessing game' wherein interested observers, including foreign diplomats and scholars, attempt to piece together fragments of information as if constructing a jigsaw puzzle.[64]

The paradox facing Gulf officials is that their global rise also increases their vulnerability to weak public diplomacy. This became clear in 2012 when growing regional and international scrutiny of Qatar's assertive Arab Spring policies met with 'walls of silence' from Qatari officials and government ministries. Michael Stephens, a Qatar-based researcher at the Doha branch of the Royal United Services Institute (RUSI) defence and security think-tank, described how

> the Qatar policy elite sit distanced from the events they are controlling, unaware often of the turbulent waters that swirl beneath. Rumours begin, often without the elite's knowledge and very quickly

spread into larger rumours; before you know it elites in the UAE fear that Qatar is funding Muslim Brotherhood cells in Ras al-Khaimah and half the world is convinced Qatar is spreading jihadist ideology in Mali.

Stephens added: 'When the rumours get so large that answers are demanded they are met with walls of silence, not because Qatar has anything to hide, but because that is the culture of governance here.'[65]

Differing value systems constitute the second factor in determining the nature of Gulf States' state-branding initiatives. Political relations between the Gulf States and the West have recovered from their cathartic post-2001 nadir, but remain unlikely to align over common *values*. In their absence, a set of common *interests* has emerged instead. These are, unsurprisingly, concentrated in economic and security issues, as there is far greater overlap of common interest in both fields. Gulf state-branding was thus focused on economic and security aspects from the start. An example of the economic dimension of branding was Bahrain's adoption of the 'Business-Friendly Bahrain' slogan that was stamped into every visitor's passport and even adorned the sides of London buses and taxis prior to the popular uprising in 2011.[66] By early 2015, the equally visible slogan had changed to 'Bahrain: Back to Business' as the government sought to reassure international investors that the political upheaval that broke out in February 2011 was resolved.[67] The security-related element of branding was evident in comments made by Qatar's Prime Minister, Sheikh Hamad bin Jassim Al Thani, after Qatar gave financial assistance to those Americans whose livelihoods and homes were devastated by Hurricane Katrina in New Orleans in 2005. When a visiting American official in Doha expressed his gratitude, the Prime Minister responded: 'We might have our own Katrina' – a reference to the fact that Qatar might one day be in need of support from the US.[68]

State-branding initiatives unfolded across a range of different fields in the 2000s, boosted by the incoming windfall in government revenues during the post-2002 oil price boom. Rarely stated publicly yet uppermost nonetheless in the minds of ruling circles in the Gulf was the legacy of Iraq's invasion of Kuwait in August 1990. Kuwait's possession of some of the largest oil reserves in the world clearly was instrumental in mobilising the swift international response to eject Saddam Hussein's forces from the emirate. Yet, once the shock of the Gulf War had subsided, one of the deeper 'takeaways' by Gulf officials was the importance of maintaining robust relationships with a diverse web of global partners.[69] This was especially the case in the smaller Gulf States, which lacked the international visibility of Saudi Arabia; one Gulf Ambassador in Washington, DC, recounted in 2009 his dismay at the low awareness among many members of Congress and their staffs of the smaller states in the GCC.[70]

In contrast with the plethora of investments made by Gulf-based sovereign wealth funds (which will be analysed in Chapter 5), a major branding objective has been aimed at winning 'hearts and minds' among key external partners. Again, a recent Qatari example serves as an illustration of the process at work among the political classes that matter inside the Washington Beltway. In 2008, Qatar provided US$2.5 million towards the US$50 million renovation of the Ford Theatre in Washington, DC, the site of the assassination of Abraham Lincoln in 1865. Fittingly for a site so resonant in US presidential history, the theatre reopened just a month after the inauguration of Barack Obama as the first black president in US history.[71] In the United Kingdom, Qatar reached a similar audience of establishment figures in June 2014 when Royal Ascot selected the ruling-family-owned QIPCO (the Qatar Investment & Projects Development Holding Company) as the first sponsor in its 303-year history. Tellingly, the chief executive of Royal Ascot, whose board is chaired by a representative of the Queen, responded to media enquiries about the suitability of the Qatari ruling family as a sponsor by stating: 'We would only do business with people who we think are suitable partners for us.'[72]

The projection of cultural influence in four sectors in particular has become synonymous with the large-scale Gulf branding efforts. These are the high-profile prestige investments in the education and cultural sectors; the targeting and hosting of major international sporting events and global sports stars; the growth of luxury-level international travel and tourism; and pioneering research and development into cleaner energy fuels. Together they sought to transform regional and international perceptions of the Gulf States and foster the perception of a dynamic 'can do' mentality among their leadership. To the extent that there was an overarching 'message,' it was that the GCC was nurturing a global reputation as a safe place to do business, live, and work, in an otherwise insecure region. Moreover, the smaller GCC states (excepting Saudi Arabia) all relied heavily on the lucrative MICE (Meetings, Incentives, Conferences, Events) circuit to place them firmly on the global map. This produced a considerable degree of one-upmanship as GCC states competed with each other to establish region-leading expertise in niche sectors.[73]

Global sport and Gulf branding

The most notable and globally visible example of the softer forms of power and influence emanating from the Gulf is in the sporting arena. From involvement in the international politics of sport to the organisation of high-profile tournaments and events and the sponsorship and outright acquisition of teams and franchises, the past decade has witnessed a succession of Gulf-based interventions. These have been part of the broader globalisation of sport as North American and (particularly) European influence in international sporting bodies has steadily diluted. Motor racing provides a clear indication of both the changing landscape and the multifaceted human, political, and commercial links with the Gulf. The number of races in the Formula One World Championship taking place in Europe fell from 11 out of 17 total races in 1995 to 9 out of 19 in 2014, by which time two Grand Prix were being run on gleaming new circuits in Bahrain and Abu Dhabi. Significantly, Bahrain's links with motor racing extended far beyond the annual Bahrain Grand Prix. Crown Prince Salman bin Hamad Al Khalifa, the oldest son of King Hamad, entered into co-ownership of a racing team that competes in the Formula One feeder series with the son of Jean Todt, the president of the Fédération Internationale de l'Automobile (FIA), while his younger brother, Sheikh Abdullah bin Hamad Al Khalifa, was appointed to the World Motor Sport Council. Moreover, Bahrain's sovereign wealth fund, Mumtalakat, not only owns the race venue (the Bahrain International Circuit) and sponsor (Gulf Air) but also a 42 per cent stake in the McLaren Group and a 50 per cent stake in McLaren Automotive, backer of one of the oldest and most successful racing teams in Formula One.[74]

A similar multipronged approach characterised Qatar's bid for the 2022 FIFA World Cup. Although it has since come under intense scrutiny over alleged improprieties in the bidding process, the successful campaign to defeat rival bids from the US, Japan, and Australia amplified the growing Gulf role in sports politics. Qatar itself has never qualified for football's premier global competition, and with the notable exception of Saudi Arabia in 1994, the other Gulf States have made very little impression on the tournament, as Table 2.2 illustrates.

This notwithstanding, Qatar's race, seemingly from nowhere, to win the rights to host the World Cup was a microcosm of the nuanced intersection of state-branding and the creation of coalitions of regional and international support. Simply put, the Qatari leadership worked the political mechanics of vote-winning more effectively than rival bidders in order to secure the support of enough of the 24 voting members on

Table 2.2   GCC states' records in FIFA World Cup finals play

Tournament	Country qualified	Outcome
1982	Kuwait	First round group stage (1 point)
1990	UAE	First round group stage (0 points)
1994	Saudi Arabia	Second in group stage, eliminated in Round of 16
1998	Saudi Arabia	First round group stage (1 point)
2002	Saudi Arabia	First round group stage (0 points)
2006	Saudi Arabia	First round group stage (1 point)

Overall World Cup finals record of GCC states

Played	Won	Drawn	Lost	Goals for	Goals against
19	2	3	14	13	49

Source: Adapted from information available on the FIFA website http://www.fifa.com/
worldfootball/statisticsandrecords/associations/index.html

the FIFA Executive Committee. Qatari officials also pitched a very persuasive portrait of a nation using sport to bridge different cultures while rooted in an Arab context, all encapsulated in its catchy slogan, 'Expect Amazing.' The compelling nature of the Qatari bid overcame the practical and health considerations of holding a competition in the searing summer heat in a country with little discernible footballing tradition.[75]

The creation of the Aspire Academy for Sports Excellence illustrated the careful build-up of Qatar's credentials in international sporting circles. Aspire was established in 2004 as a world-class training and development facility for young athletes across a range of different sports. The complex combines the Aspire Dome – one of the largest multipurpose indoor arenas in the world, which hosted the 2010 IAAF World Indoor Championships in track and field – as well as a dedicated research track into sports science and healthy living, and tailored programmes aimed at aspiring athletes from resource-poor developing countries. Two notable examples of such tailored programmes specifically targeted footballers: an initiative launched in 2007 to identify and nurture talented young players in 15 developing countries in full cooperation with their national football association, and a programme established in 2009 to host and train players from 10 countries throughout Africa.[76] Yet, suspicion later focused on the ways in which the Qatari bid team secured the votes on the 24-person FIFA Executive Committee. These included allegations that Qatar had targeted specific countries with voting members on the Executive with Aspire programmes and promises of support, as well as questions relating to the presence of Qatar's Mohammed bin

Hammam as the president of the Asian Football Confederation between 2002 and 2011.[77]

Qatar was not alone among Gulf States in seeking to leverage its influence within FIFA and utilise the soft power of world football. Bin Hammam resigned as head of the Asian Football Confederation following allegations of corruption in 2011 and was succeeded as president by a member of the Bahraini ruling family, Sheikh Salman bin Ibrahim Al Khalifa. Dubai's Emirates Airline, meanwhile, spent more than US$100 million over the 2010–2014 World Cup cycle on becoming one of FIFA's Official Worldwide Partners, alongside Visa, Sony, Adidas, Coca-Cola, Hyundai Motor, and Kia Motor. The estimated one billion viewers of the 2014 World Cup final between Germany and Argentina witnessed the surreal sight of a row of Emirates flight attendants handing the victorious German team their medals.[78] Even the comparatively more conservative Saudi Arabia attempted to harness the international soft power of FIFA when it created and hosted the King Fahd Cup in 1992, 1995, and 1997. The kingdom initially paid all the expenses of participating nations and successfully brought six continental champions to Riyadh, before the competition was taken over by FIFA in 1997 to become the Confederations Cup.[79]

In addition to the abovementioned sponsorship of the FIFA World Cup, Emirates and other Gulf corporations also sponsored and, in some cases, actually purchased prominent European football clubs. Examples of teams featuring the Emirates logo on their shirts include the 2014 European Champions Real Madrid, Arsenal in England, and AC Milan in Italy. Arsenal also play their home games in the Emirates Stadium under the terms of a 15-year naming rights agreement signed in 2004, when the team still played at the fabled Highbury Stadium. Moreover, since 2010 Qatar has been associated with FC Barcelona, one of the most attractive and successful football teams in the world, through the sponsorship first of the Qatar Foundation and then of Qatar Airways. The five-year, US$180 million deal with Qatar Sports Investment (QSI), a subsidiary of the Qatar Investment Authority (QIA), was notable for Barcelona breaking with tradition by placing for the first time a commercial sponsor on their famous blue and red shirts. The then coach of Barcelona Pep Guardiola spent two years with Al-Ahli in the Qatar Stars League towards the end of his playing career and was working, at the time of the agreement, as a global ambassador for the Qatar 2022 World Cup bid.[80]

More ambitious still has been the takeovers of Manchester City and Paris Saint-Germain by investors from Abu Dhabi and Qatar respectively.

The 2008 takeover of Manchester City by the Abu Dhabi United Group for Development and Investment, a private equity vehicle owned by Sheikh Mansour bin Zayed Al Nahyan, a younger half-brother of the Ruler of Abu Dhabi (and President of the UAE), catapulted a middling team into the richest club in Europe and led to Premier League triumphs in 2012 and 2014. Manchester City also renamed their new stadium – built for the 2002 Commonwealth Games through lottery and local council funding – the Etihad Stadium after Abu Dhabi's airline. In July 2013, following a mass trial of opposition and human rights activists in the UAE, Human Rights Watch issued a critical report on the UAE and noted specifically how ownership of Manchester City enabled Abu Dhabi to 'construct a public relations image of a progressive, dynamic Gulf state, which deflects attention from what is really going on in the country.'[81] Another facet of growing Emirati involvement at the highest and most prestigious levels of European football came with the October 2014 announcement of a strategic partnership between ten-time European champions Real Madrid and the Abu Dhabi government-owned International Petroleum Investment Company (IPIC). This tied into and built upon the existing links between Real Madrid and their shirt sponsor, Emirates, with the additional revenue going to fund the refurbishment of Madrid's historic Santiago Bernabeu stadium.[82]

The acquisition of a majority stake by QSI in the French club Paris Saint-Germain (PSG) in 2012 illustrates how the purchase of individual teams can also fit into a bigger picture. The takeover followed a lunch hosted by French President Nicholas Sarkozy for Qatar's Heir Apparent, Sheikh Tamim bin Hamad Al Thani, and the French president of the European football association, Michel Platini, at the Elysee Palace in November 2010. Quite apart from rejuvenating a team that had dominated French football in the 1990s and signing global superstars such as Zlatan Ibrahimovic and David Beckham, the QSI takeover occurred only months before Al Jazeera Sports purchased the broadcasting rights for the French Ligue 1. The Al Jazeera Sports move saved French football from financial crisis after the previous holder announced it would not be able to continue paying for the television rights. The self-reinforcing paths of Qatari inroads into French football deepened when the director of Al Jazeera Sports, Nasser al-Khelaifi, became president of PSG and the Qatar National Bank and Qatar Tourism Authority unveiled major sponsorship agreements with the team. A subsequent report by the *Financial Times* noted that 'Qatar is the first country to attempt nation-branding through club football' and quoted Ibrahimovic as stating that 'today we represent Paris, France, and Qatar.'[83]

The support of international sporting events has therefore functioned as a crucial mechanism for leveraging Gulf States' soft power to a global audience. Moreover, the sense of attachment and loyalty that many fans feel for 'their team' provides potent branding opportunities, particularly in cases where the financial wherewithal of Gulf sponsorship translates into relatively immediate sporting success, as in the cases of Manchester City and PSG. While such positive outcomes are not guaranteed, as the flawed and short-lived takeover of Spain's Malaga football club by an individual Qatari Sheikh or Portsmouth FC's unhappy experience with Dubai investor Sulaiman al-Fahim illustrate, they nevertheless have served to embed the Gulf States in the global conscience in more ways far more benign than other possible associations such as those with terrorism, conflict, or sectarian tension. As such, in a relatively short period of time, global sports has helped to imprint the Gulf States onto the world stage in a highly visible manner.

3
State Capitalism and Strategic Niches

This chapter builds upon the enabling factors identified in Chapter 2 to analyse in specific detail the mechanisms of the Gulf States' projection of power and influence at a regional and global level. Officials in GCC states responded pragmatically to the evolving changes in the international system by adapting and implementing a Gulf-specific model of state capitalism and concentrating on developing expertise in clearly defined strategic niches. Underpinning the pursuit of state capitalism and strategic niches was a reliance on small circles of concentrated policymaking clustered around ruling elites. This was at its strongest in the smaller Gulf States of Qatar and the UAE, particularly Dubai and Abu Dhabi, where the younger generation of rulers who came to power in the 1990s and 2000s governed far more in the style of executive leaders than political rulers, and was harder in the larger states of Saudi Arabia and Oman and in the particular circumstances of Bahrain, where authority has been dispersed among several competing factions within the ruling family, to replicate the propitious conditions for successful state capitalism.

The opening sections of this chapter describe the evolution of state capitalism and the search for strategic niches as integral components of the broader programmes of national development and economic diversification unveiled in the 2000s. These were guided by typically multi-decade 'visions' often drafted by Western management consultants and designed as part of the comprehensive state-branding initiatives described in the previous chapter. The second half of the chapter focuses on specific niche developments in the Gulf, with particular emphasis on renewable and alternative energy in the UAE and Saudi Arabia, refined products and petrochemicals in Saudi Arabia, and higher education and research in Qatar and, to a lesser extent, Oman. The inclusion of case studies from Saudi Arabia and Oman demonstrates that the difficulties of implementing state capitalism in the larger Gulf States did not necessarily preclude attempts to identify and fill niches of regional and world-leading expertise.

National development visions

Beginning in the 1990s but accelerating after 2000, all of the GCC states unveiled grandiose visions of economic diversification and national development drafted for the most part by teams of international strategy consultants. This was not an entirely new phenomenon as an earlier generation of Gulf policymakers also had turned to Western consultants to develop the master plans that had guided the initial phase of oil-fuelled socio-economic development. As early as 1950, officials in Kuwait commissioned a British town-planning firm, Minoprio and Spencely, along with an English planner, P. W. Macfarlane, to draw up a plan to remodel Kuwait City; working without any local knowledge, the result was a blueprint for urban development based heavily on the English model of garden cities then in fashion but wholly unsuited to Kuwait.[1] A decade later, in Dubai, the English architect John Harris was appointed by the new ruler, Sheikh Rashid bin Saeed Al Maktoum, to prepare a master plan for urban development; such, however, was the rapidity of growth that Harris had to issue a second report in 1971, which itself was quickly overtaken by the post-1973 oil price boom.[2] Similar fates befell the master plan to develop Riyadh drawn up by Doxiades Consultants of Greece between 1968 and 1972,[3] and the urban design for Doha commissioned by a British planning company, Llewellyn-Davies, in 1972.[4]

The development of planning in Saudi Arabia illustrates also the pivotal role of international organisations. A planning agency was established in 1958 on the advice of the International Monetary Fund (IMF) and was expanded into the Central Planning Organization in 1965, but its remit was limited by financial constraints. In the 1960s, both Aramco and the Ford Foundation in the US helped the Saudi government plan ministry activities and establish a civil service. By the end of the decade, the collection of statistics on non-oil related activities was becoming more urgent as the information was required by the growing number of international companies that sought to invest in Saudi Arabia. A start was made in 1970, when the newly appointed head of the Central Planning Organization (which became the Planning Ministry in 1975 and still later the Ministry of Economy and Planning), Hisham Nazer, inaugurated the cycle of five-year development plans and contracted the

Stanford Research Institute (today, SRI), a private American consulting firm, to draw up both the first (1970–1975) and second (1975–1980) five-year plans.[5]

The national development visions of the twenty-first century went far beyond the urban master plans and planning agencies of the 1960s and 1970s and were intended both to underpin and to convey the more nuanced projection of power, influence, and interest that ran both into and out of the Gulf. Attracting a steady inflow of global figures reinforced the benevolent image of a dynamic region that ruling elites sought to portray to their own publics and the wider world alike. One example of this process at work was former US President Bill Clinton's speech at the inaugural commencement ceremony marking the first graduating class of New York University's Abu Dhabi campus in May 2014,[6] at a time of considerable media interest in the apparent ill-treatment of the migrant labour workforce that constructed the campus; another was the appointment of soccer legends such as Real Madrid and Barcelona superstars Zinedine Zidane and Pep Guardiola as 'Qatar Bid Ambassadors' during the run-up to the successful campaign to win the hosting rights to the 2022 FIFA World Cup.[7] Former British Prime Minister Tony Blair was another frequent visitor to the Gulf following the end of his political career in the United Kingdom, and he developed close relations with ruling elites in Kuwait and the UAE, while his successor as British Prime Minister, Gordon Brown, gave four speeches in the Gulf – two in Qatar and one apiece in the UAE and Kuwait – that topped the list of external earnings in the House of Commons Register of Members' Interests in 2012.[8]

The plethora of national 'visions' that emerged in the 1990s and 2000s set out ambitious targets and objectives for diversifying GCC economies and expanding the productive base to ease the eventual transition towards a post-oil political economy. As such, the visions typically were multi-decade in length and contained key 'buzzwords' about the development of social and human capital designed to appeal to a global audience of potential investors and business partners. Table 3.1 illustrates the timeline behind the unveiling of national visions and development plans across the GCC.

The earliest plan was Oman's *Vision 2020*. This was formulated in the mid-1990s as the country, together with Bahrain, possesses the lowest oil reserves among the Gulf States and thus the most pressing need to diversify beyond energy. To this end, *Oman 2020: Vision for Oman's Economy* was launched in June 1996 and designed to run in conjunction with an ongoing series of five-year development plans that focused directly on economic diversification and expanding the private and non-oil sectors.

Table 3.1   National visions in GCC states

Year	Country	Vision
1995	Oman	Oman 2020: Visions for Oman's Economy
2008	Bahrain	Economic Vision 2030
2008	Qatar	Qatar National Vision 2030
2010	Kuwait	Kuwait Vision 2035
2010	UAE	Vision 2021

Source: Martin Hvidt, 'Economic Diversification in GCC Countries: Past Record and Future Trends,' *LSE Kuwait Programme Working Paper* No. 27, January 2013.

The Vision aimed to reduce the oil sector's share of Omani GDP from 41 per cent in 1996 to 9 per cent in 2020, while raising the share of gas and non-oil industry from under 1 per cent to 10 per cent and from 7.5 per cent to 29 per cent respectively. The plan also sought to improve the human development of Omani citizens, particularly women, and to equip them with the skills and qualifications to compete in the private sector against cheaper expatriate workers.[9]

Vision 2020 provides the most detailed opportunity to assess the interim results of Gulf development visions as the timeframe of the plan is (as of 2015) four-fifths complete. The challenge for policymakers has been that the results of the plan were decidedly mixed as it entered its second decade. Oil as a share of GDP actually rose to 42.6 per cent in 2012, due more to surging prices rather than production, which fell marginally from 0.972 million barrels per day in 2000 to 0.92 million in 2012.[10] The figures illustrated the extent of the Omani economy's continuing dependence on oil in spite of the attempt to broaden the economic base. Similarly slow progress marked the effort to 'Omanise' the private sector labour force by replacing expatriate workers with Omani nationals, and the implementation of several initiatives had to be postponed. Moreover, while the number of Omani employees in private sector jobs rose by 138 per cent between 2003 and 2010, much of the progress was reversed by the policy responses to the Arab Spring in 2011. The announcement of 35,000 new public sector jobs in the spring of 2011 reportedly led 30,000 Omanis to resign from private sector employment. The issuing of work permits to hire foreign workers also surged in a bid to placate major business and economic elites looking to keep labour costs low, meaning that the overall number of non-nationals working in Oman in 2012 was 1.3 million – more than three times the 2003 figure of 400,000.[11]

Bahrain was the first country in the GCC to debate and implement substantive reforms to labour markets that encompassed changes to the system of sponsorship and wage differentials between the public and private sectors. *Economic Vision 2030* was launched in November 2008 and was complemented a year later by a National Economic Strategy, which aimed to formulate short-term spending plans in order to achieve the longer-term vision. Bahrain 2030 was formulated by the Economic Development Board (EDB) as part of a package of measures that included labour market reform and educational and vocational training reform to boost a pro-business agenda based on the branding of 'Business Friendly Bahrain'. The EDB was an entity created in 2000 and chaired since then by Crown Prince Salman bin Hamad Al Khalifa with a mandate to facilitate the strategic development of the Bahraini economy and attract foreign direct investment (FDI).[12] Like the EDB itself, Bahrain 2030 relied heavily on international management and strategy consultants only to later be undermined by the upheaval generated by the Arab Spring in 2011. Similar to its Omani counterpart, Vision 2030 sought to boost the role of the private sector and create sufficient new jobs to absorb the fast-growing and more highly qualified labour force.[13]

While Oman and Bahrain were early movers in diversification, their efforts have since been surpassed in order of magnitude by the UAE, Qatar, and Saudi Arabia, with Kuwait a regional laggard. In the mid-2000s, Dubai grabbed the media headlines with its array of ostentatious and eye-catching initiatives such as the Palm Islands and The World archipelago. These built upon the very first branding campaign in the Gulf that was inaugurated in Dubai as early as 1992 when the 'Decide on Dubai' initiative was launched to a target audience of potential tourists and shoppers.[14] While the campaign was successful in marketing Dubai to the British market, in particular, and the inaugural Dubai Shopping Festival took place in 1996, it was dwarfed by the scale of the later visions that were unveiled during the boom years of the mid-2000s. These included the *Vision for Dubai* unveiled in 2000, whose targeted increase in GDP to US$30 billion by 2010 was achieved by 2005, and the Dubai Strategic Plan, announced in February 2007, which mapped growth strategies for Dubai by concentrating economic development in sectors where the emirate already enjoyed a comparative advantage. Following the financial crisis of 2008 and the bailout of Dubai by Abu Dhabi, the focus shifted to the federal level in the form of the *UAE Vision 2021* intended to commemorate the fiftieth anniversary of the country.[15]

In Qatar, the General Secretariat for Development Planning unveiled its own ambitious *Qatar National Vision 2030* in 2008. This outlined five major policy challenges facing Qatar as the state embarked upon a period of gas-driven breakneck growth. The challenges included meeting the needs both of current and of future generations and aligning economic growth with social development and environmental management. To meet these overarching goals, the vision recommended four interdependent pillars that focused on human, social, environmental, and economic development. Also central to the vision is the creation of a knowledge economy that would create a regional hub for research and development, services, and value-added technologies.[16] As with Bahrain, publication of the longer-term vision was accompanied by a more immediate *Qatar National Development Strategy 2011–2016* to align the reforms at macroeconomic and institutional levels with specific short-term projects. The winning of the hosting rights to the 2022 FIFA World Cup injected a third element into Qatari planning considerations owing to the scale of infrastructural construction associated with the bid. However, progress on all three levels – immediate (2011–2016), medium (2022), and long-term (2030) – was complicated by the sheer speed of Qatari demographic and economic growth which meant that the data in each plan rapidly became outdated.[17]

The Qatari emphasis on human and sustainable development becomes vividly evident in the sprawling Ras Laffan Industrial City that lies 70 kilometres north of Doha. Since its inception in 1996, Ras Laffan has emerged as one of the fastest-growing industrial cities in the world and evolved into an integrated hub for the production and export of liquefied natural gas (LNG) and gas-to-liquid (GTL). The city is wholly owned by Qatar Petroleum (QP) and also contains a major gas processing plant servicing the Dolphin cross-border refined gas transmission project linking Qatar with the UAE and Oman. By 2009, Ras Laffan employed more than 100,000 people in 22 local and international companies and had developed a reputation for one of the world's leading green industrial zones through a focus on clean gas technologies. It also established a fully integrated port for shipping LNG around the world in specially designed Q-Max carriers that are among the largest ships ever built, with 80 per cent greater capacity than conventional carriers. The port is the largest artificial harbour in the world and features the world's largest LNG export facility.[18]

Economic diversification in Saudi Arabia has followed a two-pronged approach and remains embedded within the regular cycle of five-year plans (dating back to 1970) alongside sector-specific national plans covering particular economic activities. One dimension focused on the creation of economic cities as hubs of agglomeration and diffusion of knowledge, while the other emphasised the development of a sophisticated downstream petrochemicals industry. The centrepiece of the first strand of development lay in the construction of six economic cities, including the showpiece King Abdullah Economic City (KAEC) on the Red Sea Coast north of Jeddah, and the King Abdullah City for Atomic and Renewable Energy (KA-CARE) near Riyadh. The King Abdullah Economic City contains an integrated seaport, industrial centre, and financial sector and is intended to hold two million people by 2020, while KA-CARE has been mandated to develop the Kingdom's nuclear and renewable energy programmes within a national framework for sustainable energy. Both mega-projects form the core of Saudi Arabia's strategy of economic diversification and job creation and build upon the 2005 accession to the World Trade Organization (WTO) and the drive to attract foreign investment in key economic sectors.[19]

Massive investment in, and rapid development of, downstream petrochemical products and capacity is the second pillar of the Saudi national development plans. By 2009, the kingdom was the fastest-growing market in the Middle East for the petrochemical, printing, plastics, and packaging industries, and accounted for 70 per cent of petrochemical production in the GCC. These created new integrative links with the global economy, and more complex industrial ties with emerging and industrialised economies across the world, as well as greater flows of FDI, technology transfer, and integration into global production and supply chains.[20] A prominent example of this at work is evident in the Saudi Basic Industries Corporation (SABIC), which employs an almost exclusively (and highly qualified) local workforce and has established its own research centres that have taken an increasing role in their own production design and innovation.[21]

Kuwait has been the laggard among the Gulf States in formulating a comprehensive national development vision. This reflects the greater level of contentious political debate in Kuwait since current Emir Sheikh Sabah al-Ahmad Al Sabah came to power in 2006 that has made it far harder to achieve consensus on political and economic reform. The troubled trajectories of Kuwait's medium and longer-term economic plans provide a case in point. A longer-term plan, Kuwait Vision 2035, was prepared at controversial public expense by Tony Blair Associates and presented by the former British Prime Minister to the Emir in March 2010. Kuwait Vision 2035 aimed to transform Kuwait into a regional financial, trading, and logistics hub for the Northern Gulf, and set out a list of ambitions and desired outcomes linked to greater accountability, more professionalisation in the civil service, and substantial educational reforms.[22] A unit was established subsequently in the office of the then Kuwait's Prime Minister, Sheikh Nasser Mohammed Al Sabah, to engage with the recommendations of Kuwait Vision 2035. However, the unit was closed following Nasser Mohammed's resignation in December 2011, and as of 2014, the report lies fallow.[23]

Alongside Kuwait Vision 2035, the National Assembly belatedly approved the government's Four-Year Development Plan for 2010–2014 (initially envisaged as a five-year plan beginning in 2009, but parliamentary ratification was delayed until February 2010). The four-year plan aimed at stimulating GDP growth and enlarging the role of the private sector in the economy with an emphasis placed on involving the private sector in implementing national projects through greater use of Public Private Partnerships (PPP). However, persistent political gridlock led to a succession of delayed spending decisions and meant that capital spending barely exceeded KD1 billion (US$3 billion) in the plan's last fiscal year (2013–2014) against a target of KD8 billion (US$28.4 billion) per year. Moreover, the non-oil sector remained tiny in comparison to the oil sector, which continued to represent 94 per cent of GDP, while major targets concerning the role of the private sector in the economy also fell far short of their targets.[24]

State capitalism in the Gulf

In addition to the formulation of the comprehensive development visions listed above, the rise of Qatar and Dubai (and later Abu Dhabi), in particular, was also aided by the relatively more streamlined models of state capitalism that emerged in the 1990s and 2000s. In these emirates, and drawing upon the absence of organised political opposition to economic development (as in Kuwait), segmented factionalism in control of overlapping and sometimes even competing institutions (as in Saudi Arabia), and dwindling levels of resource wealth (as in Bahrain and Oman), a relatively small circle of senior figures operating with considerable autonomy from societal pressure was able to take executive decisions quickly and effectively. The personalisation of policymaking intersected with the ability to draw in resources to facilitate the mobilisation of different elements of state institutions and state-owned enterprises in pursuit of common objectives.

There has been a revival in recent years of academic and practitioner interest in the concept of state capitalism, with an article in *Foreign Affairs* in 2009 suggesting it had 'come of age,'[25] *The Economist* magazine somewhat begrudgingly devoting an issue to its rise in January 2012,[26] and

Bloomberg Businessweek referring more optimistically to its 'innovative potential,' also in 2012.[27] The global financial crisis that started in 2007 exposed failings in the aggressively pro-market Washington Consensus economic agenda and required officials in Western capitalist economies to intervene politically to direct high levels of economic resources to state-driven recovery measures. Simultaneously, at the end of a decade of high oil prices and substantial capital accumulation, the resolutely state-led approach of the Gulf States began to look more robust in light of the failings of the Bretton Woods system of economic governance. Writing about Dubai in 2009, shortly before the emirate's own economic slowdown, Danish economist Martin Hvidt might well have been writing about Qatar in his description of how

> the extremely centralised and capable decision-making structure and significant government involvement in the economy have made it possible to coordinate sizeable state investments, incoming foreign investments, and most likely a good part of private-sector investments . . . the centralised state paradigm (one of the defining characteristics of the developmental state paradigm in Dubai) has been reinforced by the traditional tribal (patrimonial) leadership style.[28]

During the late 2000s, macroeconomic trends converged with the pressures generated by the global financial crisis to accentuate the shift in global economic power from the market to the state, and, broadly, from West to East. From China to the East Asian 'tiger' economies, officials in the GCC states absorbed and distilled policymaking lessons that sometimes differed significantly from those of the International Monetary Fund (IMF) or the World Bank. In the Gulf, the East Asian model of the developmental state in general, and its implementation by Lee Kuan Yew in Singapore in particular, was very influential. This was based on a pragmatic combination of state guidance and private initiative, underpinned by significant government interventions in the economy. Another attraction of Singapore to Gulf elites was the broadly similar nature, as a small (and politically authoritarian) polity that nevertheless overcame the limitations of size to diversify into a knowledge-based and internationalised economy.[29]

Both Qatar and the UAE witnessed the creation of a lean and efficient business landscape that contained a number of high-profile and increasingly successful state-owned enterprises (SOEs). The models of state capitalism applied in Qatar and Dubai differ in their precise macroeconomic approaches and sector-specific focuses, yet certain commonalities exist.[30] Broadly, the SOEs operate across economic sectors and have acquired reputations for strong corporate management in line with international standards of governance, efficiency, and leadership, especially when compared to bloated and poorly regulated public sector counterparts. Significantly, they blend public and private sector representation on their boards, with members of ruling families serving alongside hand-picked businesspeople. This has ensured rapid and high-level access to the top of the decision-making structure and enabled the mobilisation of key state assets in support of particular policies. In addition, the SOEs can be (and in practice are) aligned with national economic plans and recipients of targeted state support. Examples of support identified by Steffen Hertog include the provision of state land, cheap petrochemical feedstock, and access to national infrastructure such as new, state-of-the-art ports and airports.[31]

Aside from state-backed airlines (Qatar Airways, Emirates, and Etihad Airways), which have grown enormously and are analysed in Chapter 7, other prominent examples of Gulf SOEs include SABIC, one of the largest diversified chemical and manufacturing companies in the world by asset value; Aluminium Bahrain (ALBA) and its Emirati counterpart Dubal (Dubai Aluminium), both among the world's largest aluminium companies; Industries Qatar, a subsidiary of Qatar Petroleum established in 2003 to specialise in the fertiliser, petrochemical, and steel sectors; and DP World, the Dubai port operator which gained unfortunate worldwide exposure in 2006 when its acquisition of P&O caused political controversy in the US (see Chapter 5). Together with the proliferation of large-scale family conglomerates, themselves an outgrowth of the traditional Gulf merchant class, by 2011 25 of the 30 largest companies in the Arab world by market capitalisation were based in GCC states (Table 3.2).[32]

Such streamlined operating procedures in Qatar and the UAE stemmed largely from the fact that the leadership of most enterprises and institutions was concentrated in a small circle of elite policymakers. In Qatar, Sheikh Hamad bin Jassim Al Thani ('HBJ'), Prime Minister between 2007 and 2013, emerged as the archetypal state capitalist and was described by one observer as a 'politician-cum-businessman.'[33] In addition to his dual ministerial positions (as Foreign Minister from 1992 to 2013 as well as Prime Minister), HBJ simultaneously served on the Supreme Council for the Investment of the Reserves of the State, was the vice chairman and chief executive officer (CEO) of the Qatar Investment Authority (QIA), and chairman of QIA's real estate arm (Qatari Diar) and direct

Table 3.2   Prominent Gulf-based state-owned entities

Entity	Country of origin	Sector
Emirates	UAE (Dubai)	Aviation
Etihad	UAE (Abu Dhabi)	Aviation
Qatar Airways	Qatar	Aviation
ADNOC	UAE (Abu Dhabi)	Energy
Kuwait Petroleum	Kuwait	Energy
Qatargas	Qatar	Energy
Qatar Petroleum	Qatar	Energy
Saudi Aramco	Saudi Arabia	Energy
Aluminium Bahrain	Bahrain	Heavy industry
Dubai Aluminium	Dubai	Heavy industry
SABIC	Saudi Arabia	Heavy industry
Industries Qatar	Qatar	Heavy industry
DP World	UAE (Dubai)	Logistics
Emaar Properties	UAE (Dubai)	Real estate
Qatari Diar	Qatar	Real estate
Batelco	Bahrain	Telecoms
Etisalat	UAE (Abu Dhabi)	Telecoms
Ooredoo	Qatar	Telecoms

Source: Organisation for Economic Cooperation and Development (OECD)

investment arm (Qatar Holding), which made multiple high-profile acquisitions in the United Kingdom, in particular. HBJ's personalised network flowed through his sons, too, as they also occupied top-level positions that strengthened his influence in the state capitalist structure, with the eldest son, Jassim bin Hamad Al Thani, being chairman of both Qatar Islamic Bank and QInvest (an Islamic investment banking company) while serving as a director with Qatar Insurance Company and a board member with Qatar Navigation, and two other sons (Sheikh Jabr bin Hamad and Sheikh Fahad bin Hamad) being represented on the board of Doha Insurance Company and vice chairman of Gulf Warehousing Company respectively.[34]

Prior to the debt crisis that rocked Dubai in November 2008, the most prominent example of the state capitalist model in the UAE was Dubai Holdings and its multiple subsidiaries, which included Jumeirah International, Dubai International Capital, the Dubai Group, and Tecom Investments, a business park operator responsible for managing Dubai Internet City and Dubai Media City. Majority-owned by the Ruler of Dubai, Sheikh Mohammed bin Rashid Al Maktoum, Dubai Holding was operated by one of the ruler's closest economic confidantes, Mohammed al-Gergawi, and at its height was believed to control more than US$15 billion of overseas assets. As the emirate's pre-eminent investment vehicle, the Dubai Holding group made high-profile investments in global brands such as Daimler-Chrysler and EADS before being hit heavily by the global economic slowdown in 2009. Another SOE majority-owned by Sheikh Mohammed bin Rashid has been Dubai World, a holding company whose assets include DP World, its property arm Nakheel, which rose to global prominence as the developer of the Palm Islands and The World archipelago, and its investment arm, Istithmar World. Dubai Holding and Dubai World both functioned as the flagship investment vehicle for Dubai intended to promote the emirate as a regional financial and commercial hub.[35]

As with Qatar, the role of the ruler in Dubai was buttressed by a small group of hand-picked senior executives who led the major holding groups. During the boom years of Dubai's dizzying economic expansion prior to the 2009 debt crisis, the three key 'lieutenants' around Sheikh Mohammed were the aforementioned al-Gergawi of Dubai Holding (also the Minister of Cabinet Affairs), Sultan bin Sulayem (CEO of Dubai World), and Mohammed Alabbar (chairman of property and real estate developer Emaar). All three men served on the Investment Corporation of Dubai, an investment vehicle for channelling funds into the myriad state-owned companies, and a competitive atmosphere emerged among them as each vied to pursue the most eye-catching initiative. Their activities were underpinned by an Executive Office, which provided strategic planning and which gradually replaced the more traditional Ruler's Court as the epicentre of decision-making in Dubai in the freewheeling years of breakneck growth.[36]

The strengthening of Dubai's reputation as an ideal place to do business benefited directly from the fact that all elements of the bureaucratic apparatus were overseen closely by the ruler and his immediate circle of core advisers as described above. This facilitated the establishment and growth of the free zones, such as the Jebel Ali Free Zone (founded in 1985 by Sultan bin Sulayem), which aimed to boost foreign (and non-oil related) investment with incentives such as full foreign ownership, specialised new cities such as Internet City and Media City (both developed by Mohammed al-Gergawi) to attract new economic sectors, and the creation of the Dubai International Financial Centre (operated by another key adviser to Sheikh Mohammed, Omar bin Suleiman) to allay investor concerns about local bureaucratic issues by drawing up its own legislative and regulatory framework based on English common law.[37]

Development of strategic niches

High levels of state resources have gone into identifying and carving out strategic niches that have positioned the Gulf States as regional hubs and even global leaders in sector-specific areas. A combination of significant resource availability and relatively few domestic political constraints on how to deploy the windfall from high oil prices enabled a series of large-scale initiatives that also aimed to generate reserves of soft power and international repute. This section illustrates several examples and demonstrates how the process of developing strategic niches has played out in the fields of renewable and alternative energy, higher education, and petrochemicals production. In each of the three case studies, the injection of substantial amounts of capital by Gulf governments and SOEs has resulted in the establishment of enclaves of genuinely cutting-edge expertise and excellence. These, in turn, have strengthened local cycles of innovation and enterprise and stimulated the growth of the non-oil sector that will one day be needed to cushion the eventual transition to post-oil economies. Yet, despite placing increasing emphasis on value creation and the 'knowledge economy,' doubts remain as to how organically the strategic niches are linked to deeper socio-economic and political currents in Gulf polities.

Renewable and alternative energies

The UAE (Abu Dhabi) and Saudi Arabia unveiled grandiose plans in the late 2000s to become world-leading centres of research and development into renewable and alternative energies. On the surface, these plans stood in direct contradistinction to the environmentally unsustainable policies of economic and industrial development underway in each country. Levels of domestic energy consumption soared during the decade between 2000 and 2010 with compound annual growth rates in all six GCC states of 4.4 per cent in oil consumption, 6.7 per cent in natural gas, and 5.4 per cent in electricity.[38] In the mid-2000s, GCC states occupied the top four places in the global ranking of carbon emissions per capita, with the figure for Qatar being more than double that of the UAE in second place, and three times that of the US.[39] The Qatari per capita figure declined subsequently as the population more than doubled in the space of six years, but the figure for all GCC states remained outliers in global terms. Water desalination plants, made possible by cheap domestic feedstock, coupled with heavily subsidised rates for water usage, compound the problem of over-consumption, with Mari Luomi finding that the average resident of the UAE uses more than four times more water per day (equivalent to 550 litres) than their counterpart in the United Kingdom.[40] Simultaneously, the Gulf States, led in this instance by Saudi Arabia and Kuwait, gained a reputation for obstructionism in successive rounds of climate change negotiation. This arose as Gulf officials concentrated their focus on the perceived negative economic implications of climate change adaptation rather than on the environmental effects of climate change itself.[41]

And yet, against this pattern of the unsustainable and environmentally destructive use of resources, officials in Abu Dhabi and Saudi Arabia invested considerable time, effort, and capital to become world leaders in renewable and alternative energy. Investment in the UAE rose substantially after 2004, building upon the strong environmental legacy of the nation's founding father, Sheikh Zayed bin Sultan Al Nahyan, who died the same year. In April 2006, the Masdar Initiative was launched under the auspices of the Abu Dhabi Future Energy Company, itself a subsidiary of Mubadala, a sovereign wealth fund established in 2002 by current Crown Prince Sheikh Mohammed bin Zayed Al Nahyan. The initiative encompassed not only the expansive Masdar City project of creating a zero-carbon city in the desert next to Abu Dhabi's international airport, but also a wider hub for research into renewable and future energies. This included the Masdar Institute for Science and Technology, which opened in September 2009, and the World Future Energy Summit, which has taken place every year since 2008. Moreover, Abu Dhabi campaigned vigorously to host the International Renewable Energy Agency (IRENA) at Masdar City, successfully beating out Germany and South Korea in the process. Together, these developments enabled the emirate to brand itself, somewhat improbably in light of its ecological footprint, as a global leader in the renewable energy field.[42]

Closer examination of Abu Dhabi's approach towards the Masdar Initiative and the IRENA bid illustrates some of the comparative advantages – and also the pitfalls – of Gulf attempts to create strategic niches in sector-specific areas. The plans for Masdar City unveiled with great fanfare in 2006 had to be scaled back significantly following the financial slowdown in 2009 and a slew of other difficulties in translating initial intent into capability. Luomi has characterised the challenges that faced the developers as including 'over-optimistic assumptions, hasty marketing, colossal promises, rushed implementation, and, most likely, bad recruitment choices.' As a result, in 2010, the operating budget for the city was cut by a quarter, the timeline for its development extended, and a number of technical features cancelled. These had the effect of transforming the original intent of creating a 'zero-carbon' city first to a 'carbon-neutral' city and subsequently merely to a 'low-carbon' city.[43]

With regard to the successful campaign to bring IRENA to Abu Dhabi, at the expense of competitors with far longer records of engaging with renewable energy, Luomi has outlined the package of financial incentives that made the Abu Dhabi bid difficult to turn down. These included a pledge by Abu Dhabi to cover 'all the building and operating costs of the agency' as part of a commitment of US$135 million to the new organisation. In addition to these fixed costs, the financial package included an offer of annual loans of US$50 million from the Abu Dhabi Fund for Development to fund IRENA-approved projects in developing states between 2009 and 2015. Luomi noted further that the largesse of the Abu Dhabi 'bid' far exceeded that of Germany's, which included US$46 million for setting up IRENA and US$3–4 million for annual operating costs, and concludes that 'Abu Dhabi's oil wealth may have been the deciding factor in its victory over Europe's leader in renewable energy, which had originally envisioned the launch of the organisation.'[44]

Policymakers in Abu Dhabi also cooperated intensively with the International Atomic Energy Agency to ensure that its civil nuclear energy plans meet the highest standards of transparency, safeguarding, and monitoring, in order to gain the support of the international community, and the US in particular.[45] US Congressional approval for the '123' nuclear cooperation deal offered by the outgoing Bush administration in January 2009 sent a powerful signal of geopolitical support for the UAE as a stable actor implementing nuclear energy in a responsible manner that addresses proliferation concerns and forms a model for other Middle Eastern states seeking a nuclear energy capability.[46] Most notably, in order to reassure the international community regarding proliferation concerns (and to stand in direct contradistinction to Iran's highly contentious nuclear programme), the UAE foreswore 'proliferation-sensitive capabilities' such as uranium enrichment and spent fuel reprocessing.[47]

Saudi Arabia joined Abu Dhabi in unveiling an ambitious and multi-pronged bid to become a regional leader in renewable and alternative energy. In April 2010, King Abdullah issued a Royal Decree establishing KA-CARE to oversee the development and implementation of a national energy sustainability programme in the kingdom. The city's launch signalled the acknowledgement, at the highest level of policymaking, of the need to diversify the sources of energy production to offset the soaring domestic levels of energy consumption and demand for electricity. Particular attention focused on projections that, absent concerted measures to conserve energy and develop alternative energies, the overall demand for fossil fuels for power, desalination, and transportation would reach 8.3 million barrels of oil equivalent by 2028. This was broadly consistent with a separate study conducted by the national oil company, Saudi Aramco, which warned that the country's crude export capacity risked falling by three million barrels of oil per day by the same year.[48]

The launch of KA-CARE was paralleled by a series of other initiatives designed to place Saudi Arabia at the forefront of the development of renewable and alternative energy. These included the 2009 establishment of the King Abdullah University of Science and Technology (KAUST) near Jeddah and the 2012 creation of a dedicated renewables investment fund by Saudi Aramco. KAUST began operating in September 2009 with a US$10 billion endowment and research tracks dedicated to examining natural resources, energy, and the environment. Notably, the university placed particular emphasis on clean combustion technologies and the science of solar and alternative energy and possessed the funding and the capability to attract world-leading faculty and equipment. In addition to hosting the first supercomputer in the Middle East, a report in *Science* suggested that each faculty member was given between US$400,000 and US$800,000 in internal support for research, sums that far outmatched those available in cash-strapped Western universities. Equally significant was the role of Saudi Aramco, rather than the Ministry of Higher Education, in assuming the lead role in financing and operating KAUST, thereby bypassing cumbersome bureaucratic processes.[49] Saudi Aramco also was pivotal in setting up the Saudi Aramco Energy Ventures fund (SAEV) in 2012 with a mandate 'to invest globally into start-up and high-growth companies with technologies of strategic importance' to the kingdom. Subsequent activity included the announcement of planned investment of up to US$120 million a year with Norwegian partners into European start-up energy and service companies.[50]

Together, the Emirati and Saudi initiatives demonstrate the importance of top-level leadership and buy-in among the most senior decision-makers. This has led to scepticism that the initiatives represent little more than 'vanity' projects whose existence may not outlive the passing of their patrons or the decline of oil prices. Yet, this notwithstanding, the scale of the resources being deployed to renewable and alternative energies is indicative of the growing urgency of local and regional debates on energy sustainability and long-term prospects. Moreover, the strategy of creating enclaves is itself an acknowledgement of the obstacles presented by the resilience of layers of vested interests with a stake in the maintenance of the political and economic status quo. As Saudi Aramco has done with KAUST, a measure of the success (or otherwise) of the projects will be their ability to generate durable new linkages not only with each other but also organically with local economic and socio-political patterns of activity.

Higher education and the 'knowledge economy'

In the 2000s, the Gulf States all embraced the concept of 'knowledge economies' as integral to their ambitious programmes of economic diversification and development. These, in turn, represented also a crucial element of the adaptation of Gulf economies to the broader processes of structural changes in the global economy, based on accelerating flows of information, capital, and people across national boundaries. Policymakers in the Gulf States directed a large share of the capital accumulation during the 2002–2008 oil price boom to investment in high-profile initiatives in higher education and scientific research and development. Underlying such moves was awareness of the necessity of producing a well-educated and highly skilled workforce of qualified nationals capable of competing in global labour markets and alleviating systemic problems of domestic unemployment and under-employment. Some of the early results have been eye-catching, as hubs of agglomeration for knowledge-intensive goods and services have already emerged, adding a new dimension to the national visions described above.

The linking of higher education to the creation of a strategic niche was most evident in the foundation and expansion of Education City and related initiatives in Qatar. Largely through the Qatar Foundation for Education, Science, and Community Development headed by Sheikha Mozah bint Nasser al-Missned, the powerful second wife of the then Emir Sheikh Hamad, Qatar sought to project itself as an intellectual (and cultural) hub for the Gulf and the Middle East. The centrepiece of this process is Education City, a vast educational hub that has developed on the dusty outskirts of Doha since its inception in the late 1990s. Education City has attracted transplant branches of eight leading global universities and has positioned Qatar at the forefront of regional higher education choices. Such growth arguably occurred at the expense of state-run Qatar University, which predates Education City by more than two decades (founded in 1973 as a College of Education before expanding into a university in 1977). Qatar University has remained outside the Education City/Qatar Foundation umbrella and has not received funding on the scale of its younger counterpart, which also operates a mixed-gender regime unlike the segregated state-run university.[51]

The first entrant into Education City was the Virginia Commonwealth University in Qatar in 1998. Since then a process of steady expansion saw the arrival of the Weill Cornell Medical College in Qatar in 2001, the Texas A&M University of Qatar in 2003, the Carnegie Mellon University in Qatar in 2004, the Georgetown University School of Foreign Service in Qatar in 2005, and the Northwestern University in Qatar in 2008. In addition to these six pioneering US institutions, 2011 saw the arrival of the HEC Paris Business School and a branch of University College London, the first British transplant of its kind. Although initial plans to have up to 15 prestige university branches and a minimum quota of 75 per cent of Qatari students proved unfeasible, by 2010, Qatari students formed about 45 per cent of the total student population of about 10,000 (although a worrying factor for Qatari educational leaders was, as overall enrolment numbers increased, the proportion of Qatari students consistently declined).[52] These universities were joined by offshoots of prestigious Western think-tanks and research institutions that chose to locate their regional offices in Qatar. These included the RAND-Qatar Policy Institute (which has since closed), the Brookings Doha Centre, and the Royal United Services Institute for Defence and Security Studies (RUSI Qatar). Together, these university campuses and research institutes ensured a constant stream of high-profile and specialised visitors that anchored Qatar as a leading hub of concentrated thinking in the region.[53]

More innovative still was the alignment and integration of academic research with Qatari developmental and strategic plans. This occurred through the launching of the Qatar National Research Fund and its National Priorities Research Programme in 2006. A part of the Qatar Foundation, these annual funding cycles attracted applications from researchers across the world in cooperation with a local academic partner in Qatar itself. Some US$121 million in project funding was announced in the May 2013 funding cycle alone, spread across 27 local research institutes and their international partners.[54] The programme represented a step up from the research councils established in other Gulf States, such as Oman and the UAE, by directly incentivising and promoting collaborative academic partnerships between local and international research networks, and by funding research that clearly met Qatar's (self-defined) needs. Moreover, as governmental funding and research grants in Western universities was squeezed relentlessly by the pressure of budget cuts in the late 2000s, the amounts of funding available in Qatar magnified its allure among academics the world over.[55]

Such developments sought to position Qatar at the forefront of regional and even international developments in research and critical thinking. They functioned as a powerful tool of soft power by extending the circles of academic and public policy debate devoted to issues facing Qatar and its environs. As tools of state-branding, they reinforced the self-branding of Qatar as a benign influence in international affairs, as a country seeking to contribute to the sum of human knowledge and push forcefully against regional boundaries of dissenting speech and independent thought. And yet, doubts remain over the depth of Qatar's commitment to the supposedly universal principles of free speech and thinking, as scepticism persists over whether and how officials would tolerate the spotlight of scrutiny being turned inward on domestic Qatari affairs. One article, published in 2014, entitled 'In Doha, a "Climate of Fear,"' painted a bleak portrait of self-censorship at one of the American campuses in Education City, and argued that 'behind the finely-tailored PR lies a harsh reality for its employees.'[56] Moreover, the travails of the Doha Centre for Media Freedom, which saw its founding director resign in frustration in 2009 and a successor removed suddenly in 2013, offers a similar tale of caution.[57]

Officials in Oman also sought to expand rapidly in higher education in the 2000s. Until that point, the public Sultan Qaboos University (SQU) was the only such entity permitted to operate in the country, but the number of private colleges proliferated following their legalisation in 1995. By 2008, no fewer than 24 private institutions were operating in the sultanate, including several in partnership with prestige international collaborators, among them the German University of Technology ('GuTech'). This was a joint venture with the reputable educational provider, RWTH Aachen, well known in Germany for its expertise in engineering and technology.[58] Like Qatar, Oman created a Research Council in 2005 in order to formulate an integrated plan for research and development in line with identified national priorities. Working with SQU, the council was tasked with becoming a leader in knowledge generation and building a world-class infrastructure for research at SQU focusing on solar energy, enhanced oil recovery, and nanotechnology.[59]

These developments notwithstanding, a 2010 study of higher education in the GCC, co-authored by a British-based academic and a former Minister for Higher Education in Oman, underscored some of the challenges still confronting university campuses in the Gulf. Gari Donn and Yahya Al Manthri noted pessimistically that the trend towards importing foreign, primarily American, campuses ran the risk of perpetuating a culture of dependency in which the Gulf States remained consumers, rather than producers, of knowledge. Donn and Al Manthri added that the influx of foreign higher education institutions further risked becoming 'a valuable economic and political cargo for the sellers/exporters but of little educational value to purchasers/importers.'[60] Additional data collected in Dubai for a study conducted by the Dubai School of Government (since renamed the Mohammed bin Rashid School of Government after the Ruler of Dubai) indicated that only a minority of the students enrolled in the international branch campuses in the UAE were actually Emirati nationals. Moreover, the study found that the substantial majority of expatriate students fully expected to return to their home countries following completion of their studies.[61]

Refined products and petrochemicals

The sustained investment in downstream refined products and petrochemicals represent arguably the most successful niche where the Gulf States have genuinely emerged as world leaders. Although refineries were first established in the Gulf at the dawn of the oil era in the 1930s (in Bahrain) and 1940s (in Kuwait and Saudi Arabia), these were geared primarily to domestic markets, and after a brief upsurge in investment in refineries during the 1970s oil price boom, total capacity remained effectively stagnant until the early 2000s. During this period, much of the investment in refined and retail products took place beyond the Gulf, as with Kuwait Petroleum International's (KPI) network of Q8-branded service stations across Europe and ownership of a refinery in the Europort in Rotterdam. Saudi Arabia also entered into refining joint ventures with international partners in the US, Greece, South Korea, and the Philippines. In Abu Dhabi, the ruling family set up the International Petroleum Investment Company (IPIC) in 1984 to invest globally in energy and energy-related industries.[62]

As international oil prices rose rapidly in the mid-2000s, a qualitative shift occurred as officials in GCC states began to integrate downstream and move beyond the simple extraction of crude oil towards the creation of sophisticated value-added petroleum products. Giacomo Luciani has noted that the rush of new refining and petrochemical ventures was a pragmatic form of economic diversification 'not away from oil but leveraging the availability of oil and gas' in sectors where the GCC states possessed a comparative advantage.[63] Moreover, the scale of the industrialisation projects unveiled in the mid-years of the decade signified an attempt both to lessen over-reliance on the volatility of international oil markets (and revenues) and to broaden the Gulf States' integration into the global economy. The role of petrochemicals in diversifying economic and commercial relations has been particularly evident in the thickening of Gulf-Asia ties based on the rapid growth of non-oil trade flows in petrochemicals, plastics, and aluminium. Notably, this impacted Gulf relations with emerging economies such as China just as much (and in different ways) as it did ties with advanced economies such as Japan, as the former provided a large market for export opportunities while the latter benefited GCC partners through technology transfers and inward investment.[64]

In the 2000s, the Gulf States became global leaders in a variety of industries that ranged from petrochemicals and aluminium to cement and construction products. By 2008, the GCC as a region accounted for 12 per cent of global petrochemical production and a series of new ventures were launched that represented the biggest such initiatives in the world. These included three in Saudi Arabia alone – the US$27 billion Ras Tanura Integrated Project joint venture between Saudi Aramco and Dow Chemical that aims to establish the kingdom as the leading producer of a vast range of petrochemical products, including ethylene, propylene, aromatics, chlorine, chlorine derivatives, polyethylene, ethylene oxide, and glycol; construction of the world's largest petrochemicals facility in the already vast Jubail Industrial City in the Eastern Province; and the upgrading of the Petro Rabigh Refinery into one of the most sophisticated integrated oil refining and petrochemical facilities of its kind.[65] Simultaneously, a 2006 partnership between SABIC and Kayan Petrochemicals illustrated the type of 'backward linkages' that officials intend to form the cornerstone of the Kingdom's economic transition into value-added products. In January 2011, the Saudi Kayan Petrochemicals Company commenced the first Middle East-originated exports of acetone (a part of the value-chain used to manufacture polycarbonates, solvents, adhesives, and paints) to the substantial Indian market.[66]

Similar developments occurred elsewhere in the GCC, most notably in petrochemicals in Qatar and Abu Dhabi and (in an earlier era in the 1970s and 1980s) in aluminium in Bahrain and Dubai. Qatar Petroleum and the Qatar Petrochemical Company (QAPCO) unveiled several high-profile projects in the mid-2000s, including a joint venture with the Chevron Phillips Chemical Company (Q-Chem-2) to produce high density polyethylene, and a joint venture between QAPCO and Total Petrochemicals (Qatofin) for the creation of a world-scale polyethylene plant in Mesaieed Industrial City. Both joint ventures utilised feedstock from ethylene provided by a third venture, an ethane cracker at Ras Laffan Industrial City established in partnership by Qatar Petroleum,

Qatofin, and QAPCO.[67] Developments in Abu Dhabi focused on the expansion of the range of products and global partnerships of Borouge, a joint venture launched in 1998 by the Abu Dhabi National Oil Company (ADNOC) and Borealis, itself co-owned by Abu Dhabi's IPIC and the Austrian oil and gas group OMV. The 'Borouge 2' project tripled the polyolefins manufacturing capacity of the petrochemical facility at Ruwais and installed the largest ethane cracker in the world, while 'Borouge 3' launched a further phase of expansion into high value-added products in partnership with South Korea's Hyundai Engineering and Construction and Samsung Engineering.[68]

The case studies therefore illustrate in action the Gulf States' strong preference for practical engagement with issue- and sector-specific areas in pursuit of tangible national (and, on occasion, regional) objectives. As the following chapter makes clear, patterns of global interaction have placed emphasis on translating the GCC states' greater leverage both into reshaping frameworks of governance and into creating new ones. Through such processes, the Gulf States have become further integrated into existing layers of intergovernmental institutions, working alongside the established Western powers where necessary and through coalitions of convenience with other groups of emerging economies on selected issues. In each case, a pragmatic and cautious approach to policymaking has characterised the rise of the Gulf States as regional powers with international reach.

4
Gulf Perspectives on the Global Rebalancing

This chapter ends Part I of this book by mapping the motivations and policy objectives that underpin the qualitative change in global engagement evident in GCC capitals since the turn of the millennium. It begins with an evaluation of the impact of the processes of globalisation on the Gulf that argues that the economic dimensions have largely been embraced whereas the political and socio-cultural aspects of globalisation have been subject to pushback. Yet, official scepticism of theoretical or normative concepts such as 'global governance' has not distanced the GCC states from actively participating in the evolving structures of global power, politics, and policymaking. Hence, the second section of this chapter explores three instances where individual Gulf States have engaged pragmatically in attempts to reshape international governing structures. These are the attempts to leverage GCC states' roles in recapitalising struggling Western institutions during the global financial crisis in 2007–2008 into greater representation in the architecture of international finance; the greater emphasis on positioning the Gulf States at the forefront of new frameworks of energy governance; and the decision to participate more fully in the international politics of climate change. In each instance, the underlying motivation to engage more substantively in global governance structures was to maximise the projection of Gulf interests at both national and regional levels. However, the more visible role played by Gulf States was not without its problems, as identification with global issues often was lacking, and policy frequently was characterised by style over substance, illustrated by a snapshot case study of Qatar's hosting of the 2012 annual climate change conference.

More positively, the sector-specific examples listed above do require GCC states to conform to international practices and thus represent highly visible examples of the interaction between the local and the global levels. Such interactions are increasing and moreover are doing so at an exponentially faster rate. Thus, the chapter ends by assessing the implications of the Gulf States' rise for the continuing evolution of global institutions in a polycentric environment with multiple centres of influence and policy objectives. This final section analyses how the GCC states formed part of loose groupings of rising powers on sector-specific issues and explores the thickening and diversification of linkages with other major emerging economies such as China, India, Brazil, and Indonesia. These ties represent new coalitions of convenience around a practical and shared interest in reframing patterns of global engagement to better manage the governance of globalisation rather than any normative affiliation with what increasingly are perceived as Western-centric norms of global governance.

Uneven impact of globalisation

Recent works on globalisation have emphasised the multiplicity of approaches to the study of the impact of global processes and flows on regions and nations. Consensus has yet to emerge on whether the rise of the Global South has the potential 'to form a real economic and political force that may move beyond dependence on the West to form a new center of power in the global political economy.'[1] While it is indeed the case that the global financial crisis opened up new pathways of opportunities for rising powers and emerging economies, they did not represent a fundamental challenge to global hegemonic norms such as neoliberal economic governance. Rather, the growth of additional engines of global growth both reflected and reinforced the intensity of non-Western connections and networks that constitute the building blocks of the international political economy of the twenty-first century. These new nodes formed part of the broader geographic shift between West and East and the geo-economic rebalancing from the global North to South.[2]

It is by no means axiomatic that the 'new' participants in debates over globalisation and the reshaping of global governance will share any affiliation with norms concerning rights, authority, and legitimacy, to take three of the most heatedly contested terms in contemporary discourse. As a result, David Held has noted that 'the meaning of some of the core concepts of the international system are subject to the deepest conflicts of interpretation.'[3] Previously hegemonic states (and norms) are coming under sustained challenge from many of the rising international actors, with profound implications for issues such as democracy, the rule of law, and human rights. As regional powers with international reach, the Gulf States are pivotally located in global conversations about the nature and form of the changing architecture of international governing frameworks. And yet, Gulf States' trajectories towards greater global integration have neither been one-directional nor free from political or economic resistance.

Throughout the GCC states, the impact of globalising processes on Gulf societies has been uneven and filtered through multiple layers of identification. Views such as those expressed by the veteran Qatar-based Egyptian cleric Yusuf al-Qaradawi that globalisation 'from the beginning has been linked to the expansion of the Western model' reflect a more widespread perception that globalisation aims at reproducing the models of Western hegemony, albeit in a benign form.[4] Other expressions of scepticism towards globalisation include perceptions that the process is merely 'another way of talking about US dominance' and 'a one-way street where the benefits and the interests are all western.' At its most extreme, the then Governor of Saudi Arabia's Makkah Province, Prince Khaled al-Faisal bin Abdulaziz Al Saud, claimed in 2009 that Saudi youth 'finds himself caught between two forms of extremism,' namely Westernisation and radical Islamist militancy, in which 'each ideology tries to take him to its side leaving him confused and in need of knowing who he is and what his culture stands for.'[5] There is nevertheless no 'Gulf consensus' on the normative aspect of globalisation; policymakers in Kuwait have, in the past, expressed greater openness to global issues borne out of the country's liberation by a 34-country multinational coalition in 1991. More recently, the neoliberal business regimes established in Bahrain and the UAE have sought specifically to appeal to niches in the international flows of trade and finance and to consumers of a 'global elite' of luxury lifestyles.[6]

It should be noted at the outset that such ambivalence about globalisation is far from unique to the Gulf States or indeed to the broader Arab or Islamic world. Rather, it reflects a degree of scepticism found in much of the non-Western world about the normative concepts frequently ascribed in much of the Western literature on issues of globalisation and global governance. Discourse in China and India, for example, illustrates a similar underlying scepticism of global norms coloured by their own national experiences of foreign intervention and colonial control.[7] Held has noted how 'the meaning of some of the core concepts of the international system are subject to the deepest conflicts of interpretation' in non-Western settings, which instead put forward their own set of views of rights, authority, and legitimacy.[8] Moreover, Held goes on to observe that globalisation has in fact stimulated powerful nation-centric responses that challenge prevailing assumptions about the erosion of state power in the face of globalising pressures. Thus, states continue to act as powerful intermediaries through which the impact of international politics (and global governance) is filtered and shaped.[9]

The port cities located up and down the Arabian coastline of the Gulf have long functioned as critical nodes in wider networks of trade and exchange, as Chapter 1 illustrated. Yet, there was little consistency in receptivity to global influences during the period of rapid modernisation of spatial and social patterns in Gulf societies that followed the beginning of oil exports in the mid-twentieth century. The most open approach was followed in Kuwait, where the Ruler, Sheikh Abdullah al-Salem Al Sabah (ruled 1950–1965) launched a wide-ranging strategy to modernise all aspects of Kuwaiti political, economic, and social activity. This was intended to confer 'upon Kuwait a distinct position among the civilised and developed world states' and included an urban master plan drawn up by a British firm of architects with no prior experience of urban planning in the region, that would make Kuwait City 'the best planned and most socially progressive city in the Middle East.'[10] At the other extreme, both Abu Dhabi and Oman were ruled by extremely conservative rulers until 1966 and 1970 respectively, delaying socio-economic patterns of development and the opening up to the outside world. Saudi Arabia, meanwhile, remained largely closed to external influences for much of the twentieth century, until a set of cautious reforms initiated during the reign of King Faisal bin Abdulaziz Al Saud in the 1970s.[11]

Emirati political scientist Abdulkhaleq Abdullah has identified a potent disconnection among the different types of globalisation that alternatively were embraced or resisted in the Gulf. Notably, he suggests persuasively that policymakers and publics broadly have welcomed the economic benefits of globalisation while they largely have resisted the political and cultural aspects. Abdulla adds that the GCC states 'acknowledge that they are in the grip of forces over which they had little power – they are also aware that the world around them is changing at an exceptionally rapid pace.'[12] Speaking at the London think-tank Chatham House in 2003, Badr bin Hamad Al bu Said, an Under-Secretary in the Omani Ministry of Foreign Affairs, underlined the importance of preserving 'the local and the specific . . . especially in the context of contemporary globalisation.'[13] GCC states also have remained heavily involved in domestic political and economic structures, thereby blunting the impact of global flows that, in other regional contexts, have eroded or bypassed notions of state sovereignty, which remained paramount in the Gulf.[14] Although to a lesser extent than other Middle East states such as Egypt, Syria, or Iraq, the broad pattern of the Gulf States' incorporation into the global political and economic system does resemble the 'differential integration' identified by Fred Halliday, in which the international influence on decision-making processes and policymaking is filtered through strong state institutions.[15]

The paradox facing scholarly analysis of the relationship between the Gulf and globalisation is that, as the editors of a 2006 volume on the subject put it, 'no part of the world has come into the global market more rapidly' than the Gulf monarchies, which 'take in capital, goods, information, and skilled labor in percentages not seen elsewhere in the world.'[16] This immediately becomes apparent to visitors to the Gulf States who cannot fail to be struck by the, at least superficial, paraphernalia of globalisation that are clearly visible all around them. Examples include some of the highest rates of smartphone penetration and social media usage in the world, alongside the plethora of Western fast-food outlets and enormous shopping malls.[17] And yet, it readily becomes apparent that such patterns are carefully regulated, whether in the form of gated residential communities where foreigners can own homes or the persistence of what Adam Hanieh refers to as entrenched features of 'khaleeji [Gulf] capital.'[18] As John Fox, Nada Mourtada-Sabbah, and Mohammed al-Mutawa succinctly put it, ruling elites in the GCC 'deliberately cushion themselves from the negative aspects of market penetration into social life' by creating 'separate spaces within Gulf society so that local and global are almost engineered to mix in prescribed ways.'[19]

Some of the most dynamic and fluid patterns of local and global interaction occur in international court systems as commercial disputes that might in the past have been contained within the Gulf now have regional and international impact. In 2009, what was ostensibly a dispute between two of the largest Saudi-run family conglomerates (Saad Group and Ahmad Hamad Algosaibi and Brothers [AHAB]) over some US$20 million in 'lost loans' during the financial crisis in 2007–2008 escalated into a global issue affecting more than 100 foreign financial institutions. These included multinationals such as Bank of America, Standard Chartered, Citigroup, and BNP Paribas, in addition to two banks in Bahrain that defaulted as a direct result of their exposure and sent shockwaves through the Bahraini financial sector.[20] The disputed transactions at the heart of the affair subsequently became the subject of court proceedings in New York, London, the Cayman Islands, Switzerland, the UAE, and Bahrain. Negotiations on potential settlements to creditors in Saudi Arabia and around the world have been hindered by the linguistic challenges of translating mountains of documents from Arabic as lawyers on three continents attempt to unravel the chain of events based on limited access to (or understanding of) the full documentation relating to the companies' holdings and operating structure.[21]

The international dimensions of the Saad-Algosaibi dispute showed the extent of modern entities' enmeshment in the evolving layers of global governance. These are transforming the spatial reach of social relations and transactions and generating new supra- and sub-national networks of interaction and power, as noted in Part I of this book.[22] More intrusive requirements of compliance with international norms and standards stimulated measures to reformulate the regional business culture and state-business relations during the 2000s boom. These included efforts to deepen transparency and accountability by unbundling the political and economic stakeholders intertwined in traditional merchant family conglomerates.[23] Policymakers' emphasis on corporate governance reflected their awareness of the need to address the challenges posed by opaque networks of familial alliances. However, the lack of transparency or disclosure of information about the Saad-Algosaibi case demonstrated the enduring tenacity of obstacles to overcoming older methods of conducting business on the basis of personal connections.[24]

All of these factors contributed to a low level of awareness of the concept of global governance in the Gulf, as in the wider Arab region. Writing in 2008, Tarik Yousef, then the dean of the Dubai School of Government, drew attention to the fact that 'we don't have a body of literature – knowledge, stories, cases, practices – that has been documented, distilled, and disseminated, and that deals with various aspects of governance in the Arab world.'[25] To the extent that global governance is about normative concepts of good governance, institutions such as the Dubai-based Hawkamah Institute for Corporate Governance raised awareness of this core component. However, other critical dimensions of the concept of global governance, including the dilution and sharing of state sovereignty and engagement with domestic and global civil society, have remained resolutely absent in the Gulf-specific context. This ties into the Gulf States' separation of economic from political and cultural globalisation in an attempt to manage their accelerating integration into the global system as much as possible on their own terms.

A similar ambivalence is evident in the Gulf States' patchy record of signing up to key international covenants. Kuwait remains the only GCC state to have acceded to the International Covenant on Civil and Political Rights and International Covenant on Economic, Social, and Cultural Rights, which it joined on 21 May 1996. Moreover, Kuwait was also the first Gulf State to sign the Convention on the Elimination of

All Forms of Discrimination against Women (CEDAW) on 2 September 1994. This preceded by more than a half-decade the accession of Saudi Arabia (2000), Bahrain (2002), and Qatar (2009) to the CEDAW.[26] Kuwait's first-mover status reflected the intersection of domestic and international pressure in the years immediately after Kuwait's liberation by the multinational coalition from Iraqi occupation in February 1991, which resulted in a degree of socialisation in global norms as Kuwaiti activists built coalitions of international support for reform at home. Nevertheless (and in common with other regional states), Kuwaiti accession to the international conventions came with broad reservations when integral articles in each were found to contravene Kuwaiti law or the Islamic *sharia*.[27]

Pragmatic engagement in the governance of globalisation

The reservations listed above have not prevented the Gulf States from engaging pragmatically with the global economy and with structures of international governance. The breadth and depth of the Gulf States' enhanced engagement in global issues extends from energy governance to the politics of climate change and the debate over reforms to the global financial architecture. This has propelled them into the global arena largely on their own terms, but has not been accompanied by any substantive identification with the notion of global governance. State-centric visions of inter-state cooperation, rather than attachment to normative concepts of global governance, still motivate GCC policymakers to project their interests globally, primarily in order to bolster their domestic and regional position. Nevertheless this engagement is taking place within a rapidly globalising environment in which complex interdependencies have emerged that bind the Gulf States to global structures and provide the parameters for their engagement within the international community.[28]

Gulf rulers thus tend to view engagement globally as a crucial pillar of their domestic and regional posture. They are also becoming more enmeshed in existing layers of global governance through membership of the WTO, which Saudi Arabia finally joined in December 2005 following 12 years of accession talks. Membership is significant as it benchmarks domestic governance to international standards, while participation in an international rules-based system introduces a new dynamic to domestic reform processes.[29] Three key issues – financial architectural reform, energy governance initiatives, and the politics of climate change – make it possible to operationalise and map the nature and intent of Gulf States' involvement in the governance of globalisation on a practical (rather than theoretical) level. This draws out the objectives that guide their integration into the international economic and institutional system and ascribes voice to the key domestic agents within the Gulf States who drive these policies forward.

With the global economy in a state of flux following the 2008 crash, the GCC states seized the opportunity to make their voices heard in the debate over the reshaping of the global financial architecture. This was particularly the case for Saudi Arabia by virtue of its position on the G20, but also for the UAE, Qatar, and Kuwait, which had accumulated sizeable sovereign wealth funds with global reach. Gulf policymakers initially expressed their 'surprise' that they were being asked for bailouts in a crisis that appeared to them to have originated in the US.[30] It was in this context that Saudi officials interpreted UK Prime Minister Gordon Brown's visit to the Gulf ahead of the G20 meeting in November 2008. Thus, the Finance Minister, Ibrahim Abdulaziz al-Assaf, rebuffed Brown's begging bowl proposal that the GCC states spend 'hundreds of billions' of dollars on an IMF rescue package for emerging markets by replying pointedly that 'we have been playing our role responsibly and we will continue to play our role, but we are not going to finance the institutions just because we have large reserves.'[31] One week later, the Governor of the UAE Central Bank, Nasser Al Suwaidi, offered a blunter perspective that outlined Gulf States' interests and motivations: 'If they [GCC states] are given more voice then they will provide money maybe . . . They will not be providing funds without extra voice and extra recognition.'[32]

In the run-up to the second meeting of the G20 in London in April 2009 the contours of a loose new alignment of emerging economies converged around calls to redress a representational imbalance in the international financial architecture. Chinese President Hu Jintao visited Saudi Arabia in February 2009 and pledged to work with the GCC 'with a view to reforming the global financial institutions.'[33] Shortly thereafter, Saudi Finance Minister al-Assaf made it clear that the kingdom advocated an increase in the shares and voting powers in international financial institutions.[34] In parallel, moves towards emerging coalitions of 'middle powers' took a step forward in June 2009 with the creation of the BRIC (Brazil, Russia, India, China) Forum in Yekaterinburg in Russia. This new annual summit of the four leading emerging economies (which subsequently met in Brasilia in 2010 and Sanya in China – with South African participation – in 2011) created a platform intended to counterbalance perceived US leadership in the global system.[35] Ahead of the third G20 meeting in Pittsburgh in September 2009, al-Assaf joined BRIC in supporting a proposal to increase emerging economies' representation in the IMF that would more accurately reflect their weight in the global economy.[36]

As the financial crisis unfolded, the eagerness with which Gulf investment was pursued contrasted sharply with the attitude of distrust which greeted previous sovereign wealth investments in the West (see Chapter 5). The importance of sovereign wealth funds became fully apparent in the aftermath of the global financial crash as European governments, led by the United Kingdom, actively sought Gulf support for the injection of short-term liquidity into European markets, while the outgoing Bush administration reportedly sought US$300 billion from Saudi Arabia, the UAE, Kuwait and Qatar to bail out the US automobile industry.[37] During the autumn of 2008, Gulf sovereign wealth funds accounted for approximately one-third of the emergency funding that European governments made available to financial institutions. The scale of these investments coincided with calls from Gulf policymakers for a new approach to handling sovereign investment and made more urgent a dialogue between investor and recipient states on their governance.[38]

A broadly similar dynamic of intersecting domestic, regional, and international interests animates GCC states' engagement in global energy governance and the international politics of climate change. The previous chapter documented the assertive attempts made by Abu Dhabi to secure the headquartering of IRENA. Qatar also has been proactive in hosting the Gas Exporting Countries Forum (GECF) and facilitating its growth into an intergovernmental organisation of 11 of the world's largest natural gas producers. Although it was founded in Tehran as early as 2001, the GECF operated without a charter and a formal membership structure until 2008, when an Executive Office and a Secretariat were established in Doha. Since then, the GECF has hosted regular annual (and sometimes biannual) ministerial meetings and, in November 2011, organised its first full summit in Doha. Opened by Qatar's Emir, the summit resulted in the Doha Declaration in support of the use of long-term gas contracts to balance risk sharing mechanisms among natural gas producers and consumers. The then Russian President Dimitry Medvedev described the Doha Summit as 'an important event, which marked a new stage in the development of the global energy sector and the gas sector in particular.'[39]

The growth of IRENA and the GECF are significant in that they illustrate how GCC states have engaged more deeply with the institutional architecture of global energy governance; what Andreas Goldthau and Jan-Martin Witte label 'the significance of the "rules of the game."'[40] Moreover, within OPEC itself, the four Gulf members – Saudi Arabia, Kuwait, Qatar, and Abu Dhabi (rather than the UAE) – have in recent years emerged as the pivotal actors in setting agendas and implementing policy outcomes. The 'return' to prominence of state players in international oil and gas markets moreover has occurred simultaneously with the rise of significant new global energy linkages. While the mismatch between supply and demand in global energy markets began to cause significant disruption in 2014, the Gulf States responded pragmatically by forging new markets for their energy flows. A case in point was the 52.7 per cent surge in Kuwaiti oil exports to China in the year to December 2014 following the signing of a ten-year crude supply deal between the state-run Kuwait Petroleum Corporation (KPC) and China's largest energy trader, Unipec. Signed in August 2014, the sales contract was the largest ever signed by KPC, both in volume and revenue, as it involved the transfer of 300,000 barrels of oil per day to Unipec reserves.[41]

Nevertheless, the state-led efforts to brand themselves as world leaders in renewable and alternative energy research (as described above and in Chapter 3) stand in direct contradistinction to the Gulf States' environmentally unsustainable development policies and obstructionist position in climate change negotiations.[42] The national and regional political economy of rent redistribution and energy-intensive economic diversification in the Arabian Peninsula mean that individually and collectively the GCC states have a considerable stake in shaping global discussion and decision-making processes. There is thus considerable tension at the heart of regional attempts to portray the Gulf States as responsible actors in global energy governance while minimising the threat to domestic interests from international pressure on the climate change issue. This demonstrates the acute linkages between the domestic and international spheres that are intertwined in policymaking in these sensitive areas.

As previously mentioned, GCC states occupy the top four global rankings in carbon dioxide emissions per capita.[43] Another report, the World Wildlife Fund's (WWF) biennial Living Planet Report, ranked the 'ecological footprint' of each country – namely, the amount of biologically productive land and water area required to produce the resources that an individual, population, or activity produces, and to absorb the carbon dioxide emissions they generate. Here, too, the Gulf States monopolised the top three positions, with the 2014 report finding that Kuwait had overtaken Qatar as the country with the world's largest per capita ecological footprint, with the UAE falling to third, yet all three GCC states continued to score far higher results than comparable industrial or emerging economies.[44] Another study, also produced in 2014, measured the countries that use the most oil per capita, and again scored three Gulf States in the top ten, with Qatar second (behind global leader Iceland), Kuwait fourth, and the UAE seventh (Tables 4.1 and 4.2).[45]

The indices listed above illustrate the task facing Gulf officials in international negotiations over the appropriate range of policy responses to the threats from environmental degradation and climate change.

Table 4.1   Largest ecological footprint per capita

Rank	Country
1	Kuwait
2	Qatar
3	UAE
4	Denmark
5	Belgium
6	Trinidad and Tobago
7	Singapore
8	US
9	Bahrain
10	Sweden

Source: WWF Living Planet Report 2014

Table 4.2   Energy use per capita (kilograms of oil equivalent), 2014

Rank	Country	Amount (kg)
1	Iceland	18.774
2	Qatar	17.418
3	Trinidad and Tobago	15.691
4	Kuwait	10.408
5	Brunei	9.427
6	Luxembourg	7.684
7	UAE	7.407
8	Canada	7.333
9	US	6.793
10	Finland	6.183

Source: Oilprice.com

With the notable exception of Oman, GCC policymakers gained a reputation for obstructionist tactics at successive rounds of climate change
negotiations by focusing on the (negative in their perception) economic
implications of a climate-changed world rather than the environmental impacts of climate change itself.[46] The enduring dominance of this
approach was clearly demonstrated in comments made to an OPEC
conference in March 2009 by Mohammed al-Sabban, head of the Saudi
delegation to the United Nations Framework Convention on Climate
Change (UNFCCC), as he warned that strict global proposals to mitigate climate change by cutting carbon emissions and dependence on
oil represented a 'very serious [threat] for oil producing countries and
in particular Gulf producing countries,' which 'stand to lose out to such
policies that are biased against oil producers.'[47] Low public awareness of
adaptation and mitigation measures had themselves been underpinned
by political and institutional policies that support the unsustainable and
environmentally destructive use of resources.[48]

In recent years, officials in GCC states began to develop more nuanced
approaches to climate change that at the minimum acknowledged the
need to participate more actively in negotiations to shape the response
mechanisms. This, again, has been most pronounced in the smaller
Gulf States, particularly the UAE, which created an Energy and Climate
Change Directorate within the Ministry of Foreign Affairs, and Qatar,
whose leadership, in particular, perfected the practice of bidding for and
hosting major international meetings. Moreover, the Qataris did so in a
manner that greatly enhanced the country's global profile by reaching
out in economic and governance sectors not commonly associated with
the Gulf region. Thus, in February 2009, Doha hosted the fourth Global
Conference of the Extractive Industries Transparency Initiative (EITI),
on the theme of 'Establishing Resource Transparency.' This was despite
the fact that Qatar was neither a compliant nor a candidate country to
actually join the EITI, or even a supporter intending to implement its
values. Association with the event nevertheless played into the Qatari
projection of an image of itself as a responsible global actor, even though
few people within Qatar appeared aware of it ever having taken place.[49]

The same may be said of the successful bid to host the 18th United
Nations Conference of the Parties (COP 18) Climate Change Conference
in Doha in November 2012. This allowed Qatar to move beyond its hitherto obstructionist image in climate change negotiations, and attempt to
differentiate itself from its Gulf neighbours. Moving away from the 'hard-
line' positions of Saudi Arabia and Kuwait in previous rounds of climate
change negotiation, hosting the COP was intended to project an image

of a state wealthy in hydrocarbons that was willing to engage with rather than block action on this pressing international issue. It also represented a domestic response to raise Qatar's profile vis-à-vis Abu Dhabi's attempt to project regional leadership on climate change and clean energy issues through its multi-billion dollar Masdar Project funded by the Abu Dhabi Future Energy Company, and its hosting of IRENA.[50]

Yet, the process and outcome of the COP 18 conference provided an opportunity to measure the degree of alignment between style and substance in Qatari (and, by extension, other Gulf States') patterns of global engagement. Qatari policymakers originally seem to have considered their bid to host COP 18 as part of the international state-branding initiatives already referred to. Interviews conducted in Qatar in the aftermath of the bid, and again at the halfway point between Qatar's successful bid and the conference itself (in December 2011 and May 2012), captured a sense of disquiet and uncertainty as policymakers realised belatedly that they would be required to formulate substantive proposals and credible initiatives to put before the conference.[51] Failure to do so, it was acknowledged, would simply reinforce negative external perceptions concerning Qatar, by dint of the world's media descending on Doha and focusing on the incongruity of hosting a pivotal climate change conference in a major hydrocarbons-producing state. As a result, a group of international experts was drafted in to augment and strengthen the Qatari negotiating team.[52]

It is evident from the foregoing that multiple and interlinking factors feed into the ostensibly contradictory policy approaches towards energy governance and the international politics of climate change at the domestic, regional, and global levels. The political economy of the oil monarchies renders them acutely vulnerable to any shifts in demand for, or perceptions toward, fossil fuels. In a climate-stressed world in which alternative and renewable sources of energy assume greater importance, it is in their interest to take proactive steps to shape the regulatory forms that emerge. Several notable features have defined the terms of Gulf States' interaction on the global level in the three cases outlined in this section. Most prominent is the continuing emphasis on state-centric approaches to issues of global governance and the lack of affiliation with the concept of *global governance* as attention focused instead on shaping emerging frameworks covering the *governance of globalisation*. Thus, the Gulf States emerged as influential actors in the global repositioning of power, exhibiting a greater willingness to take proactive steps in reshaping the institutional design of global frameworks of governance, particularly in the energy sector.[53]

In response to the new demands posed by a globalising world environment and the diffusion of the loci of power- and decision-making, these 'post-traditional' polities increasingly chose to pursue nuanced and multidimensional strategies designed to manage the impact of the processes of globalisation. The result has been greater visibility and voice in existing international organisations as well as the new institutional architecture that emerged out of the global financial and economic crisis. Evolving patterns of global engagement placed particular emphasis on translating greater leverage into reshaping international financial institutions and emerging frameworks of energy governance. Furthermore, as the final section in this chapter illustrates, the Gulf States form part of a broader realignment within the global order as GCC officials build coalitions of convenience with other emerging powers also sceptical of the normative concept of global governance, yet receptive to shaping the practical governance of globalisation.

New 'coalitions of convenience'

Scholarly attention has in recent years focused on the concept of the 'world economic centre of gravity' (WECG) to provide empirical evidence for the redistribution of global economic activity. Danny Quah of the London School of Economics constructed a model that extrapolates economic growth from 700 locations across the world to indicate that the WECG shifted 4,800 kilometres eastward between 1980, when it was located roughly midway in the Atlantic Ocean, and 2010, when it reached a longitude equivalent to Izmir in Turkey or Minsk in Belarus. Quah's research further suggests that by 2050 the WECG will have moved another 4,500 kilometres to the east, to lie at a point between India and China.[54] As described in other chapters of this book, the Gulf States have in effect functioned as a pivot around which broader shifts in the global balance of power took place, particularly as oil prices soared in the 2000s. Greater economic linkages and new patterns of trade with Russia, China, India, and South and East Asian nations shifted the Gulf States' orientation eastward during the first decade of the century.[55]

With the Gulf region's share of global oil and natural gas production projected to rise from 28 per cent (including Iraqi and Iranian output) in 2000 to 33 per cent in 2020, and most of that increase going to Asian markets, it is likely that the GCC states will continue to diversify and broaden economic interdependencies.[56] Already, the majority of oil exported from the UAE goes eastward to Asia as does a rapidly increasing share of Qatari liquefied natural gas. China alone accounted for nearly 40 per cent of the increase in world oil consumption between 2004 and 2007, and is forecast to account for a further 40 per cent of the increase in world demand for oil through 2030.[57] In 2009, moreover, it surpassed the US in the volume of oil imported from Saudi Arabia for the first time. This symbolic milestone occurred as surging Chinese demand intersected with a 50 per cent drop in US requirements during the global economic downturn. It underscored the internationalisation of the Gulf through the rise of new linkages with emerging economies everywhere.[58]

Although already underway before 2008, the global economic crisis hastened this process as Asian economies led the world out of recession and recovered market share at the expense of Western competitors. A blunt assessment by the Emir of Qatar in March 2009 captured the mood as he said that 'China is coming, India is coming, and Russia is on its way, too . . . I don't know if America and Europe will still be leading.'[59] Qatar's Prime Minister and Minister of Foreign Affairs, Sheikh Hamad bin Jassim Al Thani, went further by suggesting that the international system be 'redefined.' HBJ called for profound changes to its organisational framework in recognition of the emergence of a multipolar order in which the West was no longer the sole or even the major player.[60] His intervention was significant, as it represented one of the most detailed statements of the objectives that guided GCC states' policymakers in seeking to leverage their influence in changing global institutions and the relative weight accorded within them. As a point of additional significance, HBJ's observation that international relations should be based on the rule of law at the global as well as the domestic level foreshadowed Qatar's later role in organising Arab support (and critical political cover and subsequent military support) for the United Nations Security Council's imposition of a No-Fly Zone over Libya in March 2011.[61]

Mention already has been made of the alignment of interest between the GCC states and the BRICS nations in seeking to address the issue of underrepresentation in the international financial architecture. Later chapters in this book will examine in greater depth the new patterns of trade and finance and the rapid growth in the interdependencies of food and resource security networks. The Gulf-Asia energy nexus remains pivotal to such linkages, with the GCC exporting more than three and a half times more oil to Japanese, South Korean, Chinese, and Indian markets in 2010 than to the US and all (then 27) member states of the European Union put together (with figures of 203 billion Euros and 58 billion Euros respectively).[62] Moreover, the Pacific Asian economies remain highly (in some instances extraordinarily) dependent on oil imported from the Gulf; Japan, in 2010, sourced no less than 81.5 per cent of its crude oil imports from the region in 2010 with the GCC states alone making up 68.7 per cent of total Japanese imports.[63] South Korea was only slightly less dependent on Gulf oil imports, which constituted 78.2 per cent of imported crude in 2010 (with 63 per cent coming from the GCC).[64]

Such economic ties frame a set of common interests and shared objectives that provide an agenda for greater inter-state cooperation in international forums and organisations within sector-specific areas. Policymakers from the GCC and the BRICS also worked closely on issues relating to the WTO and on specific matters such as Brazil's call for a new concept of humanitarian intervention, 'responsibility while protecting.' All six GCC states joined the Asia Cooperation Dialogue (ACD) between its establishment in 2002 and 2005, with Qatar and Bahrain being founding members of the organisation. Unsurprisingly, cooperation on energy issues has been one of the major areas of priority for the Gulf States within the ACD. In May 2006, Qatar hosted the fifth ACD Ministerial Meeting and launched an ACD Energy Forum to promote and achieve energy accessibility and affordability. The Energy Forum subsequently drew up an ACD Energy Action Plan that advocated, among other issues, the creation of a regional energy infrastructure network. In 2012, Kuwait spearheaded and organised the inaugural ACD Summit in Kuwait City, during which participants endorsed the Energy Action Plan drawn up in 2006. At the ACD Summit, the Emir of Kuwait also urged members to donate US$2 billion to assist underdeveloped Asian (non-Arab) states in financing medium-sized projects aimed at meeting the Millennium Development Goals, and donated US$300 million to the fund.[65]

In a different setting, Qatar joined with Switzerland and Singapore in the Global Redesign Initiative (GRI) of the World Economic Forum (WEF). This organisation was set up to channel the views of 28 small and medium-sized states into the G20 process and it also spawned a Global Governance Group (3G) as well. Qatar hosted a Global Redesign Summit that took place in Doha on 30–31 May 2010, producing a final communiqué entitled *Strengthening International Cooperation in a More Interdependent World*. This outlined 'the parameters of an optimal system of global cooperation as well as a set of pragmatic, actionable steps in specific areas of international cooperation.' Qatar additionally hosted one of the initiative's three supplementary hearings, focusing on energy security governance (the other two hearings were hosted by Switzerland on United Nations reform and by Singapore on Asia's role in global governance).[66]

A third example of Gulf States' involvement in new frameworks of inter-regional dialogue over specific issues is the Abu Dhabi Dialogue established in 2008 by the International Organization of Migration (IOM). From its inception, the UAE has provided a support structure for the 18-country group of labour-sending and labour-receiving countries, which (as of 2014) was under the rotating leadership of Kuwait. All six GCC states have joined the dialogue in tandem with 11 of the main states of origin for migrant workers (Afghanistan, Bangladesh, China, India, Indonesia, Nepal, Pakistan, the Philippines, Sri Lanka, Thailand, and Vietnam). These 11 states had earlier come together to form the 'Colombo Process' of regional dialogue in 2003. Five years later, the UAE government hosted and funded the deepening of the collaborative initiative by bringing the major destination states of the Gulf (including Yemen) into a process of sustained dialogue and consultation. The meeting culminated in the Abu Dhabi Declaration that announced the launch of 'a new collaborative approach to address temporary labor mobility and maximize its benefits for development . . . based on the mutual interests of labor origin and destination countries.'[67]

Another example of Gulf participation in regional (and inter-regional) dialogue occurred in the defence and security sphere with the formation of the Indian Ocean Naval Symposium (IONS) in 2008. Conceived by the Indian Navy as a biennial forum for naval delegations to explore common threats from challenges to maritime trade, energy, and economic security as well as explore collective approaches to humanitarian aid and natural disaster responses, the symposium has 35 members, and the UAE hosted its second meeting in Abu Dhabi in May 2010 with the Commander of the UAE Navy assuming the rotating leadership for 2010–2012.[68] Gulf navies have in addition operated alongside navies from myriad European and Asian partners in anti-piracy controls in the Gulf of Aden and off the coast of Somalia. These operations are intended in no small measure to secure the maritime lines of communication into and out of Gulf ports and mark a significantly new and multilateral approach to the overarching concept of Gulf security.[69]

GCC officials also have participated fully in the triennial summit of the Non-Aligned Movement that met shortly after the global financial crash in June 2009 to focus on how to restructure international governance and embed developing country participation into formal decision-making structures. The summit called for reforming international institutions that, in the words of the then Indian Prime Minister Manmohan Singh, 'continue to be based on charters written more than sixty years ago, though the world has changed greatly since then.'

Kuwaiti officials used the summit to announce two donations to the value of US$500 million to a fund supporting small and medium-sized development projects in emerging economies and US$300 million to a fund combating poverty in Africa.[70] The donations anticipated the previously described pledges made by Kuwait in 2012 to the ACD Summit. Gulf charities also became far more active in Southeast Asia during the 2000s, particularly in Indonesia, Thailand, Malaysia, and the Philippines, where they operated development aid and Islamic relief projects focusing on poverty alleviation and social welfare. This included immediate and very substantial responses to natural disasters such as the 2004 Aceh earthquake and tsunami, the 2006 Java earthquake, and the aftermath of Typhoon Haiyan in the Philippines in 2013.[71]

A final instance of the greater proactivity in regional approaches to global issues lay in Kuwait's organisation of the first Arab Economic Summit that met in Kuwait City in January 2009. Convened in response to the global financial crisis, the summit called for the coordination of policies among regional central banks and greater regional cooperation among Arab economies. Notably, the summit came shortly after a similar regional meeting of African ministers of finance and central bank governors in Tunis in November 2008 and the inaugural Latin American and Caribbean Summit for Integration and Development that met in Brazil in December. All three gatherings were part of a worldwide attempt to mobilise regional solutions to the unfolding global financial crisis that could serve as subsequent 'stepping stones for global integration.'[72]

The Gulf States have emerged as influential actors in the global repositioning of power, exhibiting a greater willingness to take proactive steps in reshaping the institutional design of global frameworks of governance, particularly in the energy sector. Questions nonetheless remain as to whether this influence will continue to be projected on a bilateral basis by the individual states, inter-regionally through the GCC, or globally through greater participation in the new institutional architecture, and whether policymakers will continue to be able to capture the processes of change or eventually be challenged by a more autonomous and powerful societal voice and supra- and sub-state pressures for meaningful and lasting reforms to the structures of governance.

Part II

Changing Patterns of Global Engagement

5
The Internationalisation
of Gulf Finance

The second part of this book analyses the emergence of the Gulf States as pivotal actors in the broader rebalancing of global geo-economic and political power. The five chapters in this section examine the greater assertiveness of GCC states in debates over new frameworks of international governance, their rise as major global actors in Islamic finance and sovereign wealth funds, their enmeshment in shifting patterns of global trade, the role of aviation as a powerful case study of the Gulf States' global repositioning, and the emergence of new security threats and challenges that may over time undermine the Gulf States' global rise.

This chapter examines the emergence of the Gulf States as regional and international hubs both for conventional and Islamic finance and contextualises their growth against broader trends in the shift in global economic power from west to east and from the market to the state. Inflows of oil revenues were transformational not only in their effect on domestic economic structures but also on the place of the Gulf States in international relations and the international political economy. From the growth of transnational family conglomerates in the 1950s and 1960s to the deployment of financial leverage in the form of enhanced aid and development flows in the 1970s and 1980s, the Gulf States developed into regional financial actors several decades before their global rise. Moreover, the capital accumulation during the second oil price boom (2002–2014) differed qualitatively from that of the first (1973–1982) as the far greater absorptive capacity of GCC economies facilitated the domestic circulation of incoming oil revenues and new investment opportunities opened up across a range of new and liberalised sectors.[1] As the 2000s progressed, Dubai, Abu Dhabi, and Doha subsequently competed with each other to carve out niches in global finance through initiatives such as free zones and regulatory reforms.

There are five parts to this chapter. It begins by examining a central characteristic of the distinct form of 'Gulf finance,' namely the agency system as a wealth-sharing mechanism at the heart of the redistributive political economy that developed during the oil era in all Gulf States. The subsequent diversification and internationalisation of many of the family-run conglomerates saw Gulf businesspeople amass significant commercial interests across the Middle East. This leads into a second section detailing how Bahrain evolved into a regional financial centre in the 1970s and 1980s following the onset of civil war in Lebanon and the resulting capital flight. Bahrain pioneered the creation of a business-friendly investor climate that has since become a hallmark of neighbouring states' construction of financial hubs of their own.

Moving from the regional to the inter-regional and the global, the third and fourth sections document the growth of Islamic finance and Sovereign Wealth Funds (SWFs) as major new players in the global financial architecture. While both trace their origins back decades, it was only in the 1990s and 2000s that Islamic finance and SWFs burst onto the international landscape. Their relatively sudden appearance forced Western officials to scramble to develop policy responses that, in cases such as the Dubai Ports (DP) World debacle of 2006, generated heated and frequently unmerited debate over Gulf States' investment objectives. Two years later, the world financial crisis demonstrated how Gulf economies were bound inextricably to broader global processes and made clear their stake in shaping the international response and recovery measures. The final section examines the shifts in Gulf capital that took place in the 2000s in response to 9/11 and the Arab Spring, the rise in international oil prices, and the changing balance of regional and global geo-economic power.

Evolution of the agency system

The capitalist class that formed out of the traditional 'merchant family' business elites in the Gulf that predated the discovery of oil followed a highly distinctive pattern of development. Implicit in the 'ruling bargain' between rulers and merchants was a trade-off whereby the merchants were allowed to pursue economic opportunities in return for steering clear of overtly political involvement. Cut out by the ruling family/government from direct ownership or control of oil and gas, the 'Gulf capitalists' pursued business opportunities in other industries that were either derivative to the oil sector or initiated with state assistance from accrued oil revenues. The most important of these opportunities initially were service and construction contracts granted to local companies by governments and foreign multinationals, either in the oil sector or for broader industrialisation and infrastructure development. Many of these groups today are characterised by their continued involvement in these types of service and basic contracting activities, which remain the core of their business even as they have diversified and developed extensive interests in other sectors, such as retail and finance.[2]

In each of the GCC states, the most significant mechanism linking the 'state-business' elite was the assignment of agency rights. This was a way of permitting the merchant elites to pursue business opportunities in other industries and sectors. It was, also, an opportunity for the ruling family to obtain and reward the loyalty of the economic and business elites by granting or revoking the licences for concessions to import goods or operate local franchises as they arose. A new ruling bargain evolved whereby merchant families close to senior decision-makers were granted the most lucrative franchise concessions, as a way of both ensuring their loyalty and giving them an economic stake in the status quo. Both the agency and the sponsorship system provided ample opportunities for local middlemen to profit from business relationships; the difference between them was that whereas foreign companies needed an agent to export to the Gulf States, a sponsor was required if a company wished to operate locally. The agency and sponsorship system initially was little more than the assignment by rulers of major import deals to specific merchants or bureaucrats, often as a direct reward for services rendered.[3] Thus, the Zainal family (also called the Alireza) claim to be the oldest family business in Saudi Arabia, tracing its origins to 1845 when Zainal Alireza began importing foodstuffs, textiles, and other goods from across the Middle East and India. The family firm was an early client of the founder of Saudi Arabia, King Abdulaziz Al Saud, as was the al-Jomaih family, which began as King Abdulaziz's grocer.[4]

An early beneficiary of the nascent agency system was Harry St John Philby (father of the notorious World War Two era spy Kim Philby) who converted to Islam and advised King Abdulaziz for many years. Philby was granted the right to the Ford dealership in the 1930s and began to import some of the first motor cars and trucks into the kingdom.[5] In his study of the Gulf merchant families, Michael Field relates how Philby 'ran his business to finance his travels and to support the pleasant life he led when he returned to London on leave' and once claimed (in a letter to his wife) that 'I hate the sight and sound of motor cars.'[6] Perhaps unsurprisingly, Philby lost the Ford agency in 1940 to the Alireza business family, which quickly acquired the rights to other prominent Western brands such as Pepsi Cola, Dunlop, and Goodyear. Such was the volume of international companies seeking local partners that among the companies the Alireza family declined to represent were Siemens and Mercedes.[7] In neighbouring UAE, Khalid al-Mezaini estimates that 'traditional merchant families' still 'constitute over 90 percent of the private companies' in the country and enjoy 'strong business partnerships' with the ruling families of the seven constituent emirates.[8]

In addition to personal connections to the ruling elites during the formative years of state-building, merchant families also filled specific niches in the breakneck early period of oil-fuelled modernisation and economic expansion. Again in Saudi Arabia, the al-Ghosaibi family group was established in the 1940s as a trading and money exchange firm in the growing oil city of Al-Khobar in the Eastern Province; the al-Olayan started as a trucking and transportation contractor for Aramco and Bechtel in 1947 before launching a food and consumer trading business in 1954; while the al-Turki group was founded in the 1950s as a supplier of retail goods for foreigners working in the oil sector.[9] During the early years of Aramco, the American officials running the company turned frequently to the merchant families to serve as agents, bankers, and provider of goods and services, as the merchants were able to guide the Aramco officials through an unfamiliar business environment. The abovementioned al-Olayan and al-Ghosaibi families both grew in this way, with Sulayman al-Olayan beginning his career as a clerk in Aramco's translation department before cultivating relationships with Aramco officials to establish an earth-moving firm and a gas distribution company, and the al-Ghosaibi family utilising its network of business activities in Aramco's operating fields in the Eastern Province.[10]

The scale and complexity of the 'family conglomerates' is evident in Adam Hanieh's exhaustive description of their holdings, with just one example – that of Kuwait's Kharafi Group, created by one of the oldest and largest merchant families in Kuwait, illustrative of a region-wide trend:

> Portland Cement Company; the United Stainless Steel Company; poultry and meat processing plants in Kuwait, Saudi Arabia, and Egypt; maintenance, servicing, and project management of refineries, pipelines, power stations, water treatment plants, and other civil engineering projects; manufactures insulation materials, aluminium, architectural products, steel products, pipes, mobile homes, glass,

and plastic products; largest paper mill in the Middle East; construction company with branches in Saudi Arabia, the UAE, Yemen, Egypt, Kenya and elsewhere building airports, pipelines, hotels, roads, power plants, petrochemical facilities, hospitals, and sewage treatment plants; designs and constructs oil and gas facilities, refineries, pipelines, and other industrial work; major shipbuilder and repairer in Kuwait; manufactures and installs oil pipes; represented on the board of the National Industries Group

In addition to these multi- and cross-sector interests, the Kharafi Group (as many others across the Gulf) is represented in ownership structures of local and regional banks, financial institutions, and other conglomerates.[11] One of M. A. Kharafi and Sons' most recognisable companies has been its majority ownership in the Kuwait Food Company, known also as Americana. With more than 1,000 outlets, Americana grew into a franchise giant operating in Kuwait and the UAE and the regional Middle East franchise partner for global food brands such as Pizza Hut, Kentucky Fried Chicken, Baskin Robbins, Costa Coffee, TGI Friday's, Hardee's, and Krispy Kreme doughnuts. These turned the company into one of the largest food companies in the Middle East as Americana accurately forecasted the surge in regional demand for fast food as Western eating habits took hold across the Middle East and the Gulf in the 1990s. Americana also showed foresight in building up investment in agribusinesses in Egypt in the 1980s, giving it a 20-year head start over competitors (both state-based and private) that sought to secure access to farmland in Asia and Africa in the 2000s. Other elements of Americana's extensive interests in Egypt include the Cairo Poultry Processing Company (Koki), which makes processed chicken nuggets, and the Egyptian Canning Company. In addition, in 1992, Americana launched a joint venture in Egypt with another long-time partner, Heinz, to produce ketchup and other Americana-branded products for the Middle East market.[12]

The Kharafi family also illustrates the crossover between the merchants' economic and political roles. Two of the sons of the family patriarch, Mohammed Abdulmohsin al-Kharafi (who died in 1993), Nasser Mohammed al-Kharafi and Jassim Mohammed al-Kharafi, became dominant figures in Kuwait's economic and political life. Under Nasser al-Kharafi's leadership, M. A. Kharafi and Sons expanded rapidly into other parts of the Middle East and pioneered the 'Build, Operate, Transfer' (BOT) contracting model in Kuwait in the 1990s and 2000s. During this period, the Kharafi Group became represented, through its network of subsidiaries and shareholdings, on the board of nearly every company on the Kuwait Stock Exchange, which fell more than 1 per cent upon hearing of Nasser's sudden death in Cairo in 2011.[13] Jassim al-Kharafi pursued an equally high-profile political career that saw him elected to the National Assembly in 1975, serve later as Minister of Finance and chairman of the Kuwait Investment Authority, and culminate in a 13-year stint as Speaker of the National Assembly between 1999 and 2012 before his own sudden death from a heart attack in May 2015. The brothers' careers epitomised the family's status as the pre-eminent political-economic family in Kuwait.[14]

Rise of Gulf financial centres

Leading merchants were instrumental in the early creation of the banking and finance industry in the Gulf. These included the first indigenous bank in the Gulf, the National Bank of Kuwait, established in 1952 by what Pete Moore labels 'the cream' of Kuwaiti merchant families, including the al-Kharafi, the al-Sagr, the al-Hamad, and the al-Sayer, while another prominent merchant, Khalid al-Marzooq, was a founding member of the Commercial Bank of Kuwait in 1960.[15] Similarly, in Saudi Arabia, Hanieh observes that the first local bank, the National Commercial Bank, which opened in 1953 'had its origins in a local money changing company run by the Bin Mahfouz family.'[16] In the UAE, representatives of most of the leading merchant families featured on the boards of directors of banks such as Emirates Bank while Mashreq Bank, one of the largest in the country, was (and remains) linked to the prominent al-Ghurair family.[17] Ruling family members also were involved in the nascent banking and financial industry, most notably in Abu Dhabi, with the Abu Dhabi Commercial Bank and First Gulf Bank,[18] and, controversially, the Bank of Credit and Commerce International (BCCI), whose Pakistani founder, Agha Abedi, reportedly 'had for more than twenty years managed personal portfolios for members of the [Al Nahyan] family' before BCCI imploded spectacularly in 1991.[19]

Lebanon emerged as the initial focal point for Arab banking in the 1960s as investors from across the Middle East, including the Gulf, took advantage of a period of relative political stability, proximity to European markets, and a laissez-faire system of relatively lax governmental controls and regulations that 'turned Lebanon into a haven for anonymous capital.' During this period, 'capital investments from the Gulf were instrumental in setting up a number of Beirut-based banks of regional/international character,' including the Beirut-Riyadh Bank in

1959, and Byblos Bank and Credit Libanais in 1962.[20] However, Lebanon slipped into civil war in 1975 and the violence escalated as first Syria and later Israel intervened and the threat from non-state Palestinian actors intensified. The civil war caused a flight of capital and signalled the end of Lebanon's centrality in the Arab banking and financial system.[21]

There were several reasons why Bahrain and the Gulf eclipsed Beirut as the new centre of (offshore) banking in the Arab world. On a regional level, the oil price shock of 1973 and the resulting inflows of substantive oil revenues meant that the Gulf gradually became the 'focal point' of Arab banking just at time that the conflict in Lebanon worsened. Capital flowed initially into Kuwait as well as Bahrain as Kuwaiti banks increased their international trading and an informal and loosely regulated stock exchange (*Suq al-Manakh*) formed in Kuwait City to trade in shares of offshore Gulf companies.[22] The *Suq al-Manakh* functioned as a parallel market to the Kuwaiti Stock Exchange, which was itself only formalised in 1977. Most of the transactions in the *Suq al-Manakh* were settled by post-dated checks while the majority of the companies trading in it (most of which were non-Kuwaiti) were in reality paper companies with little or no real assets.[23] Through 1981 and the first half of 1982, feverish speculation inflated the market rapidly amid a cacophony of 'get rich quick' publicity and a trebling of share value. A flourishing secondary market also developed as 'the post-dated checks were then traded back and forth' at interest rates of up to 100 per cent.[24] A contemporary article in the *New York Times* described what happened next:

> The panic began in early August, when a creditor holding a post-dated check for nine million dinars, or about $30 million, attempted to cash it. The bank rejected it, declaring that the check writer's account was empty. The debtor was one of the most prominent businessmen in Kuwait. Word spread quickly, resulting in a run on the banks.[25]

The collapse of the *Suq al-Manakh* had an enormous impact both on Kuwait and on investors from other GCC states, particularly the emirate of Ajman in the UAE, which was heavily exposed to the crisis. Investigators estimated the outstanding value of the 28,000 post-dated checks at US$94 billion spread among 5,000 to 6,000 investors, large and small alike. Further, almost every Kuwaiti bank save for the National Bank of Kuwait was involved in financing the transactions in the *Suq al-Manakh*. After the crash, many of the banks were threatened with insolvency and received support from the Central Bank of Kuwait. The Kuwaiti government also stepped in to bail out private investors through a Difficult Credit Facilities Resettlement Program and the Kuwait Clearing and Financial Settlement Company. It nevertheless took years to work through all of the bad debt. Shortly after Kuwait's liberation from Iraqi occupation in 1991, the government sought to resolve all lingering effects by purchasing Kuwait's entire domestic debt load existent on 1 August 1990, at an estimated cost of US$20 billion.[26]

Whereas the growth of the *Suq al-Manakh* was in part triggered by the controls placed on the (formal) Kuwait Stock Exchange, where only government bonds and securities of companies registered in Kuwait could be traded, officials in Bahrain actively constructed a business-friendly environment designed to appeal to international investors from the beginning. This contrasted also with the tightening of banking regulations in Saudi Arabia that further restricted the ability of international banks to operate in the kingdom by making it a requirement that all such banks incorporate as a local company with majority Saudi ownership.[27] In 1975, the year that the Lebanese civil war started, the Bahraini government followed the Cayman Islands and Singapore and introduced regulations that allowed the creation of offshore banking units (OBUs). Exemptions from corporate tax and low start-up fees increased further the attractiveness of Bahrain as a regional hub for financial organisations and the number of OBUs in the country rose to 48 in 1978 and peaked at 76 in 1984.[28] During the same period, the volume of assets managed by OBUs in Bahrain increased from US$23.4 billion to US$62.7 billion.[29] Among the leading international banks that relocated their regional headquarters to Bahrain were Chase Manhattan, Citibank, Credit Suisse, the Société Générale, and the Bank of Tokyo. By 2010, the 'vast majority' of the 133 banks registered in Bahrain operated offshore, as did a further 270 financial institutions such as insurers and fund management companies.[30]

The abovementioned measures transformed Bahrain into the first financial hub in the Gulf in the 1980s and 1990s, but in the 2000s they were surpassed in order of magnitude by regulatory and institutional developments in the UAE (Dubai) and Qatar. A key component of the market liberalisation and corporatisation programmes underway in each case was the adoption of Western formal institutions and rules. These independent regulatory agencies (IRAs) were designed to reassure and attract international investors with the promise of predictable, efficient, and fair domestic governance.[31] Dubai led the way in the creation of a new financial hub after a change to the federal UAE constitution in 2004 that allowed the individual emirates to establish free trade zones. That same year, the Dubai International Financial Centre (DIFC) was legally established with its own stock market, the Dubai International Financial Exchange (DIFX). Significantly, the DIFC and the DIFX operated under the regulatory auspices of the Dubai Financial Services Authority (DFSA), which was based largely on the Anglo-Saxon legal system. As a result, 'almost all dealings within the DIFC were exempt from UAE civil law.'[32]

The DIFC and its related entities were integral to the development and diversification of Dubai's non-oil economy by the then Crown Prince of Dubai (and, since January 2006, the Ruler) Sheikh Mohammed bin Rashid Al Maktoum. In the decade since its formation, the DIFC dominated the regional financial scene and also moved beyond its initial status as a regulatory 'island.' In particular, the DIFC Judicial Authority (known as DIFC Courts) become increasingly available to the business community at large as, in 2011, the Dubai government significantly expanded the jurisdiction of the DIFC Courts to allow any parties, even those not incorporated within the DIFC free zone, to use the DIFC Courts to resolve commercial disputes. Previously, only companies based in the DIFC or those that had an issue related to the DIFC could use the DIFC Courts, although the court will only hear a dispute if both parties agree to it. Based on the common law English model and using international judges from common law jurisdictions such as England, New Zealand, and Malaysia, the DIFC Courts developed a reputation among multinationals as more predictable and transparent, with English as the working language and mechanisms in place for the winning party to claim costs from the losing party. For these reasons, the DIFC Courts emerged as the jurisdiction of choice for many international contracts and a major centre for dispute resolution not only in Dubai but also for the region as a whole.[33]

Less than a year after the founding of the DIFC, Qatar followed suit with the 2005 creation of an outwardly similar Qatar Financial Centre (QFC) nested within a distinct Qatar Financial Centre Regulatory Authority (QFCRA) using a bespoke legal system based on international law. The institutional similarities between the Dubai and Qatar models are in part attributable to the fact that they were designed by the same British expert, Philip Thorne, himself a former managing director of the Financial Services Authority (FSA) in London.[34] There were, nonetheless, significant differences between the QFC and the DIFC, as the QFC did not launch a separate exchange like the DIFX. In addition, officials and regulators in Doha focused on creating niche expertise in areas such as reinsurance, captive insurance, and asset management rather than competing directly with the DIFC's broad-brush approach. However, the results fell short of initial expectation as the QFC largely failed to 'entice reinsurance firms away from their existing global hub of Bermuda or even captive insurance companies from neighbouring Bahrain.'[35] In response, the QFC drew up a new strategy in 2014 designed to attract more non-financial firms and amended its regulations to create further tax incentives for Qatari companies to utilise the centre.[36]

The planned launch in 2015 of the Abu Dhabi Global Market (ADGM) and the phased opening of the King Abdullah Financial District (KAFD) in Riyadh will add further concentrations of expertise to an already crowded regional sector. The ADGM is intended to form the centrepiece of a new financial free zone in Abu Dhabi that will focus broadly on asset management, private banking, and wealth management. Again, a strong element of institutional diffusion is evident as the executive adviser to the ADGM, Jan Bladen, was earlier a part of the team that put together the Dubai Financial Services Authority in 2004.[37] The hiring of ADGM's top leadership demonstrated also the internationalisation of Gulf finance as the chief regulatory officer of the Singapore Exchange (SGX), Richard Teng, resigned in October 2014 to become chief executive of the regulator of ADGM.[38] Two months later, ADGM engaged Sir Hector Sants, the former chief executive of Britain's FSA, on a consulting contract to advise ADGM's regulatory framework in the run-up to its formal launch.[39]

In June 2013, global index compiler Morgan Stanley Capital International (MSCI) upgraded Qatar and the UAE from 'Frontier' to 'Emerging Market' (EM) status after five unsuccessful reviews that dated back to 2008. The move, which took effect in June 2014, signified a new era for capital flows in the UAE and Qatar as well as greater access to global funds.[40] The upgrade meant that investors in funds that track MSCI's popular Emerging Markets Index would be allocated weighted shares in each country. This gave Qatar and the UAE weighted access to the estimated US$1.4 trillion in funds linked to the Emerging Markets Index, more than a hundredfold greater than the value of funds tied to the MSCI Frontier Markets Index.[41] Later in 2014, rival index compiler S&P Dow Jones Indices also promoted Qatar and the UAE to its own S&P Emerging Market BMI index series at the same time as the compiler downgraded Greece from Developed to Emerging status.[42]

Any liberalisation of the Saudi Arabian stock exchange (*Tadawul*) would far exceed in scale and potential opportunity the measures outlined above in Dubai, Doha, and Abu Dhabi. An important step in this regard occurred in July 2014 when the Saudi Cabinet approved the (cautious) opening of the stock market to foreign financial institutions. With a market capitalisation of US$530.5 billion in mid-2014, the cumulative

Table 5.1 Market capitalisation of GCC stock exchanges, 2014

Country	Market	Capitalisation (US$ in billions)
Saudi Arabia	Tadawul	530.5
Qatar	Qatar Exchange	202.4
UAE (Abu Dhabi)	Abu Dhabi Securities Exchange	115.3
Kuwait	Kuwait Stock Exchange	114
UAE (Dubai)	Dubai Financial Market	79.7
Oman	Muscat Securities Market	38.7
Bahrain	Bahrain Bourse	22

Source: *Gulf States Newsletter*, 38(974), 17 July 2014, p. 12.

value of the *Tadawul* was two and a half times larger than its nearest competitor (the US$202.4 billion Qatar Exchange) and four times that of the Abu Dhabi Securities Exchange (US$115.3 billion).[43] In April 2015, the Capital Markets Authority in Riyadh announced it would issue guidelines for (cautiously) opening up the *Tadawul* to very large international investors by mid-June. Reuters captured the sense of anticipation at 'one of the most eagerly awaited economic reforms in the region in recent times,' adding that, 'worth more than stock markets in Russia, Malaysia, or Turkey, the Kingdom is also one of the last major global bourses to open itself for foreigners to directly invest in the exchange'[44] (Table 5.1).

The growth of Islamic finance

The earliest modern examples of *Sharia*-compliant Islamic financial institutions emerged in Egypt and Pakistan in the 1960s with the development of local cooperative and savings banks in predominantly rural areas of both countries. Nazih Ayubi has noted how the first recognisably 'Islamic' bank, Mit Ghamr, was created in the Nile Delta region of Egypt in 1963 and took its inspiration 'not from Islamic economics, but from the theory and experience of German cooperative and mutual savings banks.' Indeed, one of the bank's initiators, Ahmad al-Najjar, had lived in West Germany and later became the secretary-general of the International Association of Islamic Banks.[45] Over the course of the following decade, Islamic finance spread slowly to the Gulf States with the launch of the Dubai Islamic Bank (1975), the Kuwait Finance House (1977), and the Bahrain Islamic Bank (1978). Four years later, the first Islamic bank opened in Qatar, but it was only in 1987 that Al Rajhi Bank was licensed to operate in Saudi Arabia. This was in part due to Saudi officials' concern that creating a separate 'Islamic' category of finance 'might highlight the interest transactions of the conventional banks in the Kingdom.'[46] In Oman, too, the Sultanate did not permit Islamic banks to operate until 2011, 'for political reasons concerned with limiting the influence of the Ibadi sect.'[47] This notwithstanding, the demand for Islamic financial instruments in Oman was evident in the estimation that up to US$11 billion worth of Omani riyals were deposited in other Islamic banks in the GCC, mainly in Bahrain and the UAE.[48]

While Islamic financial institutions originated outside the Gulf, the Dubai Islamic Bank was the first such institution specifically to label itself as an Islamic Bank per se. The Dubai Islamic Bank and the Kuwait Finance House pioneered the growth of financing based on *murabaha* contracts, in which the banks would purchase imports on behalf of local merchants and re-sell them to the merchant for a mark-up, in lieu of interest. Such trades were deemed *Sharia*-compliant because the bank assumed temporary ownership of the goods being sold, and thereby avoided lending against interest. Many of the early Islamic financial institutions in the Gulf thus operated in partnership between ruling families and the major merchant families, with the 49 per cent state shareholding in the newly formed Kuwait Finance House a case in point.[49] As the levels of affluence and liquidity increased rapidly within the GCC states in subsequent decades, Gulf-based Islamic financial institutions evolved a comprehensive range of new financial products to meet surging local and regional demand. These included *Sharia*-compliant deposit facilities, consumer credit, real estate finance, Islamic investment banking, and (following Malaysia's lead) the issuance of securitised Islamic financial instruments (*sukuk*).[50]

The Gulf States have not yet challenged Malaysia as the global centre of Islamic finance either in terms of overall volume or through 'thought leadership' whereby the Central Bank of Malaysia has established its own *Sharia* board. Moreover, most of the legal and regulatory innovations concerning the governance of Islamic financial institutions have originated either in Malaysia or in London. As Rodney Wilson has observed, 'GCC governments have not felt pressurised to introduce Islamic banking laws; rather, they take a pragmatic approach and introduce regulation where it is necessary.'[51] Bahrain was the notable exception owing to the significance of Islamic (as well as conventional) banking to the country's abovementioned growth as a regional financial hub. In 1991, Bahrain founded the Accounting and Auditing Organization for Islamic Financial Institutions (AAOIFI) and has continued to host the group ever since. Over the quarter-century since its launch, the AAOIFI has become accepted as a credible reporting and regulatory organisation for Islamic financial institutions worldwide.[52] This notwithstanding, the Islamic Financial Services Board in Kuala Lumpur remains the premier international standard-setting organisation that, in 2006, defeated a UAE-led GCC proposal to establish a rival International Islamic Financial Policy Forum to be based in the Gulf.[53]

GCC-based Islamic banks nevertheless have contributed heavily to the global expansion of Islamic Finance and have carved out a major regional hub in the Gulf itself. Data released in September 2014 by the Islamic Finance Development Indicator (IFDI) set up by ICD/Thomson Reuters in 2013 illustrate the market dominance of GCC states after Malaysia, as illustrated in Tables 5.2 and 5.3.

Thus, the Al Rajhi Bank in Saudi Arabia has grown into one of the world's largest Islamic banks by capital while institutions such as Kuwait Finance House (KFH) have developed extensive branch networks that operate across regions. In 1989, KFH became the first GCC-based Islamic bank to operate outside the region when it established a Turkish subsidiary, the Kuveyt Turk Participation Bank. KFH also has created a network of branches in Malaysia and used Kuala Lumpur as a base for further expansion into Singapore and Australia. Al Rajhi Bank has surpassed KFH in the number of branches it operates in Malaysia, while the Dubai Islamic Bank has grown significantly in Pakistan since 2006.[54] Meanwhile, Qatari and Kuwaiti institutions have been instrumental in the creation of Islamic Financial Institutions abroad. The Qatar Islamic Bank opened the European Finance House in London, the Asia Finance House in Kuala Lumpur, and the Arab Finance House in Beirut.[55] Kuwaiti investors were pivotal in the founding of the Bank of

Table 5.2 Leading Islamic finance markets

Rank	Country	Indicator value
1	Malaysia	93
2	Bahrain	76
4	UAE	57
5	Qatar	40
6	Kuwait	38
9	Saudi Arabia	31

Source: http://gulfbusiness.com/2014/09/bahrain-ranked-gccs-leading-islamic-finance-market-report/#.VTPgb8KPJjo

Table 5.3   Amount of Islamic financial assets

Rank	Country	Market value (US$ in millions)
1	Malaysia	423,385
2	Saudi Arabia	338,106
4	UAE	140,289
5	Kuwait	92,403
6	Qatar	81,027
7	Bahrain	64,644

Source: http://gulfbusiness.com/2014/09/bahrain-ranked-gccs-leading-islamic-finance-market-report/#.VTPgb8KPJjo

London and the Middle East, the largest standalone Islamic Bank in the United Kingdom.[56] By 2011, the four largest Islamic investment banks in London were all owned by GCC-based institutions in an indication of the growing global reach of Gulf financial institutions.[57]

Sovereign wealth funds in the Gulf

Much academic and policymaking attention focused on the rise of GCC-based sovereign wealth funds (SWFs) in the 2000s. The Sovereign Wealth Fund Institute defines a sovereign wealth fund as 'a state-owned investment fund or entity that is commonly established from balance of payments surpluses, official foreign currency operations, the proceeds of privatisations, governmental transfer payments, fiscal surpluses, and/or receipts resulting from resource exports.'[58] Although many of the largest sovereign wealth funds by asset value originate in the GCC states, other significant funds are based in countries such as Norway, Hong Kong, Singapore, and China. These include the largest sovereign wealth fund in the world in 2014, the Norwegian Government Pension Fund – Global. Table 5.4 illustrates the preponderance of Gulf-based SWFs in 2014, with four in the largest ten global funds as estimated by the Sovereign Wealth Fund Institute.

It was in the Gulf that the first such fund was established more than six decades ago. In 1953, the Ruler of Kuwait created an account at the Bank of England to manage the growing influx of oil revenues following the beginning of oil exports in 1946. Two Bank of England directors were among the four trustees of the Kuwait Investment Board and were charged with ensuring the prudent investment of oil revenues. Following the

Table 5.4   Largest SWFs by assets under management

GCC rank	Global rank	Fund	Country
1	2	Abu Dhabi Investment Authority	UAE
2	3	SAMA Foreign Holdings	Saudi Arabia
3	6	Kuwait Investment Authority	Kuwait
4	9	Qatar Investment Authority	Qatar
5	13	Abu Dhabi Investment Council	UAE
6	20	Investment Corporation of Dubai	UAE
7	21	International Petroleum Investment Corporation	UAE
8	22	Mubadala Development Company	UAE
9	39	Emirates Investment Authority	UAE
10	41	State General Reserve Fund	Oman
11	42	Mumtalakat Holding Company	Bahrain

Source: Sovereign Wealth Fund Institute: 'Sovereign Wealth Fund Rankings'
http://www.swfinstitute.org/fund-rankings/

termination of the British protectorate over Kuwait in 1961 and Kuwaiti independence, the Kuwait Investment Board was renamed the Kuwait Investment Office (KIO). The KIO managed the Future Generations Fund (FGF, created in 1976 to invest 10 per cent of Kuwait's annual oil revenue in long-term assets) from London until 1984, when the Kuwaiti government established the Kuwait Investment Authority (KIA). Since then, the FGF has been co-managed by the KIA in Kuwait City and the KIO in London through a division of responsibilities. Hence, the KIA invests assets in foreign bonds and equities through external fund managers working from separately managed accounts while the KIO oversees real estate investments and invests more actively by taking strategic stakes in European companies, with the KIA investing about 60 per cent of the total assets in relation to the KIO's 40 per cent. In addition to the FGF, the Kuwaiti government also established the General Reserve Fund (GRF) in 1976 in order to invest surplus funds domestically and abroad.[59]

The Abu Dhabi Investment Authority (ADIA) is the other long-established sovereign wealth fund in the Gulf. Founded in 1976, five years after the creation of the UAE, ADIA is owned and operated by the government of Abu Dhabi through the Abu Dhabi Investment Council (ADIC), itself founded in 2006 as a successor to the Abu Dhabi Investment Company. ADIC was established with a mandate to invest both domestically and internationally and was pivotal in the creation of Etihad Airways as well as other Abu Dhabi-based sovereign wealth funds such as Mubadala, the International Petroleum Investment Company (IPIC), and the Abu Dhabi National Energy Company (known as Taqa).[60] Each of the subsidiary sovereign wealth funds was set up to fulfil a specific, and increasingly strategic, purpose. IPIC was established in 1984 by ADIA and the Abu Dhabi National Oil Company (ADNOC) to invest globally in energy and energy-related industries. Mubadala was launched in 2002 as a wholly owned Abu Dhabi government investment vehicle to focus on investment in capital-intensive industries such as healthcare, semiconductor computer chip manufacturing, aerospace, and renewable energy, including the iconic Masdar City cleantech development in Abu Dhabi. Taqa was formed in 2005 as an energy holding company for the government of Abu Dhabi and subsequently made substantial international investments in the North Sea, Canada, Africa, and Asia. Sara Bazoobandi has shown how, in practice, there has been significant overlap among ranking officials and board members across ADIA and the other three sovereign wealth funds, with individuals serving on multiple and, in the case of Taqa chairman Hamad al-Hurr al-Suwaidi, all four boards simultaneously.[61]

ADIA, in common with the KIA and all other sovereign wealth funds based in the Gulf, does not make public its holdings, which remain a matter of considerable speculation, with estimations ranging from as low as US$150 billion to an unlikely figure of US$875 billion in 2007 alone. Various reasons are put forward for this secrecy, including a sensitive point made by former Gulf-based banker-turned-academic Jean-Francois Seznec that

> one can argue that the funds of Abu Dhabi do not belong to the ruling Al Nahyan family but to the people of Abu Dhabi and, by extension, to the people of the United Arab Emirates. The Al Nahyan are the stewards of this money, not the owners. Hence, it could be awkward for the ruling family to have the country be overly informed of the amounts, investments and procedures of the funds under their fiduciary responsibility.[62]

The abovementioned launch of Mubadala and Taqa in the 2000s was part of a broader proliferation of Gulf-based SWFs as incoming oil revenues surged during the decade. Bahrain established the Mumtalakat Holding Company in June 2006 as the government's investment arm with a mandate to diversify away from government-linked companies and provide value creation in strategic assets. However, its holdings have remained small by regional standards; by the end of 2013, Mumtalakat had US$10.6 billion in assets and majority or minority stakes (worth US$7.2 billion) in 38 companies. By far the most high-profile of Mumtalakat's stakes was also its first – the acquisition of a 30 per cent stake in McLaren Group in 2006 that grew subsequently to 42 per cent.[63] In echoes of the state-branding initiatives analysed in Chapter 2, Mumtalakat's investment in one of the most successful Formula One participants came two years after the launch of the Bahrain Grand Prix first put the country on the international sporting map.[64]

The Qatar Investment Authority (QIA) was another of the region's sovereign wealth funds established in the mid-2000s. Launched in 2005, the QIA has competed alongside a bewildering array of subsidiary groups and private ventures that also invest on behalf of the Qatari government and, on occasion, individual members of the ruling Al Thani family. Like several of its regional counterparts, the QIA was founded with the intention of diversifying the Qatari economy by investing oil and gas reserves into new asset classes. What marks the QIA as distinct is its overlapping network of subsidiaries that operate in sector-specific areas. Thus, Qatar Holding has functioned as the direct investment arm of the QIA and has conducted some of the highest profile Qatari investments in Harrods, Barclays Bank, and the London Stock Exchange. Qatari Diar, the wholly owned property arm of the QIA, has been another particularly visible investor in London, with the acquisition of landmark real estate assets such as the Olympic Village and Chelsea Barracks.[65]

In addition to the state-run funds described above, leading Qatari 'private' investors also have made frequent use of personal investment vehicles. Some of these investment vehicles appear to have been established solely for involvement in one-time acquisitions, and the operations of all of them remain shrouded in opacity. The most well-known investment vehicle is Challenger, which came to prominence during the Qatari acquisition of the Barclays stake in late 2008. Qatar's stake was split between Qatar Holding and Challenger, the special purpose vehicle owned 'privately' by the then Prime Minister and head of the Qatar Investment Authority, Sheikh Hamad bin Jassim Al Thani (HBJ).[66] Another such vehicle, Paramount Services Holding, was involved in the aborted 2011 merger of troubled Greek lenders Alpha Bank and EFG Eurobank. Even less is known about Paramount than Challenger, as the vehicle was described only as representing the interests of Qatar's 'most prominent' family, although it was assumed both within Qatar and the international investor community to refer to HBJ.[67]

A 2008 profile of HBJ in the *Financial Times* drew attention to this overlap between state-run and 'private' investment as it noted that HBJ 'leads the QIA's investment strategy but often invests his own wealth in similar deals to the QIA's.'[68] Other examples of special purpose vehicles linked to HBJ and his immediate family included a third investment vehicle, Precision Capital, based in Luxembourg and with HBJ on its board. Precision was the vehicle used to acquire stakes in troubled Belgian bank KBC and struggling Luxembourg bank Dexia BIL in October and December 2011 respectively.[69] A fourth instance was Al Mirqab Capital, with HBJ's oldest son as chief executive officer, which became embroiled in a 2012 legal battle between Irish developer Paddy McKillen and the Barclay brothers (Sir David and Sir Frederick Barclay) over the ownership of Coroin, the parent company that owns Claridge's, the Berkeley, and the Connaught hotels in London. It emerged later that Tony Blair had intervened personally to arrange an initial meeting between McKillen and Jassim bin Hamad to discuss the financing deal while Blair was visiting Doha in February 2012 to meet with HBJ.[70]

Saudi Arabia does not possess a fund that meets the classical definition of a sovereign wealth fund. However, the Saudi Arabian Monetary Agency (SAMA) is responsible for managing the kingdom's foreign assets, which it does in a highly conservative manner mostly in low-risk US Treasury notes, and is often included in rankings of SWFs. SAMA also manages funds on behalf of local state entities, of which the largest are the Public Investment Fund (PIF), the General Organization for Social Insurance (GOSI), and the Saudi Industrial Development Fund (SIDF).[71] These funds are invested locally rather than internationally and were used to fund the large budget deficits in the 1980s and early 1990s. This allowed the kingdom to avoid having to take loans from international financial institutions during the long period of low oil prices as the US$190 billion borrowed by Saudi Arabia at this time came entirely from local banks and GOSI. The funds also are used to invest in the large-scale infrastructure projects that form the backbone of job creation and economic diversification schemes in Saudi Arabia.[72] The use of Saudi investment funds to more actively support economic reforms and development has also been evident in the creation of specialised funds such as the Saudi Aramco Energy Ventures[73] (SAEV) in 2012 (to invest in renewable energy projects) and the 2014 approval of a US$530 million industrial investment company managed jointly by PIF, Saudi Aramco, and SABIC.[74]

During the oil price boom in the mid-2000s, growing international interest began to focus on how the policy decisions to deploy the revenues that accrued to GCC states enhanced their profile and position-ing within the global economy. This occurred as, collectively, the six Gulf States acquired an estimated US$912 billion in the five years that elapsed between the start of the oil price rise in 2003 and the peak of the mar-ket in June 2008.[75] As such, the significant holdings possessed by SWFs were perceived to be part of the wider shift of economic leverage from west to east and from the market to the state in the allocation of capi-tal.[76] At about the same time, increasing political and public attention in the US and Europe began to be paid to the growth of sovereign wealth funds, many of them from the Gulf, amid a slew of exaggerated predic-tions about their size and potential influence. Typical in this regard was a Morgan Stanley report published in May 2007 that suggested that the value of SWFs could reach US$12 trillion by 2015.[77] Moreover, the rise of Russian and Chinese funds, in particular, heightened broader anxie-ties over the origin of sovereign investment flows. This contributed to wariness in investment-recipient countries, notably the US, about the potential for political motivations driving investment decision-making.[78] Thus, the then Director of National Intelligence in the George W. Bush administration, John McConnell, remarked in 2008: 'Concerns about the financial capabilities of Russia, China, and OPEC countries and the potential use of their market access to exert financial leverage to achieve political ends represents a major national security issue.'[79]

The most egregious example of this was the visceral Congressional reaction to the 2006 Dubai Ports (DP) World takeover of a ports man-agement contract in the US. The DP World case caught the Gulf States in the crossfire of a populist xenophobic domestic backlash against per-ceived geopolitical swings against US interests. Policymakers in the Gulf expressed concern at the inability of American officials to provide them with a list of 'national security' no-go sectors for future investment.[80] The tawdry episode also led to a counterintuitive situation whereby DP World was defended staunchly by the largest shipping firm in Israel, Zim Integrated Shipping, with whom DP World had entered into a joint venture.[81] During the political firestorm that followed the attempted ports management takeover in February 2006, Zim's Israeli CEO became a vocal defender of DP World against political critics in the US who opposed the move on national security grounds. In a letter to New York Senator Hillary Clinton, Idon Offer criticised the 'misinformation about DP World in the US media' and added that '[a]s an Israeli company . . . we are very comfortable calling at DP World's Dubai ports.'[82]

In reality, pre-financial crisis estimates of the value and poten-tial trajectory of Gulf-based SWFs proved to be over-estimations that subsequently were eroded further by losses sustained during the down-turn.[83] Across the GCC, SWF assets soared during the oil boom years from US$205 billion in 1999 to US$883 billion in June 2008 before falling away to US$667 by December as losses mounted.[84] Attitudes towards the funds also shifted as austerity-hit states and companies embraced new sources of inward investment; during the initial stages of the global financial crisis, Gulf-based sovereign wealth funds were important sources of liquidity for Western financial institutions such as Merrill Lynch, Barclays Bank, and Citigroup.[85]

However, initial hopes in the autumn of 2008 that the financial contagion might bypass the Gulf proved misplaced as oil prices plunged, project financing dried up, and the real estate speculative bubble burst.[86] This was in spite of an optimistic analysis by the Ruler of Dubai, Sheikh Mohammed bin Rashid Al Maktoum, who commented in September 2009 (two months before the bursting of the Dubai debt bubble) that the global crisis was 'a passing cloud that will not stay longer, despite pessimistic speculations and analyses by economists and financial experts.'[87] Individual Gulf states felt the impact in different ways. In Dubai, the crisis exposed the fragility of its economic diversification based on the real estate industry, high-end tourist development, and the financial sector, underpinned by conglomerates such as Dubai World and Dubai Holding relying on continuous FDI and access to cheap international credit.[88] Kuwaiti financial institutions were exposed to a combination of weakening domestic property markets and local equity markets and the tightening of international credit. In January 2009, Kuwait's biggest investment bank, Global Investment House, defaulted on the majority of its debt after failing to repay maturing loans.[89] Later, in May, Investment Dar defaulted on a US$100 million *sukuk* issue. These followed the emergency rescuing of Gulf Bank after it lost US$1.05 billion in (unauthorised) derivatives trading and experienced a run on deposits in December 2008.[90]

Despite these setbacks, and after weathering the initial shock, regional financial institutions proved more resilient than many had expected, even as GCC stock markets dropped in value by an estimated 50 per cent during the crisis. Central banks and SWFs (led by the KIA and the QIA) eased the pressure on local banks by investing up to US$350 billion in domestic stock markets in 2008–2009.[91] The emergency rights issue in Gulf Bank by KIA had the effect of diluting the bank's ownership by the al-Ghanim merchant family, which was blamed for mishandling the derivatives trades.[92] Moreover, the swift recovery of international oil prices from 2010 onward meant that capital outflows from the GCC remained high, with Bessma Momani setting the figure at US$430 billion between June 2008 and June 2010 alone. The sharp contrast between the GCC states' continuing capital accumulation and Western economies struggling to cope with the impact of austerity projects meant that attitudes towards Gulf investors also changed significantly as policymakers actively sought to attract, rather than resist, Gulf investment, as had happened to Dubai Ports World in 2006.[93]

Shifts in Gulf capital flows

Over the course of the 2000s, and particularly in the aftermath of the 9/11 terrorist attacks in the US, GCC-based SWFs (together with Gulf state-owned enterprises and private investors) began also to diversify their portfolios and move beyond holdings in North American and European markets. Even before the DP World case, concerns were raised among Gulf officials that their investments in Western markets could be mischaracterised and cause reputational damage. Momani cites the UAE Minister of Economic and Planning Affairs at the time of 9/11, Sheikha Lubna bint Khalid Al Qassimi, describing how '9/11 was an economic turning point. Anxiety about travelling, freezing assets, and the extra scrutiny of people entering the United States made a lot of businessmen here more inclined to invest at home.'[94] Speaking nearly a decade later, a senior banker in Kuwait recalled issues such as the response to 9/11 and the DP World firestorm, commenting caustically that 'they [US investors] need the money and then they politicise it. Perhaps they think we are all bin Laden. Either they want the investment or they don't.'[95]

The greater diversification in trade, investment, and other financial flows between the GCC states and the Middle East and North Africa is connected to wider global trends whereby total FDI sent by developing countries to other developing countries accelerated both in absolute and in relative terms. Hence, the growth in FDI from the BRICS group (particularly to low income countries in Africa), outstripped the growth in global FDI in the 2000s, before the Arab Spring, rising from less than US$10 billion in the late 1990s to a peak of almost US$150 billion in 2008 before falling back to about US$100 billion in 2009. Over the same period, the BRICS' share in global FDI rose from about 1 per cent to almost 10 per cent.[96]

Gulf Arab investments in regional (Middle Eastern and North African) economies also increased markedly after 2001. Both SWFs and private Gulf investors engaged in 'a gradual structural reorientation away from US markets and toward an increasingly regional, as well as global, focus.'[97]

At the same time, the maturation of Gulf financial sectors allowed them to play a greater role in recycling the surpluses generated by the decade-long oil boom that began in earnest in 2003. In addition to the afore-mentioned creation of new SWFs in the 2000s, the number of Gulf-based investment banks, private equity funds, and venture capitalists prolifer-ated during the decade.[98] A significant repatriation of Arab capital from the US also occurred as institutional and private investors feared becom-ing entrapped in a post-9/11 political and security backlash.[99]

These trends had practical consequences on the routing of Gulf capi-tal flows. Whereas Gulf 'petrodollars' accrued during the first oil price boom between 1973 and 1982 were spent unproductively on unnec-essary prestige or 'white elephant' projects or were largely channelled through Western banks and financial institutions, the emergence of 'Gulf capitalism' meant that more of these flows remained within the region during the second oil price boom in the 2000s. Although the core of GCC-based SWF activities continued to favour low-risk investments in Western economies, greater emphasis was placed on identifying and tapping higher-risk strategic investments in emerging and regional mar-kets. Prominent examples of greater 'South-South' investments included a tie-up between the KIA and leading private investors in Kuwait to cre-ate the Kuwait China Investment Company in 2005 as well as the KIA's purchase of US$720 million in shares in the Industrial and Commercial Bank of China in one of China's first Initial Public Offerings (IPOs) in 2006;[100] the QIA's 2012 acquisition a 22 per cent stake of CITIC Capital, a subsidiary of China's own sovereign wealth fund (the China Investment Corporation [CIC]) and the subsequent creation in 2014 of a US$10 bil-lion joint investment fund between the two;[101] and Mubadala's US$2 billion investment in a strategic partnership with Brazilian magnate Eike Batista's troubled EBX Group in 2012.[102]

In an interview with the Oxford Business Group in 2008, the manag-ing director of KIA, Bader al-Saad, commented on the growing value placed on investments in Asia:

> It's part of our location strategy. Two and a half years ago, we started focusing on the emerging and Asian markets, particularly in countries where there is higher-than-usual growth (8–10 percent growth), and are shifting our activities accordingly . . . In India and Pakistan, we are focusing on infrastructure projects, encouraged in part by recent governmental reforms. In China and Korea, we are looking primarily at the financial sectors, including brokerage, leasing, assets manage-ment and banking, in addition to real estate.[103]

In a similar vein, the (then) CEO of the QIA, Ahmed al-Sayed, noted on the occasion of the launch of the Qatar-CITIC joint investment fund: 'We've just done a deal in Europe, and we'll continue doing deals in Europe. But as a global fund, also we need to diversify asset allocations and geographical location.'[104] The joint investment fund was one of numerous agreements reached during the November 2014 state visit by the young new Emir of Qatar, Sheikh Tamim bin Hamad Al Thani, to China. Potentially the most significant over the long-term was the signing of a memorandum of understanding between the People's Bank of China and the Qatar Central Bank to establish a clearing and settlement facility in Qatar for Chinese renminbi. The Industrial and Commercial Bank of China was nominated as the clearing bank for renminbi in Qatar and a US$5.7 billion three-year swap agreement was set up to boost bilateral trade and investment. China had earlier made a similar swap agreement with the UAE in January 2012, but as of November 2014 it had failed to lead to a full clearing agreement between the two countries.[105]

On the regional level, GCC entities became far more visible across the Middle East and North Africa throughout the 2000s. Adam Hanieh has observed that investments from GCC states in Jordan, Lebanon, Egypt, Palestine, and Syria totalled 69.2 billion Euros between 2003 and 2009 compared with 22.9 billion Euros from Europe and 5.2 billion from North America in the same period. FDI from the Gulf constituted, moreover, in excess of 70 per cent of total FDI in Syria and Lebanon by 2008 and rocketed from 4.5 per cent of total Egyptian FDI in 2005 to more than 25 per cent two years later.[106] In post-war Iraq, 'the investments of US companies were soon surpassed by those from the GCC,' which accounted for more than half the total investment in the country from 2003 to 2009. Hanieh adds that 'Khaleeji Capital' consists primarily of family-based conglomerates, SWFs, and private equity groups that invest across sectors, in addition to the dominance of regional banking systems with '58 of the top 100 banks headquartered' in the six GCC states.[107]

Successive waves initially of Qatari and later of UAE pledges of investment in Egypt in the turbulent aftermath of the 2011 upheaval reinforced the primacy of Gulf capital across the region and tied it far more closely to region-wide political objectives. This occurred as Gulf governments sought to influence developments in Egypt as part of the broader struggle to shape the trajectory of the volatile post-Arab Spring landscape. Indeed, the maelstrom of post-transition politics in Egypt provides a case study of the Gulf States' emergence as assertive regional

powers. As previous chapters make clear, their growth as visible participants in regional and international politics predated the Arab Spring,
but this process accelerated and acquired a potent new dimension once
the initial shock of the Arab Spring had subsided.[108]

GCC states took the lead in responding to the initially wide-ranging
political and economic challenges triggered by the Arab Spring. The
three years after the Arab Spring thus saw the Gulf States align their
growing capabilities (in the political, economic, and security arenas) with
a far more expansive *policy intent*. This was as evident within the Gulf
itself, when Saudi Arabia and the UAE led GCC forces into Bahrain to
restore order following the Pearl Roundabout uprising in March 2011,
as it was in policy responses to the escalating violence in Syria and the
uncertain aftermath of regime changes across North Africa. The scope
and scale of economic assistance to Egypt provides a clear example of
the practical and policy implications of this process in action, but highlights also how Gulf actors were far from impartial in picking sides and
choosing how and to whom to provide aid. Gulf support differed significantly from more conventional forms of international development and
aid by being linked indelibly to particular political *currents* rather than
being tied to *outcomes* such as reforms to governance or improvements
in transparency.[109]

While policies towards the unrest in the Arabian Peninsula (Yemen
as well as Bahrain) were generally coordinated and more multilateral in
nature, no such uniformity extended towards developments in North
Africa or, indeed, Syria. GCC states moved quickly to back competing
interests that highlighted the very divergent visions regarding the reordering of Egyptian (and Arab Spring) politics. Thus, after Mubarak's fall,
Saudi Arabia and the UAE backed the Supreme Council of the Armed
Forces (SCAF) with financial support and diplomatic recognition in the
16 months to June 2012. During this period, officials in both Riyadh and
Abu Dhabi opted for regime-type continuity in a bid to limit the impact
and contain the overspill of such rapid and unexpected change.

The UAE initially pledged US$3 billion in aid for Egypt in 2011
although delivery was subsequently put on hold after the Muslim
Brotherhood prevailed in the Egyptian presidential election in June
2012. In June 2012, shortly before Mohammed Morsi's electoral success,
Saudi Arabia approved US$430 million in support from the Saudi Fund
for Development aid, and gave Egypt access to a US$750 million line
of credit to import oil products.[110] Qatar took a diametrically opposed
position to that of its Gulf neighbours and extended a comprehensive
package of support to Morsi's Muslim Brotherhood government. During

Morsi's year in office (June 2012–July 2013), Qatar transferred more than US$7 billion in emergency loans and direct financial aid to Egypt. In addition, Qatar's Prime Minister pledged in September 2012 to invest US$18 billion over five years in tourism, industry, and infrastructure projects to revive the Egyptian economy, although little, if any, of the promised investment materialised in practice.[111]

The speed with which Qatar's GCC neighbours backed the 2013 restoration of military rule in Egypt with direct budgetary support, shipments of fuel products, and large amounts of bilateral aid spoke volumes. Having largely succeeded in containing the political upheaval at home, the conservative Gulf States rapidly deployed their financial largesse and political support in Egypt. With the toppling of the Muslim Brotherhood government in Cairo effectively signalling the end of the Arab Spring, at least in its initial post-2011 phase, Saudi and Emirati officials moved quickly to seize the regional initiative away from Qatar. Together with Kuwait, the three GCC states immediately provided some US$12 billion in aid to Egypt to assist the new military-led government to boost its foreign reserves and meet its import needs.[112] By the end of 2014, the total Gulf support to President Abul Fattah al-Sisi's government had risen to an estimated US$23 billion in the form of oil shipments, cash grants, and central bank deposits.[113] In March 2015, the same three states each made further pledges of US$4 billion each at the Egypt Economic Development Conference designed to kick-start the Egyptian economy after four years of turmoil.[114] Kuwait's Emir, Sheikh Sabah al-Ahmad Al Sabah, added that Kuwaiti private investors would take advantage of the Egyptian government's New Investment Law. Dubai-based real estate giant Emaar also was assigned to deliver the opening phase of the US$85 billion Capital Cairo project optimistically scheduled to open by 2020.[115]

Against this backdrop of greater regional assertiveness, the halving of international oil prices from US$115 per barrel in June 2014 to US$57 at year-end will pose difficult questions for Gulf policymakers, particularly if oil prices remain low for any significant period of time. Although oil prices plunged even more precipitously in 2008 from a high of US$145 in July to a low of US$33 by November, they recovered relatively quickly, so GCC budgets avoided taking a major hit. The challenge for policymakers in early 2015 has been that the international oil price showed signs of stabilising at between the US$50 and US$60 per barrel range, below the break-even oil prices needed to balance budgets in most of the GCC states. This has risen inexorably over the decade of high current and capital spending during the oil price boom. In Saudi Arabia the break-even price rose from US$20 in the early 2000s to at least US$90 by the start of the Arab Spring in 2011, with a further increase likely in view of the generous welfare packages designed to pre-empt and blunt any unrest within the kingdom.[116] Bahrain already faces a break-even price exceeding US$120, while in the UAE the break-even price soared from US$23 per barrel in 2008 to an estimated US$92 in 2011.[117] Even in Kuwait, the acting Minister of Finance claimed in March 2012 that the state's current rates of expenditure would require an oil price of US$109.50 to balance the budget in the 2012–2013 fiscal year, and that, if spending patterns remained unchanged, by 2030, Kuwait would need to be producing three million barrels of oil per day at the price of US$213.50 to meet its fiscal requirements.[118]

Although much depends on how long prices remain low, any prolonged slump will call into question the multi-billion dollar investment programmes planned over the next decade, especially in Dubai and Qatar as they prepare respectively for the World Expo in 2020 and the FIFA World Cup in 2022. Thus, before the fall in oil prices, Dubai had announced a new spate of glitzy mega-projects in 2014 to add to the more than US$130 billion in planned spending in the infrastructure and construction sectors, while officials in Qatar expected to award at least US$168 billion in contracts for World Cup-related projects between 2014 and 2022 with spending expected to peak in 2017 on 20 simultaneous mega-projects in the city.[119] Abu Dhabi and Saudi Arabia also had planned enormous investment in energy and infrastructure, with more than US$100 billion worth of spending in the construction, transport, and energy sectors in Abu Dhabi, and upward of US$500 billion in planned investment in infrastructure, health, education, logistics, and infrastructure projects in Saudi Arabia through the remainder of the decade.[120]

With the exception of Bahrain, which by 2014 was already running a budget deficit equivalent to more than 40 per cent of its GDP, and Oman, the four other (more resource-rich) Gulf States will be able to draw on their substantial capital accumulation to finance budget deficits for several years. However, this will be a short measure at best and will risk accelerating the drawdown of foreign reserves, within little more than a decade in the case of Saudi Arabia,[121] and possibly even sooner in the case of Kuwait, where the IMF warned, as early as May 2012, that, at current trends, 'government expenditure will exhaust all oil revenues by 2017, which means that the government will not be able to save any portion of these revenues for future generations.'[122] By January 2015, the impact of the halving of international oil prices was underscored as the

IMF revised downward its projection for GCC states' oil export earnings by US$300 billion.[123]

And yet, the unwillingness of Gulf monarchies to risk social or political unrest by reducing spending on subsidies or welfare for the national population poses an acute dilemma for ruling elites in all GCC states. In consequence, it is likely that any spending cuts will fall first on capital projects, as policymakers try to shield their national populations from cutbacks to current spending. Across the GCC, there have been signs of projects being scaled back and budgets being slashed among prestige projects that have extended far beyond 'soft' sectors such as education and the arts to encompass a reassessment of several large-scale energy and infrastructure projects as well. Emblematic in this regard was Qatar's announcement in late 2014 that it was cancelling two large-scale petrochemical projects that were to have been built in joint ventures with international partners amid evidence that all 'non-essential' capital expenditure was being scaled back.[124]

6
Shifting Patterns of Global Trade

This chapter develops the empirical evidence of the Gulf States' greater role in patterns of global trade and production. It examines how the large-scale economic diversification programmes initiated in the 1990s and 2000s and described in previous chapters have created new integrative linkages with the global economy as the GCC states grew into world-leading centres of production for a variety of industries ranging from petrochemicals and aluminium to cement and the construction industry. Simultaneously, the direction of Gulf hydrocarbons and non-oil trade shifted to the East in response to the Asian economic boom in the 2000s. The result has been the creation of more complex industrial ties with emerging (as well as industrialised) economies, primarily at bilateral levels but also on a multilateral basis as well. These ties have contributed to the shifting patterns of international trade that cumulatively are reshaping the contours of the global economy. Set against this has been the far slower progress on global trade agreements such as the WTO's Doha Development Round, which remained at an impasse in 2014, more than a decade after its launch in the Qatari capital in 2001.

An opening section in this chapter explores the attempts by the GCC to negotiate free trade agreements both with bilateral and regional partners around the world and examines why the majority of these efforts have thus far failed to yield substantive results. The stalling of multilateral talks has not, however, impeded the rapid expansion of bilateral connections which simultaneously are reflecting and reinforcing new patterns of global trade. Thus, the second section in this chapter analyses the significant diversification of Gulf States' trade relationships not only with existing states such as those in Pacific Asia but also with new partners in South and Southeast Asia. China also falls into this category as a late-developer in Gulf-Asia trade, owing to the historical factors that held back ties during the Cold War. The chapter then ends with an extended case study of the emerging nexus of food and energy security that is creating durable new connections between the Gulf States and a range of partners across Africa and Asia.

Free trade agreements

All six GCC states acceded to the WTO during the 1990s and 2000s with Saudi Arabia the last to join in 2005 after a lengthy (and difficult) process of negotiation that lasted for more than ten years and 'involved a complex bundle of cross-cutting regulatory reform issues.'[1] Saudi accession also was complicated by US concerns over the kingdom's boycott of Israeli goods (and persons), which officials in Washington, DC, viewed as discriminatory.[2] In addition, by 1998, every GCC state had joined the World Intellectual Property Organization (WIPO) as well. Membership in the WTO was actively pursued even though oil and gas remained outside the organisation's remit. In addition to giving the Gulf States 'the potential to exert influence on some areas of international trade,' policymakers were propelled by an elemental geopolitical rationale as they

> realised that they would have little choice but to join the international community and to become part of the north-south argument, particularly as they tried to broaden and develop their national economic bases . . . it was, in effect, a game of do or die – either accede to the WTO or face global isolation.[3]

WTO accession integrated the Gulf States more firmly into the international rules-based trading system and was intended to facilitate commerce, reduce uncertainty, and increase investor confidence. This necessitated further reforms not only to regulatory regimes in each GCC state but also to foundational issues such as intellectual property rights and protection.[4] The Agreement on Trade-Related Aspects of Intellectual Property Rights (TRIPS, to which all six GCC states are signatories) provides an illustration of the embedding of international norms and trends in legal and legislative frameworks across the GCC (Tables 6.1 and 6.2).[5]

The stalling of the Doha Development Round of world trade negotiations highlighted the structural barriers separating blocs of developed and developing economies on key issues such as industrial tariffs and agricultural subsidies (which are also a point of contention between the US and the European Union). As the deadline for completion of the Doha Round was put back repeatedly, inter-regional trade agreements

Table 6.1   Accession to the agreement on TRIPS

Country	Year
Bahrain	1995
Kuwait	1995
Qatar	1996
United Arab Emirates	1996
Oman	2000
Saudi Arabia	2005

Source: List of Parties to International Treaties Protecting
Rights Relating to Copyright

Table 6.2   Accession to WIPO

Country	Year
United Arab Emirates	1974
Qatar	1976
Saudi Arabia	1982
Bahrain	1995
Oman	1997
Kuwait	1998

Source: World Intellectual Property Organisation:
Member States

and frameworks proliferated.[6] Thus, from the 1990s on, the Gulf States have been involved in various sets of negotiations for free trade agreements with international partners, both on a bilateral and on a multilateral basis. The outcomes of the negotiation processes have varied widely and have provided in themselves an indication of the evolving motivations and policy objectives at national and regional levels. The multiplicity of such inter-regional trade agreements has, moreover, contributed to the wider fragmentation of the prospects for a cohesive and multilateral international trading system.[7]

By far the longest-running and also the most fruitless negotiating process has been with the European Union. The negotiations that began in the autumn of 1990 had their origins in a framework Cooperation Agreement between the (then) European Economic Community (EEC) and the GCC in 1988. This agreement came into force two years later and institutionalised the relationship between the two regional entities. It also advocated the creation of a Free Trade Agreement (FTA) as part of an intensification of mutual trade and investment ties.[8] Both sides initially hoped to gain from closer economic relations, with EEC countries seeking closer energy ties and GCC states prioritising access to the substantive European petrochemical market and other trade concessions. The talks got underway in the midst of the crisis occasioned by the Iraqi invasion of Kuwait, which merely heightened their urgency, and were modelled on the EEC agreements with Association of Southeast Asian Nations (ASEAN) states.[9]

It was, nevertheless, not long before negotiations ran into difficulty. The initial round failed when GCC states objected to EEC attempts to restrict their access to the European petrochemical market, necessitating the re-launch of a second negotiating round in 1992. European negotiators cited the GCC states' failure to create a customs union as an obstacle to an FTA and, as the 1990s wore on, focused increasingly on the task of deepening and broadening the European Union. During this period, the thrust of European policymaking in the Middle East was also focused on issues such as the European Neighborhood Policy and the Euro-Mediterranean Partnership (also known as the Barcelona Process), both of which prioritised strategic partnerships with proximate states in North Africa and the Levant rather than the more geographically distant Gulf.[10]

The sudden launching of the GCC Customs Union in 2003 revived the negotiations as it enabled the Gulf States to assume a unified external trade policy. Once again, contentious issues quickly arose, with European concerns about subsidies to Gulf-based aluminium and petrochemical firms that exported to EU economies, and GCC displeasure with EU tariffs on aluminium and petrochemical products. GCC negotiators additionally objected to EU reservations over Gulf States' stances on political reform, human rights, and environment protection, particularly when it appeared agreement was close. For these reasons, the long-running talks collapsed in acrimony in December 2008 due to the EU's insistence upon imposing what the GCC states saw as 'political' conditions in any final agreement. Thus, the Deputy Prime Minister of Qatar, Sheikh Abdullah bin Hamad al-Attiyah, criticised the 'hidden agenda' of the EU that included 'irrational issues that have nothing to do with free trade,' and added that '[o]ur experience with the discussion we've had with the EU, has been that on reaching the signing stage, the EU surprised us with issues that have nothing to do with free trade.'[11]

Against this backdrop of stalled negotiations with the EU, the GCC made efforts to reach agreements with less politically constrained partners in Asia. An example was the 2008 FTA with Singapore, which followed just two years of discussions, although it subsequently took five years to ratify, and only came into force in September 2013. The ratification was welcomed in Singapore as part of the efforts to enhance the city-state's 'role as a Gateway City by connecting the two large regions of Asia and the Middle East and North Africa.'[12] The FTA granted preferential treatment for GCC citizens in Singapore in sectors ranging from retail and engineering to law and reduced tariffs for Singapore-produced goods and refined oil products in the GCC. While the FTA initially failed to reverse a slump in GCC-Singapore trade, which declined by a fifth in 2013, partly due to lower Saudi oil shipments, trade ties between Singapore and the UAE deepened significantly in the energy sector.[13]

Elsewhere, the GCC's record in securing FTAs has been equally mixed, as intermittent discussions with Australia, India, Japan, Jordan, Korea, New Zealand, ASEAN, and MERCOSUR had not yielded substantive results by 2014. As with the EU negotiations described above, the 'threat' of cheap GCC petrochemicals products to local and regional host economies frequently has constituted a stumbling block to agreements.[14] The very first free trade agreement signed by the GCC as a bloc, with Syria, in 2005 was overtaken by the civil conflict that has engulfed the country since 2011. Meanwhile, the protracted negotiations with China increasingly resemble the talks with the EU given the major differences in position over key issues, some of which have been political rather than economic in nature. Indeed, the on-off discussions with China illustrate how ostensibly greater alignment in political positions (notably a shared distaste for 'conditionality' and human rights clauses) does not by itself prevent serious gaps over economic positions. Thus, the original talks that started in July 2004 came to a halt after five rounds in 2009 after China sought to limit the access of GCC petrochemical exporters to its markets out of what Gulf negotiators suspected was a desire to shield domestic producers from international competition.[15]

GCC officials subsequently suspended the FTA negotiations altogether and China-Gulf ties also were negatively impacted further by the political fallout from the escalating civil war in Syria as Chinese backing for the Assad regime was fiercely criticised in Gulf capitals. Simultaneously, a GCC-China Strategic Dialogue was also suspended as a result of the disagreement over the international response to the Syrian conflict. Political relations only began to thaw following a visit from Chinese Foreign Minister Wang Yi to Saudi Arabia in December 2013 that paved the way for the resumption of the strategic dialogue – after more than a two-year hiatus since May 2011 – in January 2014. The strategic dialogue saw the two sides agree to restart the free trade negotiations as Foreign Minister Wang reassured his hosts that 'China is working closely with its allies in the Middle East, including Saudi Arabia, to ensure peace and security in the region.' Two months later, the negotiating process was reaffirmed at the highest level when Chinese Premier Li used the visit of (then) Crown Prince Salman of Saudi Arabia to repeat his country's support in restarting the talks.[16]

There are numerous reasons for the sustained lack of success in GCC efforts to negotiate successfully as a bloc. One is the deep structural weaknesses within the GCC that account also for the slow progress in unifying external trade positions (and relations). Along with the launch of a GCC common market in 2008 and a planned single currency in 2010, the 2003 customs union was intended to accelerate the transformation of the Gulf into a unified economic bloc. However, each initiative has been beset by difficulty in aligning policy among the six member states, leading to the indefinite suspension of the single currency project and repeated delays in the full implementation of both the customs union and common market. Other difficulties included continuing obstacles to cross-border mobility within the GCC alongside low-levels of internal trade and the persistence of differing legal and regulatory frameworks among the six Gulf States. The impasse was belatedly resolved at the annual GCC Summit that took place in Qatar in December 2014, which agreed to impose a unified tariff of 5 per cent on foreign imports from 1 January 2015 and create a single port of entry dedicated to collecting the unified customs fees.[17]

Individual states' approaches to trade and investment additionally remained stubbornly resilient as a succession of bilateral trade deals undermined moves towards a collective GCC platform. Moreover, international trade partners preferred, for different reasons, to engage bilaterally with individual GCC states rather than with the bloc as a whole. Thus, the EU-GCC negotiations were hampered for years by the reluctance of European nations to work with the Gulf on a multilateral basis.[18] This 'competitive bilateralism' has undermined bloc-to-bloc negotiations as the United Kingdom, France, and Germany, in particular, have jostled for contracts in pursuit of closer bilateral economic and commercial ties with individual Gulf partners. Abdulla Baabood and Geoffrey Edwards note an occasion in 2005 when German Chancellor Angela Merkel visited the Gulf in her capacity as the President of the European Council, only to emphasise the opportunity for Germany to 'expand its energy ties with the Persian Gulf region.' As if to reinforce the message, a spokesperson for Chancellor Merkel added: 'This is a very important economic zone for us, and alongside the stabilisation of the political situation, it will be about expanding trade links to our mutual benefit.'[19]

The trend towards bilateralism and the reluctance to engage with the GCC as a bloc was even more pronounced during the George W. Bush presidency in the US. During its eight-year tenure (2001–2009), the Bush administration negotiated bilateral FTAs with Bahrain in September 2004 and with Oman in January 2006. After ratification, the agreements came into effect in August 2006 and January 2009 respectively. Simultaneously, the Bush administration also entered into bilateral talks for FTAs with Qatar and Kuwait in 2006 although neither of these processes bore results and subsequently were abandoned.[20] In fact, the Bush administration adamantly refused to negotiate with the GCC as a trade bloc, borne in part out of a desire to dilute its collective bargaining power.[21] Saudi officials responded with fury to the US bilateral negotiations with Oman and Bahrain and Foreign Minister Prince Saud al-Faisal Al Saud stated that the separate agreements were not compatible with the spirit of the GCC charter. He added that 'they diminish the collective bargaining power and weaken not only the solidarity of the GCC as a whole but also each of its members . . . what is more important, these agreements impede the progressive steps needed to achieve full Gulf economic integration.'[22]

The political row that followed the signing of the Bahrain-US and Oman-US FTAs is indicative of the core-periphery tensions that have hampered closer Gulf integration in multiple spheres. From monetary integration to security coordination and political unification, the six GCC member states have consistently been unable to reach consensus on major 'big-ticket' items. Moreover, the GCC Secretariat has yet to develop any substantive mechanisms for the pooling of sovereignty and it lacks an integrative supra-national decision-making institution akin to the European Commission. Further, the GCC has no explicit treaty-based foreign policymaking power as its founding charter called only for a coordination of foreign policy. Its member governments have retained responsibility for almost all aspects of political and economic policy and resisted any limitations on their sovereignty. As a result, these internal weaknesses make it harder for the GCC to leverage influence as a bloc and contribute to the preference of individual states to pursue bilateral economic and commercial relations.[23]

Diversification of trade relationships

The slow progress in formal FTAs has done little to impact the rapid expansion of commercial ties linking the GCC to trading partners across the world. Indeed, the scale of their growth in the 2000s merely reinforces the impression that the Gulf States managed their integration into the global trading system primarily on a national basis. Hence, while the GCC-ASEAN free trade negotiations failed to make substantive head-way at the bloc-to-bloc level, bilateral trade among the member states of both organisations increased fivefold between 2004 and 2011. This reflected the GCC states' acknowledgment of the geo-economic potential of Southeast Asian states, not least as regional petrochemical and refining hubs for the wider Asian market. The energy sector remained pivotal to bilateral relationships although proactive efforts also were made to broaden the spheres of cooperation through numerous trade and investment missions in both directions.[24]

The geographical redistribution of trade flows reflected and reinforced the deeper shifts in patterns of global trade. Trade among developing countries ('South–South trade') rose rapidly from only 8 per cent of world trade in 1990 to 16 per cent in 2005 and 24 per cent in 2011 while the global share of 'North-North trade' declined from 56 per cent to 36 per cent during the same period. Developing countries also increased their share of world exports between 1980 and 2011 from 34 per cent to 47 per cent and of world imports from 29 per cent to 42 per cent. New centres of geo-economic power arose in major emerging econo-mies such as China and India as the relative influence of North America, Europe, and Japan declined. As such, Brazilian diplomat Braz Baracuhy observed in early 2015: 'International trade is one of the forces contrib-uting to shifts in the global distribution of economic power and the geo-economic landscape' (Tables 6.3 and 6.4).[25]

Oil and gas ties nevertheless illustrated the growing interdependen-cies between the two regions as joint ventures proliferated and moved far beyond simple transactions between buyers and sellers of energy to encompass developments across the upstream and downstream sectors.

Table 6.3 Largest export partners

Country	Largest export partners
Bahrain (2013)	Saudi Arabia (3.2%), UAE (2.1%), Qatar (1.8%)
Kuwait (2013)	South Korea (17.1%), India (16%), Japan (12.3%)
Oman (2013)	China (38.2%), Japan (10.3%), UAE (10%)
Qatar (2013)	Japan (26.7%), South Korea (19%), India (12.1%)
Saudi Arabia (2013)	China (13.9%), US (13.6%), Japan (13%)
UAE (2012)	Japan (14.6%), India (11.4%), Iran (10.5%)

Source: CIA World Factbook

Table 6.4 Largest import partners

Country	Largest import partners
Bahrain (2013)	Saudi Arabia (27.9%), China (10.1%), Japan (6.2%)
Kuwait (2013)	China (10.9%), US (10.6%), Saudi Arabia (7.9%)
Oman (2013)	UAE (24.1%), Japan (11%), India (10.4%)
Qatar (2013)	US (14.2%), UAE (11.1%), Saudi Arabia (8.6%)
Saudi Arabia (2013)	US (13.1%), China (12.9%), India (8.1%)
UAE (2013)	China (14.7%), India (14%), US (10.8%)

Source: CIA World Factbook

Abu Dhabi government-owned Mubadala Development Company has been particularly active in the upstream sector across Southeast Asia through a joint venture in gas exploration with the Malaysian National Petroleum Company (PETRONAS) in the offshore Sarawak field in addition to participation in oilfield development in Vietnam, Thailand, and Indonesia.[26] The UAE also, in 2013, signed a US$6.75 billion agreement to establish a petroleum storage facility with a capacity of 60 million barrels of crude oil at Tanjung Piai in the Malaysian state of Johor.[27] The same year, another Abu Dhabi investment vehicle, Aabar Investments, announced the formation of a US$3 billion joint venture with 1MDB, a strategic development company owned by the Malaysian government, to invest in energy projects in the two countries.[28]

Qatar, by contrast, has invested heavily in downstream projects in ASEAN states, including a US$5 billion investment by Qatar Holding (a subsidiary of the Qatar Investment Authority) in the Pengerang Integrated Petroleum Complex also located in Johor state in Malaysia. Signed in 2013, the project is intended to enable Malaysia to compete with Singapore to become a regional petrochemicals hub for Southeast Asia.[29] Four months later, Qatar Holding joined with two fellow state-owned entities (Qatar Petroleum International and the Qatar Electricity and Water Company) to launch a new overseas fund to invest in overseas energy infrastructure.[30] Qatar Petroleum additionally acquired a stake in a US$4 billion petrochemicals complex in Vietnam in 2012 while Qatargas signed a 20-year gas supply agreement with Thailand's PTT the same year as well as similar such long-term gas supply deals with Singapore and Malaysia. In Kuwait, KPC also moved into the ASEAN energy sector with a US$9 billion joint refinery project in Hanoi and a partnership with Indonesia's Pertamina Limited to develop a refinery complex in East Java.[31]

As an example of the expansion of trade at an individual country level, the volume of trade between Malaysia and the Gulf States surged from US$1.6 billion in 1996 to US$14.5 billion in 2011 and diversified from the energy sector to encompass significant linkages in the financial, agricultural, and real estate sectors as well.[32] Chapter 5 examined the synergies in Islamic Finance connecting Malaysia with the Gulf States, but it is instructive to observe, as Sean Foley does, that bilateral investment flows accelerated and diversified in the late 2000s. Thus, investors from Saudi Arabia invested US$733 million in Malaysia in 2011 alone while their counterparts in Malaysia reciprocated with more than US$4.5 billion in investments in Saudi Arabia between 2007 and 2010. Both Qatar Holding and the Kuwait Investment Authority made significant acquisitions through participation in initial public offerings in companies listed on the Kuala Lumpur Stock Exchange. Moreover, Foley notes that in 2009 Malaysia's Federal Land Development Authority became the first foreign entity to receive a licence to form a fully foreign owned (100 per cent) company in Saudi Arabia.[33]

Similar trajectories are evident in other regions where surging bilateral trade and investment in both the energy and non-energy sectors also have occurred despite the continuing absence of FTAs. In this regard, the development of closer ties between China and the Gulf States has followed the ASEAN trajectory as bilateral relations have deepened and broadened as multilateral negotiations have stalled. Chapters 1 and 2 gave an overview of the historical background to Gulf-China ties and noted that, with the partial exception of Kuwait and Oman, they remained very limited until the end of the Cold War. In the 1990s, however, domestic challenges caused by rapid population growth and emerging resource scarcities propelled Chinese policymakers to devise a geo-economic strategy to address these issues, much as South Korea and Japan earlier had done. For Degang Sun, a professor at the Shanghai International Studies University, this relied on the Chinese government's ability to 'expand its overseas investment and foster energy and trade cooperation' in order to 'maintain [domestic] stability and reshape the world economic order.'[34]

Economic links initially focused around hydrocarbons, with a Strategic Oil Cooperation agreement in 1999 (a year after the then Crown Prince Abdullah made the first high-level visit by a Saudi leader to China) paving the way for Saudi Arabia to become China's leading oil supplier by 2002. A mutual upstream-downstream interdependence later formed as the GCC states invested in Chinese oil refining and petrochemical industries, and Chinese entities invested in oil exploration and production in the Gulf States.[35] In 2009, a 25-year agreement between Qatargas and the China National Offshore Oil Company (CNOOC) to provide five million tonnes per year of LNG captured the new dynamics at play. The agreement created a long-term interdependency, reflecting (in the words of CNOOC President Fu Chengyu) the 'great complementarities' between the two countries, as 'China can guarantee a long-term reliable market for Qatar, while Qatar can be a stable supplier for [the] Chinese market.[36] An announcement by Kuwait's General Administration of Customs that crude oil exports to China were 52.7 per cent higher in December 2014 than a year earlier provided a snapshot on the energy relationship between the Kuwaiti and Chinese governments, encompassing all aspects of the oil sector, ranging from crude oil trading, crude reserves storage, and refinery engineering services. The rise in Kuwait exports to China came four months after state-run KPC signed the biggest sales contract in its history with China's largest energy trader, Unipec. Under the August 2014 ten-year agreement, KPC agreed to supply the trading arm of Sinopec with 300,000 barrels per day of crude oil with the possibility of raising this to 500,000 barrels per day by 2017. The agreement replaced an earlier one for 160,000 barrels per day and amounted to about 15 per cent of total Kuwaiti crude oil exports. The lack of spare crude production capacity in Kuwait meant the additional supplies to Unipec were diverted from other markets, such as Europe and Japan, where demand for Kuwaiti crude had been weakening. KPC and Sinopec separately are engaged in a joint venture to construct a refinery with a 300,000 barrels per day capacity at Zhanjiang in China's Guangdong province. However, the project has been beset by major delays since it was announced in 2011. Progress revived in June 2014 following a meeting between Chinese President Li Keqiang and Kuwaiti Prime Minister Sheikh Jabir Mubarak Al Sabah. It is now intended that KPC will supply the feedstock when the refinery eventually goes on-stream in 2017.[37]

Data from the Economist Intelligence Unit (EIU) indicate that the overall value of trade between the Gulf States and China expanded substantially after 2001 both in relative and absolute terms. Thus, China's share of GCC exports increased threefold in the twelve years to 2013 and grew faster than any other trade partner between 2010 and 2013. The EIU further expects this growth to continue and projects that China will become the GCC's largest export market in 2020, by which time the value of Chinese imports into the GCC is expected to double from its 2013 level.[38] The volume of investment and trade between all GCC states and China also surged through initiatives such as the Kuwait-China Investment Company (KCIC – established in 2005).[39] In Saudi Arabia,

SABIC also drew up a strategic 'China plan' intended to create strong supply partnerships and joint ventures that can meet China's rapidly growing demand.[40] Nevertheless, with both China and Gulf States such as Qatar and Saudi Arabia investing heavily in petrochemicals, the EIU notes a possibility that competitive rivalries may eventually develop, particularly if rates of economic growth slow. Parallel efforts by the Gulf and China to secure food security through 'agri-business' investment and acquisitions of agricultural land in parts of Africa and Asia represent another area where competition for similar resources might yet emerge, as the conclusion to the final section of this chapter contends.[41]

In contrast with the surging trade with China and ASEAN nations, links with India have been slower to expand beyond their traditional focus around issues of labour migration (which will be analysed in Chapter 8). The GCC is India's largest regional trade partner with levels of trade that far exceed India-ASEAN and India-EU flows while the UAE and Saudi Arabia are India's fourth and fifth largest bilateral trade partners respectively. Moreover, Rahul Roy-Chaudhury has observed that India's largest overseas joint venture is the US$969 million Oman India Fertilizer Company that produces granulated urea and ammonia for the Indian market. However, India has proven unable to attract significant flows of foreign direct investment or sovereign wealth investment from the Gulf and several GCC-based investors that did enter the Indian market have faced a challenging operating environment. An example was the withdrawal of UAE telecommunications operator Etisalat from India and the loss of US$827 million of planned investment after the Indian Supreme Court cancelled a 2G spectrum allocation in 2012.[42]

More surprising, in view of the geographical distance and lack of historical connection, has been the strong growth in Gulf trade with Latin America. Formal meetings between political and economic leaders slowly gathered pace during the 2000s beginning with a visit by the then Brazilian President Luis Inacio da Silva ('Lula') to the UAE (as well as to Egypt, Libya, and Syria) in 2003. Two years later, Lula organised the first South American-Arab Countries Summit (ASPA) in Brasilia but Qatar's Emir Hamad bin Khalifa Al Thani was the only Gulf head of state to attend. Later in 2005, however, the inaugural GCC-MERCOSUR summit took place in Riyadh and Qatar then hosted the second ASPA summit in Doha in 2009, and a spate of new Gulf embassies opened across Latin America between 2007 and 2010. Erick Viramontes has documented how Brazil was the driving force behind the solidification of Gulf-Latin American ties based around greater levels of economic cooperation; in 2009, the country accounted for 85 per cent of all Latin American trade with the Gulf.[43] Yet, by the time that the 34 heads of state met again for the third ASPA gathering in Lima in October 2012, the volume of trade between Latin America and the region had nearly trebled from US$11 billion in 2008 to US$30 billion, and the number of bilateral trade relationships had diversified far beyond the initial Brazilian focus.[44]

Much of the Gulf interest in Latin America was centred on food imports (as analysed in the next section of this chapter) although Gulf investors also displayed interest in Latin American real estate and energy markets as well as infrastructural projects such as mass transit and LNG terminals. However, one of the first high-profile examples of Gulf investment in Latin America was a US$2 billion investment by Abu Dhabi's Mubadala in Brazilian mining and energy magnate Eike Batista's EBX Group in 2012. This was part of an extensive 'Strategic Framework' that covered the cement, fertiliser, entertainment, and technology sectors and formed part of 'Mubadala's development of strategic opportunities in Brazil and Latin America.'[45] The agreement soured the following year following the collapse of the EBX Group and Batista's losses in the precious metals mining industry. Mubadala later acquired a string of assets across Brazil in the subsequent restructuring of EBX debt, including a 10.52 per cent stake in the MMX Mineracao & Metalicos SA mining company and a 10.44 per cent stake in Prumo Logistica SA. Furthermore, Mubadala partnered with commodities trader Trafigura Beheer BV to purchase a US$400 million controlling stake in the Sudeste port in Rio state as a foothold for the export of iron ore.[46]

The food–energy security nexus

The final section in this chapter provides an overview of the food security strategies that have been adopted in the Gulf States and analyses how they are creating significant new inter-regional linkages, particularly with the rise of a 'food–energy' nexus with Southeast Asia. A commonality of interest has developed among food-scarce GCC states, which overwhelmingly remain reliant upon imported foodstuffs, and highly populated food-exporting nations, many of which are relatively energy-poor. High rates of population growth, urbanisation, and industrialisation also mean that domestic demand for energy in ASEAN states doubled between 1990 and 2007 and is projected to be three times its 2007 level by 2030.[47] One recent analysis observed not only that 'ASEAN will struggle in the years ahead to secure enough energy resources as it will have to compete fiercely with countries whose demand is also growing, such as China and India' but also that it will face a mounting challenge 'as more and more individuals enter the global middle class, putting enormous strain on ASEAN's domestically-produced natural resources.' Much of these additional energy requirements will come from GCC suppliers, as illustrated in the previous section of this chapter.[48]

From the Gulf perspective, the rise of food security up domestic policy agendas reflected a series of decisions taken in GCC states in the late 2000s to outsource the production of food through strategic agro-investments overseas. An important rationale for doing so was the mounting alarm in official circles at the potential for the rapid escalation of commodity prices in 2007 and 2008 to trigger domestic social and economic anger. Notably, in May 2008, rising food prices triggered riots among migrant labourers in the UAE and in Bahrain while the following month it was revealed that food prices in Oman had increased by 36 per cent annually.[49] The figures highlighted the Gulf States' acute vulnerability to inflationary pressures caused by rising commodity prices owing to their near-total reliance on imported food stocks, exposing them both to volatility in pricing and to potential disruption in supply. A *Chatham House* study in 2013 found that imports accounted for between 80 and 90 per cent of total food consumption in GCC states and had the potential quickly to become politicised; the same study added, that across the broader region, the price spike of 2008 in wheat has been attributed in part 'as a precursor of the wider social, political, and economic grievances that became the Arab Spring' in late 2010.[50]

In response to the inflationary pressures caused by rising food prices, policymakers in GCC states intervened to set prices and expand subsidies for basic foodstuffs such as bread and rice. Such measures did not, however, address the supply-side issues that had been identified as a key area of GCC states' vulnerability to external volatility. The absence of significant amounts of arable land and water deposits across much of the Arabian Peninsula meant that attempts to boost domestic agriculture achieved only very limited results, and often at great cost. Prior agricultural policies neither succeeded in increasing food self-sufficiency nor were sustainable in their careful use of scarce water resources. Kuwait was ranked the most water-scarce country in the world in 2006 and three other GCC states featured among the top ten water-scarce nations – the UAE third, Qatar fifth, and Saudi Arabia eighth.[51] Another ranking of water scarcity by Maplecroft of 186 countries lists Bahrain, Qatar, Kuwait, and Saudi Arabia in the top four positions and notes also that Saudi Arabia consumes 936 per cent of its total renewable water resources each year.[52]

Recent developments in Saudi Arabia illustrate how narrow approaches that fail to take a holistic approach to the overarching concept of 'resource security' can paradoxically magnify issues of food or water insecurity. In February 2008, Saudi officials announced that the Kingdom would cease all production of grain by 2016 in order to alleviate growing water shortages attributed to the depletion of non-renewable underground fossil water supplies. In the 1970s, Saudi Arabia had initiated an extensive state-sponsored agricultural development programme that aimed to increase the country's self-sufficiency in selected food items. Wheat production soared subsequently from 3000 tons per year in 1970 to a peak of 3.4 million tons in 1991 before falling back to 2.5 million tons by 2008. However, the wheat programme depended entirely upon central pivot irrigation that drew its water from fossil water reserves, the drawdown of which clashed with rapidly rising demands for water from other sectors of Saudi society.[53] Another prominent example of the disjuncture between agricultural water use and the wider challenge of water scarcity is the Al-Safi Dairy Farm in Riyadh. The largest integrated dairy farm in the world and more than double the size of the biggest dairy farm in the USs, the farm contains 37,000 Holstein cows producing more than 58 million gallons of milk each year, at an average water cost of nearly 2300 gallons of water per gallon of milk produced.[54]

Officials in Saudi Arabia, as in other Gulf States, therefore developed a more diverse range of policy responses to the issue of food security as acknowledgment of the intertwined nature of overall resource security grew. Policymakers in Riyadh launched the King Abdullah Initiative for Saudi Agricultural Investment Abroad and set up a food security panel affiliated with the Chamber of Commerce and Industry, which subsequently identified wheat, barley, corn, soybeans, maize, rice, and sugar as strategic crops for further investment.[55] In 2011, another wholly state-owned investment fund, the Saudi Agricultural and Livestock Investment Company (SALIC) was set up to reduce expenditure on imported foodstuffs and meet the Kingdom's food requirements. In April 2015, SALIC partnered with the global agricultural trading house Bunge to purchase a 50.1 per cent stake in the Canadian Wheat Board. The move came three years after the Canadian government ended its monopoly on purchases of wheat and barley from Canadian farmers and opened the market to international competition. The chief executive of the newly created joint venture, G3 Global Grain Group, stated of SALIC that the majority stake 'fits exactly with their vision. Canada produces some of the best-quality grain in the world. We have surplus exportable grain that's available in Canada, and we will have it for the foreseeable future.'[56]

Meanwhile, the King Abdullah Initiative established a new SR 3 billion (c. US$800 million) investment fund to purchase agricultural land overseas and to prioritise investment in wheat and rice to meet internal demand within Saudi Arabia. This fund initially targeted land acquisitions in Pakistan, Sudan, and Thailand and also supported investments by Saudi private sector companies in agricultural projects abroad.[57] Thus, in February 2009, the Hail Agricultural Development Company announced a two-year investment of US$45.3 million in the development of 9000 hectares of farmland in Sudan. Another Saudi company, the Star Agricultural Development Company, invested in the cultivation of rice and other crops on 1.2 million acres in Ethiopia.[58] However, Star made unwelcome headlines in April 2012 when an armed group ambushed and killed five local Ethiopian employees. Human Rights Watch attributed the attack to opposition to Ethiopian government moves to resettle local villagers in order to clear the land for commercial farming.[59]

News also emerged (in September 2009) of Saudi negotiations with Pakistan for the lease of 202,400 hectares of farmland representing an area nearly twice the size of Hong Kong. Significantly, a spokesperson from the Pakistani Ministry of Agriculture stated that the ministry would deploy special security forces to protect the farmland, and claimed that 'the land we will provide Saudi Arabia will be divided among the four provinces and they will using it to grow a variety of produce such as wheat, fruits, and vegetables.'[60] Left unsaid was any mention of the consent (or not) of local inhabitants or the nature of the legal jurisdiction under which they would operate. The announcement thus introduced a potentially new flashpoint of localised tension into internal discussions of security and sovereignty in Pakistan, as in other recipient states of GCC states' agro-investments.[61]

Saudi Arabia was not alone in following a dual strategy of overseas land acquisition and agro-investment policies. Qatar established the Hassad Food Company in July 2008 as a US$1 billion subsidiary of the national sovereign wealth fund, the Qatar Investment Authority, and the new entity quickly entered into major agreements with international partners. These included a US$500 million deal in 2009 to grow wheat and rice in Sudan and the purchase in 2010 of a sugar manufacturing plant in Brazil that was capable of meeting Qatar's entire annual demand for raw and refined sugar.[62] Investments in India included the 2013 acquisition of Bush Foods Overseas Ltd to facilitate the production of rice, coffee, cardamom, and 'ready-made foods.'[63] Hassad Food also created a Sydney-based subsidiary, Hassad Australia, to purchase farmland in Australia for wheat and livestock production. In its first four years to 2014, the group built up a portfolio of 14 major wheat and sheep farms across four states in southern and western Australia that covered a total of 287,000 hectares.[64] One purchase of agricultural land in South Australia in 2013 attracted local concerns over an apparent lack of transparency after it emerged that Hassad Australia was requiring sellers sign confidentiality agreements, in addition to paying up to 40 per cent above the market rate for the land.[65]

At a governmental level, the Qatari and Sudanese governments agreed in 2008 to establish a joint holding company to boost the production of wheat, animal fodder, and oilseeds in Sudan, while in 2009, the Government of Qatar commenced a strategic dialogue with Thailand covering cooperation and joint investment in the energy and food sectors.[66] To complement these external-focused schemes, Emir Hamad bin Khalifa Al Thani launched the Qatar National Food Security Programme (QNFSP) at the World Summit on Food Security in Rome in 2009. Created in order to reduce Qatar's 90 per cent reliance on imported foodstuffs, the programme aimed to enhance domestic food production in a more ecologically sustainable manner. This notwithstanding, its director acknowledged that investment in farmland abroad would remain key to attaining security in water-intensive crops such as rice and wheat.[67]

The UAE also was active in forging bilateral links with food-producing countries in Asia and Africa through a range of state-led and private ventures. Similar to its GCC neighbours, in the immediate aftermath of the food price spike of 2008, the UAE government examined the possibility of acquiring farmland in Pakistan, Egypt, and Yemen while the Abu Dhabi Fund for Development launched a large agricultural project in Sudan. In addition, the UAE undertook further strategic purchases of land in Tanzania, Mozambique, and Ethiopia,[68] while the UAE Economy Minister, Sultan bin Said al-Mansuri, acknowledged that investment in agriculture abroad was 'part of our strategic investment in general.' Dubai hosted the first Middle East-Pakistan Agricultural and Dairy Investment Forum in 2008 which resulted in more than US$3 billion in new investment into the agricultural and dairy sectors in Pakistan with a focus on milk and fruit production.[69] A Food Security Center was later set up by the Abu Dhabi Executive Council in 2010 to coordinate activity across the seven emirates of the UAE and to facilitate overseas investment in agriculture.[70]

These state-led initiatives were complemented by the growing regional portfolio of agro-investments held by private companies registered in the UAE. Prominent examples included Dubai-based Hakan Agro DMCC, one of the largest food trading companies in the Gulf, and the Pharos Miro Agricultural Fund, a joint venture between the Pharos Financial Group and Miro Holdings International. The latter was notable for being the first agricultural investment fund in the Gulf when it launched in 2009 with a focus on rice farming in Africa and cereal cultivation in Eastern Europe and the former Soviet Union.[71] Dubai-based private equity firm Abraaj Capital purchased large areas of farmland in Pakistan (although subsequent investment plans failed to take off) and by 2008 private companies based in the UAE held 800,000 acres in the country. In Abu Dhabi, Al Dahra partnered with the UAE government in several agricultural projects overseas before going it alone in March 2013 when it purchased eight agricultural companies for US$400 million in Serbia. Another Abu Dhabi-based investment company, Jenaan, acquired a total of 67,200 hectares of arable land in Egypt between 2007 and 2013 although a local backlash against plans to utilise the land to produce fodder for livestock in the UAE triggered a shift towards producing wheat for the Egyptian market instead.[72]

The manifold examples given above of agro-investment in Asia, Africa, Latin America, Australia, and elsewhere demonstrate how specific modalities of cooperation are contributing to the reshaping of inter-regional and international patterns of trade. The critical importance of energy issues in driving and deepening multilateral relationships between the GCC states and other blocs of emerging economies became evident during the first GCC-ASEAN ministerial meeting that took place in Bahrain in June 2009. Despite the slow progress on the FTA negotiations, officials discussed plans to transition towards a trading relationship that balanced ASEAN states' energy security requirements with their GCC counterparts' need to attain food security. ASEAN Secretary-General Suring Pitsuan drew attention to this emerging interdependency as he noted presciently: 'You have what we don't have, and we have in plenty what you don't have, so we need each other.' Food–energy security connections between individual GCC and ASEAN states also thickened at bilateral levels with Qatar being particularly active in forging closer trade links with major food-exporting countries such as Indonesia, Thailand, Vietnam, and the Philippines.[73]

Nevertheless, the closer food-related ties are not without controversy. GCC agro-investments in Asia and Africa, in particular, have led to allegations of 'agro-investment' and 'neo-colonialist land-grabbing.'

After the first delivery of a cargo of rice from a Saudi-financed farm in Ethiopia, an article in the Financial Times pointed out that a series of crop failures had left 11 million Ethiopians dependent on the World Food Program for sustenance. Other media coverage focused on the lack of international regulations or legal safeguards to protect local farmers and accused the Gulf States of 'a frantic rush to gobble up farmland all around the world.'[74] A further vulnerability is the heightened political risk that accompanies such acquisitions, evidenced in one instance in the maelstrom of post-Mubarak Egypt when the new government froze a major agricultural deal that the ousted regime had reached with Saudi Arabia's royally owned Kingdom Holdings.[75] The overall picture is more nuanced and has been acknowledged as such by the United Nations Food and Agriculture Organization. While recognising the 'complex and controversial economic, political, institutional, legal, and ethical issues,' it noted also that Gulf States were investing in agricultural development and productivity gains in recipient states.[76]

In addition, the Gulf States' moves into the acquisition of large tracts of foreign farmland may yet inject sources of tension into GCC ties with countries such as China over access to land. The GCC and China were the two largest-scale movers in this regard in 2008 with China's policies being guided by its aggressive 'Go Abroad' outward investment strategy. This resulted in more than 30 agricultural cooperation agreements throughout Asia and Africa that gave China access to 'friendly country' farmland in exchange for Chinese technologies, training, and inflows of infrastructural development funds.[77] In addition to the potential for direct friction, the Chinese experience carries a further warning for the Gulf States arising from the considerable local resentment it stoked. Tension focused on local cultivators' perceptions that their land and labour were being diverted to meet Chinese requirements with little benefit to themselves. In this context, it would behove the Gulf States to structure their engagement in such a way as to ensure that both producing and consuming states benefit from the agreements.[78]

The interlocking interests between food and energy security among GCC and partners across Asia and Africa may well provide a level of mutual benefit (if only to ruling elites) that means the Gulf States do not make the same missteps that befell Chinese agro-investors. So, too, might enhanced GCC investment or aid flows into host societies, particularly where they overlap with an ideational or religious appeal to fellow Arab and Islamic states, in whose countries many of the agro-investments have occurred. Major recipients of Gulf States' Overseas Development Assistance (ODA) in the 2000s included Pakistan, Sudan,

Eritrea, and Mauritania. Furthermore, the Arab Bank for Development in Africa financed road projects to promote trade among Burkina Faso, Chad, Sierra Leone, Rwanda, and Cameroon while the Kuwait-based Arab Fund for Economic and Social Development (AFESD) partnered with the Islamic Development Bank to support regional integration in Africa through the Trans-Sahara and Trans-Sahel roadways.[79] GCC state-run development funds also contributed heavily to the financing of the Merowe Dam on the Nile north of the Sudanese capital, Khartoum, in the early 2000s, admittedly with a strong self-interest in subsequently utilising the greater agricultural capacity of local land.[80]

Any such moves might mitigate the concerns of local inhabitants and international observers alike at the apparently limited base of stakeholders in GCC agro-investments abroad. Food security strategies in the Gulf States have contributed to the creation of new inter-regional linkages even as some of their more ambitious initial targets have been scaled back. This notwithstanding, the acquisition of significant land assets overseas undoubtedly injects new considerations into GCC states' interests that hold the potential to take on political and security dimensions. An example came in February 2013 with unusually robust comments by the (then) Saudi Deputy Defence Minister Prince Khalid bin Sultan Al Saud about Ethiopian plans to proceed with the construction of the Grand Renaissance Dam on the Blue Nile. Prince Khalid went so far as to allege that '[t]here are fingers messing with [the] water resources of Sudan and Egypt which are rooted in the mind and body of Ethiopia. They do not forsake an opportunity to harm Arabs without taking advantage of it.'[81]

7
Global Aviation and the Gulf

This chapter provides an empirical case study of one of the areas in which the Gulf States have been the most visible and dynamic generators of global change. The startling rise of Emirates, Etihad, and Qatar Airways has reshaped global aviation markets around the three hubs of Dubai, Abu Dhabi, and Doha, as the Gulf airlines have developed into what the *Economist* magazine has labelled 'global super-connectors' capable of connecting any two points in the world with one stopover in the Gulf.[1] This culminated in the January 2015 announcement that Dubai International Airport had overtaken London's Heathrow Airport to become the world's busiest airport for international passengers. Significantly, the 6 per cent annual rise in Dubai's international passengers (to almost 70 million in 2014) contrasted with the far smaller rate of increase caused by Heathrow operating at near-peak capacity owing to space and regulatory constraints. Moreover, Emirates, Etihad, and Qatar Airways have benefited further from the relative absence of political or legal constraints compared with European and North American 'legacy carriers' in addition to the 'state capitalist' development models described in Chapter Three.[2]

A brief overview of aviation in the Gulf constitutes the opening section in this chapter and illustrates how, for much of the twentieth century, Kuwait, Bahrain, and (briefly) Sharjah led the Gulf in aviation with Qatar and the UAE marginalised and peripheral. The development of Gulf Aviation (now Gulf Air) illustrated how the airline emerged as a symbol of pan-Gulf aspiration in the 1970s, with ownership divided among Bahrain, Abu Dhabi, Oman, and Qatar. Bahrain also made aviation headlines in 1976 when it was the destination for the inaugural British Airways Concorde flight from London's Heathrow Airport. Yet, it was Gulf Air's relative neglect of Dubai that prompted the ruling circle in that emirate to form their own airline, Emirates, with two leased aircraft in 1985 and begin the process of transforming first regional and then global aviation patterns. The rapid expansion of Emirates in the 1990s and the growth of regional rivals Qatar Airways (established 1993) and Etihad (2003) forms the centrepiece of the chapter's second section, which compares and contrasts the three airlines' development and operational models.

The third and final section of the chapter examines how the Gulf airlines have contributed in practice to the deeper changes to the GCC states' role in the world economy. This is evident in the announcement of new destinations which simultaneously reflect and reinforce the broader shifts in patterns of international trade and investment. Moreover, the announcement of lucrative aircraft orders has provided Boeing and Airbus with vital revenue flows at a time of contraction and consolidation elsewhere in the aviation industry. This has given the Gulf airlines further leverage over manufacturers and created significant sources of friction among their commercial rivals. Yet, the chapter ends by questioning whether the Gulf can sustain three aggressively expanding airlines within such a concentrated region (and market) and examines the fate of low-cost carriers as well as Kuwait Airways and Gulf Air as they struggle to compete and survive. Hence, the impact of the Gulf on global aviation is a microcosm of the GCC states' emergence as rising yet potentially unsustainable longer-term powers in the contemporary international system.

Gulf aviation in context

The geographical location of the Arabian Peninsula has made the region a strategic cog in the map of global aviation since the earliest period of intercontinental flight. This initially revolved around the British-protected sheikhdoms' positioning within the wider sphere of imperial communications that linked the United Kingdom with India, Hong Kong, and Australasia. When Imperial Airways (the forerunner of the British Overseas Airways Corporation and, still later, of British Airways) launched its Eastern Route from London's Croydon Airport to Brisbane in Australia in 1932, it established an overnight stop and constructed an airfield in the Trucial State of Sharjah. The resonance of this move echoed across the decades in a decision 80 years later, when Emirates and Qantas established a code-sharing partnership that saw the Australian airline reroute its European traffic through Dubai, a mere few miles from Sharjah, rather than through Singapore.[3] Imperial Airways paid the Ruler of Sharjah, Sheikh Sultan bin Saqr Al Qasimi, a monthly fee of 800 rupees for landing rights and fees at the new airfield as well as a monthly subsidy of 500 rupees. For his part, the ruler constructed a rest-house at the Al Mahatta Fort, which became one of the first hotels in the Gulf, while Britain's Royal Air Force (RAF) continued to use the Sharjah airfield as a regional base until Britain's military withdrawal from the Gulf in November 1971.[4]

Sharjah's pioneering role in regional aviation was superseded in the 1950s by the formation of Saudi Arabian Airlines in 1945, Gulf Aviation in Bahrain in 1950, and Kuwait Airways in 1953 (Table 7.1).

Gulf Aviation was established by former British RAF pilot Freddie Bosworth as a private shareholding company and commenced regular scheduled services to Doha, Sharjah, and Dhahran in Saudi Arabia. Following Bosworth's death in 1951 while test-flying a larger plane for the company, BOAC acquired a 22 per cent stake in Gulf Aviation, only to be bought out by the governments of the newly independent Abu Dhabi (UAE), Bahrain, Oman, and Qatar in 1973. Each of the governments took a quarter-share in the new holding company, Gulf Air, which became the carrier for the four states/emirates. In 1990, Gulf Air became the first Middle Eastern airline to fly to Australia and added direct flights to South Africa after the end of the country's apartheid-era isolation, but the evolving aviation market and the rise of Emirates as a regional

Table 7.1 Founding of airlines in the Gulf

Year	Airline	Current status
1945	Saudi Arabian Airlines	Operating as Saudia
1950	Gulf Aviation	Gulf Air/national carrier of Bahrain since 2007
1953	Kuwait Airways	Operating
1985	Emirates	Operating
1993	Oman Air	Operating
1994	Qatar Airways	Operating
2003	Etihad	Operating
2003	Air Arabia	Low-cost carrier based in Sharjah
2004	Jazeera Airways	Low-cost carrier based in Kuwait
2005	Wataniya Airways	Kuwaiti carrier ceased operating in 2011
2006	RAK Airways	Ceased operating in 2014
2007	Flynas	Low-cost carrier operating in Saudi Arabia
2007	Bahrain Air	Low-cost carrier ceased operating in 2013

Source: Information compiled by Kristian Coates Ulrichsen

competitor hit hard. In particular, the decision by Qatar and Abu Dhabi to follow Dubai and establish their own national airlines led them to withdraw from Gulf Air in 2003 and 2005. Oman followed suit in May 2007, whereupon Gulf Air became the national airline of Bahrain.[5]

Although an airport and regular air services had been established in Kuwait as early as 1927 and 1932 respectively, it was not until 1953 that two Kuwaiti businessmen launched the Kuwait Airways Corporation (KAC) with government participation in the form of a 25 per cent stake (which became a 50 per cent share in 1955 and full state ownership in 1962, after Kuwaiti independence). Flights to London and other European destinations began in 1964 (seven years before Gulf Air) and Kuwait Airways built up an extensive network of Middle Eastern and Asian routes during the 1960s and 1970s. However, Kuwait International Airport was among the first targets attacked in the opening phase of the Iraqi invasion of Kuwait on 2 August 1990, and the majority of the Kuwait Airways fleet was either destroyed or seized and taken to Iraq. This precipitated a long-running legal claim for compensation against Iraqi Airways that led in 2010 to the impounding of the first Iraqi Airways commercial flight to land in the United Kingdom since the Gulf War.[6] Kuwait Airways struggled to recover from the scale of the losses sustained during the occupation and developed a reputation as a bloated and inefficient state-run organisation with a heavily unionised labour force that lagged far behind its regional rivals in the 2000s. Long-running attempts to privatise Kuwait Airways started in the mid-1990s but the stop-start negotiations failed repeatedly to find a suitable buyer willing or able to take on such a loss-making asset.[7]

While Gulf Air and Kuwait Airways have been far surpassed by the exponential growth of Emirates, Qatar Airways, and Etihad since the 1990s, it is instructive to bear in mind the sheer rapidity and scale of the growth in aviation in the UAE and Qatar. As late as 1962, an international official arriving in Abu Dhabi for the first time described his arrival thus:

"Oh my God, we've crash landed!" I'm afraid this was my first thought as the small commuter plane of Gulf Aviation hit the ground. It took a while to realise that we had actually landed at Abu Dhabi. This was because looking out of the window upon landing just showed gravel on the ground and no tarmac, no runway as one was accustomed to seeing at airports . . . . Stepping out, there was little semblance of an airport; no terminal building, just a shade by the wayside in what appeared to be total wilderness . . . A red and white Abu Dhabi flag hoisted upon a pole was the only indication that this was indeed Abu Dhabi. A lone date palm standing tall at a distance was the only welcome sign.[8]

A British official who also arrived in Abu Dhabi in 1962 to take up a post in the growing local bureaucracy described further how the airport manager would wave a flag to incoming pilots to indicate whether the dirt runway was firm enough to land on, and that, while there were no night flights, 'in emergencies, as many vehicles as possible would be rounded up to line both sides of the runway and switch on their headlights to guide the pilot down.'[9]

Rise of the global airlines

As stated in the section above, the decline of the 'early movers' in Gulf aviation began in earnest with the creation of Emirates in 1985. The standoff between Gulf Air and the Ruler of Dubai began in 1984 after the company reduced the number of weekly flights from Dubai from 80 to 39. In response, Sheikh Mohamed bin Rashid Al Maktoum, the third son of the Ruler, Sheikh Rashid bin Saeed Al Maktoum (and, from January 2006, the Ruler of Dubai) resolved to create a new airline. With US$10 million in seed funding from the ruling family together with a US$88 million gift of two Boeing 727s from the royal fleet and an Airbus and a Boeing leased from Pakistan International Airways, Emirates' four-strong fleet commenced operations with a flight from Dubai to Karachi on 25 October 1985. Throughout its history, Emirates has benefited from the close support of Dubai's ruling family through the chairmanship of Sheikh Ahmed bin Saeed Al Maktoum, an uncle of the present Ruler, Sheikh Mohammed. Moreover, the airline was one of the few in the Gulf that maintained a full service throughout the Gulf War (January-February 1991) and picked up additional traffic during the conflict, especially from the temporarily grounded Kuwait Airways.[10]

Emirates based its early growth on the mass markets used by labour migrants to the Gulf with Mumbai, Delhi, Colombo, and Dhaka quickly joining the initial route from Dubai to Karachi. This was followed by expansion into regional markets (Cairo and Amman) and subsequently, in 1987, into Europe with flights to London's Gatwick, Frankfurt, and Istanbul. The London flight was noteworthy as Emirates offered alcoholic beverages to all passengers in a move that marked out the airline as distinct from its regional competitors and able both to anticipate and cater to customer demand, which surged as a result. In response,

Emirates subsequently made alcohol available in all classes of service on all routes save those to and from Saudi Arabia (and while over Saudi airspace). This was a highly innovative concept for a Middle Eastern airline to introduce at the time. Routes to East Asia (Bangkok, Singapore, and Hong Kong) and Manila followed in the late 1980s and early 1990s, and by the time of Emirates' tenth year of operation in 1995, it was already serving 30 different countries.[11]

Two significant factors lay behind (and made possible) the great acceleration of Emirates' growth in the late 1990s. The first was the decision of Dubai's leadership to aggressively market the emirate as an international shopping and mass tourism destination and thereby create the demand for visitors that Emirates would tap. The launch of Emirates Holidays in 1992 marked an early attempt to raise brand awareness of Dubai as a destination, and later events included the annual Dubai Shopping Festival (first held in 1996) in the winter months and the Dubai Summer Surprises Festival to overcome the traditional lull in summer visitors. Christopher Davidson has observed that commerce and tourism represented the two planks of Dubai's early efforts in economic diversification and 'transformed it into a city of shopping malls.'[12] Integral components of this strategy encompassed the construction of the largest mall in the world (Dubai Mall), the launch of an artificial Ski Dubai slope in another signature mall (Mall of the Emirates), and such iconic hotels and buildings as the sail-shaped Burj Dubai and the 2,722 feet high Burj Khalifa, the tallest manmade structure in the world when it was opened with a lavish ceremony in 2010.[13]

As the number of visitors to Dubai soared from just 400,000 in 1985 to over 3 million in the mid-2000s and 5.8 million in the first six months of 2014 alone,[14] the second element of Emirates' breakneck expansion was the series of massive new orders for long-range aircraft. The influx of state-of-the-art Boeing 777s in the 1990s and Airbus A340s and A380s in the 2000s gave the airline a transcontinental reach that offered passengers the option of bypassing traditional European hubs such as London, Frankfurt, Paris, and Amsterdam. The first Boeing 777s entered the fleet in 1996, but it was the arrival of the A340 in 2003 that enabled Emirates to launch direct services to the lucrative North American market. By 2014, Emirates linked Dubai with nine cities across the US, the most of any Gulf airline, and flew as far afield as Houston, Los Angeles, San Francisco, and Seattle. Another successful approach saw the airline fly to hitherto 'secondary' airports in key European countries, allowing travellers direct routings that would previously have required a stop in their capital's hub airport: examples in the United Kingdom include Glasgow, Manchester, and Newcastle (bypassing London Heathrow), Hamburg and Dusseldorf in Germany (bypassing Frankfurt), and Nice and Lyon in France (bypassing Paris Charles de Gaulle).[15]

The success of Emirates in branding Dubai as an internationally known city and destination resonated with the leadership in neighbouring Qatar after the new Emir, Sheikh Hamad bin Khalifa Al Thani, took power in 1995. As Chapter Two made clear, the generational shift that took place in Qatar brought to power the architects of Qatar's robust internationalisation strategy, spearheaded by the Emir and his ambitious Foreign Minister, Sheikh Hamad bin Jassim Al Thani. Qatar Airways launched operations in 1994, the year before Sheikh Hamad bin Khalifa became Emir, but the new leader relaunched the airline three years later having installed its (current) chief executive, Akbar al-Baker, in 1996.[16] Following its rebranding, Qatar Airways expanded quickly and mirrored Emirates in placing large new orders for next-generation aircraft. After being one of the earliest airlines to operate Boeing's 787 Dreamliner, Qatar Airways took delivery of the very first Airbus A350 to enter commercial service in December 2014. Notably, Qatar Airways had been the first airline to place an order for the A350 in 2007 and its subsequent orders for 80 A350s were instrumental in driving the demand for the new wide-body aircraft.[17]

Qatar Airways gained a truly global reach as the size of its fleet rose from 4 aircraft in 1997 to 28 in 2003, 50 in 2006, and 146 by the end of 2014, with double-digit growth both in the number of destinations served each year and in percentage rises in passenger traffic. However, the airline followed a very different business strategy from Emirates that reflected in part the unwillingness of the Qatari authorities to follow the 'Dubai model' and brand the country for the mass tourism market. Qatar has remained instead a relatively low-volume tourist destination, with an estimated 95 per cent of all visitors coming for business rather than pleasure, and Qatar Airways has marketed itself more as a hub and connector rather than as a destination in itself.[18] Statistics for March 2014 found that just over 40 per cent of all incoming passengers to Doha's old (and about to be replaced) international airport were in transit rather than arrival (737,000 out of 1.817 million passengers).[19] Moreover, the Qatar Airways leadership was disinclined to purchase stakes in other airlines, with its chief executive, Akbar al-Baker, noting pointedly: 'We will always go after goldsmiths, not scrap dealers.'[20] Qatar Airways did nevertheless become the first Gulf airline to formally join a global alliance, Oneworld, in 2012, and in January 2015 purchased a 10 per cent stake in the International Airlines Group, the parent company of British Airways and Iberia.[21]

The appeal to business (and transit) travellers reflected a decision of Qatari officials to target the lucrative MICE (Meetings, Incentives, Conferences, and Events) circuit as a key dimension of their effort to place Qatar firmly on the global map in the 2000s. Chapter Two described the emphasis placed by Qatar, Dubai, and Abu Dhabi and their respective airlines on the hosting and sponsorship of major international sporting events. In the case of Qatar, the 2022 FIFA World Cup will give a major boost to Qatar Airways, particularly if the airline becomes one of FIFA's six Official Worldwide Partners after rival Emirates ended its sponsorship in November 2014.[22] Meanwhile, Emirates and Etihad each have attached their name to major soccer stadia in London and Manchester respectively and entered the global sporting lexicon in much the same way as Old Trafford and Wembley. In 2010, Etihad increased by 60 per cent the capacity of its flights to Manchester after their sponsorship of Manchester City's stadium (and the club's takeover by the ruling family) increased greatly the emirate's profile (and soft appeal) in the north-west of England.[23]

As the youngest of the three major Gulf airlines, Etihad nevertheless has moved fast to develop a global profile and compete in a highly concentrated regional market. Established by an Emiri Decree in July 2003 and chaired by Sheikh Hamad bin Zayed Al Nahyan, a half-brother of the President of the UAE (and Ruler of Abu Dhabi), Etihad commenced operations in November and almost immediately made a large, multi-billion dollar acquisition of new aircraft from Boeing and Airbus. Later, in 2008, the airline made international headlines when it announced the largest aircraft order in history with the planned purchase of up to 205 new planes worth more than US$20 billion. The arrivals facilitated the rapid expansion of the Etihad network, which like Qatar Airways added new destinations at an often dizzying speed. Comments by Etihad's chief executive, former Gulf Air head James Hogan, captured the bullish mood among Gulf airlines: 'The size of our order also mirrors the rising prominence of the Middle East and its increasing emergence as a new focal point for global aviation. The Gulf is a natural air bridge between East and West.'[24]

Etihad has followed its own distinct growth model that differs both from Emirates' organic expansion in tandem with Dubai's growth and the Qatar Airways emphasis on business and transit passengers. The most notable feature of this strategy has been the formation of 'equity alliances' with struggling airlines, many in Europe, that enabled Etihad to 'add more spokes to its Abu Dhabi hub' and differ sharply from the Qatar Airways perspective on growth.[25] These equity alliances include 49 per cent stakes in Alitalia and Air Serbia, 40 per cent in Air Seychelles, a 34 per cent stake in Darwin, a Swiss regional airline since rebranded as Etihad Regional, 29.21 per cent in Germany's Air Berlin, 24.2 per cent in Virgin Australia, and 24 per cent in India's Jet Airways. The stakes were intended to give Etihad a foothold in regional markets and provide feeder traffic for the long-haul flights operated by the parent airline, but the Darwin acquisition, in particular, faced fierce local opposition by Swiss and its parent company, Lufthansa. Embattled European carriers also turned to the European Commission for support in their campaign to limit foreign ownership of European airlines, with an investigation into the issue launched in 2014.[26]

Redrawing global maps

The emergence of the three Gulf airlines has shaken global aviation markets to their core. An example of the speed and scale of their rise was evident in a February 2015 report by the US aviation industry that indicated that the Gulf carriers' share of bookings between the US and the Indian subcontinent rose from 12 per cent in 2008 to 40 per cent by 2015. This surpassed the share of the international US carriers (American Airlines, Delta Air Lines, and United Airlines) and their alliance partners such as British Airways and Air France, which fell from 39 per cent to 34 per cent over the same period.[27] Such trends and shifts in market share have generated widespread concern among competitors who perceive the state-backed carriers benefit from unfair competitive advantages. Particular resentment focused around a 'home market rule' preventing European and North American airlines originating from countries where Airbus and Boeing construct aircraft from using export credit agencies from assisting their carriers to buy aircraft. This regulation impacted all US carriers due to Boeing, and most of the larger airlines in Europe owing to the pan-European nature of Airbus, but left Gulf airlines unaffected. Scepticism towards the Gulf airlines was strongest in Germany, where Lufthansa alleged vociferously that Gulf carriers utilise public subsidies to finance aircraft deals, and in Canada, where the government transport agency initially declined (in 2010) to make additional landing slots available to Emirates and Etihad.[28]

Ottawa's action triggered a damaging spat between Canada and the UAE as the Emirati government retaliated by closing a military facility near Dubai that was being used to support Canadian troops in Afghanistan.

An additional flexing of bilateral muscles occurred when the Emirati authorities suddenly introduced steep visa fees for Canadian citizens wishing to enter the UAE, even as visas for most other European and North American visitors remained free at the port of entry. In a direct attempt to retaliate by gaining market share from Canadian airlines, Emirates and Etihad offered passengers significant discounts if they arranged their visas and their travel through the UAE carriers.[29] The new regulations remained in place for nearly three years as officials struggled to rebuild the bilateral relationship with Canada's largest export market in the Middle East. In April 2013, the announcement of a code-share agreement between Air Canada and Etihad that would open up the Canadian market signified the end of the Ottawa government's effort to protect the national airline that increasingly came at the cost of Canadian trade relations.[30]

European and North American carriers' concerns were not without foundation. The CEO of American Airlines acknowledged in September 2014: 'I worry about our ability to compete with other countries that are much more understanding and supportive of global aviation.'[31] Indeed, the three Gulf airlines fall within the nebulous state-business landscape in the Gulf where the line between public and private enterprise (as well as state and ruling family wealth) can be opaque at best. As documented above, Emirates and Etihad are chaired by the uncle and half-brother of the respective rulers. Meanwhile, in May 2014, Qatar Airways chief executive Akbar al-Baker noted: 'We became fully government owned in July last year' after the state bought out private investors who previously had a 50 per cent shareholding in the airline. Significantly, it emerged that the largest private shareholder had been former Prime Minister Sheikh Hamad bin Jassim Al Thani, although it remained unclear how large his personal shareholding had been, how much the state had paid for the shares, and whether Sheikh Hamad had purchased the shares in his capacity as a member of the ruling family, a private businessman, Qatar's Prime Minister, Foreign Minister, or head of the Qatar Investment Authority.[32]

For their part, the three Gulf airlines responded robustly to the criticisms and allegations levelled against them, which include that they benefit from an un-unionised and lower-wage workforce in addition to access to cheaper fuel or financing options. Many of the international airlines' accusations against Gulf airlines revolved around subtle matters of interpretation of direct and indirect government support that, at times, resembled the splitting of hairs. Thus, Qatar Airways chief executive al-Baker denied that his airline received government subsidies, but added that '[w]hat the government has given us is equity into an airline which they own.'[33] His counterpart at Etihad, James Hogan, was equally vague as he acknowledged – under pressure from negative publicity in the US – that '[l]ike any new airline, there was seed money and there was shareholder equity.' Suspicion around such arrangements was magnified by the fact that neither Qatar Airways nor Etihad have allowed public scrutiny of their finances, in marked contrast to Emirates, which does disclose its financial accounts and use international auditors.[34]

In February 2015, the three largest US carriers – American, Delta, and United – revived the subsidy issue as their chief executives claimed that the Gulf airlines received an 'unfair advantage' from state support and called on the Obama administration to review the US government's air treaties with Gulf partners. This represented a major step away from the Open Skies policies that US airlines had for years advocated. In meeting with Obama administration officials, the three US airlines compiled a 55-page dossier detailing alleged irregularities in Gulf airlines' financing, which they did not make public. According to a report that appeared in the *New York Times*, the dossier alleged that the three Gulf airlines had received more than US$38 billion in government subsidies. The dossier suggested that Etihad alone had benefited from US$17 billion in government subsidies in its first decade of existence, including US$6 billion in interest-free loans from the Abu Dhabi government to fund new airplane acquisitions and a further US$6.5 billion to cover operating losses. Belligerently, the report suggested that the dossier also claimed that

> Etihad's argument fundamentally misunderstands the international consensus on the definition of subsidy. Given the company's dismal financial performance over the last 10 years, if not for the subsidies, Etihad would have gone out of business.[35]

Qatar Airways, it was suggested, derived similar levels of state support in the form of an alleged US$7.7 billion in interest-free loans from the Qatari government and US$6.8 billion in reduced interest charges owing to sovereign debt guarantees. Moreover, the dossier suggested that Emirates had benefited from varying levels of support from the leadership in Dubai, which allegedly included their assumption of a US$2.4 billion loss from fuel hedging, a further US$2.3 billion in savings from artificially low airport charges, and, rather intangibly, US$1.9 billion in savings from the airline's non-unionised workforce.[36] However, Emirates chairman Sheikh Ahmed bin Saeed Al Maktoum responded bluntly to the allegations of uncompetitive advantage by calling on the US carriers to 'improve their service' and stating, 'Offer the best to the passengers and people will fly with you.'[37]

More substantively than the allegations contained in the dossier, which the US airlines declined to make publicly available, an investigation conducted by Reuters in February 2015 found that local cash-rich banks increasingly were playing a greater role in aircraft financing for the Gulf airlines, in addition to the traditional reliance on the controversial use of export credit agencies and cash injections to fund acquisitions. Whereas only 17 per cent of aircraft deals in the Middle East (as a whole) were funded by local banks in 2013, the figure rose substantially to 47 per cent in 2014. *Reuters* suggested that this was in part due to the fact that '[a]fter years of piling lending into the region's volatile property sector, local bankers see aircraft financing as a way to diversify risk into an asset class where the likely pitfalls are smaller.'[38]

The above notwithstanding, the Gulf airlines have taken advantage of a more benign set of domestic circumstances and have, on occasion, been robust in saying so. In a 2010 interview, chief executive James Hogan explained the benefits Etihad derives from operating within the political economy of Abu Dhabi, and as a latecomer relative to established European 'legacy' carriers:

> I don't have to tackle the union issues of these other carriers and I don't have additional costs because we can outsource a lot of things. When it comes to other carriers, we are both similar service airlines, but they are bound by agreements, employment agreements, 15, 20, 30, or 40 years old that are very hard to renegotiate. They are bound by infrastructure – facilities and bases that were right for them 30 years ago or even 20 years ago, but aren't today. I am fortunate that I have a clean sheet of paper.[39]

Such comments encapsulate the commercial advantages to Gulf operators of working without the constraints imposed by organised labour on European and North American competitors, and by the less stringent social welfare requirements that impart a certain advantage over Western rivals.[40]

Gulf airlines have also been recipients of major levels of what might be construed as indirect or 'soft' support by their parent emirates through the construction of some of the largest and most modern airports and associated infrastructure in the world. Both Dubai and Doha opened new airports in 2013 and 2014 respectively, while Abu Dhabi is engaged in a large-scale expansion of its own international airport. In addition to Dubai International Airport, officials in Dubai have started to open in phases what will eventually become the world's largest airport, Al Maktoum International, reinforcing the emirate's role as the preeminent logistical and infrastructural hub in the region. The centrepiece of the *Dubai World Central* economic, commercial, and residential zone, the airport is expected to have a capacity of 160 million passengers a year when it becomes fully operational. Remarkably, the construction of the massive new airport will complement the existing Dubai International Airport, which already contains the largest terminal building in the world. As mentioned above, Dubai International handled almost 70 million international passengers in 2014 and work is underway to add a new concourse that would raise capacity to more than 90 million. This has induced a weary acceptance from long-established competitors such as Heathrow, as evidenced in a statement following the news that Dubai had become the busiest international airport in the world: 'Britain has benefited from being home to the world's largest port or airport for the last 350 years. But lack of capacity at Heathrow means we have inevitably lost our crown to Dubai'[41] (Table 7.2).

A different form of leverage has been exercised by Abu Dhabi, which built up a close political, defence, and security relationship with the US government, focused around (but not limited to) the emirate's plans to develop civilian nuclear energy. Such ties were illustrated by the January 2014 launch of the first customs and border pre-clearance facility to open outside the US since the 1980s. The pre-clearance facility encountered strong opposition from aviation leaders in the US, who worried it would give a further competitive advantage if passengers from Abu Dhabi could avoid potentially long lines on arrival at US airports. These concerns were offset by an agreement that Abu Dhabi would meet 80 per cent of the cost of the facility, including the salaries of the

Table 7.2 World's busiest airports by international passenger traffic

Rank	2013	Traffic	Rank	2014	Traffic
1	London Heathrow	66,689,466	1	Dubai	69,954,392
2	Dubai	65,872,250	2	London Heathrow	68,091,095
3	Hong Kong	59,294,439	3	Hong Kong	62,929,420
4	Paris CDG	56,767,748	4	Paris CDG	58,623,111
5	Singapore	52,775,360	5	Amsterdam	54,940,534

Source: Airports Council International

Customs and Border Patrol officers needed to staff it. Fourteen members of Congress argued in a letter to the Department of Homeland Security in Washington, DC, that the facility in Abu Dhabi represented a 'dangerous precedent' of basing customs and border control on third-party financing rather than national security interests.[42] Ironically, the pre-clearance facility was beset by chronic overcrowding in its first year of operation, leading to persistent delays on US-bound flights and causing frustration among passengers and Etihad staff alike.[43]

The three Gulf airlines therefore have emerged as leading players in a global market that itself is undergoing major restructuring and consolidation. The importance of the Gulf airlines is reflected in numerous indicators such as the size of their order books for new aircraft – US$107.5 billion for Emirates, US$57.7 billion for Qatar Airways, and US$28.5 billion for Etihad as of 2015. In addition to generating significant new demand at Airbus and Boeing, the scale of the orders are themselves reshaping patterns of international trade. By 2012 for example, the UAE was the fourth-largest export partner of Washington state after China, Canada, and Japan, but far ahead of far larger industrialised economies such as South Korea, the United Kingdom, and Germany.[44] With nearly all of the bilateral trade between Washington and the UAE generated by Boeing, the launch of a daily Emirates flight from Dubai to Seattle in 2013 was symbolic. Elsewhere, the launch of new routes provided an illustration of the new intra-regional ties binding the Gulf into the global economy. These included heavy emphasis on new destinations throughout China as well as direct flights to Latin America, and made it possible for travellers to fly to any two points in the world with a single stop in the Gulf, with Johannesburg-Doha-Tokyo only one example of many.

Questions nevertheless remain over whether three such aggressive and expansionary airlines can coexist in such a concentrated region, no matter how global their activity. So long as Emirates, Etihad, and Qatar Airways are taking market share from international rivals they are likely to continue to grow. However, should the aviation market ever reach saturation point or the host emirates begin to experience long-term fiscal challenges, this will put to the test the Gulf carriers' ability to turn a profit and operate as genuine standalone entities independent of any state support. Moreover, their dominance also has resulted in a 'two-tier' regional market that has made it far harder for operators such as Kuwait Airways and Gulf Air to be competitive with their powerful rivals while other airlines, such as Wataniya Airways (in Kuwait), Sama Airlines (a low-cost private carrier in Saudi Arabia), Bahrain Air, and RAK Airways in the UAE, ceased operating altogether between 2010 and 2014.

The case of Bahrain Air, in particular, was notable for the illustration of Gulf airlines' vulnerability to regional and political instability. The airline never fully recovered from the Bahraini government's decision to suspend direct flights to Lebanon, Iraq, and Iran following the 2011 Shia-led uprising in the country. The loss of some of Bahrain Air's highest-yield and most profitable routes was compounded by the denial of a request to the government for compensation; the airline cited the 'unstable political and security situation' and 'sustained considerable financial losses' as the reasons for its closure in February 2013.[45] Shortly thereafter, the chief executive officer of Bahrain Air, Richard Nuttall, spelled out the challenging operating conditions facing the 'other' Gulf carriers:

> In a part of the world where almost every other airline is subsidised, and flying from a small Kingdom which is currently going through its own issues, it was always going to be difficult to be truly profitable. There is not enough point to point traffic, and regional connecting traffic yields are too low to sustain an airline. So it was always going to struggle by traditional measures.[46]

In such a context, the discrepancy between the local aviation market in the Gulf and the global ambitions of its three largest carriers becomes readily apparent. Should state support, in all its soft forms, ever be withdrawn or scaled back, it is likely that Emirates, Etihad, and Qatar Airways would face similar restructuring and downsizing challenges as Kuwait Airways and Gulf Air, their predecessors as the aviation symbols of the Gulf. This may, however, be averted should the large Gulf carriers succeed in creating a critical mass of customers, destinations, and innovative products that take advantage of the region's central geographical location and upwardly mobile clientele. With more than three billion people living within an eight-hour flight from GCC capitals, including in the rapidly growing Chinese and Southeast Asian markets, such trends both reflect and reinforce the broader rebalancing of the global economy and the opportunities within this for Gulf airlines.

8
Migrant Labour in the Gulf

This chapter explores how the Gulf States developed into the largest recipients of inward labour migration, primarily from the Global South, in the world. It examines how the rise of dual labour markets, split between public/private sectors and citizens/expatriates, is linked inextricably to the political economy of the redistributive welfare state models that developed with the oil era. This has created a segmented workforce with pronounced hierarchies among both the citizen population and the foreign communities that make up the contemporary demographic pyramid in the Gulf. Although the scale of the demographic imbalance varies considerably across the six Gulf States, with Oman and Saudi Arabia having the lowest proportion of non-nationals and Qatar and the UAE the highest, they share certain characteristics in common. These include the hard truth that many of the region's 'mega-projects' and development plans would likely not have been possible without the 'cheap and transitory labour power' of migrant workers.[1]

Labour migration additionally constitutes a highly visible if inequitable element of the relationship of the Gulf States to the labour-sending states of the Global South, which account for the vast majority of the incoming migrants. The tenfold increase in the population of the six Gulf States, from 4 million in 1950 to 40 million in 2005, was among the highest in recorded human history, and much of this was attributable to inward migration. Together, the GCC states now host more than 23 million migrants, although the precise figure is unknown due to incomplete data and a large amount of 'irregular' migration to the Gulf, and non-nationals constitute about 48 per cent – nearly half – of the total population.[2] This forms a web of human and socio-economic ties between the Gulf and South Asia, in particular, illustrated and monetised by the value of remittances sent home by workers to their families.

However, such dependence provides GCC rulers with a political tool that they can wield at times of crisis, as happened with the expulsion of tens of thousands of Palestinians and Yemenis from Gulf countries after the Iraqi invasion of Kuwait in 1990. Recent large-scale deportations of expatriate workers from Saudi Arabia and Kuwait in 2013 and 2014 moreover indicate the continuing vulnerability of such groups to blowback from domestic tensions.

Accordingly, there are four sections to this chapter, beginning with an opening section that analyses the practical challenges facing the study of migration and demographic issues in the absence of comprehensive and reliable statistics. Significant research has in recent years added depth and nuance to the 'demographic debate' in (and on) the Gulf, but the raw data available to practitioners and researchers remains very limited by comparison with international standards. This constitutes an ongoing obstacle to scholarly efforts to place migration flows to (and within) the Gulf within their full and proper context, although important efforts are being taken to address some of the lacunae. The following section sets out the historical parameters of migrant labour in the Gulf and demonstrates how and why migration became such a deeply embedded feature of the region's political economy as it developed from the 1950s onward. State-building and rapid urbanisation transformed both the spatial and the demographic profiles of the newly independent Gulf States during this period. This occurred as the accrual and utilisation of oil revenues transformed the hitherto resource-starved and relatively employment-surplus regional political economy into a resource-rich and comparatively labour-deficient one.

The third section in this chapter explores the domestic impact of migration in sustaining the political economy of the Gulf States by distorting domestic labour markets and empowering key business actors with a vested interest in maintaining access to a low-cost workforce. This has complicated efforts to reform such flashpoints as the sponsorship (*kafala*) system and fully implement labour nationalisation programmes throughout the GCC states in recent years. Nevertheless, as unemployment and under-employment have become critical public policy issues, and doubts have mounted about GCC states' ability to generate sufficient new jobs to absorb a generation of new entrants into the workforce, a new interplay among demography, labour markets, and more intangible concepts of citizenship and identity has emerged. The fourth section analyses migration as a case study of the tense relationship between the Gulf States on the one hand, and international NGOs and global civil society, on the other. Thus, the chapter ends by assessing the pressures that the internationalisation of the Gulf is creating for enhanced scrutiny and transparency in the treatment of migrant labourers, particularly in Qatar as the country prepares for the 2022 FIFA World Cup.

Gaps in statistics and data

Much of the data on migration in the Gulf has been produced by national governments, but difficulties of access and questions about the quality and reliability of the information persist. Further, many of the existing statistics are fragmentary and are scattered across multiple, overlapping, and sometimes incompatible sources. Both individually and collectively, the Gulf States lack a centralised platform for making available information on migration and demographic issues to policymakers, let alone scholarly and research organisations. In part, this reflects official unease at revealing the scale of migration to the region and the physical and spatial dominance – in many Gulf cities – of non-nationals in society. Table 8.1, based on data compiled by Kasim Randeree, reveals that Emirati citizens constituted a mere 2 per cent of the workforce of Dubai in 2005 (compared with more than 50 per cent for Indian nationals), illustrating the sensitivity surrounding such figures in a context of local debates over the perceived loss of identity and national 'values.'[3]

A further case in point was the political furore in Bahrain in 2008 when opposition MPs walked out of parliament in anger at the revelation that

Table 8.1   Workforce breakdown by nationality in Dubai, 2005

Group	Percentage of total workforce
Indian	54
Pakistani	13
Other Asian	11
Arab	9
Bangladeshi	4
Iranian	3
UAE nationals	2
European	2
Other	2

Source: Kasim Randeree, 'Workforce Nationalization in the Gulf Cooperation Council States,' Georgetown School of Foreign Service in Qatar, Centre for International and Regional Studies Occasional Paper No. 9, 2012, p. 8

the official population of the country suddenly had jumped by nearly 40 per cent from 700,000 to 1.1 million.[4]

The care and caution with which data and statistics are treated has contributed to a palpable feeling of political and public unease as intangible concepts such as identity and belonging have become entwined in policy debates on the high dependence of GCC states on migrant labour (Table 8.2).

This was evident in comments by the then Minister of Labour of Bahrain, Majeed al-Alawi, in August 2009: 'The issue of expatriate labour is not a time bomb; it is a bomb that has already gone off,' and added that unless policy solutions were put in place, 'the fate of Gulf States will be at stake.'[5] This backdrop of uncertainty caused by the void of reliable information has provided a fertile ground for rumour and populist countermeasures such as the large-scale rounding up and deportation of tens of thousands of migrants from Saudi Arabia and Kuwait in 2013 and 2014 and the popularity of T-shirts proclaiming 'The UAE is full. Go home!' among young Emiratis in Abu Dhabi around 2010.[6] It also has contributed to significant gaps in 'official' understanding of such basic issues as the very number and presence of illegal immigrants in the GCC as well as the safety nets that have emerged to sustain them. Examples from the UAE have included the creation by undocumented migrants of their own insurance and education systems that have for years operated below (and beyond) the official radar.[7]

Recent research by Nasra Shah has illustrated the challenge posed by poor availability of data for the study of migrant workers in Kuwait. Shah compared the two data sets that provide the main sources of population data in Kuwait – census records from the Central Statistical Bureau (CSB) and the civil registration database held by the Public Authority for Civil Information (PACI). Each of the three years examined by Shah – 1995, 2005, and 2011 – revealed substantial discrepancies between the

Table 8.2   Estimated citizen/expatriate breakdown

Country	Nationals	Expatriates	Total
Bahrain (2011)	584,688	610,332	1,195,020
Kuwait (2013)	1,242,499	2,722,645	3,965,155
Oman (2013)	2,172,000	1,683,000	3,855,000
Qatar (2014)	278,000	1,845,160	2,123,160
Saudi Arabia (2013)	20,271,058	9,723,214	29,994,272
UAE (2013)	1,400,000	7,800,000	9,200,000

Sources: CIA World Factbook, Gulf Labor Markets and Migration, World Bank

two sets of figures with the PACI figures considerably higher in all three cases. Whereas in 1995, the PACI figure for the population of Kuwait (1,881,250) was 305,680 higher than the CSB census, by 2005 the discrepancy had more than doubled to 673,237 before narrowing slightly to 566,159 in 2011. Shah observed: 'In a population numbering only about 3.6 million in 2011, these discrepancies are indeed huge' and concluded:

A major problem arises for planners and policymakers faced with the discrepant data . . . Planning for the future requires population projections which would differ greatly depending on which of the two sources is used . . . In view of the apparent undercounts in the last three censuses, a fundamental question arises about the validity of the previous censuses collected between 1965 and 1985.[8]

Shah noted further that the compilation of such diverging official statistics by distinct yet overlapping organisations has constituted 'a massive duplication of effort and resources' that could be diverted elsewhere.[9] A similar lack of accuracy in demographic data has been evident in Saudi Arabia as well; in the mid-2000s, estimates of the population of the city of Jeddah ranged from 2.4 million to 3.6 million, while the reliability of data on the expatriate population was also elastic.[10] It has further been the case that the data on migration has been among the most incomplete owing to the lack of information on the presence of considerable numbers of undocumented workers or others who overstayed their visas or transferred from one sponsor to another once in-country.[11]

Such gaps in the raw data and statistics make it far harder for officials in GCC states to devise and implement evidence-based policy solutions across the range of government in a time of rapid population growth. A senior policymaker in the healthcare sector in Qatar noted that during the average seven-year time-span for the construction of a hospital in Doha, the population of Qatar approximately doubled, leaving the facility as originally planned too small to meet the surging demand for care.[12] Similar dilemmas exist throughout the six Gulf States, as the introduction of large-scale data sets over the past decade have struggled to keep pace with the pace of demographic change, and it remains unclear how existing data informs the policymaking process in GCC states.[13] Another lacuna in the migration literature has concerned the study of the 'migration cycle' in its entirety, with a path-breaking edited volume in 2012 offering the first comprehensive study of the issue from a multidisciplinary perspective.[14]

In Saudi Arabia, veteran American journalist Thomas Lippman has been a regular visitor to the kingdom since the 1970s, when he was the regional correspondent for the Washington Post, and describes the ongoing challenge of accessing reliable data and statistics thus:

> Economists and political analysts who write about Saudi Arabia often say that the most difficult part of their research is finding accurate statistics about the Kingdom. Population, food production, water resources, oil and gas reserves, industrial output – many kinds of data that are essential to sound planning and accurate evaluation cannot be taken at face value, especially if they are generated by Saudi government agencies.[15]

In his 2005 book on the country, Lippman noted: 'In the late 1970s, researchers found that government statistics were literally manufactured in the ministries of Finance and Planning.'[16] Such comments reflect the unreliability of statistics in Saudi Arabia, which vary from ministry to ministry and in some sectors, particularly the labour market and employment, are neither coordinated nor centralised. Thus, in 2007, while the Saudi Ministry of Labour reported the labour force to be 6.7 million strong, the Ministry of Economy and Planning's statistics gave a figure of 8.2 million. The difficulty in reconciling such discrepancies is made harder by the fact that the most comprehensive annual data source, the Statistical Yearbook that has been produced annually since 1975 by the Central Department of Statistics and Information, does not include employment-related statistics.[17]

Gulf migration in historical context

While previous chapters in this book have documented how the Arabian Peninsula has for centuries been a zone of dynamic interaction between cultures and peoples, the region as a whole was sparsely populated until the twentieth century. Such settlements as did exist were primarily concentrated on the western and eastern coastlines or in upland areas in the mountainous regions of modern-day Saudi Arabia, Yemen, Oman, and the UAE. James Onley and Sulayman Khalaf have described how 'there was fierce competition between and within tribes and ruling families for control of the Gulf's scarce resources.'[18] Guy Michaels has additionally noted that 'economies that are currently resource-rich were not necessarily considered resource-rich in the past,' as in the Arabian Peninsula prior to the period when oil was discovered and became commercially extractable.[19]

The inability of regional economic structures to generate sufficient employment opportunities for their local population led to internal and external migration throughout the pre-oil period. Such flows of pilgrims, merchant traders, imperial functionaries, and foreign slaves means that the presence of large numbers of expatriates in the Arabian Peninsula is not a new phenomenon. An important case in point was the Sultanate of Oman. Territorial expansion during the nineteenth century peaked in the 1840s when its (short-lived) maritime empire extended across the Indian Ocean from Zanzibar to Baluchistan in modern-day Pakistan. Dynastic struggles led to the separation of Zanzibar in 1861, but the Omani enclave around Gwadur was only ceded to Pakistan in 1958.[20] The acquisition of territory was accompanied by waves of migration from both directions, with particularly large numbers of Baluch from the Makran settling in the Sultanate, where today they are estimated to form between 10 and 13 per cent of the Omani population.[21] Oman experienced another wave of inward migration in the violent aftermath of the Zanzibar Revolution of 1964 when tens of thousands of people of Arab origin fled persecution and returned to their ancestral homeland.[22]

Similarly, the case of Dubai demonstrates the fluidity and mobility that characterised regional movements of peoples and goods in the early twentieth century. The emirate had long competed with the Persian port city of Lingah for regional trade in the lower Gulf. In 1903, the imposition of high taxes by a newly centralising Persian state on the merchants of Lingah led many of them (both Arab and Persian) to migrate across the Gulf to Dubai. There, they formed the backbone of Dubai's takeover as the key regional trading post role, as they brought with them their businesses, shipping experience, and the Indian associates who formed the middlemen between the Gulf pearl merchants and their worldwide markets.[23] One contemporary businessman concluded that 'this drain of expertise from Lingah was to be the foundation for Dubai's strong growth after 1902 . . . Persia's loss was Dubai's gain.'[24] This early experience of the beneficial acquisition of migrants' skills fostered the outward-looking trading mentality that has seen Dubai develop into the most cosmopolitan city in the world, with a population of non-nationals that exceeds that of nationals by up to 15 to 1.

The onset of the oil era fundamentally changed the nature of migration in the Gulf as new labour flows met the demands of the oil sector and derivative industries and were intended, at least initially, to be short-term in nature. Simultaneous state-building and urbanisation projects rapidly transformed both the spatial and the demographic profiles of the newly independent Gulf States in the 1960s and 1970s. Incoming oil revenues thus redrew the international political economy within the Middle East, as substantial flows of labour and money (in the form of workers' remittances as well as direct aid) crossed regional frontiers.[25]

The first wave of labour migration to the Gulf mainly comprised Arabs from regional Middle Eastern states and Palestine. After the creation of the State of Israel in 1948 and the series of Arab-Israeli wars that followed, tens of thousands of Palestinians migrated to the Gulf States, with two notable spikes occurring in 1948 and 1967 respectively. The flow of Palestinian refugees was largely a function of labour supply and demand as the Palestinians possessed the educational and professional skills to staff the new bureaucracies in the rapidly developing oil states. This was particularly significant in health and education, as Palestinians and other Arab expatriates plugged shortfalls in the pool of skilled indigenous manpower to meet the transformative needs of modernisation.[26] In Kuwait, for example, the number of Palestinian and Jordanian workers rose from 14,000 in 1957 to 78,000 by 1965 – a figure that, by comparison, would have exceeded the entire population of the sheikhdom in 1938.[27]

Palestinians filled numerous leadership positions in Kuwaiti institutions during this formative period of state-building immediately prior to and after Kuwait's independence in 1961. Examples included the City Secretary of Kuwait as well as the Electricity Office, which was labelled informally 'The Jaffa Colony' as the director, 'Abd al-Muhsin Qattan, employed many fellow Palestinians from his hometown of Jaffa. The second wave of Palestinian migrants occurred after the 1967 Six-Day War, and included the future leader of Hamas, Khaled Mishaal, whose family settled in Kuwait, where he first became active in Palestinian politics. The nascent oil industries in the Gulf were another source of large-scale recruitment of Palestinian workers, including by Aramco in Saudi Arabia, Petroleum Development Qatar, and the Kuwait Oil Company.[28]

Egyptians also were instrumental in constructing the educational systems in Kuwait and the other Gulf States during their formative years of state-building; in 1956, 44 out of 64 teachers in boys' secondary schools in Kuwait were Egyptian.[29] In Bahrain, too, Egyptians were dominant in the formative development of the education system from the 1920s onwards and were active in shaping notions of Arab solidarity and class politics, aided by Iraqi dissidents exiled from Baghdad in the 1950s.[30] Many of the Egyptians who moved to the Gulf in the 1950s and 1960s were members of the Muslim Brotherhood fleeing the crackdown on their organisation by President Gamal Abdul Nasser. Their influence was particularly strong on the subsequent development of education and curricula in Qatar, where Egyptians went on to become the first Director of Education and the Director of Islamic Sciences at the Ministry of Education.[31]

The influx of Palestinians and Egyptians as well as Syrians, Jordanians, and Yemenis thus acted as a transmitter of ideological and pan-Arab sentiments that fused local and regional political currents. Students in Kuwait began to protest against the rise in Jewish immigration to mandate-era Palestine as early as the 1920s in some of the first recorded political demonstrations in the Gulf.[32] In the 1930s, the cosmopolitan merchant elites in Kuwait, Bahrain, and Dubai were at the forefront in developing local support for pan-Islamic and Arab nationalist movements. In the period before the opening of the first Arabic printing press in the Gulf, the Dubai merchants imported Arab books and nationalist magazines from Cairo for onward transmission to subscribers across the Gulf.[33] In the 1950s, popular Arab nationalist movements were particularly strong in Kuwait and Bahrain and gathered additional momentum following the Suez Crisis of 1956. Anti-British protests occurred in both British-protected emirates and culminated in the resignation of the Emir of Bahrain's longstanding adviser, Sir Charles Belgrave, in 1957.[34] Two years later, Yasser Arafat co-founded Fatah in Kuwait, where he and other leading Palestinian activists were located, and based the movement's Central Committee in Kuwait City until it moved to Damascus in 1966.[35]

This first phase of significant labour migration to the Gulf differed greatly from its subsequent evolution. The prominent Kuwaiti sociologist Khaldoun al-Naqeeb has described how Arab migrants were pivotal to 'the revolutionary, Arab nationalist tide which inundated the Gulf and Arab peninsula region in the 1950s.'[36] John Chalcraft has illustrated that Arab migrants were integral to domestic politicisation through 'oppositional assemblages, involving renegade princes, disaffected officers, merchants, professional and intermediary classes, workers, and migrants.'[37] Bahraini sociologist Abdulhadi Khalaf has calculated that, between 1945 and 1973, Arab migrants constituted some 85 per cent of all migrant labour in the Gulf, but that a momentous shift in the composition of migrants occurred during the immediate aftermath of the 1973 oil price boom. This occurred as the rapid influx of non-Arab migrants, particularly from South and Southeast Asia, steadily eroded the proportion of Arab migrants in Gulf States' workforce. The proportion of Arabs in the total migrant population fell from 72 per cent in 1975 to 56 per cent in 1985, and the decline accelerated after the 1991 Gulf War to between 25 and 29 per cent by 2002.[38]

Numerous reasons account for the radical shift in migrant policy as Gulf governments succeeded largely in depoliticising labour forces and replacing politically 'troublesome' migrant communities with groups holding no linguistic, religious, or cultural affinity to the local population. The political sensitivity of over-reliance on Arab migrants initially became an issue for Gulf governments in the 1970s, when rising Palestinian activism in the National Assembly contributed in large part to the Emir's decision to prorogue the constitution and suspend political life in 1976.[39] By contrast, Forstenlechner and Rutledge have noted that 'Asians were less likely to claim citizenship, could more easily remain disenfranchised, and were seen as generally more likely to remain passive observers of political processes.'[40]

Yet, it was the Gulf crisis of 1990 that represented the decisive turning point in the use of migration as a political tool to punish (or reward) recalcitrant (or quiescent) communities as hundreds of thousands of Yemenis and Palestinians were deported from the Gulf in retaliation for their leaderships' stance on the Iraqi invasion of Kuwait. After Yemen abstained from a United Nations Security Council resolution condemning the Iraqi invasion and resisted attempts to build a coalition to liberate Kuwait, more than one million Yemenis were expelled from Saudi Arabia. Their return to Yemen presented the newly reunified republic with an immediate economic and humanitarian crisis in a country where foreign remittances had constituted 44 per cent of GDP in North Yemen and 40 per cent in South Yemen in 1980.[41] Mass expulsions of Palestinians from Kuwait (where they were also targeted for reprisals) and other Gulf States also took place after the conclusion of the Gulf War in February 1991. Over 400,000 Palestinians were deported from the Gulf in response to Yasser Arafat's high-profile support for Saddam Hussein, including 350,000 from post-liberation Kuwait alone.[42] The vast majority returned either to Jordan, the West Bank, or the Gaza Strip, where the loss of remittances and the resulting surge in unemployment had a similarly decimating effect as in Yemen.[43]

The broader use of migration as a tool of ruling family control has been encapsulated by Khalaf, who has noted how

> ruling families have gradually incorporated migration in their arsenal of tools to maintain the stability of their rule. Migration control and migration management policies provide the GCC states with several new tools to enable them to shape their societies at the micro level, and to control the activities of all the inhabitants within their territories.[44]

In his seminal yet provocative *After the Sheikhs*, Christopher Davidson argued persuasively that that the presence of large numbers of migrant labourers served the rulers' interest, since expatriates 'have no real interest in the politics of their host countries, and certainly never revolutionary politics. In many ways, they become a loyal, silent support base for the ruling families.' Davidson added, with respect to Dubai, that

> as the emirate's indigenous population has continued to shrink, relative to the influx of hundreds of thousands of expatriates each year, the government has regularly announced new initiatives to hold the situation in check. But in many ways it has suited the ruler's interests well – even if it has alarmed the citizenry – to govern over a city made up of temporary migrants.[45]

In his summary of how 'migration took on a completely different political significance' between the 1960s and the 1990s, John Chalcraft observed that migration 'became an adjunct rather than a challenge to the resurgent power of patrimonial ruling families.' In addition to the geopolitical decisions outlined above, careful control of migration management also played a major role in the emergence of the Gulf States' pronounced regional distinctiveness.

Domestic political economy of migration

Within GCC states, migration has simultaneously shaped, and been shaped by, the political economy of wealth redistribution. The most distinctive, as well as the most contentious, feature of the domestic political economy of migration is the *kafala*, or sponsorship, system whereby all foreign residents acquire a permit to work from a sponsor and guarantor (a *kafeel*). This was put in place by the nascent Gulf States as their own distinct regulatory framework of migration management and control. As a tool of labour market protectionism that aimed to benefit local (and largely unskilled) workers, the *kafala* system originated in the 1950s and 1960s with measures such as the 1959 Aliens Residence Law in Kuwait. Such laws codified and replaced hitherto fluid notions of identity and belonging as citizenship became far more restrictive, and the presence of foreign labourers tightly regulated and placed on an impermanent basis. The *kafala* system has aptly been described as 'a citizen-devolved system of governance' that has played 'an integral role in bolstering the existing division of power between citizens and foreign residents.'[46]

From the beginning, the *kafala* system was a critical component of an asymmetrical relationship of power between migrants and their employers. To a former head of the Employment Service Bureau at the Bahrain Ministry of Labour, Mohammed Ditto, 'the link between wealth distribution and exclusion is critical' to understanding how the system evolved. Moreover, Ditto suggested that the system developed a path dependency of its own as it grew 'from being a consequence of rentier state policies to becoming a principal enabler of this system in later years.'[47] The delegation of the authority to permit a migrant to enter the country from the state to the (citizen) employer also served to 'fuse the power of both the state and employers, with both spheres controlling the right of entry of the migrant into the Gulf.'[48] In her study of Kuwait, Anh Nga Longva added that the 'shifting [of] the state's power of control over the migrants' onto Kuwaiti civil society ensured that dominance became 'a central component in the relationship between individual citizens and individual migrants'.[49]

Regional and international attention has focused on the widespread abuses within the *kafala* system in both the labour-sending and labour-receiving states. Heavy recruitment and transit fees imposed by recruiters and middlemen in the countries of origin mean that workers often arrive in the Gulf with substantial debts and spend their first months and years in a state of debt bondage. Once in the Gulf, many unskilled migrants and domestic workers have their passports confiscated by their sponsors and are placed in substandard housing or in labour camps located far from urban areas.[50] Common forms of exploitation include delayed or non-payment of salaries, hazardous working conditions often in extreme temperatures that exceed 50 degrees Centigrade (122 degrees Fahrenheit) in the summer, and the inability to create unions or engage in collective bargaining. Moreover, the delegation of *kafala* from the state to individual sponsors has ensured that 'employers have the unilateral power to cancel residency permits, deny workers the ability to change employers, and deny them permission to leave the country.'[51]

These abuses notwithstanding, it has nevertheless been the case that, as American sociologist Andrew Gardner has pointed out, 'unskilled and low-skilled migrants continue to stream to the Gulf States in spite of the difficult conditions and exploitative labour relations many of them encounter in the region.'[52] Several reasons account for this, including a degree of economic rationality arising from the fact that 'salary levels in the Gulf remain competitive in the global context.' Thus, the majority of migrant labourers are able to begin sending home remittances once their initial debts have been repaid; a study of out-migration from Kerala found that inflows of remittance payments from the Gulf did boost the local economy. As a province, Kerala supplied more than half of all Indian labour to the Gulf in the 2000s, and much of this was concentrated within several districts alone. One such district – Malappuram – was found to have a per capita income that exceeded the regional GDP by 69 per cent, while per capita consumption levels in Kerala as a whole have been among the highest in all of India.[53]

The *kafala* system fulfilled an important function as it was designed initially as a mechanism to provide a temporary, rotating labour pool that could rapidly be imported during periods of economic growth and later expelled if or when times grew harder. This reflected the desire of officials in all the Gulf States to view the presence of foreign workers as strictly temporary in nature and limited to a defined duration. Tied to this was the near impossibility of policy pathways to the granting of eventual citizenship. In a recent study of migrant labour in Qatar, Zahra Babar found that one of the only formal avenues for gaining Qatari citizenship was by petitioning the Emir for naturalisation and that even this was open only to individuals resident in Qatar for 25 successive years.[54] In such a restrictive context where Qatari citizenship was limited to individuals who could prove their ancestors' presence in Qatar in 1930, it was perhaps hardly surprising that the number of Qatari nationals constituted only about 225,000 of the overall population of about 1.84 million in 2012. More remarkable still was the fact that Qataris numbered a mere 85,187 of the 1.35 million people active in the labour force in Qatar the same year.[55]

Episodes of 'political naturalisation' nevertheless have occurred at periodic intervals in the Gulf as ruling elites responded to socio-political pressures with attempts to recalibrate the demographic composition of their societies. Two notable instances, in Kuwait and Bahrain, illustrate the inherently political nature of such processes of population management. Between 1965 and 1981, Kuwait naturalised up to 220,000 Bedouin from tribes inhabiting the borderlands with Iraq and Saudi Arabia. This occurred as the Kuwaiti government encouraged the Bedouin to settle in Kuwait and meet the surging demand for manual labour in the construction sector as Kuwait City rapidly urbanised. In part, Kuwaiti officials hoped the Bedouin would prove more 'loyal' and less politically radical than the Egyptian, Syrian, and Palestinian workers, as has been described above.[56] A second motivation was domestic as the government sought to counterbalance the political (and parliamentary) dominance of the liberal merchant elites by enfranchising a new set of voters whose dependence on state jobs would – it was hoped – produce an electoral base of government support.[57]

Large-scale naturalisations in Bahrain have been linked to alleged efforts by the ruling family to alter the sectarian makeup of the country by diluting the Shiite majority who formerly made up between 50 and 70 per cent of the national population (reliable figures are hard to come by owing to the acute sensitivity of such data, and the inaugural census in 1941 remains the only occasion when the Sunni-Shiite demographic was measured). An estimated 100,000 naturalisations took place during the 2000s with up to 90 per cent of those granted citizenship said to be Sunnis from Saudi Arabia, Syria, Yemen, or Pakistan. Many of the newcomers worked in the security and defence forces, and their arrival sharpened sectarian tensions in the already volatile archipelago.[58] The issue of political naturalisation exploded into public and political discourse in the 2006 parliamentary election, as a British advisor to the Cabinet Affairs Ministry alleged that government officials were engaged in a systematic attempt to manipulate the sectarian balance in the country.[59] While the allegations were never formally proven, a US diplomatic cable described how 'Bandargate' triggered 'an avalanche of public accusations, counter-accusations, conspiracy theories, and unanswered questions' in Bahrain.[60]

The two examples above illustrate how ruling elites have wielded the granting – as well as the revocation – of citizenship as a tool either to ensure political loyalty or alternatively to punish political dissent. An example of the latter occurred in 2005, when the citizenship of up to 6,000 members of the Al-Murra tribe in Qatar was taken away as a collective punishment for the involvement of several of their number in an alleged coup attempt.[61] Since the onset of the Arab Spring in 2011, the stripping of citizenship has occurred with greater regularity across the GCC states, but particularly in Bahrain, which also faced the most disruptive opposition protests. Thirty-one Bahrainis had their citizenship revoked in November 2012 for 'causing damage to state security,' including the sociologist Abdulhadi Khalaf, whose work has been cited numerous times in this chapter. Writing about the incident shortly thereafter, Khalaf suggested that, in the Gulf, 'a passport is not a right of citizenship, but rather an honour bestowed by the ruling family' who 'reserves the right to grant or revoke this gift at any time.'[62]

Public and political concerns among Gulf nationals tend to have focused on the scale and apparent irreversibility of the demographic imbalance, although such fears downplay the role of individual sponsors (*kafeel*) in continuing to employ foreign workers. In response, officials in every GCC state launched wide-ranging labour nationalisation schemes that aimed gradually to replace expatriates with suitably trained local workers. The origin of these policies lay in the economic slowdown and falling oil revenues that lasted for much the 1980s, and in the emergence of growing local socio-economic discontent as mechanisms for redistributing wealth became strained. Yet, three decades of official support for labour nationalisation produced very few tangible results, as the absolute number of expatriates in the Gulf surged and even their relative proportion increased. Efforts were undermined and complicated by the decade of high oil prices that began in 2003 and by the resulting proliferation of prestige mega-projects and economic diversification plans, both of which led to a further substantial rise in the foreign workforce.

This growth was at its most pronounced in the UAE and in Qatar, as first Dubai and then Abu Dhabi and Doha developed into regional hubs and aspirant 'global cities.'[63] Even in less oil-wealthy Bahrain, however, the number of expatriates in the country more than doubled from 261,000 in 2000 to 570,000 just eight years later. The link between the 'spatial-demographic fix' in Bahrain (as elsewhere) was underscored in 2005 when acute shortages of labour developed in construction projects after restrictions were (temporarily) imposed on foreign work permits in an effort to nationalise the sector.[64] In Saudi Arabia, a Royal Decree in 1995 that mandated an annual 5 per cent increase in the proportion of Saudis in all companies with more than 20 employees proved unworkable in practice; Steffen Hertog has related how the measure, together with a subsequent plan to incentivise the hiring of Saudis in the mid-2000s, 'failed in the face of massive business lobbying, particularly from the business sector,' which stood to lose from its access to a cheap foreign workforce.[65]

Tensions arising from the impact of Arab Spring unrest across the region have since 2011 sharpened the volatile nexus between demographic and labour market patterns, and more intangible concepts of citizenship and identity. These, in turn, built upon policy decisions that had been taken during the 2000s to liberalise the real estate sector and open up categories of residential visas to expatriates in GCC states. Beginning in Dubai in the late 1990s, longstanding national laws that banned the ownership of property by non-nationals began to be superseded by large-scale property developments that targeted specifically high-end Western or expatriate buyers. One of the earliest such instances occurred in 1997 with the launch by Emaar Properties of the 'Emirates Hills' residential project in which direct foreign ownership was not only marketed but encouraged.[66] The largest real estate company in the GCC, Emaar was established by Mohammed Alabbar, a close aide of the Ruler of Dubai and member of the Dubai Executive Council. Initially, the company was fully owned by the Government of Dubai before listing on the Dubai Financial Market in 2000 and becoming one of the first traded companies to offer shares to foreign nationals.[67]

Bahrain was the first GCC state to allow expatriates to buy real estate in 2001, with Dubai formalising its own position the following year. Qatar and Oman followed in 2004 and 2006, as did four of the other six emirates in the UAE, including Abu Dhabi. These measures typically permitted foreigners to purchase properties in pre-approved, mostly gated communities. Saudi officials then stated in 2010 that they would permit foreign ownership in the massive new King Abdullah Economic City, then under construction. This left Kuwait the only GCC state yet to follow suit.[68] Omar AlShehabi has calculated that, at the peak of the oil price and real estate boom in 2008, at least 1.3 million housing units were being planned for foreign ownership in Bahrain, Oman, Qatar, and the UAE. This startling figure had 'the potential to house more individuals than the total of all the citizens of these four countries,' assuming an average three inhabitants per unit, had they all subsequently been built.[69]

The regional real estate boom, which resumed in earnest in 2013 after a hiatus caused by the 2008 crash, has altered the political economy of migrant communities in the Gulf in two significant ways. The first is the passage of legislation in Bahrain, Oman, Qatar, and the UAE, of legislation linking residency visas to the purchase (and continuing ownership) of real estate, thereby modifying the role of the *kafeel* for at least one group of internationally mobile and affluent expatriates.[70] Such measures will accelerate the impact of the second shift in regional trends, which is the rise of second-generation migrants whose have been born in the region and yet have no possibility to access full rights of citizenship in the countries they call home. A 2013 study of second-generation non-nationals in Kuwait found that no fewer than 18 per cent of all non-nationals had been born in the country and lived in Kuwait for at least half their life.[71] Elsewhere, in *Dubai: Gilded Cage*, Syed Ali explored the phenomenon of 'legally invisible' second-generation immigrants who identified instinctively with Dubai as their home, thereby 'contradicting the official interpretation of expatriates as guest workers and thus temporary foreigners.'[72]

Migration as contested international politics

The emergence of the GCC states onto the global stage in the 2000s was accompanied by a rising chorus of international criticism over the alleged abuse of migrant labourers. Many of the concerns of intergovernmental organisations and international civil society groups were linked to the maintenance of the *kafala* system. In 2006, just as the development of Dubai into a regional hub was accelerating, Human Rights Watch set the tone with a deeply critical report entitled *Building Towers, Cheating Workers: Exploitation of Migrant Construction Workers in the United Arab Emirates.* The report laid bare a pattern of exploitative conditions endemic in the construction industry as the cityscapes of Dubai and Abu Dhabi took shape. These included 'wage exploitation, indebtedness to unscrupulous recruiters, and working conditions that are hazardous to the point of being deadly.' In addition, Human Rights Watch suggested that the government was failing 'adequately to address these issues,' and urged the authorities in the UAE to become a signatory to international conventions such as the International Convention on the Protection of the Rights of All Migrant Workers and Members of their Families.[73]

Other publications, such as the Trafficking in Persons (TIP) reports produced annually by the US Department of State, continue to list the Gulf region as one of the worst in the world for human trafficking and migrants' rights. None of the GCC states have risen above a Tier 2 ranking, which denotes that they are failing to comply with the international standards of the Trafficking Victim's Protection Act. Kuwait and Saudi Arabia, moreover, are designated Tier 3 states, which means that they are failing even to demonstrate any effort to comply with the Act. The Trafficking in Persons Report for 2014 was particularly blunt on Kuwait:

> Kuwait lacks a domestic labour law to govern the relationship between domestic workers and sponsors; thus, many workers report work conditions that are substantially different from those described in the contract . . . Nascent efforts to help abused workers, such as by issuing exit and travel documents to those whose passports had been confiscated by their employers, were not accompanied by any enforcement activities against the employers from whom the workers had fled.[74]

The same report also placed Bahrain and Qatar on the Tier 2 Watch List and warned that both countries risked being downgraded to Tier 3 in future reports.[75]

Bahrain and Qatar are illustrative of the varying levels of domestic and international pressures that influence the development of government policies to address migrant issues. The Government of Bahrain enacted the most pioneering, and initially the most potentially far-reaching, reforms of the *kafala* system in August 2009 when immigration regulations were modified to permit 'mobility transactions.' This allowed migrant workers to change employers with or without the permission of the sponsor. The reforms also established a Labour Market Regulatory Authority (LMRA), which introduced two flagship measures – imposing fees on business owners for every foreign worker hired, and the imposition of minimal quotas for hiring local workers – as efforts to nationalise the labour force stepped up. However, their impact was reversed under the pressure of the 2011 popular uprising as the Bahraini government sought to buttress its political support among the business community, which had not fully supported the reforms. Thus, the flat fee of 200 Bahraini Dinars on every expatriate hired on a two-year visa (along with a 10 BD monthly charge) was suspended in April 2011 and only partially reintroduced (at a lower level) in August 2013. As a result, Bahraini scholar Hasan Tariq Alhasan commented in July 2012 that the government had 'driven the last nail into the coffin of the economic and labour market reforms . . . in an attempt to secure political support from the business community.'[76]

The fate of Bahrain's reforms illustrates the challenges of making meaningful and sustained policy changes that confront powerful layers of vested 'political-economic' interests and can survive any resulting pushback by these influential actors. Similar difficulties have been evident in Saudi Arabia with regard to the imposition of national quotas (*nitaqat*) in economic sectors and the resulting anger among economic actors directed towards policymakers and officials.[77] Meanwhile, in Qatar, the glare of the global spotlight on domestic issues such as the treatment of migrant workers has intensified manifold since the awarding of the 2022 FIFA World Cup in December 2010. The furore over the condition of migrant workers that erupted in the British media in the autumn of 2013 provided an early foretaste of the trial by hostile media that awaits all host cities of major sporting events. Front-page headlines in the *Guardian* newspaper investigated the deaths of 49 Nepalese labourers from heart failure or workplace accidents on Qatari construction sites and publicised claims by the International Trade Union Confederation (ITUC) that World Cup preparations could 'cost the lives of at least 4,000 migrant workers before a ball is kicked.'[78] Further articles followed with lurid titles such as 'Revealed: Qatar's World Cup "Slaves,"' 'Qatar's World

Cup "Slaves": the Official Response,' 'Qatar: the Building Site from Hell,' and 'Qatar's World Cup "Slaves": FIFA's UK Representative "Appalled and Disturbed."'[79]

The October 2013 arrest and detention of two German journalists for filming workers on a nearby construction site from the balcony of their Doha hotel highlighted the challenges that lie ahead in adapting to and accommodating greater public interest and media attention.[80] Additional news stories in the following months drew widespread attention to reports of the soaring numbers of deaths among migrant workers, leaving the Qatari authorities struggling to keep up with the sustained level of media interest in the issue.[81] While this may sound surprising for a country that, like Dubai, has thrived on generating high-impact newsworthy stories, the capacity to acknowledge and tolerate legitimate concern and criticism is an area where all GCC states have to date shown serious shortcomings. Moreover, the path dependency of the decision to seek the hosting rights of the 2022 World Cup means that the leadership in Qatar will have to deal with the fallout from each new revelation in the full glare of the international media spotlight. It will not be easy for Qatari officials to shift the narrative away from an issue that large sections of the press have identified as the major public and human interest story surrounding the 2022 World Cup.[82]

The abovementioned issues are all critical factors that will shape and reshape international perceptions of the Gulf States in the years to come. Chapter 4 described some of the inter-regional frameworks, such as the Abu Dhabi Dialogue that brought together the major labour-sending and labour-receiving states in 2008. While subsequent progress towards an equitable minimal working standard has been slow, it remains the case that the Gulf States are among the largest sources of global remittance flows. In 2006, Saudi Arabia was the second-highest remittance sending country in the world and Bahrain the fourth-highest, while Saudi Arabia and Kuwait remitted sums equivalent to 5 and 4 per cent of GDP respectively, with this figure rising to 5.8 per cent for Oman in 2007.[83] By 2012, the aggregate remittance outflow from the Gulf exceeded US$75 billion, a figure 50 per cent higher than the amount remitted from the US that year. In 2014, a study by the newly formed Gulf Labour Markets and Migration (GLMM) network found that the share of remittance outflows from the GCC states came to about one-fifth of the total global remittance flows for 2010, 2011, and 2012.[84] The study also found a high correlation between local instabilities in Gulf economies and the monetary remittance transfers, although it concluded that micro-level data studies of remittance flows 'are non-existent' and need to be developed further order to understand their full impact on sending and recipient economies.[85]

With Dubai set to host the 2020 World Expo and Qatar the FIFA World Cup two years later, the number of large-scale infrastructure projects is likely to accelerate. This, in turn, will create additional demand for migrant labour in the construction sectors in both regions, at least in the short-term, and thicken still further the economic and human linkages between labour-sending states and the Gulf. And yet, commercial interests in securing a supply of cheap labour may clash increasingly with rising societal unease over issues such as the perceived loss of identity or erosion of cultural values. In this regard, public discussion of the demographic imbalance in GCC societies has become a value-laden frame of reference that has added resonance in the politicised post-Arab Spring atmosphere. Emotive and highly charged debates over the idiosyncratic nature of Gulf labour markets will continue to accompany the formulation and implementation of public policies on reforms to migration management and control. Moreover, as the final chapter in this book makes clear, if the deeper structural weaknesses in the political economy of GCC states gradually become fiscally unsustainable, it is the most vulnerable segments of Gulf societies that will be impacted first. For these reasons, the large-scale roundup and deportation of tens of thousands of expatriates from Saudi Arabia and Kuwait may be a harbinger of future flashpoints both within the Gulf States and between the GCC and labour-sending states across Southeast Asia.

9

The Illusion of Security?

This final chapter starts by examining how the regional security land-scape is changing in response to non-traditional and longer-term challenges to stability. The large themes explored in this book, such as the internationalisation of the Gulf, increasingly must coexist alongside potent sources of insecurity stemming from state failure in Yemen, ongoing state weaknesses in Iraq, and the ideational and material threat from Iran. Since late 2010, the Arab Spring has injected powerful new pressures and highlighted the weaknesses of authoritarian regimes in regulating or stemming the flows of new ideas, methods of communication, or patterns of mobilisation. Thus, the rapid technological advances in information and communications pose a qualitatively different threat to Gulf rulers, who have responded with a series of technocratic measures that largely ignored or downplayed the social dimension of the Arab Spring.

The opening section of this chapter focuses on the deeper transitions underway in regional and global security as wars between states gradually give way to conflicts within societies as primary causes of instability. This leads into a second section that charts the growth of non-state threats in the Gulf and the rise of such volatile new actors as al-Qaeda in the 1990s and, a decade later, its regional offshoot, al-Qaeda in the Arabian Peninsula (AQAP). The issues examined in these two sections took place against the backdrop of the fallout from the 2003 US-led invasion, and subsequent occupation, of Iraq. The third section describes the 'geopolitical straitjacket' that arose when Gulf policies to counter the perceived rise of Iranian and Shiite influence in the region became a liability following the sudden emergence of the Islamic State of Iraq and Syria (ISIS, later IS) in 2014. Sections four and five examine how the GCC states responded to the outbreak of Arab Spring protests by developing more assertive and autonomous regional policies designed to protect

and project Gulf leverage over the pace and direction of states and societies in transition.

Regional and global security in transition

The Gulf remains an extremely volatile sub-region of the Middle East,
with multiple interlinking threats to internal and external security alike.
It did not share in the transformation of security that occurred in Latin
America and Eastern Europe in the 1980s and the 1990s. In both regions,
the emergence of new concepts of cooperative security was associated
with a shift away from realist approaches predicated largely on a zero-
sum notion of national security. No such comparative shift took place in
the Gulf, which instead experienced three major inter-state wars based
on regional balance-of-power considerations in the period between 1980
and 2003.[1] And yet, each of the three conflicts – the Iran–Iraq War of
1980–1988, the Iraqi invasion of Kuwait and the subsequent Gulf War in
1990–1991, and the US-led invasion of Iraq in 2003 and its violent aftermath – illustrated how threats to security operated at the transnational
and inter-cultural, as well as traditional inter-state, levels.[2]

The three Gulf Wars decisively altered the positioning of the GCC
states vis-à-vis Iran and Iraq and accelerated their integration into the
Western military and security umbrella, as was noted in Chapter One.
Significantly, they led also to the gradual meshing of US-led and Gulf
States' strategic objectives into an interlocking relationship founded
upon shared interests in regional security. While the US only acquired
large-scale basing rights in the aftermath of the Iraqi invasion of Kuwait
in August 1990, it was developments between 1986 and 1988 that introduced a sizeable external naval force into the Gulf for the first time
since Britain's 1971 military withdrawal from the region. The internationalisation of Gulf waters after 1986 occurred as the US, the United
Kingdom, France, Italy, and the Soviet Union all sent warships to conduct convoy operations that protected Kuwaiti re-flagged and chartered
vessels during the 'Tanker War' phase of the Iran–Iraq War. By the end
of the conflict in August 1988, there were 82 Western vessels, including
33 combat ships, in the Gulf and adjacent waters, along with 23 Soviet
ships, minesweepers, and support vessels.[3]

While the international response to the Tanker War was important,
it was the legacy of decisions taken between August 1990 and February
1991 that subsequently exerted the decisive influence on the evolution
of the Gulf security architecture. The permanent – and increasingly
visible – presence of US troops and bases in the Arabian Peninsula led

to a growing divergence between political and public opinion, as the American military footprint deepened throughout the 1990s. The joint defence agreements signed between the US and Gulf partners shortly after the liberation of Kuwait proved inadequate to deter Saddam Hussein and were hastily reassessed in October 1994 after the Iraqi President massed two Republican Guard divisions near the Kuwaiti border. In response to this act, the Clinton administration in Washington, DC, expanded its naval and military assets in GCC states as part of the 'Dual Containment' approach to Iraq and Iran.[4]

Part of the resulting backlash among segments of Gulf societies arose as a result of the growing influence of Islamism as a social and political force in all GCC states. It also reflected greater popular scepticism of US motives and perceptions of regional threats, particularly after the election of the reformist Mohammed Khatami as President of Iran in 1997. Khatami's election was greeted with cautious optimism in GCC capitals and by efforts to normalise relations between the Gulf States and Iran.[5] The emerging gap between regime and public opinion over foreign and security policy opened up a space for oppositional voices to register their discontent at what Kuwaiti sociologist Ali al-Tarrah labelled the 'smothering embrace' of the US military presence in the Gulf.[6] In Qatar, too, the close official rapport between Qatari and US military and defence interests was not universally acclaimed. Shortly after 9/11, Muhammad al-Musfir, a professor of political science at Qatar University, bluntly told Mary Ann Weaver of *National Geographic*:

> Your military is a very provocative element, and it's not just my students who are saying this. Go to the *suq*. Go downtown. Go to any café. The attitude is decidedly anti-American.[7]

Such ambivalence was most evident among Islamists in the Gulf, although it also encompassed secular and nationalist strands of opinion as well. Most notably, it provided the background to Osama bin Laden's notorious declaration of 'Jihad against Jews and Crusaders' on 23 February 1998. In this proclamation, the dissident ex-Saudi founder of al-Qaeda stated menacingly that

> for over seven years the United States has been occupying the lands of Islam in the holiest of places, the Arabian Peninsula, plundering its riches, dictating to its rulers, humiliating its people, terrorizing its neighbors, and turning its bases in the Peninsula into a spearhead through which to fight the neighboring Muslim peoples.[8]

This statement represented an existential threat to the ideational and moral legitimacy of the Gulf monarchies and was especially potent in Saudi Arabia. Moreover, the advent of the Internet and Arab satellite television channels from the mid-1990s greatly facilitated the spread of oppositional messages and provided new forums for discussion and mobilisation. Although the King Fahd University of Petroleum and Minerals (KFUPM) was the first Saudi institution to connect to the Internet as early as 1993, and Saudi Aramco followed suit in 1995, it was only in January 1999 that public access became widely available through commercial providers. Subsequent usage rose rapidly and the spread of smartphones in the 2010s magnified further the penetrative reach of the Internet in general and online spaces for debate in particular.[9]

Growth of non-state threats

The rise of oppositional movements that benefited from the spread of new information and communication technology highlighted how the internal and external dimensions of security in the Gulf States were interconnected and bound together in the 2000s as never before.[10] The threat this posed both to regional and to global security became dramatically clear when Gulf nationals comprised 17 of the 19 airplane hijackers on 11 September 2001.[11] The attacks on New York and Washington, DC, highlighted the myriad linkages between globalisation and security in an era of intensely transnational and increasingly non-state threats.[12] Al-Qaeda's exploitation of globalising flows of finance and people as it prepared and executed the attacks illustrated the dark side of global interconnections. It also underscored how a profoundly regressive form of globalisation existed as organisations mobilised across states and within societies to compete with progressive (and more conventional) global civil society groups in the new spaces opened up by global processes.[13]

The impact of these changes around the turn of the millennium also accelerated the rise of new forms of 'imagined communities' that both tapped into and fuelled the growing awareness of 'Islamic issues.'[14] For Saudi Arabia, in particular, its leaders' projection of pan-Islamism as a tool of regime legitimacy exposed them to contestation on the same grounds, as Saudi militants travelled abroad to participate in jihad in places as diverse as Afghanistan, Bosnia, Chechnya, and Kashmir. This threat was amplified after the mid-1990s, as the new Arab satellite television channels broadcast daily footage of Muslims suffering elsewhere in the world. The Norwegian academic Thomas Hegghammer cites a Saudi official, responding to the 2003 upsurge of terrorist activity in the kingdom, who acknowledged: 'We encouraged our young men to fight for Islam in Afghanistan. We encouraged our young men to fight for Islam in Bosnia and Chechnya. We encouraged our young men to fight for Islam in Palestine.'[15]

In 2002–2003, the emergence of AQAP and the fallout from the US-led invasion and subsequent occupation of Iraq demonstrated how non-state violence was replacing inter-state conflict as the primary threat to regional security and stability in the Gulf. The declared AQAP objective of forcing the withdrawal of Western forces and influences from the Arabian Peninsula was directed at the core of the Gulf States' domestic and international political economy. Attacks on Western targets and compounds as well as operations such as the failed February 2006 assault on the Abqaiq oil-processing facility were aimed at the heart of the social and commercial contract binding GCC regimes to their societies and to the international system. The choice of Abqaiq was audacious, as the facility is situated close to the massive Ghawar oilfield and up to two-thirds of Saudi oil production passes through it on route to the Ras Tanura refinery and export terminal, itself the largest offshore oil-loading facility in the world.[16]

Shortly afterward, international security expert Paul Rogers noted that al-Qaeda quickly claimed responsibility for the operation as 'part of the project to rid the Arabian Peninsula of the infidels' and intended to stop the 'pillage of oil wealth' from Muslims.[17] For Rogers, the adoption of such economic targets meant that

> the key lesson here is that determined and dedicated insurgents have a capacity to damage the economy of a country that far outweighs their numbers . . . the Abqaiq attack is a sharp reminder of what the Al Qaeda movement could do if it chose to take this route.[18]

Although AQAP was defeated and dismantled within Saudi Arabia by a series of concerted counter-terrorism measures, the January 2009 reconstitution of the organisation in Yemen revived the threat to Saudi Arabia from violent non-state actors. The second iteration of AQAP developed into one of the most dangerous offshoots of al-Qaeda, as it demonstrated both the intent and the capability to undertake attacks against Saudi Arabia and further afield. These included an attempt to assassinate the head of counter-terrorism in Saudi Arabia (and, as of January 2015, the Deputy Crown Prince), Prince Mohammed bin Nayef Al Saud in August 2009 and the abortive effort to bring down a Northwestern airliner over Detroit on Christmas Day 2009. Both attacks only narrowly failed, as did a subsequent plot to detonate two bombs hidden in printer cartridges on US-bound aircraft in October 2010. Memories of the Abqaiq incident also were rekindled by the arrest in 2010 of three AQAP cells, totalling 113 militants (including 58 Saudis and 52 Yemenis) who allegedly were planning suicide assaults on oil facilities in Saudi Arabia.[19]

Contemporaneous developments in Iraq underscored further the growing capacity of non-state actors to destabilise state structures, even if the GCC states predominantly remained largely untouched by any direct spillover from Iraq's multiple and overlapping local conflicts. Thus, the impact on regional stability of the third Gulf war differed qualitatively from its two predecessors, between 1980 and 1991, which primarily were inter-state in nature. The major difference in 2003 was the dynamic interplay between domestic actors and regional and international events in a globalised arena of difficult-to-regulate flows of people, finance, information, and ideas. And yet, the Gulf States not only avoided the worst overspill of conflict from the third Gulf War that began in 2003 but also ensured that patterns of destabilisation actually ran in the opposite direction, as they originated in the GCC and flowed into Iraq.[20]

Governments in the six GCC states all gave varying levels of political logistical assistance to the US-led invasion of Iraq in 2003. The Gulf States' role as administrative facilitators left them vulnerable to considerable levels of domestic opposition, with up to 97 per cent of Saudis opposed to any cooperation with an American attack. Anti-war demonstrations occurred in other Gulf States as well, with those in Bahrain particularly well-attended and prolonged. Policymakers in the GCC were put therefore in the awkward position of having to balance their security ties with the US with high levels of popular opposition to the invasion. This security dilemma prompted many Gulf rulers to distance themselves publicly from the US, while privately offering greater encouragement and support to the effort to oust Saddam Hussein's regime.[21]

The elevated levels of public anger at US actions in Iraq formed part of a broader chorus of anger at the George W. Bush administration's Middle East policies more generally. In March 2007, King Abdullah of Saudi Arabia went as far as to denounce the 'illegitimate foreign occupation' of Iraq in an unprecedented public display of anger at the kingdom's primary security partner. In this environment, the GCC states might have expected significant blowback due to both their geographical proximity to Iraq and their leaders' military and political ties with Washington. This, notably, did not happen, as the Gulf States implemented a range of hard security measures that ensured they remained relatively immune to the cross-border overspill of the multiple indices of human insecurity, such as sectarian conflict, terrorism attacks, and flows of refugees and displaced persons, which impacted Syria and Jordan far more.[22]

Instead, the destabilising flows of men and money ran largely in the opposite direction, from the GCC into Iraq. Between 1,500 and 3,000 Saudi militants joined the Sunni insurgency and constituted a significant proportion (up to 60 per cent) of the total number of foreign fighters in Iraq.[23] In Kuwait, members of two organisations of radical militants – the Peninsula Lions and the Mujahideen of Kuwait – also channelled fighters to the insurgency and mounted a number of attacks on US forces in Kuwait itself. Notably, the emergence of such groups – both in Kuwait and in Saudi Arabia – took the security services by surprise. The then Interior Minister of Kuwait (and, since 2006, Crown Prince) Sheikh Nawaf al-Ahmad Al Sabah linked the growth of the Peninsula Lions to the militant al-Haramain Brigade in Saudi Arabia, and went so far as to allege that 'Initial investigations have proved that the financing of the terrorist elements came from outside the country, specifically from one of the neighboring brotherly countries.'[24]

Such observations fed into broader concerns over the role of Gulf-based individuals and organisations in terror financing networks. After 9/11 but prior to the invasion of Iraq, an independent task force set up by the Council on Foreign Relations to examine the issue concluded bluntly that

> for years, individuals and charities based in Saudi Arabia have been the most important source of funds for Al Qaeda. And for years, Saudi officials have turned a blind eye to this problem.[25]

Four years later, the Iraq Study Group appointed by the US Congress in 2006 to assess the worsening violence and civil war in the country observed that 'funding for the Sunni insurgency comes from private individuals within Saudi Arabia and the Gulf States.'[26] Particular attention focused on the activities of the Saudi-based International Islamic Relief Organization (IIRO), a transnational Muslim humanitarian group, owing to its operations in Falluja and other insurgent strongholds and its exclusion from Saudi charitable regulations.[27] Later, in 2008, the US Treasury ordered the assets of a Kuwaiti charity – the Revival of Islamic Heritage Society – to be frozen owing to its alleged links with al-Qaeda, to a chorus of disapproval among Kuwaiti politicians.[28] A December 2009 diplomatic cable subsequently released by WikiLeaks indicated that Gulf involvement in terror financing remained an issue of concern for US authorities. The cable quoted Secretary of State Hillary Clinton referring to an 'ongoing challenge to persuade Saudi officials to treat terrorist funds emanating from Saudi Arabia as a strategic priority.'[29]

A geopolitical straitjacket

With the direct threat from Iraq contained, regional discourse in the (Arab) Gulf focused instead on the perceived geopolitical and strategic implications of post-occupation Iraq for the balance of regional power. This revolved around GCC leaders' concerns at the expansion of Iranian influence following the removal of Teheran's main counterweight in the Gulf. The Sunni regimes in the Gulf repeatedly expressed varying levels of alarm at the empowerment of Iraqi Shiites, which they feared could stoke unrest or greater political demands from their own Shiite communities. As early as February 2003, Saudi Foreign Minister Prince Saud al-Faisal Al Saud warned President Bush that he would be 'solving one problem and creating five more' if Saddam Hussein was removed by force. In 2005, the prince added that the US was 'handing the whole country over to Iran without reason.' Saudi policy thus focused on preventing certain scenarios, such as the disintegration of Iraq or the complete disempowerment of its Sunni communities, by supporting Sunni Islamist movements within Iraq.[30]

The sectarian lens therefore constituted a powerful filter through which GCC ruling elites viewed developments in Iraq, especially as sectarian violence spiralled between 2005 and 2007. Officials deeply distrusted the government led by Nuri al-Maliki, whom they suspected to be an Iranian proxy and an ideational threat to their own conservative status quo polities. This had significant implications in framing GCC states' policy towards Iraq, generating a self-fulfilling prophecy as the Gulf States' reluctance to expand their political and economic engagement with Baghdad actually enabled Iran to take the lead in many reconstruction and development projects. Thus, while investment from Kuwait and the UAE increased, notably in Iraqi Kurdistan, Saudi Arabia still had not (by 2014) posted a resident Ambassador in Baghdad. Notably, too, the Emir of Kuwait was the only GCC head of state to attend the Arab League Summit that took place in Baghdad in March 2012.[31]

In the aftermath of the final withdrawal of US troops in December 2011, the threat posed by Iraq to Kuwait and its GCC partners was one of a weak state struggling to assert political authority and a monopoly of the use of force over the panoply of non-state groups still operating in the country. This differed significantly from the challenge of a 'strong' Iraq that under Saddam Hussein had faced the region, but ties between Iraq and the GCC struggled to revive during the premiership of Iraqi Prime Minister Nuri al-Maliki (2006–2014). In addition to the aforementioned Gulf scepticism at Maliki's leadership, which intensified as Maliki's authoritarian tendencies became more apparent, the Iraqi Government itself harboured anger and resentment at the GCC states' role in fuelling the insurgency that gathered pace after 2003. The ill-feeling on both sides ultimately magnified the vulnerability of the Gulf monarchies to the threat from IS as it emerged as a destructive regional force in late 2013 and early 2014.[32]

The IS threat to the Gulf States grew rapidly in 2014 as the group seized control of large areas of northern Syria and western Iraq. This meant that the region, and particularly Saudi Arabia, confronted a virulent new non-state threat, nearly a decade after AQAP was banished to Yemen, and new flows of recruits and networks of financing and support from within Gulf societies. Whereas AQAP specifically targeted Western interests in the Gulf States, IS focused on ruthless territorial consolidation in, and resource extraction from, the areas under its control in Iraq and Syria. The Gulf States' subsequent participation in the US-led air campaign against IS targets in Iraq and Syria once again posed a security dilemma for officials forced to balance their security relationship with the US against the threat of backlash from domestic IS sympathisers.[33]

A spate of attacks in Saudi Arabia and one in Abu Dhabi in late 2014 suggested initially that the threat posed by IS to the GCC states arose primarily from 'lone wolf' operations and 'copycat' attacks. Two shootings involving American employees of defence contractor Vinnell left one dead and another wounded in Riyadh in November 2014 and two more employees wounded in the oil-rich Eastern Province in January 2015.[34] Also in November 2014, supporters of IS claimed responsibility for the shooting of a Danish national in the Eastern Province, while a Canadian was stabbed in a random attack at a shopping mall the same month.[35] Most disturbingly, an American teacher was brutally murdered in an upscale shopping mall in Abu Dhabi in early December 2014, weeks after the US Embassy in the UAE warned of jihadi threats to attack Americans in the country.[36] Although there was no evidence that the separate attacks were linked to each other, they constituted an emerging pattern that rattled expatriates and Gulf security services alike.

The above notwithstanding, the GCC states also faced a deeper challenge both internally from networks of IS cells and externally from the flow of Gulf nationals to the IS battlefronts in Iraq and Syria. Risk of blowback was, moreover, amplified in Saudi Arabia and Bahrain owing to the rise in sectarian identity politics and social polarisation in both countries in recent years. The uncovering of several organised IS-linked cells and groups in Saudi Arabia in 2014 illustrated the growing challenge to internal security in the Gulf. The 62 arrested in the first discovery of a terrorist network attributed to IS in May 2014 included 59 Saudis. The group had allegedly been plotting assassinations and other attacks within Saudi Arabia. Four months later, in September, 88 people, including 84 Saudis, were arrested for terrorist recruiting and planning attacks both inside Saudi Arabia and abroad.[37] In November, an assault on Shiite worshippers in the Eastern Province that left eight dead was carried out by a network that had pledged loyalty to the IS leader, Abu Bakr al-Baghdadi, and was in frequent communication with IS in Iraq. Just as three Saudis were behind the November attack, so four Saudis carried out an audacious suicide bombing that killed the commander of Saudi Arabia's border operations in January 2015 after re-entering the kingdom from Iraq's volatile Anbar province.[38]

A disturbing trend that alarmed Saudi officials was the discovery that between half and two-thirds of those detained had previously been arrested on terror-related charges. This called into question the effectiveness of the high-profile de-radicalisation and rehabilitation programme set up by Prince Mohammed bin Nayef Al Saud in the aftermath of the May 2003 AQAP bombings of residential compounds in Riyadh. In addition, the targeting of Saudi Shiite in the November 2014 attack also illustrated the Gulf States' vulnerability to the extremist sectarian narratives propagated by IS. Sectarian tensions rose sharply in the Gulf after 2011 as officials in Saudi Arabia and Bahrain attributed the Arab Spring protests to Iranian (and Shiite) interference. Direct sectarian blowback has been most visible and acute in Bahrain, where the Sunni ruling family and security forces crushed a largely Shiite-led uprising in 2011 that left the country divided along sectarian lines.[39]

An IS video released in September 2014 featured a former official of the Ministry of Interior denouncing Bahrain's decision to join the US-led air strikes on IS and calling on officers in the security services to defect, while another Bahraini from the same influential Sunni al-Binali tribe with close ties to the ruling Al Khalifa family emerged as one of the most senior clerics within the IS 'caliphate' in northern Iraq.[40] Bahraini government unease at the potential danger from within the security forces was evident in their reluctance to take action against IS sympathisers even in the face of public expressions of support for the group. This included acknowledgment by government officials that 'the threat is real, the issue is very serious. These are people from within the security services, from the police and the military.'[41] Alarmingly for the Bahraini authorities, it emerged that IS penetration may have been facilitated by the recruitment (and naturalisation) of thousands of Sunnis from neighbouring states to staff the security services and shift the demographic composition of Bahrain, as detailed in the previous chapter. Veteran journalist Bill Law quotes the aforementioned government source as asking, rhetorically, 'What guarantees do the Al Khalifas [the ruling family] have of protection from the police if the police are not Bahraini but Syrian, Jordanian, Yemeni? What guarantee [is there] that the police are not themselves extremists?'[42]

Having spent much of the period after the 2003 invasion lamenting the plight of Iraq's Sunni communities, and most of 2012 and 2013 channelling support to Sunni rebel groups in Syria, Gulf officials find themselves caught in a geopolitical straitjacket. Policymakers are aware that tactical involvement in the international coalition against IS sits uneasily alongside strategic sympathy with the re-empowerment of Sunnism in Iraq and Syria. Moreover, the gap is likely to widen if the military campaign against IS expands and US forces operating from bases in the Gulf get drawn deeper into the conflict. The interlinking of such sensitive internal (in)security and external (in)stability considerations means that policy responses are likely to be incomplete and ineffective. Saudi Arabia led the Gulf States in listing IS as a terrorist organisation in March 2014 and warning that membership in the group would be punished by lengthy jail sentences. However, countermeasures such as the construction of elaborate boundary defences struggle to address the ideological appeal of IS as long as the sectarian fissures and other tensions in Gulf societies that feed into deeply held grievances remain unresolved.[43]

The Arab Spring

During 2011 a wave of popular protests and intensifying opposition to authoritarian governance began to sweep the Middle East and North Africa. What developed into the Arab Spring led to the rapid fall of long-standing Presidents and leaders in Tunisia, Egypt, Libya, and Yemen and posed a grave challenge to the regime in Syria. Popular anger at economic stagnation and political repression intersected with a disenchanted youthful population wired together as never before. Its size and contagious overspill distinguished the civil uprisings from other previous expressions of discontent.[44] They also revealed the narrow social base of support underpinning longstanding authoritarian rulers, and their reliance on the use of coercion or the threat of force. The popular mobilisation did not spare the GCC states, although the nature and depth of protest varied widely within the Arabian Peninsula. Thus, Qatar and the UAE were relatively less affected by the instability than Bahrain, Oman, and parts of the Eastern Province of Saudi Arabia, while protests in Kuwait followed a distinctly local trajectory that predated 2011.

Although the unrest originated (and was most transformative in) North Africa, it did not spare the Gulf States. The civil uprisings that swept Presidents Ben Ali and Hosni Mubarak from power in Tunisia and Egypt galvanised the popular opposition to the ruling Al Khalifa family in Bahrain. Emboldened protestors voiced demands ahead of the 14 February day of protest for greater political freedom and equality for all Bahrainis. These targeted the regime's policies of fomenting sectarian division to inhibit the emergence of any popular cross-community opposition movement. Moreover, they facilitated the expansion of an already existing social movement of young Bahrainis desiring political reform. Recognition of this popular uprising against them prompted the Al Khalifa ruling family to violently restore political order, ultimately through the use of (Saudi-led) GCC forces and the declaration of a three-month state of emergency that lasted until June 2011.[45] Moreover, attempts to convene a national dialogue in the summer of 2011 and again throughout 2013 faltered as moderate advocates of political compromise became outflanked by hardliners and extremist voices on all sides. At the time of writing in April 2015, there remained little prospect of a lasting political settlement to Bahrain's deep-rooted social and economic inequalities, even though the immediate period of danger to the ruling Al Khalifa family had long since passed.[46]

Kuwait also experienced sustained and large-scale public demonstrations, which escalated sharply following allegations of a massive political corruption scandal in August 2011, and culminated in the dramatic storming of the National Assembly in November and the resignation of the embattled Prime Minister, Sheikh Nasser al-Muhammad Al Sabah, the following month. Predominantly tribal and Islamist opposition candidates then secured a substantial majority in the February 2012 elections to the National Assembly, winning 34 of the 50 seats. Four months later, with tensions between the elected parliament and appointed government soaring, the Constitutional Court annulled the February electoral result on a technicality, and reinstated the previous parliament elected in 2009. This decision sent shockwaves through the political establishment in Kuwait as the reinstated Assembly attempted – and failed – to reconvene. When new elections were finally called in October 2012, they were accompanied by a controversial Emiri decree reducing the number of votes each Kuwaiti could cast from four to one. Opposition politicians and political societies boycotted the subsequent election in December, resulting in an overwhelmingly pro-government parliament before that, too, was declared void by the Constitutional Court in June 2013.[47]

Widespread demonstrations among Shiite communities in Saudi Arabia's Eastern Province began contemporaneously to the Bahraini uprising, and since have turned into 'the largest and longest protest movement in Saudi Arabia's modern history.'[48] However, while protests also occurred in other areas of Saudi Arabia, such as among female university students in the southern city of Abha and among families of detainees in the regime's Najdi heartland of Burayda, they remained isolated from one another and did not coalesce into a concerted protest movement.[49] In Oman, protests in the industrial town of Sohar took place in February and March 2011 and were met with deadly force by state security, while officials in the UAE responded to a petition for political reform by arresting dozens of prominent human rights and opposition activists, closing down non-governmental organisations and international branches of think-tanks, and taking over local civil society organisations.[50] Only Qatar, with its fortuitous combination of large hydrocarbon wealth and a small citizen population, escaped unrest, although even in Doha there were mutterings of discontent at the speed and scale of breakneck economic growth and consequent fears among Qatari nationals of the loss of identity and erosion of values.[51]

The civil uprisings shook the political economy of authoritarian state structures across the Arab world. Mohamed Bouazizi's desperate act of self-immolation in Tunisia in December 2010 resonated powerfully among youthful populations lacking sufficient opportunities for employment or advancement. Additionally, it widened an intergenerational gap between rising demands and the perceived failure of gerontocratic regimes to manage or meet expectations. The spread of the unrest to Bahrain and (to a lesser degree) Oman indicated that mounting discontent was capable of affecting the comparatively richer GCC states as well as the less resource-rich states of North Africa.[52] Notably, the Gulf States shared many of the same conditions – bulging young populations, high youth unemployment and imbalanced labour markets, and authoritarian regimes' reluctance to open up to meaningful political reform – that characterised the protests in Egypt and Tunisia. An example is unemployment among Saudi nationals between the ages of 20–24, which was a reported 38.4 per cent in 2008, with the figure rising to 72 per cent for women alone.[53]

Globalising pressures also played a significant role in creating an enabling environment for the expression and overspill of popular frustration. The appearance of a form of global politics occurred alongside the revolution in information and communication technologies (ICTs). This created new forms of private, public, and increasingly virtual spaces in which to mobilise, organise, and channelise societal demands.[54] Political bloggers were active during the parliamentary elections in Bahrain in 2006 and Kuwait in 2008 and 2009, while online youth networks were important organisers of the 'Orange movement' that secured important changes to the electoral process in Kuwait in 2006.[55] Social networking sites such as Facebook and Twitter, and encrypted communications technologies such as Skype and Blackberry Messenger, emerged as forums for debate, coordination, and unregulated exchanges. In addition, *Al Jazeera*'s coverage of the Egyptian uprising spread transformative images of largely peaceful demonstrations defying political suppression and refusing to submit to the security regimes that had kept authoritarian leaders in power. This was immediately evident in Bahrain, where cafes that usually showed Lebanese music videos instead aired non-stop footage from the enormous demonstrations in Cairo's Tahrir Square.[56]

These new forms of media and communication had the greatest impact on a youthful generation who are highly technology savvy. Their synthesis eroded the system of controls and filters constructed by ministries of information and official government media outlets. Significantly, they constituted social as well as technological phenomena as powerful agents of social change and political empowerment.[57] The social dimension of the Arab Spring transformed notions of entitlement and demands for social justice, public accountability, and political freedoms. It also made possible the leaderless nature of the initial protest movements that successfully enabled demonstrators to evade capture or co-optation by the security services of beleaguered regimes. In addition, the lack of centralised leadership was a first qualitative difference between the Arab Spring and previous bouts of political unrest across the region. Its 'headless' character was critical both to the mass-mobilisation around the universal values of freedom, justice, dignity and human rights in Tunisia and Egypt, and to the emergence of large-scale opposition in the face of intense regime suppression in Libya, Syria, and elsewhere.[58]

Local policy responses to the Arab Spring focused overwhelmingly on short-term measures to blunt or pre-empt the social and economic roots of potential political tensions. These included hand-outs of cash (Kuwait, Bahrain, and the UAE), creating jobs in already saturated public sectors

(Saudi Arabia, Bahrain, Oman), and raising workers' wages and benefits (Qatar, Saudi Arabia, Oman). Steffen Hertog correctly has identified how the most lasting and troubling legacy of the regional upheaval will likely be the legacy of the economic, rather than political decisions, taken to counter the unrest. This is because 'expectations are easy to raise but difficult to curb, creating a ratchet effect that demands ever larger outlays during every political crisis.'[59] The scale of the additional government spending was enormous, with state spending in the six GCC states soaring by 20 per cent during 2011 alone as the measures came into effect.[60]

Saudi Arabia announced two emergency welfare packages collectively worth US$130 billion. This figure exceeded every annual government budget until 2007 and included a provision to employ 60,000 additional Saudis in the Ministry of Interior alone. It also contained stipulations for increasing the minimum wage of public sector employees (but not private sector workers), offering a one-time bonus of a month's pay to all public officials, and constructing 500,000 new homes to combat a crippling shortage of social housing.[61] In Bahrain, the Ministry of Interior promised to create an additional 20,000 new jobs in the public sector, while in Oman, Sultan Qaboos announced 50,000 new public sector jobs as well as a pay increase in February 2011.[62] In the UAE, the federal government in Abu Dhabi moved ahead with infrastructure and welfare spending to quell discontent in the poorer Northern Emirates. Even Qatar, with little to no threat of domestic unrest, announced 60 per cent increases in basic salary, social allowance, and pensions for public officials and 120 per cent rises for military officers in September 2011.[63]

The GCC states also took the regional lead in responding to the unprecedented political and economic changes triggered by the Arab Spring, although they did not operate as a monolithic bloc as Qatar adopted policies that diverged sharply from its Gulf neighbours. Saudi Arabia initially announced generous financial aid packages to Bahrain, Oman, Egypt, and Jordan, pledging US$10 billion aid packages to the former two countries, US$5 billion to Jordan, and significant bilateral assistance to Morocco in 2011.[64] All six GCC states also accelerated their purchase of arms, with weapons sales to the Gulf rising by 70 per cent over five years (and soaring more than 24-fold in the case of Oman) and Saudi Arabia purchasing four times as many major weapons systems between 2010 and 2014 as in the previous five years immediately prior to the Arab Spring (Table 9.1).[65]

King Abdullah also engineered the surprising offer of GCC membership to Jordan and Morocco in May 2011 before announcing his aspiration for closer 'Gulf Union' at the GCC Summit in Riyadh that

Table 9.1   Arms imports by GCC states, 2010–2014 (US$ millions)

Country	2010	2011	2012	2013	2014
Bahrain	17	1	26	76	10
Kuwait	85	113	31	65	591
Oman	30	21	120	490	738
Qatar	30	198	319	73	55
Saudi Arabia	1,020	1,215	899	1,192	2,629
UAE	605	1,210	1,088	2,252	1,031

Source: Stockholm International Peace Research Institute (SIPRI)

December. However, despite Saudi Foreign Minister Prince Saud al-Faisal Al Saud fleshing out the proposals for an integrated military and regional security policy, neither an extraordinary mid-year GCC Consultative Summit in Riyadh in May 2012 nor subsequent annual Summits in Bahrain (December 2012) or Kuwait (December 2013) were able to reach a consensus on the move towards closer political union.[66]

The case of Egypt is worthy of closer study as it not only is the largest and most direct recipient of GCC states' assistance, but also because it highlights the complexities and competing agendas embedded within such support. After the 2011 revolution that ousted President Hosni Mubarak, Saudi Arabia and the UAE backed the Supreme Council of the Armed Forces (SCAF) with financial support and diplomatic recognition. Officials in both Riyadh and Abu Dhabi opted for regime-type continuity in a bid to limit the impact of such rapid and unexpected political change, while Qatar threw its backing behind the Muslim Brotherhood government in Egypt, as Chapter Six documented. Egypt therefore developed into the barometer of post-Arab Spring politics in the Middle East, while Qatar's strained relationships with its Gulf neighbours became a microcosm for the broader tensions between status quo advocates and supporters of political change across the region.[67]

This occurred as Qatar and the UAE clashed sharply over domestic- and regional-level approaches to the perceived Islamist threat in general, and the Muslim Brotherhood in particular. This had immediate and negative consequences in the uprising in Libya against the Gaddafi regime that erupted in Benghazi and Eastern Libya in February 2011. Both Qatar and the UAE were instrumental in rallying the Arab League for intervention and aligning with NATO in support of the creation of a No-Fly Zone in March. However, neither country coordinated their military assistance to the Libyan opposition and in fact supported different rebel brigades on the ground. This complicated the task of unifying the anti-Gaddafi movement from its earliest phase, and contributed to the subsequent splintering of the movement once it was in power after October 2011.[68]

Along with Saudi Arabia and Kuwait, Qatar played a leading role in supporting the opposition to Bashar al-Assad since the beginning of the Syrian uprising in 2011. While Kuwait emerged as a key (unofficial) conduit for financial transfers from the Gulf States to Syria and backing from Saudi Arabia initially took the form of illicit flows of militants and weapons to groups of opposition fighters, Qatar from the start adopted a political approach to organising the Syrian opposition, in addition to providing tens of millions of dollars to rebel groups. Qatari support became increasingly controversial, as it was perceived to be tied to groups linked to the Syrian Muslim Brotherhood. During 2012, Qatar and Saudi Arabia backed competing groups, contributing to the fragmentation of the opposition, before responsibility for the 'Syria file' passed decisively from Doha to Riyadh in spring 2013.[69]

The examples of post-Mubarak Egypt and also of Syria during the civil war suggest that Gulf power players are less inclined to listen to what they perceive as increasingly discredited Western-centric approaches that have, in their view, exacerbated instability in transition states since 2011. Moreover, the Egyptian example also highlights how Gulf actors are not impartial actors that do not take sides in choosing how and to whom to provide aid. The amounts proffered not only were far larger than those from international agencies and had fewer conditions attached to them but also were indelibly linked to particular political *currents* rather than being tied to *outcomes* such as reforms to governance or improvements in transparency. Over the four years since the Arab Spring, the Gulf States therefore aligned their *growing capabilities* (in the political, economic, and security arenas) with a far more expansive *policy intent*. Engaging with a muscular Gulf across the Middle East and North Africa thus is likely to be a feature of the regional landscape for at least the immediate future. It already has presented Western policymakers with difficulties in balancing political and commercial objectives with human rights concerns, notably in Bahrain.

Changing regional enmeshment

As the turmoil across the Middle East and North Africa entered a fourth year in 2015, the role of Gulf countries in influencing the processes of change across the region had evolved substantially. The development of assertive regional policies covering states in political transition and supporting fellow monarchical regimes took place against the backdrop of rising uncertainty about the future role of the US in the Middle East arising from the Obama administration's 'pivot toward Asia.' Kuwaiti academic and foreign policy advisor Abdullah al-Shayeji summarised the sense of regional unease at US and Western approaches: 'The drift and incoherence of US foreign policy under the Obama administration has not gone unnoticed in the Arab world and the Middle East, especially among America's Gulf allies.'[70]

The rise of the Gulf States as regional powers with international reach thus raises a new set of challenges for policymaking in the Middle East and North Africa as the region emerges unsteadily from the Arab Spring. Chief among them is the growing evidence that Gulf officials increasingly seem prepared to 'go it alone' and act unilaterally or, at best, as a loose regional bloc to secure their interests in transition states. This became clear in the launching of air strikes against Houthi rebels in Yemen by a coalition of Gulf and other Arab states led by Saudi Arabia in March 2015 in an effort to restore the ousted President Abd Rabbu Mansour Hadi, whose own appointment as President had been engineered by the GCC states in a carefully negotiated transition of power in 2012.[71]

Set against this backdrop of greater Gulf engagement in international affairs is the gradual reorientation of US foreign policy, away from the Middle East and towards Pacific Asia. While the much-touted 'pivot to Asia' is not about to signify a US disengagement from the Gulf or the broader Middle East region, it illuminated a major strategic rebalancing that reflected how the Obama White House viewed the Pacific Asia region as a new geopolitical centre of gravity. A recent study on the 'pivot' observed how, 'as regional power balances have shifted and US global priorities have changed, Washington's strategy toward the region has likewise evolved.' This encompassed multiple dimensions, included a free trade agreement between the US and South Korea, sustained negotiations to expand and enhance the Trans-Pacific Partnership, participation in the East Asia Summit, and closer military cooperation with the Philippines and the deployment of additional US troops to Australia and Singapore.[72] And yet, the US has a powerful set of overlapping interests with Asian partners when engaging with the Middle East in general and with the Gulf States in particular. With Asian economies all looking to the Gulf as a stable supplier of oil and gas and far more reliant on 'Gulf oil' than the US is (or ever was), there is a shared nexus of US-Asian-Gulf interests in such issues as the security of supply through international sea lanes and regional chokepoints in addition to the maintenance of regional stability more generally.[73]

Although unconnected with wider strategic realignments, US relations with its Gulf partners came under unprecedented strain over the course of the Obama presidency. Beginning with the withdrawal of US support for embattled Egyptian President Hosni Mubarak at the start of the Arab Spring and continuing with (muted) American criticism of the security response in Bahrain as the Al Khalifa ruling family restored order with GCC support, officials in the GCC states began to question US motives as never before. As early as May 2011, influential Saudi foreign policy commentator Nawaf Obaid wrote of a 'tectonic' shift in the US-Saudi relationship and lamented that 'Washington has shown itself in recent months to be an unwilling and unreliable partner' against the supposed regional threat from Iran. In a sign of the growing autonomy of Saudi and other Gulf States' policy calculations, Obaid warned that 'in areas in which Saudi national security or strategic interests are at stake, the Kingdom will pursue its own agenda.'[74]

As Gulf States' frustrations with US policy towards the Arab Spring mounted, declaratory and policy pronouncements became shriller. The failure to take military action against the Bashar al-Assad regime in Syria following the 21 August 2013 use of chemical weapons in Ghouta was greeted with dismay in GCC capitals, as were the signs of a rapprochement between the US and Iran following the election of Hassan Rouhani as President in June 2013. Saudi Arabia's decision that October to turn down one of the ten rotating, non-permanent seats on the United Nations Security Council, weeks after snubbing the annual meeting of the UN General Assembly, revealed the depth of regional alarm at the direction of US policy in the Middle East. The extent of unease became abundantly clear in a characteristically blunt interview given by billionaire Saudi businessman Prince Alwaleed bin Talal Al Saud to the *Wall Street Journal* in November 2013, when he stated belligerently: 'The US has to have a foreign policy, well-defined well-structured. You don't have it right now, unfortunately. It's just completely chaos, confusion.'[75] Shortly after the November 2013 breakthrough at Geneva which produced an interim agreement on Iran's nuclear programme, former Saudi Ambassador to the US Prince Turki al-Faisal Al Saud told an audience at the European Council on Foreign Relations (ECFR) that 'How we feel is that we weren't part of the discussions at all, in some cases we were – I would go so far as to say we were lied to, things were hidden from us.'[76]

Although US–Gulf relations improved somewhat with the shared threat from IS and cooperation in the air campaign in Iraq and Syria in late 2014 as well as logistical and intelligence cooperation in the air strikes against Houthi positions in Yemen in 2015, the Gulf States will continue to adopt more assertive and autonomous regional positions in the immediate future. This reflects the deep scepticism of Gulf officials towards the Obama administration's lengthy negotiations with Teheran that began in 2013 and continued through to the conclusion of the framework agreement in March 2015. Since the Iranian revolution that ousted the Shah in 1979, Saudi Arabia and Iran emerged as bitter rivals for regional ascendancy in the Gulf, with the Saudis providing large-scale support to Saddam Hussein's Iraq during the 1980–1988 Iran–Iraq War. Disputes between Riyadh and Teheran, as leading proponents respectively of Sunni and Shia Islam, frequently took on a sectarian dimension that raised tensions sharply across the Middle East in the decade following 2003.[77]

In addition to the aforementioned Saudi anger at the Iranian nuclear negotiations in Geneva, policymakers in GCC capitals also accused Iran of an escalating intervention in Yemen following the rapid assertion of Houthi rebel control in 2014. Tensions peaked following the Houthi takeover of Sana'a in late 2014 and the ouster of embattled Yemeni President Hadi on the same day in January 2015 as the death of King Abdullah of Saudi Arabia. After Hadi escaped to the southern port city of Aden and re-established a base of control in the city, a further Houthi advance in March 2015 threatened to over-run the city and entrench Houthi – and, in GCC eyes, Iranian – power in Yemen. This led to Saudi Arabia and nine other Arab states, including every Gulf State bar Oman – to launch air strikes on Houthi strongholds in Yemen in Operation Decisive Storm, as the proxy struggle for influence between Iran and Saudi Arabia escalated into outright regional conflict.[78]

The conflict in Yemen highlighted the new assertiveness in GCC policies as the Gulf States acted collectively in a bid to secure regional interests, however narrowly defined. It constituted an important evolution in regional security structures as the locus of decision-making shifted to (Arab) Gulf capitals rather than external partners in Washington, DC, or, earlier, in London. Notably, the Yemen operation marked the first use of the joint military command that was created by the GCC in November 2014, alongside joint naval and police forces.[79] Together with the upsurge in major arms purchases mentioned earlier, they demonstrated the greater willingness of Gulf officials to take decisive action to project (and protect) their regional interests. However, GCC officials do not currently possess a viable alternative to the US-led security guarantee that continues to underpin regional stability. For all their attempts to remake the region in the post-Arab Spring era, it is likely that GCC policies will retain an innate conservatism in an attempt to preserve the interests of status quo powers and limit or contain the prospects for transformative change.

The global emergence of the Gulf States and the new challenges posed by the Arab Spring therefore constitute two diverging trends for the contemporary Gulf. On the one hand is the broader shifts in geo-economic power and the rebalancing of the global order towards multiple centres of political and economic influence, while on the other is the new sense of vulnerability that stability may be more elusive than previously imagined. Thus, the Gulf States find themselves caught between two paradoxical trajectories; able to project their influence and shape changing global institutions and structures, while susceptible to domestic contestation arising from the interlinking of local discontent with regional and international pressures for reform. The interaction of these two diverging trends will profoundly shape the dynamics of the Gulf States' international political economy and international relations in the years and decades ahead.

Conclusion: The Gulf Paradox

Over the decade and a half since the turn of the millennium, the Gulf States have evolved into regional powers with international reach. The chapters in this book have illustrated the scope and scale of the new linkages binding the GCC states to a global order that itself is in a state of flux following the world financial crisis of 2007–2008. Using their substantive energy resources and capital accumulation as leverage, Qatar, the UAE, and even Saudi Arabia became more active in global issues. The emergence of the Gulf States as visible global actors predated the Arab Spring, but accelerated and acquired a potent new dimension once the initial shock of the upheaval had subsided. As a result, the Gulf States led the regional response to the pressures triggered by the political upheaval in a display of 'hard' power that went far beyond the projection of 'soft' and 'smart' power prior to 2011.

Engaging with a muscular Gulf across the Middle East and North Africa already has required Western policymakers to carefully balance security and commercial objectives against concerns for human rights abuses and the constriction of the political space and tolerance of dissent in every GCC state. This has on occasion caused great mistrust and suspicion in the highly charged post-Arab Spring atmosphere, as the GCC states have become more assertive in the international arena and gaps have opened up between established and emergent regional players. Syria offers a salutary example of the difficulties that arise when the international community is divided, and when regional and international actors pursue unilateral policies that follow competing or even contradictory lines.

Even as the GCC states have emerged as key players shaping (and reshaping) the pace and direction of political and economic development in the states that experienced regime transition in 2011, the regional upheaval profoundly impacted their own economic and security dynamics as well. Most notably, the Arab Spring injected urgency into the looming transition from oil-dependent economies towards competitive post-oil economic (and political) structures. In particular, it is likely that policymakers in the Gulf will struggle to roll back subsidies and patterns of wasteful consumption, and that their failure to do so in times of comparative plenty raises the risk that change instead will occur during periods of relative hardship. One can even go so far as to make the argument that current economic models of development, and the current high-intensity consumption of energy, place at risk the viability of the political model that has maintained stability for the past four decades.

This is the acute policy dilemma that may confront officials in GCC states in coming years, as the trade-off between political stability in the short term and economic sustainability in the longer term increasingly resembles a zero-sum game whereby one comes at the expense of the other. It has not been lost on close observers of the Gulf that the instinctive response of ruling elites to the outbreak of the Arab Spring was to intensify the politics of patronage in an effort to pre-empt or blunt socio-economic grievances. In this, they were largely successful in enabling the GCC states to weather the protests, thereby confirming on one level the monarchies as the great survivors of Middle East politics. Taking a longer view, however, it is apparent that the GCC states opted to pursue strategies that maintain the status quo at the expense of the systemic changes to domestic political and economic structures that will inherently be needed to smooth the eventual shift towards a post-oil political economy in the Gulf. This transition will inevitably take place, albeit at different speeds in individual countries, although it may be sooner rather than later, as rising break-even prices of oil and surging domestic consumption eat into export sales and government revenues.

The global emergence of the Gulf States and the new challenges posed by the Arab Spring therefore constitute two diverging trends for the contemporary Gulf. On the one hand are the broader shifts in geo-economic power and the rebalancing of the global order towards multiple centres of political and economic influence, while on the other is the new sense of vulnerability that stability may be more elusive than previously imagined. The sharp drop in international oil prices that commenced in June 2014 and the reconfiguration of the global energy landscape with the rise of shale oil and gas production in North America inject further uncertainties into the policymaking landscape for GCC officials. It is still (at the time of writing) unclear whether recent breakthroughs in tight oil and shale gas extraction amount to an energy 'revolution' or the extent to which they will affect large established players in world energy markets such as Saudi Arabia. Nevertheless, they retain the potential to shift the centre of gravity in world energy markets away (possibly decisively) from the Middle East if capital-intensive development continues to drive down the costs of production.

Moving forward, it is likely that several trends will predominate in the next phase of the Gulf States' global engagement. The first is that it is more likely that future Gulf leverage will be projected on a bilateral basis by individual states rather than inter-regionally through the GCC, which will continue to struggle on 'big issue' consensus (as opposed to practical cooperation on internal security mechanisms). Continued emphasis on state sovereignty and a preference for bilateral policymaking with international partners means that the second trend is the risk that, instead of combining efforts in collaborative initiatives designed to maximise *khaleeji* (Gulf, as opposed to Saudi or Qatari or Emirati) influence, GCC states will end up with overlapping regional financial/logistical/aviation/transportation hubs in an environment already well known for its intense competition. While this carries the danger of oversaturation, it links to the third likely feature of policy, which is that the internationalisation of the Gulf will continue to be based around bilateral economic and strategic partnerships, especially of the kind seen with food-producing nations in Asia and Africa. This is consistent with the Gulf States' record of engaging globally on their own terms so far as possible, working to maximise their leverage within existing and new institutions of (state-centric) international governance.

Notes

Introduction

1 Mohammed al-Fahim, *From Rags to Riches: A Story of Abu Dhabi* (London: London Center of Arab Studies, 1995), p. 55.

2 Abdul Hafeez Yawar Khan Al Yousefi, '50 Years in Al Ain Oasis – Memoirs of Khabeer Khan,' *Liwa: Journal of the National Centre for Documentation and Research*, 5(9), 2013, p. 57.

3 Ibid., p. 15.

4 'Abd Al-Aziz ibn 'Abd-Allah al-Khwaiter, 'King Abdul Aziz: His Style of Administration,' in Fahd al-Semmari (ed.), *A History of the Arabian Peninsula* (London: I.B. Tauris, 2010), pp. 201–2.

5 Tim Niblock with Monica Malik, *The Political Economy of Saudi Arabia* (Abingdon: Routledge, 2007), p. 32.

6 Michael Field, *The Merchants: The Big Business Families of Saudi Arabia and the Gulf States* (Woodstock, NY: The Overlook Press, 1985), p. 321.

7 Michael Herb, *All in the Family: Absolutism, Revolution, and Democracy in the Middle Eastern Monarchies* (Albany, NY: State University of New York Press, 1999), pp. 87–88.

8 The 1990 photograph and a similar view taken in the late 2000s have been reproduced in Jim Krane, *Dubai: The Story of the World's Fastest City* (London: Atlantic Books, 2009).

9 'Photos from 1960s Portray an Abu Dhabi Long Gone,' *The National*, 10 April 2013.

10 Marc Valeri, *Oman: Politics and Society in the Qaboos State* (London: Hurst, 2009), pp. 64–67.

11 J. E. Peterson, 'Oman: Three and a Half Decades of Change and Development,' *Middle East Policy*, 11(2), 2004, p. 126.

12 Jerry Harris, 'Desert Dreams in the Gulf: Transnational Crossroads for the Global Elite,' *Race and Class*, 54(4), 2013, p. 86.

13 John Fox, Nada Mourtada-Sabbah, and Mohammed al-Mutawa (eds.), *Globalization and the Gulf* (London: Routledge, 2006).

14 David Held and Kristian Ulrichsen, *The Transformation of the Gulf: Politics, Economics, and the Global Order* (Abingdon: Routledge, 2011).

15 Kristian Coates Ulrichsen, 'The GCC States and the Shifting Balance of Global Power,' Occasional Paper No. 6, Georgetown University School of Foreign Service in Qatar, 2010; 'Rebalancing Global Governance: Gulf States' Perspectives on the Governance of Globalization,' *Global Policy*, 2(1), 2011a, pp. 65–74; 'Repositioning the GCC States in the Changing Global Order,' *Journal of Arabian Studies*, 1(2), 2011b, pp. 231–247; 'South-South Cooperation and the Changing Role of the Gulf States,' *Brazilian Journal of Strategy & International Affairs*, 1(1), 2012a, pp. 103–124.

16 Thomas Oatley, *International Political Economy* (Cambridge: Pearson, 2nd edition, 2011b).

17 Thomas Oatley, *Debates in International Political Economy* (Cambridge: Pearson, 5th edition, 2011a).
18 Andrew Walter and Gautam Sen, *Analysing the Global Political Economy* (Princeton: Princeton University Press, 2008).
19 John Ravenhill (ed.), *Global Political Economy* (Oxford: Oxford University Press, 2nd edition, 2008).
20 Robert Gilpin, *The Political Economy of International Relations* (Princeton: Princeton University Press, 1987); *Global Political Economy: Understanding the International Political Order* (Princeton: Princeton University Press, 2001); *The Challenge of Global Capitalism: The World Economy in the 21st Century* (Princeton: Princeton University Press, 2002).
21 Richard Beardsworth, *Cosmopolitanism and International Relations Theory* (Cambridge: Polity Press, 2013), p. 2.
22 David Held, 'Global Challenges: Accountability and Effectiveness,' *Open Democracy*, 17 January 2008.
23 David Held, *Global Covenant: The Social Democratic Alternative to the Washington Consensus* (Cambridge: Polity Press, 2004).
24 Fred Halliday, 'Global Governance: Prospects and Problems,' in David Held and Anthony McGrew (eds.), *The Global Transformations Reader: An Introduction to the Globalization Debate* (Cambridge: Polity Press, 2003), p. 496.
25 Jan Aart Scholte, 'Civil Society and Democratically Accountable Global Governance,' in David Held and Matthias Koenig-Archibugi (eds.), *Global Governance and Public Accountability* (Oxford: Blackwell and Wiley, 2005), p. 90.
26 Mary Kaldor, Helmut Anheier, and Marlies Glasius, 'Global Civil Society in an Era of Repressive Globalization,' in Mary Kaldor, Helmut Anheier, and Marlies Glasius (eds.), *Global Civil Society 2003* (Oxford: Oxford University Press, 2003), p. 4.

1   The Gulf and the Global Economy

1 Anoushiravan Ehteshami, *Globalisation and Geopolitics in the Middle East: Old Games, New Rules* (London: Routledge, 2007), p. 110.
2 D. T. Potts, 'The Archaeology and Early History of the Persian Gulf,' in Lawrence Potter (ed.), *The Persian Gulf in History* (New York: Palgrave Macmillan, 2009), pp. 30–32.
3 Thomas Metcalf, *Imperial Connections: India in the Indian Ocean Arena, 1860–1920* (Berkeley, CA: University of California Press, 2007), p. 1.
4 Fahad Ahmad Bishara, 'Mapping the Indian Ocean World of Gulf Merchants, c.1870–1960,' in Abdul Sheriff and Engseng Ho (eds.), *The Indian Ocean: Oceanic Connections and the Creation of New Societies* (London: Hurst, 2014), pp. 78–79.
5 Ibid., p. 79.
6 Michael Field, *The Merchants: The Big Business Families of Saudi Arabia and the Gulf States* (Woodstock, NY: The Overlook Press, 1985), p. 24.
7 James Onley, 'Transnational Merchants in the Nineteenth Century: The Case of the Safar Family,' in Madawi al-Rasheed (ed.), *Transnational Connections and the Arab Gulf* (Abingdon: Routledge, 2005), pp. 68–69.
8 James Onley and Sulayman Khalaf, 'Shaikhly Authority in the Pre-oil Gulf: An Historical-Anthropological Study,' *History and Anthropology*, 17(3), 2006, p. 191.

9   Jill Crystal, *Oil and Politics in the Gulf: Rulers and Merchants in Kuwait and Qatar* (Cambridge: Cambridge University Press, 1990), p. 5.

10 James Onley, 'Britain and the Gulf Shaikhdoms, 1820–1971: The Politics of Protection,' *Occasional Paper* No. 4 (2009), Georgetown School of Foreign Service in Qatar, p. 10.

11 Kamal Osman Salih, 'The 1938 Kuwait Legislative Council,' *Middle Eastern Studies*, 38(1), 1992, p. 77.

12 Mary Ann Tetreault, 'Autonomy, Necessity, and the Small State: Ruling Kuwait in the Twentieth Century,' *International Organization*, 45(4), 1991, p. 577.

13 Michael Herb, *All in the Family: Absolutism, Revolution, and Democracy in the Middle Eastern Monarchies* (Albany, NY: State University of New York Press, 1999), p. 147.

14 Joel Migdal, *Shifting Sands: The United States in the Middle East* (New York: Columbia University Press, 2014), p. 3.

15 Jeffrey Macris, *The Politics and Security of the Gulf: Anglo-American Hegemony and the Shaping of a Region* (Abingdon: Routledge, 2009), p. 99; W. Taylor Fain, *American Ascendance and British Retreat in the Persian Gulf Region* (Basingstoke: Palgrave Macmillan, 2008), p. 133.

16 Ibid.

17 Onley, 'Politics of Protection,' p. 18.

18 Christopher Davidson, *The United Arab Emirates: A Study in Survival* (London: Lynne Rienner, 2005), p. 66.

19 Letter from the Permanent Representative of the People's Democratic Republic of Yemen to the Secretary General of the United Nations, 26 November 1973. London: The National Archives, File FCO 8/2037.

20 Odd Arne Westad, *The Global Cold War: Third World Interventions and the Making of Our Times* (Cambridge: Cambridge University Press, 2005), p. 3.

21 Migdal, *Shifting Sands*, pp. 54–55.

22 Abdul-Reda Assiri, *Kuwait's Foreign Policy: City-State in World Politics* (Boulder, CO: Westview Press, 1990), p. 26.

23 Mahmoud Ghafouri, 'China's Policy in the Persian Gulf,' *Middle East Policy*, 16(2), 2009, p. 83.

24 Fred Halliday, *The Middle East in International Relations: Power, Politics, and Ideology* (Cambridge: Cambridge University Press, 2005), pp. 122–123.

25 Roger Hardy, 'Ambivalent Ally: Saudi Arabia and the "War on Terror,"' in Madawi al-Rasheed (ed.), *Kingdom without Borders: Saudi Arabia's Political, Religious and Media Frontiers* (London: Hurst, 2008), p. 101.

26 John Bullock, *The Gulf: A Portrait of Kuwait, Qatar, Bahrain and the UAE* (London: Century Publishing, 1984), p. 119.

27 Crystal, *Oil and Politics in the Gulf*, pp. 5–6.

28 Rosemarie Said Zahlan, *The Making of the Modern Gulf States* (Reading: Ithaca Press, 1998), p. 26.

29 Tim Niblock with Monica Malik, *The Political Economy of Saudi Arabia* (Abingdon: Routledge, 2007), p. 36.

30 Sarah Yizraeli, *The Remaking of Saudi Arabia* (Tel Aviv: The Moshe Dayan Center for Middle Eastern and African Studies, 1997), pp. 102–103.

31 Michael Casey, *The History of Kuwait* (Westport, CT: Greenwood Press, 2007), pp. 58–59.

32   Matthew Gray, *Qatar: Politics and the Challenges of Development* (Boulder, CO: Lynne Rienner, 2013), pp. 30–32.
33   Davidson, *The United Arab Emirates*, pp. 100–101.
34   Christopher Davidson, *Abu Dhabi: Oil and Beyond* (London: Hurst, 2009), p. 50.
35   Marc Valeri, *Oman: Politics and Society in the Qaboos State* (London: Hurst, 2009), pp. 72–73.
36   Niblock with Malik, *Political Economy*, pp. 36–37.
37   Ibid., p. 39.
38   Said Zahlan, *Modern Gulf States*, p. 39.
39   Laura El-Katiri, Bassam Fattouh, and Paul Segal, 'Anatomy of an Oil-Based Welfare State: Rent Distribution in Kuwait,' in David Held and Kristian Ulrichsen (eds.), *The Transformation of the Gulf: Politics, Economics and the Global Order* (Abingdon: Routledge, 2011), p. 167.
40   Pascal Menoret, *Joyriding in Riyadh: Oil, Urbanism, and Road Revolt* (Cambridge: Cambridge University Press, 2014), p. 125.
41   Yizraeli, *Remaking of Saudi Arabia*, p. 184.
42   Pete Moore, *Doing Business in the Middle East: Politics and Economic Crisis in Jordan and Kuwait* (Cambridge: Cambridge University Press, 2004), p. 85.
43   Giacomo Luciani, *The Arab State* (London: Routledge, 1990), p. 69.
44   Simon Bromley, *Rethinking Middle East Politics: State Formation and Development* (Cambridge: Polity Press, 1994), p. 120.
45   'Bahrain-Saudi Arabia Ties Stronger than Ever,' *Saudi Gazette*, 28 July 2011.
46   Robin Mills, *The Myth of the Oil Crisis* (Westport, CT: Praeger Publishers, 2008), p. 58.
47   David Roberts, 'British National Interest in the Gulf: Rediscovering a Role?,' *International Affairs*, 90(3), 2014a, p. 671.
48   Roger Owen, 'One Hundred Years of Middle Eastern Oil,' *Middle East Brief* No. 24, Brandeis University, Crown Center for Middle East Studies (January 2008), p. 1.
49   Sara Bazoobandi, *The Political Economy of the Gulf Sovereign Wealth Funds: A Case Study of Iran, Kuwait, Saudi Arabia and the United Arab Emirates* (Abingdon: Routledge, 2013), pp. 38–39.
50   Sharon Shochat, 'The Gulf Cooperation Council Economies: Diversification and Reform,' London: LSE Kuwait Programme Introductory Paper, 2008, pp. 7–8.
51   Steffen Hertog, 'The Current Crisis and Lessons of the 1980s,' *Arab Reform Bulletin*, July 2009.
52   Hazem Beblawi, 'The Rentier State in the Arab World,' in Giacomo Luciani (ed.), *The Arab State* (London: Routledge, 1990), pp. 87–89.
53   Giacomo Luciani, 'Allocative vs Production States: A Theoretical Framework,' in Luciani (ed.), *The Arab State*, pp. 71–72.
54   Ibid., p. 76.
55   Niblock with Malik, *Political Economy*, pp. 56, 75, 91.
56   Steffen Hertog, *Princes, Brokers, and Bureaucrats: Oil and the State in Saudi Arabia* (Ithaca, NY: Cornell University Press, 2010), pp. 28–29.
57   Gwenn Okruhlik, 'Rentier Wealth, Unruly Law, and the Rise of Opposition: The Political Economy of Oil States,' *Comparative Politics*, 31(3), 1999, pp. 27–28.

58 'Interview with Dr. Ali Khalifa Al Kuwari, Author of "The People Want Reform . . . in Qatar, Too,"' *Heinrich Boll Stiftung*, October 2012, http://www.lb.boell.org/web/52-1170.html (accessed 3 February 2014).

59 Robert Vitalis, *America's Kingdom: Mythmaking on the Saudi Oil Frontier* (Stanford, CA: Stanford University Press, 2007), pp. 218–224.

60 Fred Halliday, *Arabia without Sultans* (London: Penguin Books, 2002 edition), pp. 443–446.

61 Nelida Fuccaro, 'Shaping the Urban Life of Oil in Bahrain: Consumerism, Leisure, and Public Communication in Manama and in the Oil Camps, 1932–1960s,' *Comparative Studies of South Asia, Africa and the Middle East*, 33(1), 2013, p. 59.

62 Ibid., p. 61.

63 Reem Alissa, 'The Oil Town of Ahmadi since 1946: From Colonial Town to Nostalgic City,' *Comparative Politics of South Asia, Africa and the Middle East*, 33(1), 2013, pp. 43–47.

64 Adam Hanieh, *Capitalism and Class in the Gulf Arab States* (New York: Palgrave Macmillan, 2011), p. 69.

65 Valerie Marcel, *Oil Titans: National Oil Companies in the Middle East* (London: The Royal Institute of International Affairs, 2006), p. 28.

66 Hanieh, *Capitalism and Class*, p. 69.

67 J. E. Peterson, 'Rulers, Merchants, and Shaykhs in Gulf Politics: The Function of Family Networks,' in Alanoud Alsharekh (ed.), *The Gulf Family: Kinship Policies and Modernity* (London: Saqi Books, 2007), p. 29.

68 Gwenn Okruhlik and Patrick Conge, 'National Autonomy, Labor Migration and Political Crisis: Yemen and Saudi Arabia,' *Middle East Journal*, 51(4), 1997, p. 556.

69 Ehteshami, *Globalisation and Geopolitics*, p. 110.

70 John Fox, Nada Mourtada-Sabbah and Mohammed al-Mutawa, 'The Arab Gulf Region: Traditionalism Globalized or Globalization Traditionalized?' in John Fox, Nada Mourtada-Sabbah and Mohammed al-Mutawa (eds.), *Globalization and the Gulf* (London: Routledge, 2006), p. 3.

71 Peterson, 'Rulers Merchant, and Shaykhs,' p. 24.

72 Author observations and interviews in Bahrain (December 2008 and October 2009), Dubai (December 2011), Abu Dhabi (May 2012), Kuwait (December 2011 and March 2013), Qatar (May 2013 and February 2015), and Saudi Arabia (March and December 2014).

73 'Kio's Spanish Inquisition: The Growing Scandal of Kuwait's Massive Losses is Exposing the Dirty Linen of One of the World's Most Secretive Investment Agencies and Ringing Government Alarm Bells. As the Feud Spills into the Courts, Justin Webster Looks at what Lies Behind the Grupo Torras Disaster,' *The Independent*, 10 January 1993.

74 Ibid.

2 Small States in World Politics

1 Anne-Marie Slaughter, *A New World Order* (Princeton: Princeton University Press, 2004), pp. 16–17.

2 David Held and Anthony McGrew, 'The Great Globalization Debate,' in David Held and Anthony McGrew (eds.), *The Global Transformations Reader* (Cambridge: Polity Press, 2003), p. 40.

3   Ngaire Woods, 'Global Governance and the Role of Institutions,' in David Held and Anthony McGrew (eds.), *Governing Globalization: Power, Authority and Global Governance* (Cambridge: Polity Press, 2002), p. 26.

4   Justin Dargin, 'Introduction,' in Justin Dargin (ed.), *The Rise of the Global South: Philosophical, Geopolitical and Economic Trends of the 21st Century* (Singapore: World Scientific Publishing, 2013), p. xxiv.

5   Yezid Sayigh and Avi Shlaim, 'Introduction,' in Yezid Sayigh and Avi Shlaim (eds.), *The Cold War and the Middle East* (Oxford: Clarendon Press, 1997), pp. 2–3.

6   Fred Halliday, *The Middle East in International Relations: Power, Politics and Ideology* (Cambridge: Cambridge University Press, 2005), p. 97.

7   Andrew Cooper and Bessma Momani, 'Qatar and Expanded Contours of Small State Diplomacy,' *The International Spectator: Italian Journal of International Affairs*, 46(3), 2011, p. 114.

8   Robert Cox, 'Ideologies and the New International Economic Order: Reflections on Some Recent Literature,' *International Organization*, 33(2), 1979, pp. 260–263.

9   Samir Amin, 'After the New International Economic Order: The Future of International Economic Relations,' *Journal of Contemporary Asia*, 12(4), 1982, p. 432.

10 Miguel Wionczek, 'The New International Economic Order: Past Failures and Future Prospects,' *Development and Change*, 10(4), 1979, p. 647.

11 Kristian Coates Ulrichsen, 'Security Policy of the Gulf States: Bahrain, Kuwait and Qatar,' *ORIENT: German Journal for Politics, Economics and Culture of the Middle East*, 52(1), 2011, p. 24.

12 J. E. Peterson, 'Sovereignty and Boundaries in the Gulf States: Setting the Peripheries,' in Mehran Kamrava (ed.), *International Politics of the Persian Gulf* (New York: Syracuse University Press, 2011), p. 21; Richard Schofield, 'Boundaries, Territorial Disputes and the GCC States,' in David Long and Christian Koch (eds.), *Gulf Security in the Twenty-First Century* (Abu Dhabi: Emirates Centre for Strategic Studies and Research, 1997), pp. 144–145.

13 Daniel Yergin, *The Quest: Energy, Security, and the Remaking of the Modern World* (London: Allen Lane, 2011), pp. 10–11.

14 Anthony Cordesman, *Kuwait: Recovery and Security after the Gulf War* (Boulder, CO: Westview Press, 1997), pp. 127–128.

15 Kristian Coates Ulrichsen, *Insecure Gulf: The End of Certainty and the Transition to the Post-Oil Era* (London: Hurst, 2011), pp. 70–71.

16 Jacqueline Armijo, 'DragonMart: The Mega-Souk of Today's Silk Road,' *Middle East Report*, 270 (Spring 2014), p. 30.

17 'Prime Minister Dr. Manmohan Singh's Speech at the Inauguration of the Centre for West Asian Studies, Jamia Millia Islamia University, New Delhi, 29 January 2005,' in I. P. Khola (ed.), *India and the Gulf* (New Delhi: Association of Indian Diplomats, 2009), p. 80.

18 Coates Ulrichsen, *Insecure Gulf*, pp. 70–71.

19 Andrew Kennedy, 'China's New Energy Security Debate,' *Survival*, 52(3), 2010, p. 142.

20 'Abu Dhabi Signs Nuclear Power Deal with South Korean Group,' *The National*, 28 December 2009.

21 'South Korea, UAE to Cooperate on Energy Exploration, Stockpiling of Oil,' *Bloomberg*, 2 August 2010.

22 'South Korea Sends More Troops to Train UAE in Counter-Terrorist Skills,' *The National*, 12 July 2011.

23 'Abu Dhabi and South Korea Form Oil Partnership in the Emirate,' *The National*, 5 March 2012.

24 Ibid.

25 Anoushiravan Ehteshami and Steven Wright, 'Political Change in the Arab Oil Monarchies: From Liberalization to Enfranchisement,' *International Affairs*, 83(5), 2005, p. 930.

26 Steven Wright, 'US Foreign Policy and the Changed Definition of Gulf Security,' in Anoushiravan Ehteshami and Steven Wright (eds.), *Political Reform in the Middle East Oil Monarchies* (Reading: Ithaca Press, 2008), p. 240.

27 Kristian Coates Ulrichsen, 'Gulf Security: Changing Internal and External Dynamics,' London: LSE Kuwait Programme Working Paper No. 3 (2009), p. 20.

28 Marina Ottaway, 'Evaluating Middle East Reform: How Do We Know When It is Significant?,' Washington, DC: Carnegie Endowment for International Peace, *Working Papers: Middle East Series*, No. 56 (2005), p. 6.

29 Gerd Nonneman, 'Political Reform in the Gulf Monarchies: From Liberalization to Democratization? A Comparative Perspective,' in Ehteshami and Wright (eds.), *Reform in the Middle East Oil Monarchies*, pp. 29–30.

30 Daniel Brumberg, 'Liberalization versus Democracy: Understanding Arab Political Reform,' Washington, DC: Carnegie Endowment for International Peace, *Working Papers: Middle East Series*, No. 37 (2012), p. 12.

31 Mary Ann Weaver, 'Democracy by Desire: Can One Man Propel a Country into the Future?,' *The New Yorker*, 20 November 2000, quoted in Anthony Cordesman and Khalid al-Rodhan, *The Gulf Military Forces in an Age of Asymmetric Warfare: Qatar* (Washington, DC: Center for Strategic and International Studies, 2006), pp. 12–13.

32 Martin Hvidt, 'The Dubai Model: An Outline of Key Development-Process Elements in Dubai,' *International Journal of Middle East Studies*, 41(2), 2009, p. 401.

33 Jim Krane, *Dubai: The Story of the World's Fastest City* (London: Atlantic Books, 2009), p. 190.

34 'Mohammed Alabbar – Uncensored,' *ArabianBusiness.com*, 12 April 2015.

35 Ibid., p. 404.

36 Kristian Coates Ulrichsen, *Qatar and the Arab Spring* (Oxford: Oxford University Press, 2014), p. 26.

37 Louay Bahry, "The New Arab Media Phenomenon: Qatar's Al Jazeera," *Middle East Policy*, 8(2), 2001, p. 89.

38 Jill Crystal, "Economic and Political Liberalization: Views from the Business Community," in Joshua Teitelbaum (ed.), *Political Liberalization in the Persian Gulf* (London: Hurst, 2009), pp. 41–42.

39 Matthew Gray, *Qatar: Politics and the Challenges of Development* (Boulder, CO: Lynne Rienner, 2013), p. 94.

40 Jean-Francois Seznec and Mimi Kirk, "Introduction," in Jean-Francois Seznec and Mimi Kirk (eds.), *Industrialization in the Gulf: A Socioeconomic Revolution* (London: Routledge, 2011), p. 8.

41 "Gas Status Puts Country at Centre of Global Forces," *Financial Times*, 17 December 2011.

42 Neil Quilliam, 'Political Reform in Bahrain: The Turning Tide,' in Ehteshami and Wright (eds.), *Reform in the Middle East Oil Monarchies*, p. 83.
43 Ibid., pp. 84–85.
44 Justin Gengler, 'Royal Factionalism, the Khawalid, and the Securitization of "the Shi'a Problem" in Bahrain,' *Journal of Arabian Studies*, 3(1), 2013, p. 57.
45 Michael Herb, *All in the Family: Absolutism, Revolution, and Democracy in the Middle Eastern Monarchies* (Albany, NY: State University of New York Press, 1999), pp. 80–83.
46 Held and McGrew, 'The Great Globalization Debate,' pp. 3–4.
47 Thomas Juneau, 'U.S. Power in the Middle East: Not Declining,' *Middle East Policy*, 21(2), 2014, p. 40.
48 Joseph Nye, *Bound to Lead: The Changing Nature of American Power* (New York: Basic Books, 1990).
49 cf. Joseph Nye, *Soft Power: The Means to Success in World Politics* (New York: PublicAffairs, 2004).
50 Ibid.
51 David Held and Kristian Coates Ulrichsen, *The End of the American Century: From 9/11 to the Arab Spring* (Cambridge: Polity Press, 2016), forthcoming.
52 Joseph Nye, *The Future of Power* (New York: PublicAffairs, 2011), p. xiii.
53 Lawrence Rubin, 'A Typology of Soft Powers in Middle East Politics,' *Working Paper* No. 5, December 2010, Dubai: The Dubai Initiative, pp. 7–20.
54 Mehran Kamrava, *Qatar: Small State, Big Politics* (New York: Cornell University Press, 2013), pp. 60–61.
55 Kristian Coates Ulrichsen, 'The GCC States and the Shifting Balance of Global Power,' *Occasional Paper* No. 6, Georgetown University School of Foreign Service in Qatar: Center for International and Regional Studies, Doha, 2010, p. 17.
56 Mary Ann Tetreault, 'Autonomy, Necessity, and the Small State: Ruling Kuwait in the Twentieth Century,' *International Organization*, 45(4), 1991, p. 567.
57 J. E. Peterson, 'Qatar and the World: Branding for a Micro-State,' *Middle East Journal*, 60(4), 2006, p.741.
58 William Hague, 'Foreword,' in John Holden (ed.), *Influence and Attraction: Culture and the Race for Soft Power in the 21st Century* (London: British Council & Demos, 2013), p. 2.
59 'The Global Race for Influence and Attraction: The Role of the State,' University of Cambridge/YouGov Cambridge Programme' online commentary, 25 September 2013.
60 Author interviews in Saudi Arabia and Qatar (December 2014).
61 Peter van Ham, 'Place Branding: The State of the Art,' *The ANNALS of the American Academy of Political and Social Science*, 616(1), 2008, p. 127.
62 Ibid., p. 126.
63 Ibid.
64 Author interviews and research in Bahrain, Kuwait, Qatar, Saudi Arabia, and the United Arab Emirates between 2008 and 2015.
65 Michael Stephens, 'Qatar's Public Diplomacy Woes,' *Open Democracy*, 4 February 2013.
66 Author interviews in Bahrain, December 2008 and October 2009.
67 Thus, posters bearing the 'Bahrain: Back to Business' slogan were displayed prominently throughout London's Heathrow Airport.

68   Coates Ulrichsen, *Qatar and the Arab Spring*, p. 71.

69   David Roberts, 'Understanding Qatar's Foreign Policy Objectives,' *Mediterranean Politics*, 17(2), 2012, p. 239.

70   Author interview, Washington, DC, January 2009.

71   Steve Coll, *Private Empire: ExxonMobil and American Power* (London: Allen Lane, 2012), pp. 541–542.

72   'Royal Ascot Breaks Tradition with Qatari Sponsorship,' *Financial Times*, 16 June 2014.

73   Coates Ulrichsen, *Qatar and the Arab Spring*, p. 61.

74   'Al-Khalifa Links with Formula One,' *Gulf States Newsletter*, 36(922), 26 April 2012, p. 3.

75   'Football Crosses New Frontier as Qatar Wins World Cup Vote for 2022,' *The Guardian*, 3 December 2010.

76   Full details of the values that drive the Aspire Academy and its various programmes are available at www.aspire.qa (accessed 24 July 2012).

77   'Plot to Buy the World Cup,' *The Sunday Times*, 1 June 2014.

78   'Emirates Said to Spend $100m on FIFA Sponsorship in Four Years,' *ArabianBusiness.com*, 18 July 2014.

79   David Goldblatt, *Futebol Nation: The Story of Brazil through Soccer* (New York: Penguin Books, 2014), p. 239.

80   'Barcelona Reveals Financial Details Behind Qatar Airways Deal,' *Goal.com*, 28 August 2013.

81   'Abu Dhabi Accused of "Using Manchester City to Launder Image,"' *The Guardian*, 30 July 2013.

82   'Real Madrid Agree "Strategic Partnership" with Abu Dhabi's IPIC,' *The Guardian*, 28 October 2014.

83   'Can Paris Saint-Germain Become the World's Richest Sports Club?,' *Financial Times*, 28 March 2014.

3   State Capitalism and Strategic Niches

1   Farah al-Nakib, 'Kuwait's Modern Spectacle: Oil Wealth and the Making of a New Capital City, 1950–90,' *Comparative Studies of South Asia, Africa and the Middle East*, 33(1), 2013, p. 10.

2   Stephen Ramos, *Dubai Amplified: The Engineering of a Port Geography* (London: Ashgate, 2012), p. 86.

3   Pascal Menoret, *Joyriding in Riyadh: Oil, Urbanism, and Road Revolt* (Cambridge: Cambridge University Press, 2014), pp. 87–101.

4   Agatino Rizzo, 'Rapid Urban Development and National Master Planning in Arab Gulf Countries. Qatar as a Case Study,' *Cities*, 39, 2014, p. 51.

5   Sarah Yizraeli, *Politics and Society in Saudi Arabia: The Crucial Years of Development, 1960–1982* (New York: Columbia University Press, 2012), pp. 62, 124, 142.

6   'Former US President Praises New York University Abu Dhabi for Tackling Labour Welfare Allegations,' *The National*, 25 May 2014.

7   'Barca Coach Joins Qatar World Cup 2022 Bid,' *ArabianBusiness.com*, 23 February 2010; 'Zidane Named Qatar's World Cup Bid Ambassador,' *ArabianBusiness.com*, 17 September 2010.

8   'Revealed: Gulf Payments to British MPs,' *ArabianBusiness.com*, 8 January 2013.
9   Kristian Coates Ulrichsen, *Insecure Gulf: The End of Certainty and the Transition to the Post-Oil Era* (London: Hurst, 2011), p. 101.
10 'Oman: Selected Economic Indicators, 2010–18,' Table 1 in 'Oman – 2013 Article IV Consultation Concluding Statement of the IMF Mission,' 14 May 2013, https://www.imf.org/external/np/ms/2013/051413.htm
11 Steffen Hertog, 'Arab Gulf States: An Assessment of Nationalisation Policies,' *Gulf Labour Markets and Migration (GLMM) Research Paper*, RP-No. 1/2014, pp. 8–9.
12 Jeffrey Nugent, 'US-Bahrain Relations,' in Robert Looney (ed.), *Handbook of US-Middle East Relations: Formative Factors and Regional Perspectives* (Abingdon: Routledge, 2014), p. 447.
13 Martin Hvidt, 'Economic Diversification in GCC Countries: Past Record and Future Trends,' London: LSE Kuwait Programme Working Paper No. 27, 2013, p. 18.
14 'DCTPB Unveils New Advertising Campaign,' *Emirates News*, 8 December 1992.
15 Ministry of Cabinet Affairs, United Arab Emirates, 'UAE Vision 2021,' available online at http://www.moca.gov.ae/?page_id=620&lang=en
16 Coates Ulrichsen, *Insecure Gulf*, p. 101.
17 Hvidt, 'Economic Diversification,' p. 26.
18 'Nakilat Building a World-Class Shipping Fleet,' *Middle East Economic Digest*, 21 January 2010.
19 Rodney Wilson, 'Economic Governance and Reform in Saudi Arabia,' in Anoushiravan Ehteshami and Steven Wright (eds.), *Political Reform in the Middle East Oil Monarchies* (Reading: Ithaca Press, 2008), pp. 137, 144.
20 Makio Yamada, 'Gulf-Asia Relations as "Post-Rentier" Diversification? The Case of the Petrochemical Industry in Saudi Arabia,' *Journal of Arabian Studies*, 1(1), 2011, pp. 101–103.
21 Steffen Hertog, *Princes, Brokers, and Bureaucrats: Oil and the State in Saudi Arabia* (Ithaca, NY: Cornell University Press, 2010), pp. 100–101.
22 'Blair's "Kuwait Vision 2035" Report Proposes Solutions to Key Issues – Min,' *Kuwait News Agency*, 15 March 2010.
23 Author interviews, Kuwait City, February 2012.
24 http://www.al-monitor.com/pulse/business/2014/04/kuwait-development-plan-fails-achieve-goals.html
25 Ian Bremmer, 'State Capitalism Comes of Age,' *Foreign Affairs*, 88(3), May/June 2012, pp. 40–55.
26 'The Rise of State Capitalism,' *The Economist*, 21 January 2012.
27 'The Rise of Innovative State Capitalism,' *Bloomberg Businessweek*, 28 June 2012.
28 Martin Hvidt, 'The Dubai Model: An Outline of Key Development-Process Elements in Dubai,' *International Journal of Middle East Studies*, 41(2), 2009, p. 412.
29 Ibid., p. 399.
30 Christopher Davidson, 'Diversification in Abu Dhabi and Dubai: The Impact of National Identity and the Ruling Bargain,' in Alanoud Alsharekh and Robert Springborg (eds.), *Popular Culture and Political Identity in the Arab Gulf States* (London: Saqi Books, 2008a), p. 143.

31 Steffen Hertog, 'Lean and Mean: The New Breed of State-owned Enterprises in the Gulf Monarchies,' in Jean-Francois Seznec and Mimi Kirk (eds.), *Industrialization in the Gulf: A Socioeconomic Revolution* (London: Routledge, 2011), p. 18.

32 Steffen Hertog, 'The Private Sector and Reform in the Gulf Cooperation Council,' London: LSE Kuwait Programme Working Paper No. 30, July 2013, p. 1.

33 Anders Holmen Gulbrandsen, 'Bridging the Gulf: Qatari Business Diplomacy and Conflict Mediation,' Unpublished MA Thesis, Georgetown University, 2010, p. 17.

34 Ibid.

35 Christopher Davidson, *Dubai: The Vulnerability of Success* (London: Hurst, 2008), p. 102.

36 Jim Krane, *Dubai: The Story of the World's Fastest City* (New York: St Martin's Press, 2009), p. 184.

37 Christopher Davidson, 'The Dubai Model: Diversification and Slowdown,' in Mehran Kamrava (ed.), *The Political Economy of the Persian Gulf* (London: Hurst, 2012), pp. 204–206.

38 Laura El-Katiri, 'Energy Sustainability in the Gulf States: The Why and the How,' Oxford: Oxford Institute for Energy Studies (2013), p. 7, Table 1.

39 Mohammed Raouf, 'Climate Change Threats, Opportunities, and the GCC Countries,' Washington, DC: Middle East Institute, *Policy Brief No. 12*, 2008, p. 15.

40 Mari Luomi, 'Gulf of Interest: Why Oil Still Dominates Middle Eastern Climate Politics,' *Journal of Arabian Studies*, 1(2), 2011, p. 252.

41 Joanna Depledge, 'Striving for No: Saudi Arabia in the Climate Change Regime,' *Global Environmental Politics*, 8(4), 2008, p. 20.

42 Kristian Coates Ulrichsen, 'Rebalancing Global Governance: Gulf States' Perspectives on the Governance of Globalization,' *Global Policy*, 2(1), 2011a, p. 71.

43 Mari Luomi, *The Gulf Monarchies and Climate Change: Abu Dhabi and Qatar in an Era of Natural Unsustainability* (London: Hurst, 2012), pp. 125–127.

44 Ibid., p. 209.

45 Ian Jackson, 'Nuclear Energy and Proliferation Risks: Myths and Realities in the Persian Gulf,' *International Affairs*, 85(6), 2009, p. 1157.

46 'US-UAE Nuclear Deal to Take Effect Soon – State Dept,' *Reuters*, 22 October 2009.

47 Christopher Blanchard, 'United Arab Emirates Nuclear Program and Proposed U.S. Nuclear Cooperation,' *CRS Report for Congress* (Washington, DC: Congressional Research Service, 2010), p. 11.

48 Glada Lahn and Paul Stevens, '*Burning Oil to Keep Cool: The Hidden Energy Crisis in Saudi Arabia,*' London: Chatham House, 2011, p. 3.

49 'The Big Gamble in the Saudi Desert,' *Science*, 326, 16 October 2009, pp. 354–357.

50 'Saudi Aramco to Invest in New Energy Ventures,' *Reuters*, 9 July 2012.

51 Kristian Coates Ulrichsen, *Qatar and the Arab Spring* (Oxford: Oxford University Press, 2014), p. 52.

52 Anh-Hao Thi Phan, 'A New Paradigm of Educational Borrowing in the Gulf States: The Qatari Example,' *Middle East Institute Viewpoints: Higher Education and the Middle East* (Washington, DC: Middle East Institute, 2010), p. 34.

53 Coates Ulrichsen, *Qatar and the Arab Spring*, p. 53.
54 'QNRF Awards $121 Million in Research Funding to National Priority Projects,' *QNRF Newsletter*, Issue 12, August 2013.
55 Kristian Coates Ulrichsen, 'Knowledge-Based Economies in the GCC,' in Mehran Kamrava (ed.), *The Political Economy of the Persian Gulf* (London: Hurst, 2012), p. 107.
56 Charles Rollet, 'In Doha, a "Climate of Fear,"' *Northwestern Chronicle*, 14 February 2014.
57 'Qatar Sacks Dutch Head of Media Freedom Centre,' *Al Arabiya*, 2 December 2013.
58 Author interviews with policymakers in Berlin and the Gulf, September 2014.
59 Coates Ulrichsen, *Knowledge-Based Economies*, p. 114.
60 Gari Donn and Yahya Al Manthri, *Globalization and Higher Education in the Arab Gulf States* (Didcot: Symposium Books, 2010), p. 15.
61 Jason Lane, 'International Branch Campuses, Free Zones, and Quality Assurance: Policy Issues for Dubai and the UAE,' *Dubai School of Government Policy Brief*, No. 20 (August 2010), p. 5.
62 Giacomo Luciani, 'The GCC Refining and Petrochemical Sectors in Global Perspective,' in Eckart Woertz (ed.), *Gulf Geo-Economics* (Dubai: Gulf Research Center, 2007), pp. 167–169.
63 Ibid., p. 167.
64 Yamada, 'Gulf-Asia Relations as "Post-Rentier" Diversification?,' pp. 101–103.
65 Coates Ulrichsen, *Insecure Gulf*, p. 103.
66 'Saudi Kayan Ships First Acetone Export,' *Saudi Gazette*, 18 January 2011.
67 Luciani, 'Refining and Petrochemical Sectors,' p. 181.
68 Ibid., p. 191.

4 Gulf Perspectives on the Global Rebalancing

1 Kevin Gray and Craig Murphy, 'Introduction: Rising Powers and the Future of Global Governance,' in Kevin Gray and Craig Murphy (eds.), *Rising Powers and the Future of Global Governance* (Abingdon: Routledge, 2014), p. 2.
2 Syed Mansoob Murshed, Pedro Goulart, and Leandro Serino, 'Globalization and the South at the Crossroads of Change,' in Syed Mansoob Murshed, Pedro Goulart, and Leandro Serino (eds.), *South-South Globalization: Challenges and Opportunities for Development* (Abingdon: Routledge, 2011), p. 17.
3 David Held, 'Democracy, the Nation-State and the Global System,' in Malcolm Waters (ed.), *Modernity: Critical Concepts. Volume IV – After Modernity* (Abingdon: Routledge, 1999), p. 411.
4 Quoted in Kristian Coates Ulrichsen, 'Rebalancing Global Governance: Gulf States' Perceptions on the Governance of Globalization,' *Global Policy*, 2(1), 2011, p. 67.
5 'Khaled Stresses Consolidation of Saudi Moderation Policies,' *Saudi Gazette*, 18 March 2009; 'Saudi Arabia Committed to Moderate Policies,' *Khaleej Times*, 2 April 2009.
6 Ibid., p. 66.
7 Lai-Ha Chan, Pak Lee, and Gerald Chan, 'Rethinking Global Governance: A China Model in the Making?,' *Contemporary Politics*, 14(1), 2008, p. 7;

Teresita Schaffer, 'The United States, India, and Global Governance: Can They Work Together?,' *The Washington Quarterly*, 32(3), 2009, p. 72.

8   Held, 'Democracy, the Nation-State and the Global System,' p. 411.

9   Ibid., p. 423.

10 Farah al-Nakib, 'Kuwait's Modern Spectacle: Oil Wealth and the Making of a New Capital City, 1950–90,' *Comparative Studies of South Asia, Africa and the Middle East*, 33(1), 2013, p. 9.

11 Sarah Yizraeli, *Politics and Society in Saudi Arabia: The Crucial Years of Development, 1960–1982* (New York: Columbia University Press, 2012), pp. 234–237.

12 Abdulkhaleq Abdulla, 'The Impact of Globalization on Arab Gulf States,' in John Fox, Nada Mourtada-Sabbah, and Mohammed al-Mutawa (eds.), *Globalization and the Gulf* (London: Routledge, 2006), p. 181.

13 Badr bin Hamad Al Bu Said, '"Small States" Diplomacy in the Age of Globalization: An Omani Perspective,' in Gerd Nonneman (ed.), *Analyzing Middle East Foreign Policies and the Relationship with Europe* (London: Routledge, 2005), p. 261.

14 Anoushiravan Ehteshami, *Globalisation and Geopolitics in the Middle East: Old Games, New Rules* (London: Routledge, 2007), p. 112.

15 Fred Halliday, *The Middle East in International Relations: Power, Politics and Ideology* (Cambridge: Cambridge University Press, 2005), p. 303.

16 John Fox, Nada Mourtada-Sabbah, and Mohammed al-Mutawa, 'The Arab Gulf Region: Traditionalism Globalized or Globalization Traditionalized?,' in John Fox, Nada Mourtada-Sabbah, and Mohammed al-Mutawa (eds.), *Globalization and the Gulf* (London: Routledge, 2006), p. 3.

17 Jane Kinninmont, *To What Extent is Twitter Changing Gulf Societies?*, London: Chatham House, February 2013, pp. 2–3.

18 Adam Hanieh, *Capitalism and Class in the Gulf Arab States* (New York: Palgrave Macmillan, 2011), p. 103

19 Fox, Mourtada-Sabbah, and al-Mutawa, 'The Arab Gulf Region,' p. 3.

20 'The Algosaibi Affair: A Saudi Saga,' *The Economist*, 21 March 2015.

21 'Al Gosaibi-Saad Dispute Drags On in Saudi Arabia,' *The National*, 6 February 2013.

22 David Held and Anthony McGrew, 'Introduction,' in David Held and Anthony McGrew (eds.), *Governing Globalization: Power, Autonomy and Global Governance* (Cambridge: Polity Press, 2002), p. 2.

23 J. E. Peterson, 'Rulers, Merchants and Shaykhs in Gulf Politics: The Function of Family Networks,' in Alanoud Alsharekh (ed.), *The Gulf Family: Kinship Policies and Modernity* (London: Saqi Books, 2007), pp. 29–30.

24 'Scrutiny Turns to Family Firms,' *Emirates Business 24/7*, 17 July 2009.

25 'Governance Newsmaker Interview with Tarik M. Yousef,' 2(5), December 2008.

26 'Ratification of International Human Rights Treaties – Kuwait,' http://www1.umn.edu/humanrts/research/ratification-kuwait.html

27 Anthony Chase and Amr Hamzawy, *Human Rights in the Arab World: Independent Voices* (Philadelphia: University of Pennsylvania Press, 2006), p. 260.

28 Gerd Nonneman, 'Determinants and Patterns of Saudi Foreign Policy: "Omnibalancing" and "Relative Autonomy" in Multiple Environments,' in Paul Aarts and Gerd Nonneman (eds.), *Saudi Arabia in the Balance: Political Economy, Society, Foreign Affairs* (London: Hurst, 2005), p. 337.

29 Rodney Wilson, 'Economic Governance and Reform in Saudi Arabia,' in Anoushiravan Ehteshami and Steven Wright (eds.), *Political Reform in the Middle East Oil Monarchies* (Reading: Ithaca Press, 2008), p. 137.
30 'Gordon Brown in the Gulf to Seek World Bailout Support,' *Khaleej Times*, 30 October 2008.
31 'Saudi Arabia Not Mulling More Cash for IMF: Minister,' *Reuters*, 16 November 2008.
32 'Gulf Central Bankers Wary of Oil, Property Declines,' *Gulf Times*, 22 November 2008.
33 'China to Boost Relations with GCC: President Hu,' *Arab News*, 12 February 2009.
34 'Govt to Set Up Loan Companies,' *Saudi Gazette*, 15 March 2009.
35 'BRIC's Get Down to Business in Yekaterinburg,' *Russia Today*, 15 June 2009.
36 'Saudi Says IMF Reforms Should Not Be at Its Expense,' *The Peninsula*, 5 September 2009.
37 'US Seeks $300bn from Gulf States to Tackle Turmoil,' *Agence France-Presse*, 21 November 2008.
38 Richard Youngs, 'Impasse in Euro-Gulf Relations,' *Madrid: FRIDE Working Paper*, 80, 2008, p. 2.
39 'Doha Summit Urges Fair Price for Gas,' *Gulf Times*, 16 November 2011.
40 Andreas Goldthau and Jan Martin Witte, 'Back to the Future or Forward to the Past? Strengthening Markets and Rules for Effective Global Energy Governance,' *International Affairs*, 85(2), 2009, p. 374.
41 'Kuwait's Oil Exports to China Hike 52.7% to 1.73 Million Tonnes in 2014,' *Customs Today Report*, 28 January 2015.
42 Author interview, Dubai, November 2009.
43 Mohammed Raouf, 'Climate Change Threats, Opportunities, and the GCC Countries,' Washington, DC: Middle East Institute, *Policy Brief No. 12*, 2008, p. 15.
44 World Wildlife Federation, 'World Living Planet Report 2014: Species and Spaces, People and Places,' p. 39.
45 Andrew Topf, 'The World's 10 Biggest Energy Gluttons,' *Oil Price*, 29 September 2014, http://oilprice.com/Energy/Energy-General/The-Worlds-10-Biggest-Energy-Gluttons.html
46 Joanna Depledge, 'Striving for No: Saudi Arabia in the Climate Change Regime,' *Global Environmental Politics*, 8(4), 2008, p. 20.
47 'Climate Action Plan to Harm Gulf Economies: Saudi Official,' *Saudi Gazette*, 20 March, 2009.
48 Andy Spiess, 'Developing Adaptive Capacity for Responding to Environmental Change in the Arab Gulf States: Uncertainties to Linking Ecosystem Conservation, Sustainable Development and Society in Authoritarian Rentier Economies,' *Global and Planetary Change*, 64, 2008, p. 245.
49 Kristian Coates Ulrichsen, *Qatar and the Arab Spring* Oxford: Oxford University Press, 2014), p. 63.
50 Author interview with public and private sector officials, Qatar, December 2011 and May 2012.

51 Personal interview with a Qatari media commentator, Qatar, December 2011 and May 2012.
52 Ibid.
53 Coates Ulrichsen, 'Rebalancing Global Governance,' p. 72.
54 Danny Quah, 'The Global Economy's Shifting Centre of Gravity,' *Global Policy*, 2(1), 2011, p. 9.
55 Christopher Davidson, *The Persian Gulf and Pacific Asia: From Indifference to Interdependence* (London: Hurst, 2010), pp. 107–108.
56 Halliday, *The Middle East in International Relations*, p. 264.
57 Ben Simpfendorfer, *The New Silk Road: How a Rising Arab World is Turning Away from the West and Rediscovering China* (Basingstoke: Palgrave Macmillan, 2009), pp. 30–32.
58 'China's Growth Shifts the Geopolitics of Oil,' *New York Times*, 19 March 2010.
59 'Qatari Emir Warns of Another Iraq if Sudan Sinks into Chaos,' *Gulf Times*, 31 March 2009.
60 'Qatari PM Stresses Rule of Law to Face Challenges,' *Gulf Times*, 31 May 2009.
61 'Libya Conflict Shows Global Reach of Emerging Polities Qatar and Turkey,' *Gulf States Newsletter*, 35(903), 24 June 2011, p. 16.
62 Thierry Kellner, *The GCC States of the Persian Gulf and Asia Energy Relations*, Paris: IFRI Note, 2012, p. 1.
63 Ibid., p. 13.
64 Ibid., p. 23.
65 Norafidah Ismail, 'The Asia Cooperation Dialogue (ACD): Progress and Potential,' Washington, DC: Middle East Institute, 22 May 2013.
66 Richard Samans, Klaus Schwab, and Mark Malloch-Brown (eds.), *Global Redesign: Strengthening International Cooperation in a More Interdependent World* (Geneva: World Economic Forum, 2010).
67 'Abu Dhabi Declaration of Asian Countries of Origin and Destination,' Ministerial Consultation on Overseas Employment and Contractual Labour for Countries of Origin and Destination in Asia, Abu Dhabi, 21–22 January 2008, available online at http://www.iom.int/jahia/webdav/shared/shared/mainsite/microsites/rcps/abudhabi/abu_dhabi_declaration_english.pdf
68 Lee Cordner, 'Progressing Maritime Security Cooperation in the Indian Ocean,' *Naval War College Review*, 64(4), 2012, pp. 71–73.
69 Rahul Roy-Chaudhury, 'India: Gulf Security Partner in Waiting?,' in Toby Dodge and Emile Hokayem (eds.), *Middle Eastern Security, the US Pivot and the Rise of ISIS* (Abingdon: Routledge, 2014), p. 235.
70 'Developing Countries Concerned Over Economic Crisis: Kuwait,' *Kuwait News Agency (KUNA)*, 13 July 2009.
71 Hilman Latief, 'Gulf Charitable Organizations in Southeast Asia,' Washington, DC: Middle East Institute, 24 December 2014.
72 Mohieddine Hadhri, 'Globalisation Challenges and New Arab Regionalism: Towards a New Deal of South-South Integration,' in Miroslav Jovanovic (ed.), *The International Handbook on the Economics of Integration: General Issues and Regional Groups* (London: Edward Elgar Publishing, 2011), p. 498.

5   The Internationalisation of Gulf Finance

1   Samer Abboud, 'Oil and Financialization in the Gulf Cooperation Council,' in Matteo Legrenzi and Bessa Momani (eds.), *Shifting Geo-Economic Power of the Gulf: Oil, Finance and Institutions* (Farnham: Ashgate, 2011), p. 101.
2   Adam Hanieh, *Capitalism and Class in the Gulf Arab States* (New York: Palgrave Macmillan, 2011), pp. 75–76.
3   Giacomo Luciani, 'From Private Sector to National Bourgeoisie: Saudi Arabian Business,' in Paul Aarts and Gerd Nonneman (eds.), *Saudi Arabia in the Balance: Political Economy, Society, Foreign Affairs* (London: Hurst, 2005), p. 151.
4   Sarah Yizraeli, *Politics and Society in Saudi Arabia: The Crucial Years of Development, 1960–1982* (New York: Columbia University Press, 2012), pp. 278–280.
5   Pascal Menoret, *Joyriding in Riyadh: Oil, Urbanism, and Road Revolt* (Cambridge: Cambridge University Press, 2014), p. 125.
6   Michael Field, *The Merchants: The Big Business Families of Saudi Arabia and the Gulf States* (Woodstock, NY: The Overlook Press, 1985), p. 36.
7   Ibid., p. 35.
8   Khalid al-Mezaini, 'Private Sector Actors in the UAE and their Role in the Process of Economic and Political Reform,' in Steffen Hertog, Giacomo Luciani, and Marc Valeri (eds.), *Business Politics in the Middle East* (London: Hurst, 2013), p. 58.
9   Field, *The Merchants*, pp. 316–317.
10   Kiren Aziz Chaudhry, *The Price of Wealth: Economies and Institutions in the Middle East* (Cornell: Cornell University Press, 1997), p. 160.
11   Taken from Hanieh, *Capitalism and Class*, p. 193.
12   Author interviews, Kuwait and London, January 2014, and information available at http://www.americana-group.net/
13   'Kuwaiti Billionaire Nasser al-Kharafi is Mourned Widely,' *Al Arabiya*, 19 April 2011.
14   J. E. Peterson, 'Rulers, Merchants, and Shaykhs in Gulf Politics: The Function of Family Networks,' in Alanoud Alsharekh (ed.), *The Gulf Family: Kinship Policies and Modernity* (London: Saqi Books, 2007), pp. 30–31.
15   Pete Moore, *Doing Business in the Middle East: Politics and Economic Crisis in Jordan and Kuwait* (Cambridge: Cambridge University Press, 2004), p. 45.
16   Hanieh, *Capitalism and Class*, p. 80.
17   Al-Mezaini, 'Private Sector Actors,' p. 58.
18   Hanieh, *Capitalism and Class*, p. 82.
19   Christopher Davidson, *Dubai: The Vulnerability of Success* (London: Hurst, 2008), p. 247.
20   Naiem Sherbiny, *Oil and the Internationalization of Arab Banks* (Oxford: Oxford Institute of Energy Studies, 1985), pp. 9–10.
21   Hanieh, *Capitalism and Class*, p. 158.
22   Sherbiny, *Internationalization of Arab Banks*, p. 28.
23   Michael Casey, *The History of Kuwait* (Westport, CT: Greenwood Press, 2007), p. 78.
24   'Kuwait in Bailout after Market Collapses,' *New York Times*, 25 December 1982.
25   Ibid.
26   Casey, *History of Kuwait*, p. 120.

27 Hanieh, *Capitalism and Class*, p. 80.
28 Ibid., p. 44.
29 Sherbiny, *Internationalization of Arab Banks*, p. 32.
30 Jane Kinninmont, 'Bahrain,' in Christopher Davidson (ed.), *Power and Politics in the Persian Gulf* (London: Hurst, 2011), p. 49.
31 Mark Thatcher, 'Governing Markets in Gulf States,' London: LSE Kuwait Program Working Paper No. 1, 2009, p. 4.
32 Ibid., p. 15.
33 'DIFC Courts Dealing with More Cases, 81% Rise in Claim and Counterclaim Value,' *The National*, 12 April 2015.
34 Thatcher, 'Governing Markets in Gulf States,' p. 17.
35 'QFC Changes Tack to Attract More Firms,' *Gulf States Newsletter*, 38(978), 2 October 2014, p. 12.
36 Ibid.
37 'Bladen to Quit Advisory Role with Abu Dhabi Global Market,' *The National*, 12 February 2015.
38 'SGX's Richard Teng Leaving to Join Abu Dhabi Global Market,' *Business Times*, 30 October 2014.
39 'Former British Regulator Sants to Advise Abu Dhabi Financial Zone,' *Reuters*, 16 December 2014.
40 'UAE/Qatar Upgraded to "Emerging Market" Status,' *Gulf States Newsletter*, 37(949), 20 June 2013, p. 10.
41 'Qatar, UAE About to Get Major Upgrade,' *CNN Money*, 29 May 2014.
42 'S&P Reclassifies Qatar, UAE to Emerging Market Status,' *ETFtrends.com*, 15 September 2014.
43 'Saudi Tadawul Edges towards Liberalisation,' *Gulf States Newsletter*, 38(974), 17 July 2014, p. 11.
44 'Saudi Bourse's Rules for Opening to Foreigners Expected by End-April,' *Reuters*, 31 March 2015.
45 Nazih Ayubi, *Political Islam: Religion and Politics in the Arab World* (Abingdon: Routledge, 1993), p. 136.
46 Rodney Wilson, 'The Development of Islamic Finance in the Gulf Cooperation Council States,' in David Held and Kristian Ulrichsen (eds.), *The Transformation of the Gulf: Politics, Economics and the Global Order* (Abingdon: Routledge, 2011a), p. 149
47 Ibid.
48 'Oman Hopes to Open Islamic Finance Floodgates,' *The Banker*, 28 January 2013.
49 Moore, *Doing Business in the Middle East*, p. 90.
50 Ibid., pp. 150–157.
51 Rodney Wilson, 'Approaches to Islamic Banking in the Gulf,' in Eckart Woertz (ed.), *GCC Financial Markets* (Dubai: Gulf Research Centre, 2011b), p. 224.
52 Wilson, 'Development of Islamic Finance,' p. 158.
53 Andrew Baker, 'International Competition and Symbiosis in the Gulf: The Politics of Efforts to Establish an International Islamic Financial Policy Forum,' in Matteo Legrenzi and Bessma Momani (eds.), *Shifting Geo-Economic Power of the Gulf: Oil, Finance and Institutions* (Farnham: Ashgate, 2011), p. 75.
54 Wilson, 'Approaches to Islamic Banking,' pp. 236–237.

55   Ibid.
56   'London Sharia Bank Targets Well-off Gulf Clients,' *Reuters*, 16 February 2010.
57   Wilson, 'Approaches to Islamic Banking,' p. 237.
58   'Sovereign Wealth Fund Definition,' Sovereign Wealth Fund Institute, available online at http://www.swfinstitute.org/sovereign-wealth-fund-definition/
59   Gawdat Bahgat, 'Sovereign Wealth Funds: Dangers and Opportunities,' *International Affairs*, 84(6), 2008, p. 1194.
60   Jean-Francois Seznec, 'The Gulf Sovereign Wealth Funds: Myths and Reality,' *Middle East Policy*, 5(2), 2008, pp. 100–101.
61   Sara Bazoobandi, *The Political Economy of the Gulf Sovereign Wealth Funds: A Case Study of Iran, Kuwait, Saudi Arabia and the United Arab Emirates* (Abingdon: Routledge, 2013), p. 83.
62   Seznec, 'Gulf Sovereign Wealth Funds,' pp. 102–103.
63   'Pedal to the Metal: Mumtalakat and McLaren,' *ArabianBusiness.com*, 8 November 2014.
64   'Al-Khalifa Links with Formula One,' *Gulf States Newsletter*, 36(922), 26 April 2012, p. 3.
65   Anders Holmen Gulbrandsen, 'Bridging the Gulf: Qatari Business Diplomacy and Conflict Mediation,' Georgetown University M.A. Thesis, 2010, p. 17.
66   'Barclays' Qatari Capital-Raising Timeline,' *EuroMoney*, 12 May 2014.
67   'Top Greek Banks Join Forces,' *The Globe and Mail*, 29 August 2011.
68   'Man in the News: Hamad bin Jassim Al-Thani,' *Financial Times*, 21 June 2008.
69   'Qatar Royal Family Swoop on Belgian, Luxembourg Banks,' *Arab Times*, 20 December 2011.
70   'Hotels Trial Finds Room for Blair and Bono,' *Financial Times*, 18 May 2012.
71   Seznec, 'Gulf Sovereign Wealth Funds,' p. 104.
72   Ibid.
73   'Saudi Aramco Starts Fund for Renewable Energy,' *The National*, 10 July 2012.
74   'Saudi State Investment Fund to Set Up New Companies,' *Reuters*, 23 July 2014.
75   Bessma Momani, 'Shifting Gulf Arab Investment into the Mashreq: Underlying Political Economy Rationales?,' in Matteo Legrenzi and Bessma Momani (eds.), *Shifting Geo-Economic Power of the Gulf* (Farnham: Ashgate, 2011), p. 168.
76   Sven Behrendt, 'Beyond Santiago: Status and Prospects,' *Central Banking*, 19(4), 2009, p. 76.
77   'How Big Could Sovereign Wealth Funds Be by 2015?' *Morgan Stanley Research*, 3 May 2007.
78   Kristian Coates Ulrichsen, 'Repositioning the GCC States in the Changing Global Order,' *Journal of Arabian Studies*, 1(2), 2011b, p. 234.
79   Benjamin Cohen, 'Sovereign Wealth Funds and National Security: The Great Tradeoff,' *International Affairs*, 85(4), 2009, p. 720.
80   Author interview with a Gulf Ambassador, Washington, DC, January 2009.
81   Jim Krane, *Dubai: The Story of the World's Fastest City* (New York: St Martin's Press, 2009), pp. 172–174.
82   'Israeli Shipper Endorses DP World,' *CNN Politics*, 4 March 2006. Text of letter from Idon Ofer to Senator Hillary Clinton available online at http://i.a.cnn.net/cnn/2006/images/03/02/zim.letter.final.pdf

83 Seznec, 'Gulf Sovereign Wealth Funds,' p. 105.

84 Rachel Ziemba and Anton Malkin, 'The GCC's International Investment Dynamics: The Role of Sovereign Wealth Funds,' in Matteo Legrenzi and Bessma Momani (eds.), Shifting Geo-Economic Power of the Gulf: Oil, Finance and Institutions (Farnham: Ashgate, 2011), p. 116.

85 Richard Youngs, 'Impasse in Euro-Gulf Relations,' Madrid: FRIDE Working Paper 80, 2009, p. 1.

86 'Gulf's Oil Wealth to Help Cushion Impact of Likely Global Recession,' Gulf Times, 17 October 2008.

87 'Sheikh Mohammed Says Financial Crisis 'a Passing Cloud,' Reuters, 5 September 2009.

88 Christopher Davidson, 'Dubai and Abu Dhabi: Implosion and Opportunity,' Open Democracy, 4 December 2009.

89 'Kuwait's Global Investment House Defaults on Most Debts,' Kuwait Times, 9 January 2009.

90 'Kuwait's Gulf Bank Reports US $1.05 Billion Loss,' Arab Times, 3 December 2008.

91 M. Raghu, 'Future Direction of the GCC Financial Sector – A Specific Look at Banking and Asset Management,' in Eckart Woertz (ed.), GCC Financial Markets (Dubai: Gulf Research Centre, 2011), pp. 25–26.

92 'Merchant Families: Power Brokers with Fingers in Many Pies,' Financial Times, 18 April 2011.

93 Momani, 'Shifting Gulf Arab Investment,' p. 165.

94 Ibid., p. 166.

95 Author interview, Kuwait, October 2009.

96 Linda Lim and Ronald Mendoza, 'Global Rebalancing 2.0,' World Financial Review, 2013, available online at http://www.worldfinancialreview. com/?p=2496 (accessed 26 November 2013).

97 Momani, 'Shifting Gulf Arab Investment,' p. 176.

98 Seznec, 'Gulf Sovereign Wealth Funds,' p. 97.

99 Yasser Elsheshtawy, Dubai: Behind an Urban Spectacle (Abingdon: Routledge, 2009), p. 142.

100 Christopher Davidson, 'Gulf-Pacific Asia Linkages in the Twenty-First Century: A Marriage of Convenience?,' in David Held and Kristian Ulrichsen (eds.), The Transformation of the Gulf: Politics, Economics and the Global Order (Abingdon: Routledge, 2011), p. 341.

101 'Qatar Buys 22 Percent Stake in China Investment Firm CITIC Capital,' Reuters, 22 August 2012; 'Qatar's Wealth Fund to Launch $10 Billion Investment Fund with China's CITIC,' Reuters, 4 November 2014.

102 'Mubadala to Invest $2 Billion in Eike Batista's EBX Group as Part of Strategic Partnership,' Mubadala Press Release, 26 March 2012.

103 'New Avenues: OBG Talks to Bader Al Saad, Managing Director, Kuwait Investment Authority,' in The Report: Kuwait 2008 (Oxford: Oxford Business Group, 2008), p. 86.

104 'Qatar's Wealth Fund to Launch $10 Billion Investment Fund with China's CITIC,' Reuters, 4 November 2014.

105 'Qatar Looks to Invest More in China,' Gulf States Newsletter, 38(981), 13 November 2014, pp. 10–11.

106 Hanieh, Capitalism and Class, p. 151.

107 Ibid., pp. 151–153.
108 Kristian Coates Ulrichsen, 'Egypt-Gulf Ties and the Changing Balance of Regional Security,' *The Cairo Review of Global Affairs*, 12 January 2015.
109 Ibid.
110 'Difficult Geopolitical Context,' *Gulf States Newsletter*, 36(926), 21 June 2012, p. 3.
111 Kristian Coates Ulrichsen, *Qatar and the Arab Spring* (Oxford: Oxford University Press, 2014), p. 89.
112 'With Gulf Aid, Egypt Economy Can Limp Through Crisis,' *Reuters*, 20 August 2013.
113 Enas Hamed, 'As Gulf Aid Dries Up, Egypt Struggles,' *Al Monitor*, 30 December 2014.
114 'Gulf States Offer $12.5 Billion Aid to Egypt,' *Al Arabiya*, 13 March 2015.
115 'Exclusive: Mohammed Alabbar – Uncensored,' *ArabianBusiness.com*, 12 April 2015.
116 Steffen Hertog, 'The Costs of Counter-Revolution in the Gulf,' *Foreign Policy*, 31 May 2011.
117 'Strong Trade, Services Support the UAE's Economic Recovery,' *IMF Survey Online*, 18 May 2012.
118 'Oil Must Hit $109.5 to Meet State Expenditure,' *Kuwait Times*, 24 March 2012.
119 'Qatar's Megaproject Mayhem,' *Gulf States Newsletter*, 37(956), 17 October 2013, p. 12.
120 'Abu Dhabi to Make a "Quantum Leap" with $100 Billion Boom in Mega Projects,' *The National*, 1 February 2014; 'US Offers to Participate in Saudi Projects Worth $500 Billion,' *Arab News*, 20 September 2013.
121 Steffen Hertog, 'Oil Prices: Eventually the Gulf States Will Run Out of Power,' *The Conversation*, 5 January 2015.
122 'IMF Tells Kuwait to Cut Spending or Risk Running Out of Oil Money,' *The National*, 17 May 2012.
123 'IMF Urges Gulf Countries to Reduce Spending as Oil Price Plunges,' *Financial Times*, 21 January 2015.
124 'Qatar Halts Plans for $6 Billion Al Sejeel Petrochemical Plant,' *Bloomberg*, 18 September 2014; 'QP and Shell Cancel $6bn Al-Karaana,' *Middle East Economic Digest*, 14 January 2015.

6 Shifting Patterns of Global Trade

1 Steffen Hertog, *Princes, Brokers, and Bureaucrats: Oil and the State in Saudi Arabia* (Ithaca, NY: Cornell University Press, 2010), pp. 223–224.
2 Rodney Wilson, 'Economic Governance and Reform in Saudi Arabia,' in Anoushiravan Ehteshami and Steven Wright (eds.), *Political Reform in the Middle East Oil Monarchies* (Reading: Ithaca Press, 2008), pp. 136–137.
3 David Price, *The Development of Intellectual Property Regimes in the Arabian Gulf States: Infidels at the Gates* (Abingdon: Routledge, 2009), p. 63.
4 Wilson, 'Economic Governance and Reform,' p. 137.
5 Price, *Intellectual Property Regimes*, p. 59.
6 'Gulf States Stand to Lose from Doha Round Collapse,' *Gulf News*, 10 August 2008.

7   Braz Baracuhy, 'The Evolving Geo-Economics of World Trade,' in Sanjaya Baru and Suvi Dogra (eds.), *Power Shifts and New Blocs in the Global Trading System* (Abingdon: Routledge, 2015), p. 33.

8   Abdullah Baaboud and Geoffrey Edwards, 'Sovereign Reluctance: The Interaction of the Gulf States and the European Union,' in Christian Koch (ed.), *EU-GCC Relations & Security Issues: Broadening the Horizon* (Dubai: Gulf Research Centre, 2008), pp. 28–29.

9   Gerd Nonneman, *EU-GCC Relations: Dynamics, Patterns & Perspectives* (Dubai: Gulf Research Centre, 2006), p. 17.

10 Roberto Aliboni, *Europe's Role in the Gulf: A Transatlantic Perspective*, Rome: Istituto Affari Internazionali, 2005, p. 11.

11 Kristian Coates Ulrichsen, 'The GCC States and the Shifting Balance of Global Power,' *Occasional Paper* No. 6, Georgetown University School of Foreign Service in Qatar, Center for International and Regional Studies, Doha, 2010, p. 18.

12 'GCC-Singapore FTA Comes Into Effect,' *Saudi Gazette*, 2 September 2013.

13 'Optimism on GCC-Singapore Free Trade Deal Despite Lower Exchange,' *The National*, 2 November 2013.

14 EIU, 'GCC Trade and Investment Flows: A Report by the Economist Intelligence Unit,' London: Economist Intelligence Unit, 2014, p. 4.

15 'Rebooting Gulf-China Trade,' *The Majalla*, 16 April 2014.

16 'China and GCC to Restart FTA Negotiations,' *Gulf States Newsletter*, 38(963), 6 February 2014, p. 8.

17 'Gulf States in Final Push Towards Customs Union,' *Al Shorfa*, 16 December 2014; 'GCC Customs Union Fully Operational,' *The Peninsula*, 3 January 2015.

18 Matteo Legrenzi, 'Gulf Cooperation Council Diplomatic Coordination: The Limited Role of Institutionalization,' in Jean-Francois Seznec and Mimi Kirk (eds.), *Industrialization in the Gulf: A Socioeconomic Revolution* (Abingdon: Routledge, 2011), p. 117.

19 Cited in Abdulla Baaboud and Geoffrey Edwards, 'Reinforcing Ambivalence: The Interaction of Gulf States and the European Union,' *European Foreign Affairs Review*, 12, 2007, p. 549.

20 Legrenzi, 'Gulf Cooperation Council,' p. 117.

21 John Fox, Nada Mourtada-Sabbah, and Mohammed al-Mutawa, 'The Arab Gulf Region: Tradition Globalized or Globalization Traditionalized?,' in John Fox, Nada Mourtada-Sabbah, and Mohammed al-Mutawa (eds.), *Globalization and the Gulf* (London: Routledge, 2006), p. 24.

22 Cited in Baaboud and Edwards, 'Reinforcing Ambivalence,' p. 548.

23 Ibid.

24 Mohd Fauzi bin Abu-Hussin, 'Gulf Arab Foreign Direct Investment (FDI): ASEAN Targets of Opportunity,' Washington, DC: Middle East Institute, 20 March 2013, http://www.mei.edu/content/gulf-arab-foreign-direct-investment-fdi-asean-targets-opportunity

25 Baracuhy, 'Evolving Geo-Economics,' p. 122.

26 Ibid.

27 'Abu Dhabi in Nearly $7bln Oil Investment in Malaysia,' *Reuters*, 12 March 2013.

28 'Abu Dhabi Link-up with Malaysia on Investing,' *The National*, 18 April 2013.

29 'Qatar to Invest $5bn in Malaysia Petrochemicals Complex,' *The National*, 29 January 2013.

30 'Qatar to Establish New Overseas Energy Infrastructure Fund,' *The National*, 20 May 2013.

31 Abu-Hussin, 'Gulf Arab Foreign Direct Investment.'

32 Sean Foley, 'Re-Orientalizing the Gulf: The GCC and Southeast Asia,' *Middle East Policy*, 19(4), 2012, p. 79.

33 Ibid.

34 Degang Sun, 'China's Soft Military Presence in the Middle East,' Washington, DC: Middle East Institute, Online, 11 March 2015.

35 Mahmoud Ghafouri, 'China's Policy in the Persian Gulf,' *Middle East Policy*, 16(2), 2009, p. 89.

36 'Qatar, China in 25-Year Gas Deal,' *The Peninsula*, 8 March 2009.

37 'Kuwait Signs Biggest Crude Supply Deal with China,' *Kuwait News Agency (KUNA)*, 22 August 2014.

38 EIU, 'GCC Trade and Investment Flows,' p. 9.

39 Steve Yetiv and Chunling Lu, 'China, Global Energy and the Middle East,' *Middle East Journal*, 61(2), 2007, p. 5.

40 Ibid., pp. 207–208.

41 EIU, 'GCC Trade and Investment Flows,' p. 10.

42 Rahul Roy-Chaudhury, 'India: Gulf Security Partner in Waiting?,' in Toby Dodge and Emile Hokayem (eds.), *Middle Eastern Security, the US Pivot and the Rise of ISIS* (Abingdon: Routledge, 2014), pp. 229–230.

43 Erick Viramontes, 'The Role of Latin America in the Foreign Policies of the GCC States,' Paper presented at the *3rd Gulf Research Meeting*, University of Cambridge, July 2012, pp. 10–11.

44 'Gulf Embraces Latin American Flavours as Trade Triples,' *The National*, 2 October 2012.

45 'Mubadala to Invest $2 Billion in Eike Batista's EBX Group as Part of Strategic Partnership,' *Mubadala Press Release*, 26 March 2012.

46 'Abu Dhabi's Mubadala to Get Stake in Batista Mines, Port,' *Bloomberg*, 5 August 2014.

47 Melissa Low, 'ASEAN's Role in Sustainable Energy for All,' *GSCleanEnergy. com Blog*, 3 April 2013, available online at http://gscleanenergy.blogspot. com/2013/04/aseans-role-in-sustainable-energy-for.html

48 Zachary Keck, 'Qatar and ASEAN: Opposites Attract?' *The Diplomat*, 27 July 2013.

49 Kristian Coates Ulrichsen, *Insecure Gulf: The End of Certainty and the Transition to the Post-Oil Era* (London: Hurst, 2011), p. 111.

50 Rob Bailey with Robin Willoughby, 'Edible Oil: Food Security in the Gulf,' London: Chatham House, *Energy, Environment and Resources Paper EER BP 2013/03*, pp. 2–4.

51 Coates Ulrichsen, *Insecure Gulf*, p. 112.

52 Jeannie Sowers, 'Water, Energy and Human Insecurity in the Middle East,' *Middle East Research and Information Project (MERIP)*, 44(271) (Summer 2014), available online at http://www.merip.org/mer/mer271/water-energy-human-insecurity-middle-east

53 'Water Concerns Prompt Saudis to Cease Grain Production,' *Financial Times*, 27 February 2008.

54 'Dairy Kingdom,' Washington, DC: Center for Strategic and International Studies, *Middle East Program Newsletter*, April 2010, p. 1.

55 'Saudi Agri Firm Eyes Investment Abroad,' *Reuters*, 20 March 2009.

56 'Saudi Arabia Buys Stake in Canadian Grain Handling Company,' *Financial Times*, 15 April 2015.

57 'Saudis Setting Up Fund to Buy Agricultural Land Abroad,' *Gulf Times*, 26 August 2008.

58 Thomas Lippman, 'Saudi Arabia's Quest for "Food Security,"' *Middle East Policy*, 17(1), 2010, p. 92.

59 'Gulf States Seek Food Security in Europe, US, after African Problems,' *Reuters*, 30 December 2013.

60 'Pakistan Offers Farmland to Saudi Arabia, UAE,' *Saudi Gazette*, 4 September 2008.

61 Coates Ulrichsen, *Insecure Gulf*, p. 114.

62 'In Bid for Food Security, Qatar Grows Seeds Globally,' *The National*, 2 September 2010.

63 'Qatar to Invest $500m in India After Bush Acquisition,' *Bloomberg*, 10 June 2013.

64 'Qatari Government Buys Up 14,000 Hectares of Prime South Australian Farmland,' *The Australian*, 17 June 2014.

65 'Middle East Secretly Targets Our Farms,' *Adelaide Now*, 22 February 2013.

66 'Qatar, Thailand Keen on Forging New Agreements,' *Gulf Times*, 6 July 2009.

67 Amena Bakr, 'Qatar Plans to Secure Food Supplies Domestically,' *ArabianBusiness.com*, 1 June 2010.

68 Coates Ulrichsen, *Insecure Gulf*, p. 115.

69 Eckart Woertz, Samir Pradhan, Nermina Biberovic, and Chan Jingzhong, 'Potential for GCC Agro-Investments in Africa and Central Asia,' *GRC Report* (Dubai: Gulf Research Centre, 2008), p. 5.

70 'GCC Food Imports Cost $10bn Last Year: Study,' *The Peninsula*, 21 July 2009.

71 'Farmland Investment Fund is Seeking More than Dh1bn,' *The National*, 12 September 2009.

72 'Gulf States Seek Food Security in Europe, US, after African Problems,' *Reuters*, 30 December 2013.

73 'Gulf States and ASEAN Eye New Trade Bloc Based on Food, Oil,' *The Peninsula*, 1 July 2009.

74 Lippman, 'Saudi Arabia's Quest for Food Security,' p. 92.

75 'Egypt Freezes Saudi Arabian Farm Land Deal,' *The National*, 12 April 2011.

76 Kristian Coates Ulrichsen, 'South-South Cooperation and the Changing Role of the Gulf States,' *Brazilian Journal of Strategy & International Relations*, 1(1), 2012a, pp. 114–115.

77 'Seized! The 2008 Land Grab for Food and Financial Security,' *Grain Briefing*, October 2008, p. 3.

78 Coates Ulrichsen, *Insecure Gulf*, p. 116.

79 Coates Ulrichsen, 'South-South Cooperation,' pp. 115–116.

80 Woertz et al., 'GCC Agro-Investments in Africa and Central Asia,' p. 5.

81 'In Unusual Rebuke, Saudi Arabia Accuses Ethiopia of Posing Threats to Sudan & Egypt,' *Sudan Tribune*, 27 February 2013.

7   Global Aviation and the Gulf

1   'Aviation in the Gulf: Rulers of the New Silk Road,' *The Economist*, 3–9 June 2010.
2   'Dubai Jumps Heathrow as "World's Busiest International Airport,"' *USA Today*, 28 January 2015.
3   'Qantas-Emirates Alliance Ends Singapore Stopover,' *The Australian*, 10 September 2012.
4   Frauke Heard-Bey, *From Trucial States to United Arab Emirates* (London: Longman, 1996), p. 298.
5   'Oman's Gulf Air Pull Out to Benefit Bahrain in Long Run,' *Khaleej Times*, 7 May 2007.
6   David Roberts, 'Kuwait's War of Words with Iraq,' *Foreign Policy*, 20 July 2011.
7   'Parliament Oks Amendments to Kuwait Airways Law,' *Kuwait News Agency (KUNA)*, 9 January 2014.
8   Abdul Hafeez Yawar Khan Al Yousefi, '50 Years in Al Ain Oasis – Memoirs of Khabeer Khan,' *Liwa: Journal of the National Center for Documentation and Research*, 5(9), 2013, p. 58.
9   John Woolfenden, 'Memories of Abu Dhabi and Al Ain in the Early Nineteen-Sixties,' *Liwa: Journal of the National Centre for Documentation and Research*, 2(4), 2010, p. 44.
10   Jim Krane, *Dubai: The Story of the World's Fastest City* (London: Atlantic Books, 2009), pp. 107–108.
11   'Emirates Airline History,' available online at http://www.airreview.com/Emirates/History.htm
12   Christopher Davidson, 'The Impact of Economic Reform on Dubai,' in Anoushiravan Ehteshami and Steven Wright (eds.), *Reform in the Middle East Oil Monarchies* (Reading: Ithaca Press, 2008b), pp. 157–158.
13   Christopher Davidson, *Dubai: The Vulnerability of Success* (London: Hurst, 2008), p. 111.
14   'Dubai Hotels Enjoy Busiest Half-Year Visitor Numbers,' *Khaleej Times*, 25 August 2014.
15   Author interviews, Dubai and London, April 2012 and January 2014.
16   'The Qatar Airways Story,' January 2015, available online at http://www.qatarairways.com/iwov-resources/temp-docs/press-kit/The%20Story%20of%20Qatar%20Airways%20-%20English.pdf
17   'Qatar Airlines Take Delivery of First Airbus A350,' *Euronews*, 22 December 2014.
18   'Q&A Mr Ahmed Al Nuaimi, Chairman, Qatar Tourism Authority, "Boosting Visitor Numbers While Improving Quality and Offerings,"' in *B'Here Annual Review Qatar 2012: The Vision Moves Forward: Towards a Knowledge-Based Society* (Doha: Arab Communications Consult, 2012), pp. 260–262.
19   'Overtaxed Doha Airport Sees 6mn Passengers in First Quarter 2014,' *Doha News*, 27 April 2014.
20   'Qatar Airways Interested in More Buyouts,' *The Peninsula*, 5 March 2015.
21   'Qatar Airways Buys 10% of British Airways Owner IAG,' *The Guardian*, 30 January 2015.
22   'Emirates Airline Pulls Out of Backing FIFA and Could be Followed by Sony,' *The Guardian*, 3 November 2014.

23   'Capacity Increase Confirmed on Etiihad's Flights to Manchester,' *Skyscanner*, 19 February 2010.

24   'Etihad Splits Massive Order Between Boeing, Airbus,' *USA Today*, 15 July 2008.

25   'Qatar Airways Stake in British Airways Parent IAG Creates Intriguing Alliance,' *The National*, 3 February 2015.

26   'EU Widens Etihad Probe to Include More European Carriers,' *ArabianBusiness. com*, 10 April 2014.

27   'U.S. Airlines Losing Asia Market Share,' *Las Vegas Review-Journal*, 10 February 2015.

28   'Lufthansa Seeks to Clip Emirates' Wings in Europe, Berlin Mayor Says,' *ArabianBusiness.com*, 16 January 2011.

29   'UAE Embassy to Charge Canadians Steep Visa Fees,' *The Globe and Mail*, 28 December 2010.

30   'Etihad and Air Canada Strike Codeshare Deal,' *The National*, 25 April 2013.

31   'Note to Abu Dhabi on Pre-Clearance: Be Careful What You Wish For,' *Forbes. com*, 14 October 2014.

32   'Qatar Airways CEO Says Company Fully Govt-Owned; Interested in IndiGo Stake,' *Reuters*, 5 May 2014.

33   'United States Escalates Arabian Gulf Airline Subsidies Row,' *Bloomberg News*, 5 March 2015.

34   'Etihad Airways' Rapid Growth Frustrates Rivals,' *New York Times*, 2 March 2015.

35   Ibid.

36   'Airline Subsidies in the Gulf: Feeling the Heat,' *The Economist*, 6 March 2015.

37   'Emirates Executives Rebuff US Airlines' Claims of $40 Billion in Subsidies to Gulf Carriers,' *The National*, 11 February 2015.

38   'Gulf Banks Helping to Underwrite Region's Aviation Boom,' *Reuters*, 3 February 2015.

39   Mark Summers, 'Etihad Airways: Staying the Course,' *The Gulf Business News and Analysis*, May 2010, available online at http://www.thegulfonline.com/ Articles.aspx?ArtID=3001

40   David Held and Kristian Ulrichsen, 'Introduction,' in David Held and Kristian Ulrichsen (eds.), *The Transformation of the Gulf: Politics, Economics and the Global Order* (Abingdon: Routledge, 2011), p. 11.

41   'Dubai Airport Claims Top Spot for Global Passenger Traffic in 2014,' *Jakarta Globe*, 27 January 2015.

42   'U.S. Customs Passenger Facility Opens in Abu Dhabi,' *USA Today*, 27 January 2014.

43   Ted Reed, 'Note to Abu Dhabi on Pre-Clearance: Be Careful What You Wish For,' *Forbes.com*, 14 October 2014.

44   'Total U.S. Exports (Origin of Movement) via Washington: Top 25 Countries Based on 2013 Dollar Value,' *United States Census Bureau: Foreign Trade*, available online at https://www.census.gov/foreign-trade/statistics/state/ data/wa.html

45   'Bahrain Air Plans to Liquidate as Unrest Disrupts Travel,' *Bloomberg*, 13 February 2013.

46   'Bahrain Air CEO Richard Nuttall Discusses the Airline's Closure,' *The Aviation Writer*, 13 March 2013.

8   Migrant Labour in the Gulf

1   Cf. Abdulhadi Khalaf, Omar AlShehabi, and Adam Hanieh (eds.), *Transit States: Labour, Migration & Citizenship in the Gulf* (London: Pluto Press, 2015) for an excellent analysis of migrant issues in the Gulf.

2   Nasra Shah, 'Recent Amnesty Programs for Irregular Migrants in Kuwait and Saudi Arabia: Some Successes and Failures,' *Gulf Labor Markets and Migration (GLMM) Explanatory Note* 09/2014 (2014a), pp. 3–4.

3   Kasim Randeree, 'Workforce Nationalization in the Gulf Cooperation Council States,' Georgetown University School of Foreign Service in Qatar: Center for International and Regional Studies Occasional Paper No. 9, 2012, p. 8.

4   Kristian Coates Ulrichsen, *Insecure Gulf: The End of Certainty and the Transition to the Post-Oil Era* (London: Hurst, 2011), p. 87.

5   'Bahrain Labor Market Reforms Bridge Gap between Nationals, Expats – Minister,' *Kuwait News Agency (KUNA)*, 30 August 2009.

6   Jane Bristol-Rhys, 'Socio-Spatial Boundaries in Abu Dhabi,' in Mehran Kamrava and Zahra Babar (eds.), *Migrant Labor in the Persian Gulf* (London: Hurst, 2012), pp. 82–83.

7   Kristian Coates Ulrichsen (ed.), 'Addressing the Demographic Imbalance in the GCC States: Implications for Labor Markets, Migration, and National Identity,' London: LSE Middle East Center Workshop Report, June 2014, p. 3.

8   Nasra Shah, 'Data Discrepancies between the Census and Civil Registration Systems in Kuwait: Reasons, Implications, and Solutions,' *Gulf Labor Markets and Migration (GLMM) Explanatory Note* 2/2014 (2014b), pp. 5–7.

9   Ibid., p. 7.

10   David Green, 'Research in Consumer and Real Estate Markets,' in Anthony Shoult (ed.), *Doing Business with Saudi Arabia: A Guide to Investment Opportunities & Business Practice* (London: GMB Publishing, 2006), p. 294.

11   Michael Bonine, 'Population Growth, the Labor Market and Gulf Security,' in Christian Koch and David Long (eds.), *Gulf Security in the Twenty-First Century* (Abu Dhabi: Emirates Center for Strategic Studies and Research, 1997), p. 227.

12   Author interview, Doha, March 2015.

13   'The Impact of Large-Scale Datasets on Evidence-based Educational Policymaking and Reform in the Gulf States,' July 2012, available at http://gulfresearchmeeting.net/index.php?pgid=Njk=&wid=MzM=&yr=2012

14   Mehran Kamrava and Zahra Babar, 'Situating Labor Migration in the Persian Gulf,' in Mehran Kamrava and Zahra Babar (eds.), *Migrant Labor in the Persian Gulf* (London: Hurst, 2012), p. 2.

15   Thomas Lippman, 'Cooperation under the Radar: The US-Saudi Arabian Joint Commission for Economic Cooperation (JECOR),' Washington, DC: Middle East Institute commentary, 1 October 2009.

16   Thomas Lippman, *Inside the Mirage: America's Fragile Partnership with Saudi Arabia* (Boulder, CO: Westview Press, 2005), p. 174.

17   Patrice Flynn, 'The Saudi Arabian Labor Force: A Comprehensive Statistical Portrait,' *Middle East Journal*, 65(4), 2011, p. 581.

18   James Onley and Sulayman Khalaf, 'Shaikhly Authority in the Pre-oil Gulf: An Historical-Anthropological Study,' *History and Anthropology*, 17(3), 2006, p. 192.

19   Guy Michael, 'Challenges for Research on Resource-Rich Economies,' London: LSE Kuwait Programme Working Paper No. 8, 2010, p. 8.

20   Marc Valeri, *Oman: Politics and Society in the Qaboos State* (London: Hurst, 2009), pp. 18–19.

21   J. E. Peterson, 'The Baluch Presence in the Persian Gulf,' in Lawrence Potter (ed.), *Sectarian Politics in the Persian Gulf* (London: Hurst, 2013), p. 233.

22   Abdul Sheriff, 'The Persian Gulf and the Swahili Coast: A History of Acculturation over the Longue Duree,' in Lawrence Potter (ed.), *The Persian Gulf in History* (New York: Palgrave Macmillan, 2009), pp. 183–184.

23   Fatma al-Sayegh, 'Merchants' Role in a Changing Society: The Case of Dubai, 1900–1990,' *Middle Eastern Studies*, 34(1), 1998, p. 89.

24   Quoted in Christopher Davidson, *Dubai: The Vulnerability of Success* (London: Hurst, 2008), p. 73.

25   Fred Halliday, *The Middle East in International Relations: Power, Politics and Ideology* (Cambridge: Cambridge University Press, 2005), p. 265.

26   Gawdat Bahgat, 'Education in the Gulf Monarchies: Retrospect and Prospect,' *International Review of Education*, 45(2), 1999, pp. 129–130.

27   Sharon Stanton Russell, 'Politics and Ideology in Migration Policy Formulation: The Case of Kuwait,' *International Migration Review*, 23(1), 1989, pp. 29–33.

28   Ido Zelkovitz, 'A Paradise Lost? The Rise and Fall of the Palestinian Community in Kuwait,' *Middle Eastern Studies*, 50(1), 2014, p. 87.

29   Miriam Joyce, *Kuwait 1945–1996: An Anglo-American Perspective* (London: Frank Cass, 1998), p. 32.

30   Abdulhadi Khalaf, 'Labor Movements in Bahrain,' Middle East Research and Information Project (MERIP) Report 132, 1985, p. 25.

31   David Roberts, 'Qatar, the Ikhwan, and Transnational Relations in the Gulf,' Project on Middle East Political Science (POMEPS), 28 March 2014b.

32   Haila al-Mekaimi, 'The Impact of Islamic Groups and Arab Spring on the Youth Political Movement in Kuwait,' *Journal of South Asian and Middle Eastern Studies*, 36(1), 2012, p. 47.

33   Al-Sayegh, 'Merchants' Role in a Changing Society,' p. 92.

34   Joyce, *Kuwait 1945–1996*, pp. 92–94.

35   Zelkovitz, 'Paradise Lost,' pp. 87–88.

36   Khaldoun Al-Naqeeb, *Society and State in the Gulf and Arab Peninsula: A Different Perspective* (London: Routledge, 1990), p. 101.

37   John Chalcraft, 'Monarchy, Migration and Hegemony in the Arabian Peninsula,' London: LSE Kuwait Programme Working Paper No. 12, 2010, p. 3.

38   Abdulhadi Khalaf, 'The Politics of Migration,' in Abdulhadi Khalaf, Omar AlShehabi, and Adam Hanieh (eds.), *Transit States: Labour, Migration & Citizenship in the Gulf* (London: Pluto Press, 2015), pp. 46–47.

39   Chalcraft, 'Monarchy, Migration and Hegemony,' p. 9.

40   Ingo Forstenlechner and Emilie Rutledge, 'The GCC's "Demographic Imbalance": Perceptions, Realities, and Policy Options,' *Middle East Policy*, 18(4), 2011, p. 31.

41   Gwenn Okruhlik and Patrick Conge, 'National Autonomy, Labor Migration, and Political Crisis: Yemen and Saudi Arabia,' *Middle East Journal*, 51(4), 1997, p. 556.

42   Omar AlShehabi, 'Histories of Migration to the Gulf,' in Abdulhadi Khalaf, Omar AlShehabi, and Adam Hanieh (eds.), *Transit States: Labour, Migration & Citizenship in the Gulf* (London: Pluto Press, 2015a), p. 25.

43   Jean-Pierre Filiu, *Gaza: A History* (Oxford: Oxford University Press, 2014), pp. 210–211.
44   Khalaf, 'Politics of Migration,' p. 48.
45   Christopher Davidson, *After the Sheikhs: The Coming Collapse of the Gulf Monarchies* (London: Hurst, 2012), p. 63.
46   Attiya Ahmad, 'Beyond Labor: Foreign Residents in the Persian Gulf States,' in Mehran Kamrava and Zahra Babar (eds.), *Migrant Labour in the Persian Gulf* (London: Hurst, 2012), pp. 26–27.
47   Mohammed Ditto, 'Kafala: Foundations of Migrant Exclusion in GCC Labour Markets,' in Abdulhadi Khalaf, Omar AlShehabi, and Adam Hanieh (eds.), *Transit States: Labour, Migration & Citizenship in the Gulf* (London: Pluto Press, 2015), p. 81.
48   Ibid.
49   Anh Nga Longva, *Walls Built on Sand: Migration, Exclusion, and Society in Kuwait* (Boulder, CO: Westview Press, 1997), p. 100.
50   Andrew Ross, 'Degrees of Danger,' *The Baffler*, No. 26, 2014, available online at http://www.thebaffler.com/salvos/degrees-danger
51   'Trafficking in Persons Report 2014,' US Department of State, p. 320, available online at http://www.state.gov/j/tip/rls/tiprpt/2014/index.htm
52   Andrew Gardner, 'Why Do They Keep Coming: Labor Migrants in the Persian Gulf States,' in Mehran Kamrava and Zahra Babar (eds.), *Migrant Labor in the Persian Gulf* (London: Hurst, 2012), p. 57.
53   John Willoughby, 'Ambivalent Anxieties of the South Asian-Gulf Arab Labor Exchange,' in John Fox, Nada Mourtada-Sabbah, and Mohammed al-Mutawa (eds.), *Globalization and the Gulf* (Abingdon: Routledge, 2006), pp. 227–230.
54   Zahra Babar, 'The Cost of Belonging: Citizenship Construction in the State of Qatar,' *Middle East Journal*, 68(3), 2014, p. 413.
55   Ibid., p. 407.
56   Shafeeq Ghabra, 'Kuwait and the Dynamics of Socio-Economic Change,' *Middle East Journal*, 51(3), 1997, p. 364.
57   Michael Herb, 'Kuwait: The Obstacle of Parliamentary Politics,' in Joshua Teitelbaum (ed.), *Political Liberalization in the Persian Gulf* (London: Hurst, 2009), p. 142.
58   Marina Ottaway, 'Bahrain: Between the United States and Saudi Arabia,' Washington, DC: Carnegie Endowment for International Peace online commentary, 4 April 2011, available at http://carnegieendowment. org/2011/04/04/bahrain-between-united-states-and-saudi-arabia/t8
59   'Report Cites Bid by Sunnis in Bahrain to Rig Elections,' *New York Times*, 29 September 2006.
60   '"Bandargate" Report Alleges Senior Power Broker Attempted to Manipulate Political System,' US Diplomatic Cable dated 28 September 2006, available at https://cablegatesearch.wikileaks.org/cable.php?id=06MANAMA1728
61   Ahmed Abdelkareem Saif, 'Deconstructing before Building: Perspectives on Democracy in Qatar,' in Anoushiravan Ehteshami and Steven Wright (eds.), *Reform in the Middle East Oil Monarchies* (Reading: Ithaca Press, 2008), p. 125.
62   Abulhadi Khalaf, 'GCC Rulers and the Politics of Citizenship,' *Al Monitor*, 26 December 2012.

63 Cf. Mehran Kamrava, 'Contemporary Port Cities in the Persian Gulf: Local Gateways and Global Networks,' in Mehran Kamrava (ed.), *Gateways to the World: The Rise and Fall of Port Cities in the Persian Gulf* (London: Hurst, 2015).

64 Omar AlShehabi, 'Radical Transformations and Radical Contestations: Bahrain's Spatial-Demographic Revolution,' *Middle East Critique*, 23(1), 2014, p. 35.

65 Steffen Hertog, 'Arab Gulf States: An Assessment of Nationalisation Policies,' *Gulf Labour Markets and Migration Research Paper* No. 1/2014, pp. 14–15.

66 Christopher Davidson, 'The Impact of Economic Reform on Dubai,' in Anoushiravan Ehteshami and Steven Wright (eds.), *Reform in the Middle East Oil Monarchies* (Reading: Ithaca Press, 2008b), p. 164.

67 Adam Hanieh, *Capitalism and Class in the Gulf Arab States* (New York: Palgrave Macmillan, 2011), p. 132.

68 Omar AlShehabi, 'Migration, Commodification, and the "Right to the City,"' in Abdulhadi Khalaf, Omar AlShehabi, and Adam Hanieh (eds.), *Transit States: Labour, Migration & Citizenship in the Gulf* (London: Pluto Press, 2015b), p. 105.

69 Ibid., p. 106.

70 Ibid.

71 Nasra Shah, 'Second Generation Non-Nationals in Kuwait: Achievements, Aspirations and Plans,' London: LSE Kuwait Programme Working Paper No. 32, 2013, p. 1.

72 Syed Ali, *Dubai: Gilded Cage* (New Haven: Yale University Press, 2010), p. 149.

73 'Building Towers, Cheating Workers: Exploitation of Migrant Construction Workers in the United Arab Emirates,' *Human Rights Watch*, 18(8E), 2006, p. 2.

74 'Trafficking in Persons Report 2014,' US Department of State, p. 236, available online at http://www.state.gov/j/tip/rls/tiprpt/2014/index.htm

75 Ibid., p. 320.

76 Hasan Tariq Alhasan, 'Bahrain Bids Its Economic Reform Farewell,' *Open Democracy*, 8 July 2012.

77 'Saudi Shoura Council Criticises Nitaqat System,' *Gulf Business*, 29 January 2014.

78 Qatar World Cup Construction 'Will Leave 4000 Migrant Workers Dead,' *The Guardian*, 26 September 2013.

79 Editorials and articles in *The Guardian* between 25 and 27 September 2013.

80 'Man Arrested for Filming Qatar Sites,' *CNN*, 14 October 2013.

81 'More Than 500 Indian Workers Have Died in Qatar Since 2012, Figures Show,' *The Guardian*, 18 February 2014.

82 Kristian Coates Ulrichsen, *Qatar and the Arab Spring* (Oxford: Oxford University Press, 2014), p. 178.

83 George Naufal and Ali Termos, 'Remittances from GCC Countries: A Brief Outlook,' Washington, DC: Middle East Institute, online, 2 February 2010.

84 George Naufal and Ismail Genc, 'The Story of Remittance Flows from the GCC Countries,' Gulf Labor Markets and Migration (GLMM), Explanatory Note, GLMM-EN-No.5/2014, p. 4.

85 Ibid., p. 7.

9   The Illusion of Security?

1   Henner Furtig, 'Conflict and Cooperation in the Persian Gulf: The Interregional Order and U.S. Policy,' *Middle East Journal*, 61(4), 2007, p. 639.

2   Arshin Adib-Moghaddam, *The International Politics of the Persian Gulf: A Cultural Genealogy* (London: Routledge, 2006), p. 29.

3   Abdul-Reda Assiri, *Kuwait's Foreign Policy: City-State in World Politics* (Boulder, CO: Westview Press, 1990), pp. 113–114.

4   Anthony Cordesman, *Kuwait: Recovery and Security after the Gulf War* (Boulder, CO: Westview Press, 1997), pp. 127–128.

5   Abdullah al-Shayeji, 'Dangerous Perceptions: Gulf Views of the U.S. Role in the Region,' *Middle East Policy*, 5(2), 1997, pp. 1–13.

6   Ibid.

7   Mary Ann Weaver, 'Qatar: Revolution from the Top Down,' *National Geographic*, March 2003.

8   'Jihad against Jews and Crusaders,' *World Islamic Front Statement*, 23 February 1998. Available at www.fas.org/irp/world/para/docs/980223-fatwa.htm

9   Khalid al-Tawil, 'The Internet in Saudi Arabia,' *King Fahd University of Petroleum and Minerals Working Paper* (undated), available at www.faculty. kfupm.edu.sa/COE/sadiq/.../Internet%20in%20SA-update1.doc

10   Kristian Coates Ulrichsen, *Insecure Gulf: The End of Certainty and the Transition to the Post-Oil Era* (London: Hurst, 2011), p. 31.

11   Fifteen of the 9/11 hijackers were from Saudi Arabia along with two from the United Arab Emirates. The remaining two hijackers were from Egypt and Lebanon.

12   Lynn Davis, 'Globalization's Security Implications.' Santa Monica: RAND Issue Paper No. 3, 2003, p. 1.

13   Mary Kaldor, Helmut Anheier, and Marlies Glasius, 'Global Civil Society in an Era of Regressive Globalization,' in Mary Kaldor, Helmut Anheier, and Marlies Glasius(eds.), *Global Civil Society 2003* (Oxford: Oxford University Press, 2003), p. 7.

14   Marc Lynch, 'Globalization and Arab Security,' in Jonathan Kirshner (ed.), *Globalization and National Security* (New York: Routledge, 2006), p. 191.

15   Thomas Hegghammer, 'Saudi Militants in Iraq: Backgrounds and Recruitment Patterns,' Oslo: Norwegian Defence Research Establishment (FFI), February 2007, p. 9.

16   Paul Rogers, 'Abqaiq's Warning,' *Open Democracy*, 2 March 2006.

17   Ibid.

18   Ibid.

19   Daveed Gartenstein-Ross, 'Large-Scale Arrests in Saudi Arabia Illustrate Threat to the Oil Supply,' *Long War Journal*, online commentary, 24 March 2010.

20   Kristian Coates Ulrichsen, 'Basra, Southern Iraq and the Gulf: Challenges and Connections,' London: LSE Kuwait Programme Working Paper No. 21, 2012b, p. 16.

21   Furtig, 'Conflict and Cooperation,' p. 638.

22   David Pollock, 'With Neighbours Like These: Iraq and the Arab States on Its Borders,' *Policy Focus No. 70*, Washington, DC: Washington Institute for Near East Policy, 2007, p. 16.

23   Thomas Hegghammer, '"Classical" and "Global" Jihadism in Saudi Arabia,' in Bernard Haykel, Thomas Hegghammer, and Stephane Lacroix (eds.), *Saudi*

Arabia in Transition: Insights on Social, Political, Economic and Religious Change (Cambridge: Cambridge University Press, 2015), p. 217.

24 Anthony Cordesman and Khalid al-Rodhan, 'The Gulf Military Forces in an Era of Asymmetric War: Kuwait,' Washington, DC: Center for Strategic and International Studies, 2006, p. 23.

25 Maurice Greenberg, William Wechsler, and Lee Wolosky, 'Terrorist Financing: Report of an Independent Task Force. Sponsored by the Council on Foreign Relations' (New York: Council on Foreign Relations, 2002), p. 1.

26 Christopher Blanchard, 'Saudi Arabia: Terrorist Financing Issues,' *CRS Report for Congress* (Washington, DC: Congressional Research Service, 2007), p. 8.

27 Ibid., p. 9.

28 Kenneth Katzman, 'Kuwait: Security, Reform, and U.S. Policy,' *CRS Report for Congress* (Washington, DC: Congressional Research Service, 2011), p. 13.

29 'WikiLeaks Cables Portray Saudi Arabia as a Cash Machine for Terrorists,' *The Guardian*, 5 December 2010.

30 Coates Ulrichsen, *Insecure Gulf*, p. 40.

31 Kristian Coates Ulrichsen, 'GCC-Iraq Relations,' in Claire Spencer, Jane Kinninmont, and Omar Sirri (eds.), *Iraq Ten Years On* (London: Chatham House, 2013), p. 45.

32 Toby Dodge, *Iraq: From War to a New Authoritarianism* (Abingdon: Routledge, 2012), p. 192.

33 'Jihadist Expansion in Iraq Puts Persian Gulf States in a Tight Spot,' *Washington Post*, 13 June 2014.

34 'American is Fatally Shot in Saudi Arabia,' *New York Times*, 14 October 2014.

35 'Saudi Probes Motive behind Attack on Canadian,' *Al Arabiya*, 30 November 2014.

36 'US Teacher Killed as Americans Targeted in Separate Abu Dhabi Attacks,' *The Guardian*, 4 December 2014.

37 Lori Plotkin Boghardt, 'Saudi Arabia's Old Al-Qaeda Terrorists form New Threat,' *Policywatch 2370* (Washington, DC: Washington Institute for Near East Policy (WINEP)), 11 February 2015.

38 Jack Moore, 'ISIS "Attack Saudi Border Post and Infiltrate Town,"' *Newsweek*, 28 January 2015.

39 Plotkin Boghardt, 'Saudi Arabia's Old Al-Qaeda Terrorists Form New Threat.'

40 'The Race to Save Peter Kassig,' *The Guardian*, 18 December 2014.

41 Bill Law, 'Bahrain: The Islamic State Threat Within,' *Middle East Eye*, 14 October 2014.

42 Ibid.

43 'Saudi: Muslim Brotherhood a Terrorist Organization,' *Al Arabiya*, 7 March 2014.

44 Kristian Coates Ulrichsen, David Held, and Alia Brahimi, 'The Arab 1989?' *Open Democracy*, 11 February 2011.

45 Jean-Francois Seznec, 'Saudi Arabia Strikes Back,' *Foreign Policy*, 14 March 2011.

46 Kristian Coates Ulrichsen, 'Bahrain's Uprising: Domestic Implications and Regional and International Consequences,' in Fawaz Gerges (ed.), *The New Middle East: Protest and Revolution in the Arab World* (Cambridge: Cambridge University Press, 2013), p. 337.

47 Kristian Coates Ulrichsen, 'Politics and Opposition in Kuwait: Continuity and Change,' *Journal of Arabian Studies*, 4(2), 2014, p. 214.

48   Toby Matthiesen, 'A Saudi "Spring?" The Shia Protest Movement in the Eastern Province 2011–2012,' *Middle East Journal*, 66(4), 2012, p. 629.
49   Abdulhadi Khalaf, 'Saudi Arabia Manages Protests, Dissent,' *Al Monitor*, 1 April 2013.
50   Kristian Coates Ulrichsen, 'Gulf States: Studious Silence Falls on the Arab Spring,' *Open Democracy*, 25 April 2011.
51   'Interview with Dr. Ali Khalifa al-Kuwari, author of "The People Want Reform . . . in Qatar, Too,"' *Heinrich Boll Stiftung*, 3 March 2014.
52   'Resources in the Gulf will Define the Region's Future Policy Options and Relationships,' *Gulf States Newsletter*, 35(900), 13 May 2011, p. 1.
53   Martin Baldwin-Edwards, 'Labour Immigration and Labour Markets in the GCC Countries: National Patterns and Trends,' London: LSE Kuwait Programme Working Paper No. 15, 2011, p. 20.
54   Emma Murphy, 'ICT and the Gulf Arab States: A Force for Democracy?,' in Anoushiravan Ehteshami and Steven Wright (eds.), *Reform in the Middle East Oil Monarchies* (Reading: Ithaca Press, 2008), p. 183.
55   Michael Herb, 'Kuwait: The Obstacle of Parliamentary Politics,' in Joshua Teitelbaum (ed.), *Political Liberalization in the Persian Gulf* (London: Hurst, 2009), p. 153.
56   Personal interviews with Bahraini activists in London, March and June 2011.
57   Ng Sue Chia, 'Social Media's Role in Revolt: A Technological or Social Phenomenon? – Analysis,' *Eurasia Review News & Analysis*, 22 March 2011.
58   Kristian Coates Ulrichsen and David Held, 'The Arab 1989 Revisited,' *Open Democracy*, 27 September 2011.
59   Steffen Hertog, 'The Costs of Counter-Revolution in the Gulf,' *Foreign Policy*, 31 May 2011.
60   'Gulf Arab States Should Cut State Spending Growth: IMF,' *Reuters*, 29 October 2012.
61   Hertog, 'Costs of Counter-Revolution.'
62   'Oman's Sultan Qaboos Responds to Popular Protests with Successive Government Reshuffles,' *Gulf States Newsletter*, 35(896), 11 March 2011, p. 3.
63   'Qatar's Pay and Pension Rises Could Store up Problems for the Future,' *Gulf States Newsletter*, 35(908), 16 September 2011, p. 16.
64   'Kuwait Transfers $250m to Jordan's Central Bank,' *ArabianBusiness.com*, 7 October 2012.
65   'Sales of Weapons to Gulf States Up 70% Over Five Years,' *The Guardian*, 16 March 2015.
66   'Summit Fails to Agree on Gulf Union,' *Gulf States Newsletter*, 36(924), 24 May 2012, pp. 5–6.
67   Kristian Coates Ulrichsen, *Qatar and the Arab Spring* (Oxford: Oxford University Press, 2014), p. 155.
68   Kristian Coates Ulrichsen, 'Small States with a Big Role: Qatar and the United Arab Emirates in the Wake of the Arab Spring,' Durham University: HH Sheikh Nasser al-Mohammad al-Sabah Publication Series No. 3, October 2012c, p. 13.
69   Coates Ulrichsen, *Qatar and the Arab Spring*, p. 143.
70   Abdullah Al-Shayeji, 'The GCC-US Relationship: A GCC Perspective,' Washington, DC: Middle East Policy Council, Journal Essay, August 2014, http://mepc.org/journal/middle-east-policy-archives/gcc-us-relationship-gcc-perspective

71 'Saudi Deploys 100 Fighter Jets, 150,000 Soldiers for Anti-Houthi Campaign,' *Al Arabiya*, 26 March 2015.

72 Abraham Denmark, 'Regional Perspectives on U.S. Strategic Rebalancing,' *Asia Policy*, 15(1), 2013, p. 2.

73 Kristian Coates Ulrichsen, 'The U.S., Asia, and the Middle East: A Convergence of Interests,' *Houston Chronicle/Baker Institute Blog*, 9 May 2015.

74 'Leading Saudi Researcher Warns West of a Newly Assertive Saudi Arabia,' *Gulf States Newsletter*, 35(901), 27 May 2011, p. 8.

75 Simon Henderson, 'No One in the Region Will Sleep,' *The Atlantic*, 25 November, 2013.

76 'Iran and P5+1 Sign Breakthrough Nuclear Deal,' *Gulf States Newsletter*, 37(959), 28 November 2013, p. 3.

77 Lawrence Potter, 'Introduction,' in Lawrence Potter (ed.), *Sectarian Politics in the Persian Gulf* (London: Hurst, 2013), p. 25.

78 David Hearst, 'Has Iran Overreached Itself in Yemen?' *Middle East Eye*, 26 March 2015.

79 Frederic Wehrey, 'Into the Maelstrom: The Saudi-led Misadventure in Yemen,' Washington, DC: Carnegie Endowment for International Peace online analysis, 26 March 2015.

Bibliography

Books

Adib-Moghaddam, Arshin, 2006. *The International Politics of the Persian Gulf: A Cultural Genealogy.* London: Routledge.

Al-Fahim, Mohammed, 1995. *From Rags to Riches: A Story of Abu Dhabi.* London: Center of Arab Studies.

Ali, Syed, 2010. *Dubai: Gilded Cage.* New Haven, CT: Yale University Press.

Assiri, Abdul-Reda, 1990. *Kuwait's Foreign Policy: City-State in World Politics.* Boulder, CO: Westview Press.

Ayubi, Nazih, 1993. *Political Islam: Religion and Politics in the Arab World.* Abingdon: Routledge.

Bazoobandi, Sara, 2013. *The Political Economy of the Gulf Sovereign Wealth Funds: A Case Study of Iran, Kuwait, Saudi Arabia and the United Arab Emirates.* Abingdon: Routledge.

Bromley, Simon, 1994. *Rethinking Middle East Politics: State Formation and Development.* Cambridge: Polity Press.

Bullock, John, 1984. *The Gulf: A Portrait of Kuwait, Qatar, Bahrain and the UAE.* London: Century Publishing.

Casey, Michael, 2007. *The History of Kuwait.* Westport, CT: Greenwood Press.

Chase, Anthony and Amr Hamzawy, 2006. *Human Rights in the Arab World: Independent Voices.* Philadelphia: University of Pennsylvania Press.

Chaudhry, Kiren Aziz, 1997. *The Price of Wealth: Economies and Institutions in the Middle East.* Ithaca, NY: Cornell University Press.

Coates Ulrichsen, Kristian, 2011. *Insecure Gulf: The End of Certainty and the Transition to the Post-Oil Era.* London: Hurst.

Coates Ulrichsen, Kristian, 2014. *Qatar and the Arab Spring.* Oxford: Oxford University Press.

Coll, Steve, 2012. *Private Empire: ExxonMobil and American Power.* London: Allen Lane.

Cordesman, Anthony, 1997. *Kuwait: Recovery and Security after the Gulf War.* Boulder, CO: Westview Press.

Cordesman, Anthony and Khalid al-Rodhan, 2006a. *The Gulf Military Forces in an Era of Asymmetric Warfare: Kuwait.* Washington, DC: Center for Strategic and International Studies.

Cordesman, Anthony and Khalid al-Rodhan, 2006b. *The Gulf Military Forces in an Age of Asymmetric Warfare: Qatar.* Washington, DC: Center for Strategic and International Studies.

Crystal, Jill, 1990. *Oil and Politics in the Gulf: Rulers and Merchants in Kuwait and Qatar.* Cambridge: Cambridge University Press.

Davidson, Christopher, 2005. *The United Arab Emirates: A Study in Survival.* London: Lynne Rienner.

Davidson, Christopher, 2008. *Dubai: The Vulnerability of Success.* London: Hurst.

Davidson, Christopher, 2009. *Abu Dhabi: Oil and Beyond.* London: Hurst.

Davidson, Christopher, 2010. *The Persian Gulf and Pacific Asia: From Indifference to Interdependence*. London: Hurst.

Davidson, Christopher, 2012. *After the Sheikhs: The Coming Collapse of the Gulf Monarchies*. London: Hurst.

Dodge, Toby, 2012. *Iraq: From War to a New Authoritarianism*. Abingdon: Routledge.

Donn, Gari and Yahya Al Manthri, 2010. *Globalization and Higher Education in the Arab Gulf States*. Didcot: Symposium Books.

Ehteshami, Anoushiravan, 2007. *Globalisation and Geopolitics in the Middle East: Old Games, New Rules*. London: Routledge.

Elsheshtawy, Yasser, 2009. *Dubai: Behind an Urban Spectacle*. Abingdon: Routledge.

Fain, W. Taylor, 2008. *American Ascendance and British Retreat in the Persian Gulf Region*. Basingstoke: Palgrave Macmillan.

Field, Michael, 1985. *The Merchants: The Big Business Families of Saudi Arabia and the Gulf States*. Woodstock, NY: The Overlook Press.

Filiu, Jean-Pierre, 2014. *Gaza: A History*. Oxford: Oxford University Press.

Fox, John, Nada Mourtada-Sabbah, and Mohammed al-Mutawa, 2006. *Globalization and the Gulf*. London: Routledge.

Gilpin, Robert, 1987. *The Political Economy of International Relations*. Princeton, NJ: Princeton University Press.

Gilpin, Robert, 2001. *Global Political Economy: Understanding the International Political Order*. Princeton, NJ: Princeton University Press.

Gilpin, Robert, 2002. *The Challenge of Global Capitalism: The World Economy in the 21st Century*. Princeton, NJ: Princeton University Press.

Goldblatt, David, 2014. *Futebol Nation: The Story of Brazil through Soccer*. New York: Penguin Books.

Gray, Matthew, 2013. *Qatar: Politics and the Challenge of Development*. Boulder, CO: Lynne Rienner.

Halliday, Fred, 2002. *Arabia without Sultans*. London: Penguin Books.

Halliday, Fred, 2005. *The Middle East in International Relations: Power, Politics, and Ideology*. Cambridge: Cambridge University Press.

Hanieh, Adam, 2011. *Capitalism and Class in the Gulf Arab States*. New York: Palgrave Macmillan.

Heard-Bey, Frauke, 1996. *From Trucial States to United Arab Emirates*. London: Longman.

Held, David, 2004. *Global Covenant: The Social Democratic Alternative to the Washington Consensus*. Cambridge: Polity Press.

Held, David and Kristian Ulrichsen, 2011. *The Transformation of the Gulf: Politics, Economics and the Global Order*. Abingdon: Routledge.

Held, David and Kristian Coates Ulrichsen, 2016, forthcoming. *The End of the American Century: From 9/11 to the Arab Spring*. Cambridge: Polity Press.

Herb, Michael, 1999. *All in the Family: Absolutism, Revolution, and Democracy in the Middle Eastern Monarchies*. Albany, NY: State University of New York Press.

Hertog, Steffen, 2010. *Princes, Brokers, and Bureaucrats: Oil and the State in Saudi Arabia*. Ithaca, NY: Cornell University Press.

Joyce, Miriam, 1998. *Kuwait 1945–1996: An Anglo-American Perspective*. London: Frank Cass.

Kamrava, Mehran, 2013. *Qatar: Small State, Big Politics*. Ithaca, NY: Cornell University Press.

Khalaf, Abdulhadi, Omar AlShehabi, and Adam Hanieh, eds, 2015. *Transit States: Labour, Migration & Citizenship in the Gulf.* London: Pluto Press.

Khola, I. P., 2009. *India and the Gulf.* New Delhi: Association of Indian Diplomats.

Krane, Jim, 2009. *Dubai: The Story of the World's Fastest City.* New York: St Martin's Press.

Lippman, Thomas, 2005. *Inside the Mirage: America's Fragile Partnership with Saudi Arabia.* Boulder, CO: Westview Press.

Longva, Anh Nga, 1997. *Walls Built on Sand: Migration, Exclusion, and Society in Kuwait.* Boulder, CO: Westview Press.

Luciani, Giacomo, 1990. *The Arab State.* London: Routledge.

Luomi, Mari, 2012. *The Gulf Monarchies and Climate Change: Abu Dhabi and Qatar in an Era of Natural Unsustainability.* London: Hurst.

Macris, Jeffrey, 2009. *The Politics and Security of the Gulf: Anglo-American Hegemony and the Shaping of a Region.* Abingdon: Routledge.

Marcel, Valerie, 2006. *Oil Titans: National Oil Companies in the Middle East.* London: The Royal Institute of International Affairs.

Menoret, Pascal, 2014. *Joyriding in Riyadh: Oil, Urbanism and Road Revolt.* Cambridge: Cambridge University Press.

Metcalf, Thomas, 2007. *Imperial Connections: India in the Indian Ocean Arena, 1860–1920.* Berkeley, CA: University of California Press.

Migdal, Joel, 2014. *Shifting Sands: The United States in the Middle East.* New York: Columbia University Press.

Mills, Robin, 2008. *The Myth of the Oil Crisis.* Westport, CT: Praeger Publishers.

Moore, Pete, 2004. *Doing Business in the Middle East: Politics and Economic Crisis in Jordan and Kuwait.* Cambridge: Cambridge University Press.

Niblock, Tim with Monica Malik, 2007. *The Political Economy of Saudi Arabia.* Abingdon: Routledge.

Nonneman, Gerd, 2006. *EU-GCC Relations: Dynamics, Patterns & Perspectives.* Dubai: Gulf Research Centre.

Nye, Joseph, 1990. *Bound to Lead: The Changing Nature of American Power.* New York: Basic Books.

Nye, Joseph, 2004. *Soft Power: The Means to Success in World Politics.* New York: PublicAffairs.

Nye, Joseph, 2011. *The Future of Power.* New York: PublicAffairs.

Oatley, Thomas, 2011a. *Debates in International Political Economy.* Cambridge: Pearson, 5th edition.

Oatley, Thomas, 2011b. *International Political Economy.* Cambridge: Pearson, 2nd edition.

Price, David, 2009. *The Development of Intellectual Property Regimes in the Arabian GulfStates: Infidels at the Gates.* Abingdon: Routledge.

Ramos, Stephen, 2012. *Dubai Amplified: The Engineering of a Port Geography.* London: Ashgate.

Ravenhill, John, ed., 2008. *Global Political Economy.* Oxford: Oxford University Press, 2nd edition.

Said Zahlan, Rosemarie, 1998. *The Making of the Modern Gulf States.* Reading: Ithaca Press.

Samans, Richard, Klaus Schwab, and Mark Malloch-Brown, 2010. *Global Redesign: Strengthening International Cooperation in a More Interdependent World.* Geneva: World Economic Forum.

Simpfendorfer, Ben, 2009. *The New Silk Road: How a Rising Arab World is Turning Away from the West and Rediscovering China.* Basingstoke: Palgrave Macmillan.
Slaughter, Anne-Marie, 2004. *A New World Order.* Princeton, NJ: Princeton University Press.
Valeri, Marc, 2009. *Oman: Politics and Society in the Qaboos State.* London: Hurst.
Vitalis, Robert, 2007. *America's Kingdom: Mythmaking on the Saudi Oil Frontier.* Stanford, CA: Stanford University Press.
Walter, Andrew and Gautam Sen, 2008. *Analysing the Global Political Economy.* Princeton, NJ: Princeton University Press.
Westad, Odd Arne, 2005. *The Global Cold War: Third World Interventions and the Making of our Times.* Cambridge: Cambridge University Press.
Yergin, Daniel, 2011. *The Quest: Energy, Security, and the Remaking of the Modern World.* London: Allen Lane.
Yizraeli, Sarah, 1997. *The Remaking of Saudi Arabia.* Tel Aviv: The Moshe Dayan Center for Middle Eastern and African Studies.
Yizraeli, Sarah, 2012. *Politics and Society in Saudi Arabia: The Crucial Years of Development, 1960–1982.* New York: Columbia University Press.

Chapters

Abboud, Samer, 2011. 'Oil and Financialization in the Gulf Cooperation Council.' In Matteo Legrenzi and Bessma Momani, eds. *Shifting Geo-Economic Power of the Gulf: Oil, Finance and Institutions.* Farnham: Ashgate.
Abdulla, Abdulkhaleq, 2006. 'The Impact of Globalization on Arab Gulf States.' In John Fox, Nada Mourtada-Sabbah, and Mohammed al-Mutawa, eds. *Globalization and the Gulf.* London: Routledge.
Ahmad, Attiya, 2012. 'Beyond Labor: Foreign Residents in the Persian Gulf States.' In Mehran Kamrava and Zahra Babar, eds. *Migrant Labour in the Persian Gulf.* London: Hurst.
Al Bu Said, Badr bin Hamad, 2005. '"Small States" Diplomacy in the Age of Globalization: An Omani Perspective.' In Gerd Nonneman, ed. *Analyzing Middle East Foreign Policies and the Relationship with Europe.* London: Routledge.
Al-Khwaiter, 'Abd Al-Aziz ibn 'Abd Al-Allah, 2010. 'King Abdul Aziz: His Style of Administration.' In Fahd al-Semmari, ed. *A History of the Arabian Peninsula.* London: I.B. Tauris.
Al-Mezaini, Khalid, 2013. 'Private Sector Actors in the UAE and their Role in the Process of Economic and Political Reform.' In Steffen Hertog, Giacomo Luciani, and Marc Valeri, eds. *Business Politics in the Middle East.* London: Hurst.
AlShehabi, Omar, 2015a. 'Histories of Migration to the Gulf.' In Abdulhadi Khalaf, Omar AlShehabi, and Adam Hanieh, eds. *Transit States: Labour, Migration & Citizenship in the Gulf.* London: Pluto Press.
AlShehabi, Omar, 2015b. 'Migration, Commodification, and the "Right to the City".' In Abdulhadi Khalaf, Omar AlShehabi, and Adam Hanieh, eds. *Transit States: Labour, Migration & Citizenship in the Gulf.* London: Pluto Press.
Anon., 2008. 'New Avenues: OBG Talks to Bader Al Saad, Managing Director, Kuwait Investment Authority,' in *The Report: Kuwait, 2008.* Oxford: Oxford Business Group.

Anon., 2012. 'Q&A Mr Ahmed Al Nuaimi, Chairman, Qatar Tourism Authority, "Boosting Visitor Numbers While Improving Quality and Offerings".' In *B'Here Annual Review Qatar 2012: The Vision Moves Forward: Towards a Knowledge-Based Society*. Doha: Arab Communications Consult.

Baaboud, Abdulla and Geoffrey Edwards, 2008. 'Sovereign Reluctance: The Interaction of the Gulf States and the European Union.' In Christian Koch, ed. *EU-GCC Relations & Security Issues: Broadening the Horizon*. Dubai: Gulf Research Centre.

Baker, Andrew, 2011. 'International Competition and Symbiosis in the Gulf: The Politics of Efforts to Establish an International Islamic Financial Policy Forum.' In Matteo Legrenzi and Bessma Momani, eds. *Shifting Geo-Economic Power of the Gulf: Oil, Finance and Institutions*. Farnham: Ashgate.

Baracuhy, Braz, 2015. 'The Evolving Geo-Economics of World Trade.' In Sanjaya Baru and Suvi Dogra, eds. *Power Shifts and New Blocs in the Global Trading System*. Abingdon: Routledge.

Beblawi, Hazem, 1990. 'The Rentier State in the Arab World.' In Giacomo Luciani, ed. *The Arab State*. London: Routledge.

Bishara, Fahad Ahmad, 2014. 'Mapping the Indian Ocean World of Gulf Merchants, c.1870–1960.' In Abdul Sheriff and Engseng Ho, eds. *The Indian Ocean: Oceanic Connections and the Creation of New Societies*. London: Hurst.

Bonine, Michael, 1997. 'Population Growth, the Labor Market, and Gulf Security.' In Christian Koch and David Long, eds. *Gulf Security in the Twenty-First Century*. Abu Dhabi: Emirates Center for Strategic Studies and Research.

Bristol-Rhys, Jane, 2012. 'Socio-Spatial Boundaries in Abu Dhabi.' In Mehran Kamrava and Zahra Babar, eds. *Migrant Labor in the Persian Gulf*. London: Hurst.

Coates Ulrichsen, Kristian, 2012. 'Knowledge-Based Economies in the GCC.' In Mehran Kamrava, ed. *The Political Economy of the Persian Gulf*. London: Hurst.

Coates Ulrichsen, Kristian, 2013a. 'Bahrain's Uprising: Domestic Implications and Regional and International Consequences.' In Fawaz Gerges, ed. *The New Middle East: Protest and Revolution in the Arab World*. Cambridge: Cambridge University Press.

Coates Ulrichsen, Kristian, 2013b. 'GCC-Iraq Relations.' In Claire Spencer, Jane Kinninmont, and Omar Sirri, eds. *Iraq Ten Years On*. London: Chatham House.

Crystal, Jill, 2009. 'Economic and Political Liberalization: Views from the Business Community.' In Joshua Teitelbaum, ed. *Political Liberalization in the Persian Gulf*. London: Hurst.

Dargin, Justin, 2013. 'Introduction.' In Justin Dargin, ed. *The Rise of the Global South: Philosophical, Geopolitical and Economic Trends of the 21st Century*. Singapore: World Scientific Publishing.

Davidson, Christopher, 2008a. 'Diversification in Abu Dhabi and Dubai: The Impact of National Identity and the Ruling Bargain.' In Alanoud Alsharekh and Robert Springborg, eds. *Popular Culture and Political Identity in the Arab Gulf States*. London: Saqi Books.

Davidson, Christopher, 2008b. 'The Impact of Economic Reform on Dubai.' In Anoushiravan Ehteshami and Steven Wright, eds. *Reform in the Middle East Oil Monarchies*. Reading: Ithaca Press.

Davidson, Christopher, 2011. 'Gulf-Pacific Asia Linkages in the Twenty-First Century: A Marriage of Convenience?' In David Held and Kristian Ulrichsen, eds. *The Transformation of the Gulf: Politics, Economics and the Global Order*. Abingdon: Routledge.

Davidson, Christopher, 2012. 'The Dubai Model: Diversification and Slowdown.' In Mehran Kamrava, ed. *The Political Economy of the Persian Gulf*. London: Hurst.

Ditto, Mohammed, 2015. 'Kafala: Foundations of Migrant Exclusion in GCC Labour Markets.' In Abdulhadi Khalaf, Omar AlShehabi, and Adam Hanieh, eds. *Transit States: Labour, Migration & Citizenship in the Gulf*. London: Pluto Press.

El-Katiri, Laura, Bassam Fattouh, and Paul Segal, 2011. 'Anatomy of an Oil-Based Welfare State: Rent Distribution in Kuwait.' In David Held and Kristian Ulrichsen, eds. *The Transformation of the Gulf: Politics, Economics and the Global Order*. Abingdon: Routledge.

Fox, John, Nada Mourtada-Sabbah, and Mohammed al-Mutawa, 2006. 'The Arab Gulf Region: Tradition Globalized or Globalization Traditionalized?' In John Fox, Nada Mourtada-Sabbah, and Mohammed al-Mutawa, eds. *Globalization and the Gulf*. London: Routledge.

Gardner, Andrew, 2012. 'Why Do They Keep Coming: Labor Migrants in the Persian Gulf States.' In Mehran Kamrava and Zahra Babar, eds. *Migrant Labor in the Persian Gulf*. London: Hurst.

Gray, Kevin and Craig Murphy, 2014. 'Introduction: Rising Powers and the Future of Global Governance.' In Kevin Gray and Craig Murphy, eds. *Rising Powers and the Future of Global Governance*. Abingdon: Routledge.

Green, David, 2006. 'Research in Consumer and Real Estate Markets.' In Anthony Shoult, ed. *Doing Business with Saudi Arabia: A Guide to Investment Opportunities & Business Practice*. London: GMB Publishing.

Hadhri, Mohieddine, 2011. 'Globalisation Challenges and New Arab Regionalism: Towards a New Deal of South-South Integration.' In Miroslav Jovanovic, ed. *The International Handbook on the Economics of Integration: General Issues and Regional Groups*. London: Edward Elgar Publishing.

Hague, William, 2013. 'Foreword.' In John Holden, ed. *Influence and Attraction: Culture and the Race for Soft Power in the 21st Century*. London: British Council & Demos.

Halliday, Fred, 2003. 'Global Governance: Prospects and Problems.' In David Held and Anthony McGrew, eds. *The Global Transformations Reader: An Introduction to the Globalization Debate*. Cambridge: Polity Press.

Hardy, Roger, 2008. 'Ambivalent Ally: Saudi Arabia and the "War on Terror".' In Madawi al-Rasheed, ed. *Kingdom without Borders: Saudi Arabia's Political, Religious and Media Frontiers*. London: Hurst.

Hegghammer, Thomas, 2015. '"Classical" and "Global" Jihadism in Saudi Arabia.' In Bernard Haykel, Thomas Hegghammer, and Stephane Lacroix, eds. *Saudi Arabia in Transition: Insights on Social, Political, Economic and Religious Change*. Cambridge: Cambridge University Press.

Held, David, 1999. 'Democracy, the Nation-State and the Global System.' In Malcolm Waters, ed. *Modernity: Critical Concepts. Volume IV – After Modernity*. Abingdon: Routledge.

Held, David and Anthony McGrew, 2002. 'Introduction.' In David Held and Anthony McGrew, eds. *Governing Globalization: Power, Autonomy and Global Governance*. Cambridge: Polity Press.

Held, David and Anthony McGrew, 2003. 'The Great Globalization Debate.' In David Held and Anthony McGrew, eds. *The Global Transformations Reader*. Cambridge: Polity Press.

Held, David and Kristian Ulrichsen, 2011. 'Introduction.' In David Held and Kristian Ulrichsen, eds. *The Transformation of the Gulf: Politics, Economics and the Global Order*. Abingdon: Routledge.

Herb, Michael, 2009. 'Kuwait: The Obstacle of Parliamentary Politics.' In Joshua Teitelbaum, ed. *Political Liberalization in the Persian Gulf*. London: Hurst.

Hertog, Steffen, 2011. 'Lean and Mean: The New Breed of State-owned Enterprises in the Gulf Monarchies.' In Jean-Francois Seznec and Mimi Kirk, eds. *Industrialization in the Gulf: A Socioeconomic Revolution*. London: Routledge.

Kaldor, Mary, Helmut Anheier, and Marlies Glasius, 2003. 'Global Civil Society in an Era of Regressive Globalization.' In Mary Kaldor, Helmut Anheier, and Marlies Glasius, eds. *Global Civil Society 2003*. Oxford: Oxford University Press.

Kamrava, Mehran, 2015. 'Contemporary Port Cities in the Persian Gulf: Local Gateways and Global Networks.' In Mehran Kamrava, ed. *Gateways to the World: The Rise and Fall of Port Cities in the Persian Gulf*. London: Hurst.

Kamrava, Mehran and Zahra Babar, 2012. 'Situating Labor Migration in the Persian Gulf.' In Mehran Kamrava and Zahra Babar, eds. *Migrant Labor in the Persian Gulf*. London: Hurst.

Khalaf, Abdulhadi, 2015. 'The Politics of Migration.' In Abdulhadi Khalaf, Omar AlShehabi, and Adam Hanieh, eds. *Transit States: Labour, Migration & Citizenship in the Gulf*. London: Pluto Press.

Kinninmont, Jane, 2011. 'Bahrain.' In Christopher Davidson, ed. *Power and Politics in the Persian Gulf*. London: Hurst.

Legrenzi, Matteo, 2011. 'Gulf Cooperation Council Coordination: The Limited Role of Institutionalization.' In Jean-Francois Seznec and Mimi Kirk, eds. *Industrialization in the Gulf: A Socioeconomic Revolution*. Abingdon: Routledge.

Luciani, Giacomo, 1990. 'Allocative vs Production States: A Theoretical Framework.' In Giacomo Luciani, ed. *The Arab State*. London: Routledge.

Luciani, Giacomo, 2005. 'From Private Sector to National Bourgeoisie: Saudi Arabian Business.' In Paul Aarts and Gerd Nonneman, eds. *Saudi Arabia in the Balance: Political Economy, Society, Foreign Affairs*. London: Hurst.

Luciani, Giacomo, 2007. 'The GCC Refining and Petrochemical Sectors in Global Perspective.' In Eckart Woertz, ed. *Gulf Geo-Economics*. Dubai: Gulf Research Centre.

Lynch, Marc, 2006. 'Globalization and Arab Security.' In Jonathan Kirshner, ed. *Globalization and National Security*. New York: Routledge.

Mansoob Murshed, Syed, Pedro Goulart, and Leandro Serino, 2011. 'Globalization and the South at the Crossroads of Change.' In Syed Manoos Murshed, Pedro Goulart, and Leandro Serino, eds. *South-South Globalization: Challenges and Opportunities for Development*. Abingdon: Routledge.

Momani, Bessma, 2011. 'Shifting Gulf Arab Investment into the Mashreq: Underlying Political Economy Rationales?' In Matteo Legrenzi and Bessma Momani, eds. *Shifting Geo-Economic Power of the Gulf: Oil, Finance and Institutions*. Farnham: Ashgate.

Murphy, Emma, 2008. 'ICT and the Gulf Arab Streets: A Force for Democracy?' In Anoushiravan Ehteshami and Steven Wright, eds. *Reform in the Middle East Oil Monarchies*. Reading: Ithaca Press.

Nonneman, Gerd, 2005. 'Determinants and Patterns of Saudi Foreign Policy: "Omnibalancing" and "Relative Autonomy" in Multiple Environments.' In Paul Aarts and Gerd Nonneman, eds. *Saudi Arabia in the Balance: Political Economy, Society, Foreign Affairs*. London: Hurst.

Nonneman, Gerd, 2008. 'Political Reform in the Gulf Monarchies: From Liberalization to Democratization: A Comparative Perspective.' In Anoushiravan Ehteshami and Steven Wright, eds. *Reform in the Middle East Oil Monarchies*. Reading: Ithaca Press.

Nugent, Jeffrey, 2014. 'US-Bahrain Relations.' In Robert Looney, ed. *Handbook of US-Middle East Relations: Formative Factors and Regional Perspectives*. Abingdon: Routledge.

Onley, James, 2005. 'Transnational Merchants in the Nineteenth Century: The Case of the Safar Family.' In Madawi al-Rasheed, ed. *Transnational Connections and the Arab Gulf*. Abingdon: Routledge.

Peterson, J. E., 2007. 'Rulers, Merchants, and Shaykhs in Gulf Politics: The Function of Family Networks.' In Alanoud Alsharekh, ed. *The Gulf Family: Kinship Policies and Modernity*. London: Saqi Books.

Peterson, J. E., 2011. 'Sovereignty and Boundaries in the Gulf States: Setting the Peripheries.' In Mehran Kamrava, ed. *International Politics of the Persian Gulf*. New York: Syracuse University Press.

Peterson, J. E., 2013. 'The Baluch Presence in the Persian Gulf.' In Lawrence Potter, ed. *Sectarian Politics in the Persian Gulf*. London: Hurst.

Potter, Lawrence, 2013. 'Introduction.' In Lawrence Potter (ed.), *Sectarian Politics in the Persian Gulf*. London: Hurst.

Potts, D. T., 2009. 'The Archaeology and Early History of the Persian Gulf.' In Lawrence Potter, ed. *The Persian Gulf in History*. New York: Palgrave Macmillan.

Quilliam, Neil, 2008. 'Political Reform in Bahrain: The Turning Tide.' In Anoushiravan Ehteshami and Steven Wright, eds. *Reform in the Middle East Oil Monarchies*. Reading: Ithaca Press.

Raghu, M., 2011. 'Future Direction of the GCC Financial Sector – A Specific Look at Banking and Asset Management.' In Eckart Woertz, ed. *GCC Financial Markets*. Dubai: Gulf Research Centre.

Roy-Chaudhury, Rahul, 2014. 'India: Gulf Security Partner in Waiting?' In Toby Dodge and Emile Hokayem, eds. *Middle Eastern Security, the US Pivot and the Rise of ISIS*. Abingdon: Routledge.

Saif, Ahmed Abdelkareem, 2008. 'Deconstructing before Building: Perspectives on Democracy in Qatar.' In Anoushiravan Ehteshami and Steven Wright, eds. *Reform in the Middle East Oil Monarchies*. Reading: Ithaca Press.

Sayigh, Yezid and Avi Shlaim, 1997. 'Introduction.' In Yezid Sayigh and Avi Shlaim, eds. *The Cold War and the Middle East*. Oxford: Clarendon Press.

Schofield, Richard, 1997. 'Boundaries, Territorial Disputes and the GCC States.' In David Long and Christian Koch, eds. *Gulf Security in the Twenty-First Century*. Abu Dhabi: Emirates Centre for Strategic Studies and Research.

Scholte, Jan Aart, 2005. 'Civil Society and Democratically Accountable Global Governance.' In David Held and Matthias Koenig-Archibugi, eds. *Global Governance and Public Accountability*. Oxford: Blackwell and Wiley.

Seznec, Jean-Francois and Mimi Kirk, 2011. 'Introduction.' In Jean-Francois Seznec and Mimi Kirk, eds. *Industrialization in the Gulf: A Socioeconomic Revolution*. London: Routledge.

Sheriff, Abdul, 2009. 'The Persian Gulf and the Swahili Coast: A History of Acculturation over the Longue Duree.' In Lawrence Potter, ed. *The Persian Gulf in History*. New York: Palgrave Macmillan.

Willoughby, John, 2006. 'Ambivalent Anxieties of the South Asian-Gulf Arab Labor Exchange.' In John Fox, Nada Mourtada-Sabbah, and Mohammed al-Mutawa, eds. *Globalization and the Gulf*. Abingdon: Routledge.

Wilson, Rodney, 2008. 'Economic Governance and Reform in Saudi Arabia.' In Anoushiravan Ehteshami and Steven Wright, eds. *Political Reform in the Middle East Oil Monarchies*. Reading: Ithaca Press.

Wilson, Rodney, 2011a. 'The Development of Islamic Finance in the Gulf Cooperation Council States.' In David Held and Kristian Ulrichsen, eds. *The Transformation of the Gulf: Politics, Economics and the Global Order*. Abingdon: Routledge.

Wilson, Rodney, 2011b. 'Approaches to Islamic Banking in the Gulf.' In Eckart Woertz, ed. *GCC Financial Markets*. Dubai: Gulf Research Centre.

Woods, Ngaire, 2002. 'Global Governance and the Role of Institutions.' In David Held and Anthony McGrew, eds. *Governing Globalization: Power, Authority and Global Governance*. Cambridge: Polity Press.

Wright, Steven, 2008. 'US Foreign Policy and the Changed Definition of Gulf Security.' In Anoushiravan Ehteshami and Steven Wright, eds. *Political Reform in the Middle East Oil Monarchies*. Reading: Ithaca Press.

Ziemba, Rachel and Anton Malkin, 2011. 'The GCC's International Investment Dynamics. The Role of Sovereign Wealth Funds.' In Matteo Legrenzi and Bessma Momani, eds. *Shifting Geo-Economic Power of the Gulf: Oil, Finance and Institutions*. Farnham: Ashgate.

Journal Articles and Working Papers

Abu-Hussin, Mohd Fauzi bin, 2013. 'Gulf Arab Foreign Direct Investment (FDI): ASEAN Targets of Opportunity.' Washington, DC: Middle East Institute online commentary.

Alhasan, Hasan Tariq, 2012. 'Bahrain Bids its Economic Reform Farewell.' *Open Democracy*, 8 July.

Aliboni, Roberto, 2005. 'Europe's Role in the Gulf: A Transatlantic Perspective.' *The International Spectator: Italian Journal of International Affairs*, 41(2).

Alissa, Reem, 2013. 'The Oil Town of Ahmadi since 1946: From Colonial Town to Nostalgic City.' *Comparative Politics of South Asia, Africa and the Middle East*, 33(1).

Al-Mekaimi, Haila, 2012. 'The Impact of Islamic Groups and Arab Spring on the Youth Political Movement in Kuwait.' *Journal of South Asian and Middle Eastern Studies*, 36(1).

Al-Nakib, Farah, 2013. 'Kuwait's Modern Spectacle: Oil Wealth and the Making of a New Capital City, 1950–90.' *Comparative Studies of South Asia, Africa and the Middle East*, 33(1).

Al-Sayegh, Fatma, 1998. 'Merchants' Role in a Changing Society: The Case of Dubai, 1900–1990.' *Middle Eastern Studies*, 34(1).

Al-Shayeji, Abdulla, 1997. 'Dangerous Perceptions: Gulf Views of the U.S. Role in the Region.' *Middle East Policy*, 5(2).

Al-Shayeji, Abdullah, 2014. 'The GCC-US Relationship: A GCC Perspective.' Washington, DC: Middle East Policy Council, Journal Essay (online).

AlShehabi, Omar, 2014. 'Radical Transformations and Radical Contestations: Bahrain's Spatial-Demographic Revolution.' *Middle East Critique*, 23(1).

Al Tawil, Khalid, n.d. 'The Internet in Saudi Arabia.' *Working Paper*, King Fahd University of Petroleum and Minerals.

Al Yousefi, Abdul Hafeez Yawar Khan, 2013. '50 Years in Al Ain Oasis – Memoirs of Kabeer Khan.' *Liwa: Journal of the National Centre for Documentation and Research*, 5(9).

Amin, Samir, 1982. 'After the New International Economic Order: The Future of International Economic Relations.' *Journal of Contemporary Asia*, 12(4).

Anderson, Lisa, 1991. 'Absolutism and the Resilience of Monarchy in the Middle East.' *Political Science Quarterly*, 106(1): 1–15.

Armijo, Jacqueline, 2014. 'DragonMart: The Mega Souk of Today's Silk Road.' *Middle East Report*, 270.

Baaboud, Abdulla and Geoffrey Edwards, 2007. 'Reinforcing Ambivalence: The Interaction of Gulf States and the European Union.' *European Foreign Affairs Review*, 12.

Babar, Zahra, 2014. 'The Cost of Belonging: Citizenship Construction in the State of Qatar.' *Middle East Journal*, 68(3).

Bahgat, Gawdat, 1999. 'Education in the Gulf Monarchies: Retrospect and Prospect.' *International Review of Education*, 45(2).

Bahgat, Gawdat, 2008. 'Sovereign Wealth Funds: Dangers and Opportunities.' *International Affairs*, 84(6).

Bahry, Louay, 2001. 'The New Arab Media Phenomenon: Qatar's Al Jazeera.' *Middle East Policy*, 8(2).

Bailey, Rob with Robin Willoughby, 2013. 'Edible Oil: Food Security in the Gulf.' London: Chatham House working paper EER BP 2013/03.

Baldwin-Edwards, Martin, 2011. 'Labour Immigration and Labour Markets in the GCC Countries: National Patterns and Trends.' London: *LSE Kuwait Programme Working Paper No. 15*.

Behrendt, Sven, 2009. 'Beyond Santiago: Status and Prospects.' *Central Banking*, 19(4).

Blanchard, Christopher, 2007. 'Saudi Arabia: Terrorist Financing Issues.' *CRS Report for Congress*. Washington, DC: Congressional Research Service.

Blanchard, Christopher, 2010. 'United Arab Emirates Nuclear Program and Proposed U.S. Nuclear Cooperation.' *CRS Report for Congress*. Washington, DC: Congressional Research Service.

Bremmer, Ian, 2012. 'State Capitalism Comes of Age.' *Foreign Affairs*, May/June.

Brumberg, Daniel, 2012. 'Liberalization versus Democracy: Understanding Arab Political Reform.' *Working Papers: Middle East Series, No. 37*. Washington, DC: Carnegie Endowment for International Peace.

Chalcraft, John, 2010. 'Monarchy, Migration and Hegemony in the Arabian Peninsula.' London: *LSE Kuwait Programme Working Paper No. 12*.

Chan, Lai-Ha, Pak Lee, and Gerald Chan, 2008. 'Rethinking Global Governance: A China Model in the Making?' *Contemporary Politics*, 14(1).

Chia, Ng Sue, 2011. 'Social Media's Role in Revolt: A Technological or Social Phenomenon – Analysis.' *Eurasia Review News & Analysis*, 22 March.

Coates Ulrichsen, Kristian, 2009. 'Gulf Security: Changing Internal and External Security Dynamics.' London: *LSE Kuwait Programme Working Paper No. 3*.

Coates Ulrichsen, Kristian, 2010. 'The GCC States and the Shifting Balance of Global Power.' *Occasional Paper No. 6*. Georgetown University School of Foreign Service in Qatar, Center for International and Regional Studies.

Coates Ulrichsen, Kristian, 2011a. 'Rebalancing Global Governance: Gulf States' Perspectives on the Governance of Globalisation.' *Global Policy*, 2(1).

Coates Ulrichsen, Kristian, 2011b. 'Repositioning the GCC States in the Changing Global Order.' *Journal of Arabian Studies*, 1(2).

Coates Ulrichsen, Kristian, 2011c. 'Security Policy of the Gulf States: Bahrain, Kuwait and Qatar.' *ORIENT: German Journal for Politics, Economics and Culture of the Middle East*, 52(1).

Coates Ulrichsen, Kristian, 2012a. 'South-South Cooperation and the Changing Role of the Gulf States.' *Brazilian Journal of Strategy & International Affairs*, 1(1).

Coates Ulrichsen, Kristian, 2012b. 'Basra, Southern Iraq and the Gulf: Challenges and Connections.' London: *LSE Kuwait Programme Working Paper No. 21*.

Coates Ulrichsen, Kristian, 2012c. 'Small States with a Big Role: Qatar and the United Arab Emirates in the Wake of the Arab Spring.' Durham University: *HH Sheikh Nasser al-Mohammad al-Sabah Publication Series No. 3*.

Coates Ulrichsen, Kristian, 2014. 'Addressing the Demographic Imbalance in the GCC States: Implications for Labour Markets, Migration, and National Identity.' *Workshop Report*. London: LSE Middle East Centre.

Coates Ulrichsen, Kristian, 2015. 'Egypt-Gulf Ties and the Changing Balance of Regional Security.' *The Cairo Review of Global Affairs*, January.

Coates Ulrichsen, Kristian and David Held, 2011. 'The Arab 1989 Revisited.' *Open Democracy*, 27 September.

Coates Ulrichsen, Kristian, David Held, and Alia Brahimi, 2011. 'The Arab 1989?' *Open Democracy*, 11 February.

Cohen, Benjamin, 2009. 'Sovereign Wealth Funds and National Security: The Great Tradeoff.' *International Affairs*, 85(4).

Cooper, Andrew and Bessma Momani, 2011. 'Qatar and Expanded Contours of Small State Diplomacy.' *The International Spectator: Italian Journal of International Affairs*, 46(3).

Cordner, Lee, 2012. 'Progressing Maritime Security Cooperation in the Indian Ocean.' *Naval War College Review*, 64(4).

Cox, Robert, 1979. 'Ideologies and the New International Economic Order: Reflections on Some Recent Literature.' *International Organization*, 33(2).

Davis, Lynn, 2003. 'Globalization's Security Implications.' Santa Monica: *RAND Issue Paper No. 3*.

Denmark, Abraham, 2013. 'Regional Perspectives on U.S. Strategic Rebalancing.' *Asia Policy*, 15(1).

Depledge, Joanna, 2008. 'Striving for No: Saudi Arabia in the Climate Change Regime.' *Global Environmental Politics*, 8(4).

Ehteshami, Anoushiravan and Steven Wright, 2005. 'Political Change in the Arab Oil Monarchies: From Liberalization to Enfranchisement.' *International Affairs*, 83(5).

El-Katiri, Laura, 2013. 'Energy Sustainability in the Gulf States: The Why and the How.' Oxford: Oxford Institute for Energy Studies working paper MEP 4.

Flynn, Patrice, 2011. 'The Saudi Arabian Labor Force: A Comprehensive Statistical Portrait.' *Middle East Journal*, 65(4).

Foley, Sean, 2012. 'Re-Orientalizing the Gulf: The GCC and Southeast Asia.' *Middle East Policy*, 19(4).

Forstenlechner, Ingo and Emilie Rutledge, 2011. 'The GCC's "Demographic Imbalance": Perceptions, Realities, and Policy Options.' *Middle East Policy*, 18(4).

Fuccaro, Nelida, 2013. 'Shaping the Urban Life of Oil in Bahrain: Consumerism, Leisure, and Public Communication in Manama and in the Oil Camps, 1932–1960s.' *Comparative Studies of South Asia, Africa and the Middle East*, 33(1).

Furtig, Henner, 2007 Hegghammer 'Conflict and Cooperation in the Persian Gulf: The Interregional Order and U.S. Policy.' *Middle East Journal*, 61(4).

Gartenstein-Ross, Daveed, 2010. 'Large-Scale Arrests in Saudi Arabia Illustrate Threat to the Oil Supply.' *Long War Journal*, online commentary, 24 March.

Gengler, Justin, 2013. 'Royal Factionalism, the Khawalid, and the Securitization of "the Shi'a Problem" in Bahrain,' *Journal of Arabian Studies*, 3(1).

Ghabra, Shafeeq, 1997. 'Kuwait and the Dynamics of Socio-Economic Change.' *Middle East Journal*, 51(3).

Ghafouri, Mahmoud, 2009. 'China's Policy in the Persian Gulf.' *Middle East Policy*, 16(2).

Goldthau, Andreas and Jan Martin Witte, 2009. 'Back to the Future or Forward to the Past? Strengthening Markets and Rules for Effective Global Energy Governance.' *International Affairs*, 89(2).

Greenberg, Maurice, William Wechsler, and Lee Wolosky, 2002. 'Terrorist Financing: Report of an Independent Task Force. Sponsored by the Council on Foreign Relations.' New York: Council on Foreign Relations report.

Gulbrandsen, Anders Holmen, 2010. 'Bridging the Gulf: Qatari Business Diplomacy and Conflict Mediation.' Unpublished MA Thesis, Georgetown University.

Harris, Jerry, 2013. 'Desert Dreams in the Gulf: Transnational Crossroads for the Global Elite.' *Race and Class*, 54(4).

Hearst, David, 2015. 'Has Iran Overreached Itself in Yemen?' *Middle East Eye*, 26 March.

Hegghammer, Thomas, 2007. 'Saudi Militants in Iraq: Background and Recruitment Patterns.' Oslo: Norwegian Defence Research Establishment FFI.

Held, David, 2008. 'Global Challenges: Accountability and Effectiveness.' *Open Democracy*, 17 January.

Henderson, Simon, 2013. 'No One in the Region Will Sleep.' *The Atlantic*, 25 November.

Hertog, Steffen, 2009. 'The Current Crisis and Lessons of the 1980s.' *Arab Reform Bulletin* 7 July.

Hertog, Steffen, 2011. 'The Costs of Counter-Revolution in the Gulf.' *Foreign Policy*, 31 May.

Hertog, Steffen, 2013. 'The Private Sector and Reform in the Gulf Cooperation Council.' London: *LSE Kuwait Programme Working Paper No. 30*.

Hertog, Steffen, 2014. 'Arab Gulf States: An Assessment of Nationalisation Policies.' *Gulf Labour Markets and Migration Research Paper*, RP-No.1/2014.

Hvidt, Martin, 2009. 'The Dubai Model: An Outline of Key Development-Process Elements in Dubai.' *International Journal of Middle East Studies*, 41(2).

Hvidt, Martin, 2013. 'Economic Diversification in GCC Countries: Past Records and Future Trends.' London: *LSE Kuwait Programme Working Paper No. 27.*

Ismail, Norafidah, 2013. 'The Asia Cooperation Dialogue (ACD): Progress and Potential.' Washington, DC: Middle East Institute online commentary.

Jackson, Ian, 2009. 'Nuclear Energy and Proliferation Risks: Myths and Realities in the Persian Gulf.' *International Affairs*, 85(6).

Juneau, Thomas, 2014. 'U.S. Power in the Middle East: Not Declining.' *Middle East Policy*, 21(2).

Kellner, Thierry, 2012. 'The GCC States of the Persian Gulf and Asia Energy Relations.' Paris: IFRI Note.

Kennedy, Andrew, 2010. 'China's New Energy Security Debate.' *Survival*, 52(3).

Khalaf, Abdulhadi, 1985. 'Labor Movements in Bahrain.' *Middle East Research and Information Project (MERIP) Report*, 132.

Khalaf, Abdulhadi, 2012. 'GCC Rulers and the Politics of Citizenship.' *Al Monitor*, 26 December.

Kinninmont, Jane, 2013. 'To What Extent is Twitter Changing Gulf Societies?' London: Chatham House research paper.

Lahn, Glada and Paul Stevens, 2011. 'Burning Oil to Keep Cool: The Hidden Energy Crisis in Saudi Arabia.' London: Chatham House research paper.

Lane, Jason, 2010. 'International Branch Campuses, Free Zones, and Quality Assurance: Policy Issues for Dubai and the UAE.' *Policy Brief No. 20.* Dubai: Dubai School of Government.

Latief, Hilman, 2014. 'Gulf Charitable Organizations in Southeast Asia.' Washington, DC: Middle East Institute online commentary.

Law, Bill, 2014. 'Bahrain: The Islamic State Threat Within.' *Middle East Eye*, 14 October.

Lim, Linda and Ronald Mendoza, 2013. 'Global Rebalancing 2.0.' *World Financial Review*, 2013.

Lippman, Thomas, 2009. 'Cooperation under the Radar: The US-Saudi Arabian Joint Commission for Economic Cooperation (JECOR).' Washington, DC: Middle East Institute online commentary.

Lippman, Thomas, 2010. 'Saudi Arabia's Quest for "Food Security".' *Middle East Policy*, 17(1).

Luomi, Mari, 2011. 'Gulf of Interest: Why Oil Still Dominates Middle Eastern Climate Politics.' *Journal of Arabian Studies*, 1(2).

Michael, Guy, 2010. 'Challenges for Research on Resource-Rich Economies.' London: *LSE Kuwait Programme Working Paper No. 8.*

Naufal, George and Ali Termos, 2010. 'Remittances from GCC Countries: A Brief Outlook.' Washington, DC: Middle East Institute online commentary.

Naufal, George and Ismail Genc, 2014. 'The Story of Remittance Flows from the GCC Countries.' Gulf Labor Markets and Migration, *Explanatory Note GLMM-EN-No.5.*

Okruhlik, Gwenn, 1999. 'Rentier Wealth, Unruly Law, and the Rise of Opposition: The Political Economy of Oil States.' *Comparative Politics*, 31(3).

Okruhlik, Gwenn and Patrick Conge, 1997. 'National Autonomy, Labor Migration and Political Crisis: Yemen and Saudi Arabia.' *Middle East Journal*, 51(4).

Onley, James, 2009. 'Britain and the Gulf Shaikhdoms, 1820–1971: The Politics of Protection.' *Occasional Paper No. 4.* Georgetown University School of Foreign Service in Qatar.

Onley, James and Sulayman Khalaf, 2006. 'Shaikhly Authority in the Pre-Oil Gulf: An Historical-Anthropological Study.' *History and Anthropology*, 17(3).

Ottaway, Marina, 2005. 'Evaluating Middle East Reform: How Do We Know When It Is Significant?' *Working Papers: Middle East Series, No. 56*. Washington, DC: Carnegie Endowment for International Peace.

Ottaway, Marina, 2011. 'Bahrain: Between the United States and Saudi Arabia.' Washington, DC: Carnegie Endowment for International Peace online commentary.

Owen, Roger, 2008. 'One Hundred Years of Middle Eastern Oil.' *Middle East Brief No. 24*. Brandeis University: Crown Center for Middle East Studies.

Peterson, J. E., 2004. 'Oman: Three and a Half Decades of Change and Development.' *Middle East Policy*, 11(2).

Peterson, J. E., 2006. 'Qatar and the World: Branding for a Micro-State.' *Middle East Journal*, 60(4).

Plotkin Boghardt, Lori, 2015. 'Saudi Arabia's Old Al-Qaeda Terrorists Form New Threat.' *Policywatch 2370*. Washington, DC: Washington Institute for Near East Policy.

Pollock, David, 2007. 'With Neighbors Like These: Iraq and the Arab States on Its Borders.' *Policy Focus No. 70*. Washington, DC: Washington Institute for Near East Policy.

Quah, Danny, 2011. 'The Global Economy's Shifting Centre of Gravity.' *Global Policy*, 2(1).

Randeree, Kasim, 2012. 'Workforce Nationalization in the Gulf Cooperation Council States.' *Occasional Paper No. 9*. Georgetown School of Foreign Service in Qatar.

Raouf, Mohammed, 2008. 'Climate Change Threats, Opportunities, and the GCC Countries.' *Policy Brief No. 12*. Washington, DC: Middle East Institute.

Rizzo, Agatino, 2014. 'Rapid Urban Development and National Master Planning in Arab Gulf Countries: Qatar as a Case Study.' *Cities*, 39.

Roberts, David, 2010. 'Kuwait's War of Words with Iraq.' *Foreign Policy*, 20 July.

Roberts, David, 2012. 'Understanding Qatar's Foreign Policy Objectives.' *Mediterranean Politics*, 17(2).

Roberts, David, 2014a. 'British National Interest in the Gulf: Rediscovering a Role?' *International Affairs*, 90(3).

Roberts, David, 2014b. 'Qatar, the Ikhwan, and Transnational Relations in the Gulf.' *Project on Middle East Political Science (POMEPS)*, 28 March.

Rogers, Paul, 2006. 'Abqaiq's Warning.' *Open Democracy*, 2 March.

Rubin, Lawrence, 2010. 'A Typology of Soft Powers in Middle East Politics.' *Working Paper No. 5*. Dubai: The Dubai Initiative.

Salih, Kamal Osman, 1992. 'The 1938 Kuwait Legislative Council.' *Middle Eastern Studies*, 38(1).

Schaffer, Teresita, 2009. 'The United States, India, and Global Governance: Can They Work Together?' *The Washington Quarterly*, 32(3).

Seznec, Jean-Francois, 2008. 'The Gulf Sovereign Wealth Funds: Myths and Reality.' *Middle East Policy*, 5(2).

Seznec, Jean-Francois, 2011. 'Saudi Arabia Strikes Back.' *Foreign Policy*, 14 March.

Shah, Nasra, 2013. 'Second Generation Non-Nationals in Kuwait: Achievements, Aspirations and Plans.' London: *LSE Kuwait Programme Working Paper No. 32*.

Shah, Nasra, 2014a. 'Recent Amnesty Programmes for Irregular Migrants in Kuwait and Saudi Arabia: Some Successes and Failures.' *Gulf Labor Markets and Migration Explanatory Note 09/2014.*

Shah, Nasra, 2014b. 'Data Discrepancies between the Census and Civil Registration Systems in Kuwait: Reasons, Implications, and Solutions.' *Gulf Labor Markets and Migration Explanatory Note 2/2014.*

Sherbiny, Naiem, 1985. 'Oil and the Internationalization of Arab Banks.' Oxford: Oxford Institute of Energy Studies working paper F6.

Shochat, Sharon, 2008. 'The Gulf Cooperation Council Economies: Diversification and Reform.' London: *LSE Kuwait Programme Introductory Paper.*

Sowers, Jeannie, 2014. 'Water, Energy and Human Insecurity in the Middle East.' *Middle East Research and Information Project (MERIP)*, 44(271).

Spiess, Andy, 2008. 'Developing Adaptive Capacity for Responding to Environmental Change in the Arab Gulf States: Uncertainties to Linking Ecosystem Conservation, Sustainable Development and Society in Authoritarian Rentier Economies.' *Global and Planetary Change*, 64.

Stanton Russell, Sharon, 1989. 'Politics and Ideology in Migration Policy Formulation: The Case of Kuwait.' *International Migration Review*, 23(1).

Stephens, Michael, 2013. 'Qatar's Public Diplomacy Woes.' *Open Democracy*, 4 February.

Summers, Mark, 2010. 'Etihad Airways: Staying the Course.' *The Gulf Business News and Analysis*, June issue.

Sun, Degang, 2015. 'China's Soft Military Presence in the Middle East.' Washington, DC: Middle East Institute online commentary.

Tetreault, Mary Ann, 1991. 'Autonomy, Necessity, and the Small State: Ruling Kuwait in the Twentieth Century.' *International Organization*, 45(4).

Thatcher, Mark, 2009. 'Governing Markets in Gulf States.' London: *LSE Kuwait Programme Working Paper No. 1.*

Thi Phan, Anh-Hao, 2010. 'A New Paradigm of Educational Borrowing in the Gulf States: The Qatari Example.' *Middle East Institute Viewpoints: Higher Education and the Middle East.* Washington, DC: Middle East Institute.

Van Ham, Peter, 2008. 'Place Branding: The State of the Art.' *The Annals of the American Academy of Political and Social Science*, 616(1).

Viramontes, Erick, 2012. 'The Role of Latin America in the Foreign Policies of the GCC States.' Paper presented at the *3rd Gulf Research Meeting*, University of Cambridge, July.

Wehrey, Frederic, 2015. 'Into the Maelstrom: The Saudi-Led Misadventure in Yemen.' Washington, DC: Carnegie Endowment for International Peace online commentary.

Wionczek, Miguel, 1979. 'The New International Economic Order: Past Failures and Future Prospects.' *Development and Change*, 10(4).

Woertz, Eckart, Samir Pradhan, Nermina Biberovic, and Chan Jingzhong, 2008. 'Potential for GCC Agro-Investments in Africa and Asia.' *GRC Report.* Dubai: Gulf Research Centre.

Woolfenden, John, 2010. 'Memories of Abu Dhabi and Al Ain in the Early Nineteen-Sixties.' *Liwa: Journal of the National Centre for Documentation and Research*, 2(4).

Yamada, Makio, 2011. 'Gulf-Asia Relations as 'Post-Rentier' Diversification? The Case of the Petrochemical Industry in Saudi Arabia.' *Journal of Arabian Studies*, 1(1).

Yetiv, Steve and Chunling Lu, 2007. 'China, Global Energy and the Middle East.' *Middle East Journal*, 61(2).

Youngs, Richard, 2008. 'Impasse in Euro-Gulf Relations.' *Madrid: FRIDE Working Paper 80.*

Zelkovitz, Ido, 2014. 'A Paradise Lost: The Rise and Fall of the Palestinian Community in Kuwait.' *Middle Eastern Studies*, 50(1).

Newspapers

Adelaide Now
Al Arabiya
Al Shorfa
Arab News
Arab Times
Business Times
Customs Today
Emirates Business 24/7
Gulf Business
Gulf States Newsletter
Financial Times
Gulf News

Gulf Times
Jakarta Times
Khaleej Times
Kuwait Times
Las Vegas Review-Journal
Middle East Economic
    Digest
Newsweek
New York Times
Saudi Gazette
Sudan Tribune
The Australian

The Banker
The Economist
The Globe and Mail
The Guardian
The Independent
The Majalla
The National
The New Yorker
The Peninsula
The Sunday Times
USA Today
Washington Post

Online and Other Sources

Agence France-Presse
Al Monitor
ArabianBusiness
Bloomberg
CNN Money
CNN Politics
Doha News
Economist Intelligence Unit
Emirates News
ETFtrends.com
EuroMoney
Euronews
Forbes.com
Goal

Grain Briefing
GSCleanEnergy.com
Houston Chronicle/Baker
    Institute Blog
Human Rights Watch
International Monetary
    Fund
Kuwait News Agency
Morgan Stanley Research
Mubadala
National Geographic
Northwestern Chronicle
Oil Report
Open Democracy

QNRF Newsletter
Reuters
Russia Today
Science
Skyscanner
Sovereign Wealth Fund
    Institute
The Aviation Writer
The Baffler
The Conversation
The Diplomat
United States Census Bureau
World Wildlife Federation
YouGov

Index